The Complete
VEGETABLE
COOKBOOK

The Complete
VEGETABLE
COOKBOOK

Easy, Delicious Recipes for
More Than 200 Vegetable Side Dishes

LORRAINE BODGER

Illustrated by Lorraine Bodger

HARMONY BOOKS/NEW YORK

Published by Harmony Books, a division of Crown Publishers, Inc., 201 East 50th Street, New York, New York 10022. Member of the Crown Publishing Group.

Random House, Inc. New York, Toronto, London, Sydney, Auckland

HARMONY and colophon are trademarks of Crown Publishers, Inc.

Manufactured in the United States of America

Library of Congress Cataloging-in-Publication Data
Bodger, Lorraine.
    The complete vegetable cookbook : easy, delicious recipes for more than 200 vegetable side dishes / by Lorraine Bodger. —
    1st ed.
    Includes index.
    1. Cookery (Vegetables)   2. Side dishes (Cookery)   I. Title.
TX801.B598   1994   93-25566
641.6'5—dc20   CIP

ISBN 0-517-58671-1

10 9 8 7 6 5 4 3 2 1

First Edition

*This book is lovingly dedicated
to my sisters-in-law Maggie Javna and Sharon Redel,
a pair of genuine food mavens*

Acknowledgments

Once again I have had the astonishingly good fortune to find the help I needed just when I needed it. I want to express my appreciation to Rosanna Gamson for her professional skills as well as her unique ability to cook and entertain simultaneously; to Maggie Javna, Jane Weiss and Marnie Mueller for their many intelligent and useful ideas; to Barnaby Levy for his amazing vegetable broth recipe; to the Earth-Works Group for allowing me to quote from *50 Simple Things You Can Do to Save the Earth* and *The Recycler's Handbook;* to Shaye Areheart, Kathy Belden, Peter Guzzardi and Diane Cleaver for their unflagging support; to all the friends and colleagues who tasted or heard about the recipes and reminded me loudly and often that they were tired of their old vegetable dishes and waiting for my new ones.

Contents

INTRODUCTION.........................1

VEGETABLE BASICS 4

ARTICHOKES 21

ASPARAGUS 30

BEANS, DRIED 38

BEANS, FRESH 54

BEETS 64

BELGIAN ENDIVE 71

BROCCOLI 78

BRUSSELS SPROUTS 90

CABBAGE 96

CARROTS 105

CAULIFLOWER.........................113

CELERY 120

CHINESE GREENS 126

CORN 135

CUCUMBERS 143

EGGPLANT 149

ESCAROLE 163

FENNEL 170

GREENS 178

Kohlrabi 185

Leeks and Scallions 193

Mushrooms.....................................201

Okra 211

Onions..219

Parsnips 226

Peas...233

Peppers 243

Plantains 251

Potatoes...259

Pumpkin..273

Rutabagas 279

Spinach 286

Squash, Summer.............................294

Squash, Winter 302

Swiss Chard....................................310

Tomatoes 317

Turnips 327

Salads..333

Index 350

The Complete
VEGETABLE
COOKBOOK

INTRODUCTION

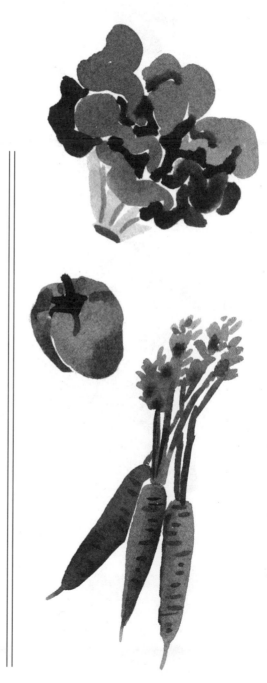

I own a very engaging traditional American cookbook copyrighted in 1940. It is 815 pages long and only 40 of those pages are devoted to vegetables. Of those 40 pages, 13 deal with potatoes, leaving 27 pages for all the other vegetables. Twenty-seven pages of recipes for boiled beans, boiled beets, boiled cabbage, boiled cauliflower—you get the idea. No wonder your grandmother had trouble getting your mother to eat her vegetables.

Fifty years later, we all firmly agree on the nutritional importance of vegetables—we read and hear about it almost daily. But we also insist just as firmly that vegetables must taste good or we won't eat them.

The Complete Vegetable Cookbook is a collection of delicious vegetable side dishes, brand-new recipes developed for the trimmed-down way we want to eat today and designed to complement everyday family suppers and important dinners for guests, too. Vegetables cooked my way never sit on the sidelines looking limp and tasting bland; they taste great, look good, and best of all, they don't require hours of fancy preparation and cooking. With more than 50 major and minor vegetables to choose from, plus salads and vegetable medleys, you'll never be at a loss for the perfect vegetable side dish to match your meal.

Each vegetable section contains at least several recipes for dishes you can easily prepare any day of the week. In addition, each section includes an extra-fast recipe designated The Vegetable Express and an extra-fancy recipe labeled Company's Coming, for guests. The one for guests usually features ingredients you wouldn't use every day (for example,

heavy cream, walnut oil, hazelnuts or brandy) or will take more time than you might ordinarily spend. But that's the point—you do it only for company.

The emphasis is on fresh vegetables, of course, but this is a practical book, so I've included recipes that make excellent use of a few frozen vegetables—such as corn, spinach and baby lima beans—that can be used in place of their fresh counterparts when the fresh ones are unavailable. On the other hand, the only canned vegetables you'll find in the recipes on these pages are the essential basics—tomatoes, assorted beans, pumpkin purée and an occasional green chile or water chestnut.

In the past, most vegetable cookbooks offered you a choice between exotic vegetables swimming in high-calorie sauces and the opposite—a lean, mean vegetarian cuisine. Not today and not in this cookbook: Tasty vegetables don't have to be too rich and healthful vegetables don't have to be too plain. The recipes in *The Complete Vegetable Cookbook* are first of all, delicious and second, thoughtfully (but not fanatically) responsive to our concern for maintaining sensible diets. Since it is in our best nutritional interest to eat vegetables, we need to focus on vegetable side dishes that don't totally deprive us of the rich tastes we love but do reduce large, unhealthy amounts of fatty ingredients.

Don't panic, though: Butter, cheese and eggs are certainly part of the dining plan, just not in great quantities and not in every dish. Instead, *The Complete Vegetable Cookbook* features a lighter style of cooking using olive and other flavorful oils, shallots and garlic, herbs, fresh lemon and lime juice, good mustard and vinegar, Italian and Asian sauces, salsa, dried tomatoes and mushrooms, fresh peppers and other tasty seasonings.

Other simple strategies cut fat and calories, too. For example, I've substituted chicken or vegetable broth (especially low-salt types) for some of the milk or cream usually required for particular sauces, or I've used plain yogurt, light sour cream, part-skim ricotta cheese, low-fat mayonnaise and other kinder-to-the-heart-and-hips ingredients—but only when the substitutions are lower in fat *and* taste great. And whenever I take out the fat, I put in something else to make the vegetable taste so good you won't even notice the deletion.

(Of course, you're always free to use the real thing in any recipe if you prefer.)

So here's my position: I'm not a vegetarian or a health food nut or a member of the Food Police trying to make you eat steamed vegetables. But, like any sensible person, I have cut down significantly on the amount of meat, dairy products and fat I eat, and that means enjoying more chicken, pasta, grains—and lots of vegetables. Back at the childhood dinner table, we were too often told that we had to get the greens down the hatch before we could have the good stuff. Well, it turns out that vegetables *are* the good stuff. And you can have as much of them as you want.

VEGETABLE BASICS

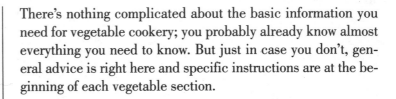

There's nothing complicated about the basic information you need for vegetable cookery; you probably already know almost everything you need to know. But just in case you don't, general advice is right here and specific instructions are at the beginning of each vegetable section.

A Vegetable by Any Other Name

This book is organized in alphabetical order from Artichokes to Turnips, and you may occasionally encounter what you think is an unfamiliar vegetable. Chances are you know it by another name, perhaps a regional or traditional name. For instance, rutabagas are also known as yellow turnips or Swedish turnips, fennel is called finocchio, and okra is called gumbo. My scallions may be your spring onions or green onions, and what I lump together as Squash, Summer (pages 294 to 301), you may think of separately as zucchini, yellow squash and pattypan squash. Or to put it the other way around: You may be looking for a vegetable called broadleaf endive or Batavia, but you won't find it unless you look at Escarole.

This slight confusion is bound to happen. The names you'll find here are the ones most commonly used in most of the country, but if there's something you can't find, be aware that it may indeed appear under another name.

How to Buy and Store Vegetables

No two vegetables are exactly alike, so there's no single rule for buying and storing all vegetables. In the beginning of each unit—Artichokes, Asparagus, Beans, Beets, etc.—you'll find a section called Buying and Storing that explains just what to look for when you make your purchase and how to store it when you get home.

Where to Buy What You Need: The Supermarket and Beyond

A good big supermarket is generally your best weekly source of vegetables, although this depends a great deal on how competent the produce manager is. I have two supermarkets within shouting distance of my home and right now, thanks to consumer demand and the astuteness of the produce managers, they both offer a wide range of vegetables (albeit of varying degrees of quality) on a regular basis. Convenience is the attraction of the supermarket, of course, since it's a definite plus to be able to do most of your shopping in one place.

However, convenience is not everything. Try to get acquainted with your smaller local groceries, too—especially the ethnic ones. They often have vegetables that may not be available in a big-chain supermarket, no matter how savvy the produce manager is. Italian greengrocers, for instance, will have escarole, broccoli rabe, sun-dried tomatoes; Asian ones will have Chinese greens, ginger, dried black mushrooms, snow pea pods, Chinese or Japanese eggplants, scallions, water chestnuts; Hispanic ones will have fresh chiles, beans, plantains, avocados, tomatillos, jícama.

Where else should you look for vegetables? Some well-stocked supermarkets now carry what used to be considered gourmet items (radicchio, baby artichokes, wild mushrooms and the like), but if yours doesn't, you're sure to find them at one of the fancy food emporia, along with baby vegetables, deluxe salad greens, French beans, etc. And don't ignore health food stores—they'll have organic vegetables, dried beans, canned beans without preservatives and more.

Last but definitely not least on the list of vegetable sources are the seasonal ones: farmers' markets, farmstands, roadside stands, greenmarkets—local farmers bringing their produce directly to you. This is where, from the first bright red radish of the season to the last deep orange pumpkin, nongardeners can see, smell and touch the genuine article, and then take it home and cook it.

And in all these markets, upscale or no-frills, look for the condiments and other interesting ingredients that make cooking and eating such a pleasure: fresh and dried herbs, Italian balsamic vinegar and wonderful olive oil, walnut oil, cold-pressed oils, chutneys, curry powder, pickled vegetables, salsa, unusual rice and grains, mustards and vinegars, buckwheat and other flours, yogurt, fine cheeses, Asian sauces and noodles, and on and on.

Keep an open mind when vegetable shopping because sometimes the eggplant you wanted for dinner is just awful-looking, while the broccoli is gorgeous. Be flexible: When you find yourself in that predicament, it makes sense to rethink your menu and serve the good broccoli instead of the bad eggplant.

Basic Preparation of Vegetables

Basic preparation is what you do before launching into the steps of a recipe. For instance, the ingredients list may specify "2 medium carrots, trimmed, peeled and diced." This means that when you begin step 1, your carrots should already be trimmed, peeled and diced—prepared and ready to be used in the recipe.

Instructions for trimming and peeling the carrot will be found at the beginning of the carrot section, under the heading Notes to the Cook, right where you need it. (Each vegetable is prepared differently, so each has its own appropriate instructions.) The dicing mentioned in this carrot example is a basic cutting technique with which you are probably familiar, but if you're not, you can learn about it on page 12.

Cleaning, washing, rinsing or scrubbing your vegetables is important, too, and—again—is covered in the Notes to the Cook in each vegetable section. These instructions will vary according to the vegetable: Belgian endive requires only a gentle wiping while russet potatoes are usually scrubbed to get them clean.

Vegetables from the supermarket or fancy food store are generally pretty clean, but when you buy from a farmstand the vegetables tend to have honest-to-goodness dirt clinging to them. Take some care in removing the dirt according to the instructions in Notes to the Cook.

Basic Cooking Equipment, Appliances and Utensils

Cookbooks are always expounding long lists of the equipment, appliances and utensils you must have for a properly functioning kitchen. I treat those lists like the magazine quizzes I used to take when I was 13: I run down the list, triumphantly checking off what I do have and feeling envious about what I don't have. In the end the list has absolutely no impact on what's in my kitchen; I simply buy what I need when I discover I need it, and I buy the best quality I can afford at the time.

There's no question that high-quality kitchen equipment (especially pots, pans and skillets) is wonderful to own and use: It yields better results and makes cooking (and cleanup) easier, more efficient and therefore more enjoyable. However, it's not important enough to obsess about unless you're planning a career in food. Here's what I use in the course of cooking vegetables:

BAKING DISHES: Baking dishes may be glass, stainless steel, ceramic or enameled cast iron, with high or low sides. It's very useful to have a selection of sizes including 1-quart, 1½-quart and 2-quart capacities.

BAKING SHEETS AND JELLY ROLL PAN: I have several sturdy metal baking sheets that have rims along one edge or on two opposite edges; you probably have some, too, which you use for baking cookies. A jelly roll pan has a rim running around all four sides, which keeps small things such as nuts or mushrooms from rolling off.

BRUSHES, ½ INCH AND 1 INCH WIDE: Although they are usually used for pastry-making chores, brushes are one of my most indispensable tools in vegetable cookery. I use them for greasing or buttering a baking dish, for applying sauce directly to vegetables, for spreading oil on vegetables before grilling, for brushing grated rind out of the holes in my grater,

etc. They suffer a lot of wear and tear, so buy high-quality brushes and keep them scrupulously clean with hot water and soap.

COLANDER; LARGE AND SMALL WIRE-MESH STRAINERS

CUTTING BOARDS: Cutting boards come in a wide variety of sizes and shapes; I have three rectangular wooden ones, small, medium and large. Wipe your wooden board with a damp cloth or sponge after each use, then dry thoroughly.

ELECTRIC HAND MIXER: In this book, an electric mixer is used mostly for beating egg whites, which—if you have a strong arm—you may certainly do by hand with a whisk.

FOOD PROCESSOR: There's only one major appliance I wouldn't want to be without and that's my food processor. If you're buying one for the first time, keep in mind that your processor doesn't have to be a super-duper fancy model, but it should have a good motor and the usual complement of blades—metal chopping blade, slicing and grating blades.

GRATER: You'll get the most use out of a stainless steel four-sided (box) grater because it has punched holes for grating, cut-out holes for shredding or grating and blades for slicing. I have both large and small box graters, for large and small jobs.

KITCHEN SCALE: This may seem like a superfluous piece of equipment, but once you have it, you'll wonder how you got along without it. Be sure yours has clear ounce, pound and gram markings and will weigh up to five pounds of food.

KITCHEN TIMER; CLOCK WITH SWEEP SECOND HAND: Timing is important in all kinds of cooking, and vegetable cooking is no exception. My timer has three channels that allow me to time three different operations simultaneously, and I'm often using two of them at once. I may, for example, be timing a dish baking in the oven while I'm keeping track of some vegetables parboiling on the stove.

A clock with a sweep second hand is useful for very short stints, such as plunging a tomato into boiling water for 45 seconds before peeling it or stir-frying ginger and garlic for two minutes.

KNIVES AND SHARPENING STEEL: I am partial to high-carbon stainless steel knives, which can be sharpened (with the sharpening steel) and cleaned beautifully. I have a small knife for paring, an eight-inch chef's knife for mincing and other tasks, and a variety of sizes in between. A sharp serrated knife is a necessity, too.

MANDOLINE: Cooks just love this nifty little manual slicing tool. It's a slanted frame with a sharp blade in the center, and there's a little space below the blade so that when you slide a hunk of vegetable—say, a cucumber—over the blade, it cuts off a perfect slice of cucumber and voilà! it drops the slice underneath the mandoline. In seconds you can slice whole cucumbers, zucchini, carrots, chunks of cabbage, almost any vegetable. And to make it even better, one of the parts is interchangeable to allow you to cut thick or thin slices, as well as beautiful matchsticks.

   A note of caution: Always use the spiked gripper for holding the vegetables as you slide them over the blade; never hold the vegetables with your bare fingers.

mandoline

MEASURING CUPS AND SPOONS: For measuring liquids, use clear glass or plastic one-cup measures with distinct markings and good pouring spouts; for dry ingredients, use a set of graduated measures ($\frac{1}{4}$ cup, $\frac{1}{3}$ cup, $\frac{1}{2}$ cup and 1 cup) with flat rims.

TIP: Having two sets of graduated measuring spoons makes cooking a lot easier.

MELON BALLER: It's not just for melons. I use it for scooping out raw and cooked vegetables—for example, for scooping the pulp out of raw tomatoes, cooked kohlrabi or zucchini, etc.

MIXING BOWLS OF VARIOUS SIZES

OVEN THERMOMETER: Correct oven temperature is important, so buy a mercury-type thermometer and leave it in the middle of the center rack of the oven each time you preheat (which takes 15 minutes). If the temperature is

*nested
steamer set*

consistently off by more than 25 degrees, have the oven adjusted by a professional.

PEPPER GRINDER: Wood, plastic or metal—it doesn't matter which you choose as long as you choose one. Preground pepper from a tin is not an acceptable substitute for freshly ground pepper from a pepper grinder.

POTS, PANS AND SKILLETS: Most of mine are easy-to-clean stainless steel with aluminum bases for good heat distribution. Some cooks prefer stainless steel over copper, copper lined with tin, enamel-coated cast iron or even glass that goes from stovetop to oven. Stay away from uncoated aluminum and iron pans—they react unpleasantly with artichokes, tomatoes and any recipe with acid (vinegar, lemon juice, etc.) in it.

You'll want a variety of large and small saucepans, stockpots and skillets, but the one you'll really need for these recipes is what I call a *large skillet*, 12 inches in diameter measured across the top, with a tight-fitting lid. You'll need tight-fitting lids for your pots, pans and other skillets, too, but not necessarily a separate lid for each; same-size pots, pans and skillets can share lids.

TIP: Pans and skillets with nonstick surfaces are very popular and a great help if you are cutting down on the fat used in sautéing.

SALAD SPINNER: For years I thought salad spinners were more trouble than they were worth—until I tried my sister-in-law Sharon's spinner. Instead of a noisy, awkward crank, her spinner has a simple pull-cord that makes the inner basket turn. It's easier, quieter, faster and more efficient, and it certainly converted me. Salad spinners are wonderful for drying spinach, lettuce, greens, herbs and every other kind of leafy vegetable.

STEAMER: There are no steamed-vegetable recipes in this book, but a steamer is occasionally used for preparation. A collapsible perforated metal rack or basket that fits into a variety of pots is inexpensive and perfectly adequate, but I use a nested steamer set consisting of a shallow pan for the water, a perforated basket for the vegetables and a tight-fitting lid.

UTENSILS: You'll want to have all the usual utensils—slotted spoons, kitchen fork, metal and wooden mixing spoons, ladle, several flexible metal spatulas and turners, several plastic spatulas, potato masher, tongs, garlic press, kitchen scissors.

VEGETABLE PEELER: I mention this separately because it is so important in vegetable cooking. I've tried half a dozen different kinds and I still find the stainless steel swivel-blade peeler to be the best.

WIRE RACK FOR COOLING: This is your basic sturdy cake-cooling rack, handy for holding any hot dish or pot while vegetables cool.

WIRE WHISKS, SMALL AND LARGE

WOK: A wok is not a necessity unless you cook a lot of Chinese-style food, but it's nice to have for stir-frying vegetables. A bamboo or perforated metal steamer rack that fits inside the wok is handy, too.

Basic Noncooking Techniques and Terms

If you are uncertain about a technique used in the recipes, check here to be sure you understand what's required.

BLEND: to combine two or more foods until they are smooth and thoroughly mixed, usually by means of a spoon, whisk, electric mixer, blender or food processor

BUTTER OR GREASE A BAKING OR OTHER DISH: to brush soft butter or oil all over the inside of a baking dish to keep food from sticking

CHIFFONADE: very finely shredded leafy herbs or vegetables, often used as garnish; easiest to do if you stack the leaves, roll them up and cut with a very sharp knife

CHOP: to cut into irregular little pieces, using a knife or food processor

CHUNK, AS IN CHUNKING A CARROT OR ONION: to cut the whole vegetable into smaller pieces, usually before dropping them into a food processor

CORE: to cut out the tough core of a vegetable such as endive, radicchio, cabbage, etc.

CORE, SEED AND DEVEIN: This is done to peppers of all kinds. It means to cut out and discard the stem end and the knob of seeds, then slit the pepper in half, rinse or brush out the seeds and trim away the pale veins or ribs, leaving just the flesh of the pepper.

CUBE: to cut into ½-inch cubes; easiest to do if you cut the vegetable in ½-inch slices, then cut the slices in ½-inch strips and the strips in ½-inch cubes

CUT CROSSWISE OR LENGTHWISE:

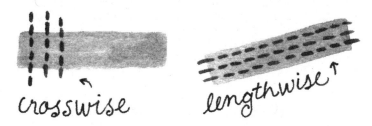

DICE: to cut into ¼-inch cubes; easiest to do if you cut the vegetable in ¼-inch slices, then cut the slices in ¼-inch strips and the strips in ¼-inch cubes

DRAIN AND RINSE UNDER COLD WATER TO STOP COOKING: to pour the vegetable and the liquid in which it was cooked into a colander or strainer (the liquid will drain off, of course) and immediately run cold water over the vegetable until it is completely cool and the cooking process stops

DRIZZLE: to pour a fine stream of liquid evenly over food, for example, salad dressing over salad greens or melted butter over a casserole

GRATE: to change a solid piece of food into very tiny pieces (as with grated lemon rind or Parmesan cheese) by rubbing it firmly over the perforated surface of a metal grater; to change a solid piece of food into narrow shreds (as with grated cheddar cheese or zucchini) by rubbing it firmly over the punched holes of a metal grater or by using the grating blade of your food processor

GRATED RIND; PEELED ZEST: To make grated rind, remove the outermost layer (the zest) of the lemon or orange by firmly rubbing it over the large or small perforations of your metal grater. To make strips of lemon or orange zest, use a vegetable peeler and peel the fruit as you would an apple. When making grated rind or peeling strips of zest, try not to take off any of the white pith just below the zest—it's bitter.

JULIENNE: to cut into matchsticks; easiest to do if you cut the vegetable in 1/8-inch slices, then stack the slices and cut them in 1/8-inch strips

MARINATE: to leave a vegetable in a seasoned liquid (such as salad dressing or Asian seasoning sauce) to soften and absorb flavor

MASH: to use a mashing tool (such as a fork or potato masher) to break down solid food into a smooth or chunky mixture

MINCE: to cut into tiny irregular pieces, with a knife or food processor

PACKED MEASUREMENTS: When the ingredients call for *1/2 cup (packed) chopped parsley*, this means you must press enough chopped parsley firmly into a 1/2-cup measure so that the measuring cup is full when the parsley is packed down. The same packing may be required for whole parsley leaves and for other chopped or whole-leaf herbs.

PEEL: to remove the skin or rind of a vegetable using a sharp knife or vegetable peeler

PURÉE: to chop or mash food until it is a thick or thin paste, usually by means of a food processor or blender

QUARTER AND CORE: to cut a vegetable (or fruit, especially apples) in wedge-shaped quarters from top to bottom, then carefully pare out the tough core

sticks

julienne (matchsticks)

quarters

cut in half

half moons

diagonal slices

SALT OR SWEAT TO DRAW OUT LIQUID: to sprinkle a vegetable (such as eggplant, cucumbers or zucchini) with salt to make it release liquid; salted vegetables are left in a colander or strainer to drain.

SEASON TO TASTE OR CORRECT THE SEASONING: to add salt, fresh pepper or any other specified herbs and spices until the flavor of the dish pleases you

SEED: to remove the seeds of a vegetable by cutting, scooping or rinsing them out

SHRED: to cut a solid piece of food into short or long narrow strips by rubbing it firmly down over the punched holes in a metal grater or by using the grating blade of a food processor; shredded pieces are slightly larger than grated pieces.

SNIP: to cut in small bits with a kitchen scissors; fresh herbs, especially chives, are often cut this way.

STEM END, ROOT END

stem *root end* *stem end* *root end*

stems

TOP AND TAIL: to remove the unwanted top and bottom of the vegetable, as we do with carrots or beets

TRIM: to remove the unusable or unwanted parts of the vegetable

WHISK: to use a wire whisk to blend wet and/or dry ingredients, for example a salad dressing, sauce or batter

Basic Cooking Techniques and Terms

Of course you know what most of these terms mean and you're familiar with most of the techniques. Consider this a refresher and please remember that the list relates not to cooking in general but to the terms and techniques used in this book.

BAKE: to cook food in the dry heat of the oven; baked vegetables are usually cooked at medium or low temperatures.

BOIL: to cook in hot liquid (212°) that is bubbling moderately at a steady rate

BRAISE: to brown vegetables in some kind of fat and then add a little liquid, cover tightly and cook over low heat until tender; vegetables are usually braised on the stove, although braising may be done in the oven.

BROWN: to cook in a skillet until nicely colored on the outside

PARBOIL: to boil for a short time, until food is partially cooked; parboiled vegetables are then usually finished by some other cooking method.

PREHEAT: to set the required oven temperature at least 15 minutes before putting food in the oven

REDUCE: to boil liquid rapidly so that some of it evaporates and the liquid thickens

REDUCE TO A GLAZE: to boil liquid rapidly and for an extended amount of time so that it thickens considerably, to the consistency of syrup

RELEASE THEIR LIQUID OR GIVE UP THEIR LIQUID: to sauté a vegetable (such as mushrooms or summer squash) until it exudes liquid, reducing the size of the vegetable as well as softening it

ROAST: to cook food in the dry heat of the oven; roasted vegetables are usually cooked at high temperatures.

SAUTÉ (OR FRY): to cook (usually for a short time) in some kind of fat in a skillet, until vegetables are lightly browned or softened

SET, AS EGG-BASED VEGETABLE CUSTARDS, TIMBALES OR PIE FILLINGS: to cook in low oven heat until the top of the egg-based mixture appears firm and a knife inserted in the center comes out clean or almost clean

SHALLOW-FRY: to cook vegetables in a shallow pool (about ¼ inch) of very hot oil until crisp and browned

SIMMER: to cook in liquid that is barely boiling, with just a few bubbles breaking the surface

STEAM: to cook vegetables in the steam given off by boiling water; usually done in a steamer (a perforated rack set above a pan of boiling water) covered tightly so the steam can't escape

NOTE: *I'm not fond of plain steamed vegetables, so you won't find any in this book. However, sometimes steaming is part of the preparation for another dish, for instance, Stuffed Zucchini Barquettes (page 300) are steamed before being stuffed and chilled.*

STIR DOWN AS THE LEAVES BEGIN TO WILT: to stir leafy greens as they are heated, so that they wilt and collapse

STIR-FRY: See the sidebar on page 132.

WILT: to cause a vegetable (usually leafy greens) to soften and lose crispness without cooking or with minimal cooking; for example, adding hot or warm dressing to leafy greens will cause them to wilt, as will stirring damp leafy greens over low heat for a few minutes; salting (page 14) will cause cucumbers and other water-laden vegetables to wilt

Basic Ingredients

Many of the basic and important ingredients (such as oil, vinegar, garlic and others that show up time and again in the ingredients lists) are discussed in some detail in individual sidebars; there's a cross-reference list of those sidebars on page 18. Other basic ingredients are discussed here.

ANCHOVIES: The anchovies used in this book are the salt-cured fillets packaged in oil in two-ounce flat cans. They are available either as flat fillets or rolled around capers.

BULGUR WHEAT: Bulgur is whole wheat kernels that have been steamed, dried and then cracked into fine, medium or coarse bits. When simmered for a short time with broth or another liquid, the bits swell and become tender, tasty grains.

BUTTER AND MARGARINE: We all know about cutting down our intake of fat in general and animal fat in particular, and that's why you'll find a moderate use of margarine and butter in this book. When butter is required in the recipes, use the unsalted (sweet) kind. When margarine is required, use solid margarine that lists *liquid oil* first in the ingredients.

CANADIAN BACON, LEAN BACON, PROSCIUTTO, PANCETTA: These four pork products are used in small amounts in some of the vegetable recipes to add a rich, smoky flavor. You can find Canadian bacon and regular bacon in any supermarket, but you'll probably have to go to a butcher to find lean bacon or bacon cured without preservatives. Prosciutto and pancetta are available in Italian groceries, as well as upscale supermarkets and gourmet stores.

CROSS-REFERENCE: BASIC INGREDIENTS

Barnaby's Vegetable Broth,
page 176

Basic Root Vegetable Broth,
page 110

Do-It-Yourself Curry Powder,
page 252

Hot Pepper in Other Forms,
page 274

More Chinese Ingredients,
page 130

Pantry: A Choice of Vinegars,
page 146

Pantry:
A Selection of Chiles,
page 248

Pantry: Bread Crumbs,
page 36

Pantry: Canned Tomatoes,
page 318

Pantry: Cheese,
page 160

Pantry: Chinese Ingredients,
page 128

Pantry: Cooking Oil
and Salad Oil,
page 156

Pantry: Dried Herbs
and Spices,
page 264

Pantry: Fresh Herbs,
page 58

Pantry: Garlic,
page 24

Pantry: Grated Cheese,
page 88

Pantry: Mustards,
page 280

CAPERS: Capers—the buds of the caper bush—are usually pickled in vinegar and have a salty, pungent flavor; to cut the saltiness, rinse the capers before using. Although there are large capers, I generally use the small ones, which are called nonpareils.

COUSCOUS: Couscous, which cooks in minutes, is granules made of semolina wheat. Buy it in the supermarket, gourmet shop or health food store.

EGGS: Use fresh eggs graded large.

FLAT-LEAF (ITALIAN) PARSLEY: There are two kinds of fresh parsley, flat-leaf and curly. Flat-leaf is tender and flavorful; it's the one I like best for both cooking and garnishing. Curly parsley is tough, spiky and not as tasty as flat-leaf; in a pinch it makes an acceptable if ordinary garnish.

FLOUR: Use all-purpose flour unless some other kind of flour (buckwheat flour, cake flour) is specified.

FRESH PEPPER: Food should be seasoned with freshly ground black pepper, not with preground pepper from the supermarket. Buy black peppercorns by the quarter or half pound and grind them in a good pepper grinder as you need them.

LEMONS, LIMES, ORANGES: Fresh lemon, lime or orange juice means just that—juice squeezed from fresh citrus fruits, not from a bottle or can. No cheating: Fresh juice (when specified) really makes a difference in the flavor of a dish.

TIP: Room temperature citrus fruits yield more juice more easily than cold ones.

To make grated rind, firmly rub the outermost layer (the rind or zest) of the lemon or orange against the large or small perforations on your grater. To make strips of lemon or orange zest, use a vegetable peeler and peel the fruit as you would an apple. When making grated rind or peeling strips of zest, try not to take off any of the bitter white pith just below the zest.

LOW-FAT OR LOW-CALORIE PRODUCTS: Whenever feasible in my recipes, I use the so-called light or lower-fat, lower-calorie versions of certain foods, on the theory that eliminating any amount of fat and calories is all to the good— as long as the final result tastes delicious. For example, I often substitute light sour cream, skim milk, part skim ricotta and low-fat mayonnaise for regular sour cream, whole milk, whole milk ricotta and regular mayonnaise. You may of course use whichever you choose in the recipes and be assured of complete success. The ingredients list will indicate the options.

On the other hand, I never use *nonfat* yogurt because I find it unpalatable, but I often use ordinary *low-fat* plain yogurt. I never use low-fat cheese (with the exception of part skim ricotta) either; instead I try to use regular cheese in sensible small-to-medium amounts rather than excessive ones.

NOTE: *Buttermilk, when made from skim milk as most commercial buttermilks are, is low-fat and wonderful to cook with.*

MILD GREEN CHILES; PICKLED JALAPEÑOS: Canned mild green chiles (whole or chopped, usually in four-ounce cans) and bottled pickled jalapeños are a great convenience for cooks in a hurry or cooks who don't like to handle fresh chiles. In some recipes they are even preferable to the fresh.

RICE: Use long-grain, basmati or any kind of rice you like as long as it's not instant.

SHERRY: When dry sherry is required, choose one labeled fino or manzanilla; medium-dry sherry is called amontillado or milk sherry, and sweet sherries are labeled oloroso, cream or golden.

TAHINI: Tahini is a thick, smooth paste made of ground sesame seeds. There are no other ingredients in tahini, but the seeds release a lot of sesame oil, so the jar or can often has a pool of oil on top of the paste. Try to stir the oil back into the paste before you measure out the amount of tahini you need.

VEGETABLE OR CHICKEN BROTH: Make your own or use canned broth, which usually comes in 13¾-ounce cans. We used only broth for testing these recipes.

Pantry: Nuts,
page 55

Pantry: Olives,
page 26

Pantry: Rice and
Other Grains,
page 217

Pantry: Shallots,
page 220

Sun-dried Tomatoes,
page 46

Also: See Salads, pages 333 to 349, for information on lettuce and other salad ingredients.

Portions and
Presentation of Vegetables

As you will see in the recipes, these vegetable dishes usually yield six servings, never less but sometimes more. Keep in mind that servings means portions, not necessarily how many people the dish will feed: Six people *may* eat one serving each, but it's just as possible for four hungry people to gobble up all six servings. Use the number-of-servings indication as a guideline, then add common sense and your own experience to judge whether a recipe will feed your family or guests adequately.

And when you're ready to put the vegetables on the table, don't ignore the importance of serving them attractively, even if that just means putting the vegetables in a pretty bowl or on a handsome platter. If you can go a step further and add a little garnish, that's even better; the sidebars on pages 186, 190 and 208 will give you some simple and fancy ideas about garnishing.

In any case, try to vary the colors and textures of the vegetables you serve at any one meal, and don't introduce too many new vegetable dishes at once or you may have a mutiny on your hands. Arrange the vegetables neatly on the platter or mound them neatly in the bowl, and if sauce or dressing splashes around the dish, wipe the rim so it doesn't look sloppy.

Making the spinach look good isn't going to lull any child into forgetting it's spinach, but attractive presentation will definitely improve the overall dining experience—and make it clear that you consider vegetables a valuable part of the meal.

ARTICHOKES

BUYING AND STORING

Artichokes come in roughly four sizes: baby, small, medium and large (or jumbo). The bud of a baby artichoke is 1½ to 2 inches high; the globe of a large or jumbo artichoke can be 4½ inches or more.

In general, look for firm, compact, thick-leaved artichokes (except the babies—their leaves are thin) that are heavy for their size and have at least an inch of stem. In spring and summer, artichokes should be a good bright green, but in fall and winter they may be bronzed or even blistered due to frost. This is perfectly harmless and doesn't affect the flavor. Avoid yellowing, dryness and spreading leaves, and watch out for wormholes in the stem and lower leaves—where there are wormholes, there may be a lot of damage inside the artichoke.

Store artichokes unwashed in a plastic bag in the refrigerator; they'll last for at least a week.

NOTES TO THE COOK

Preparing a large or jumbo artichoke: Cut off the stem close to the globe. Pull off the lowest layer of leaves and trim around the stem to remove any dark green or fibrous bits. Use a serrated knife to cut off an inch at the top of the artichoke and a

Artichokes have always reminded me of lobsters: A certain amount of work is required to get at the good parts, but the payoff is definitely worth the effort. With artichokes, there are a few steps of preparation to get through, but none are difficult and they don't add up to more time than it takes to cut up, peel and wash a bunch of broccoli.

LARGE ARTICHOKES

cut off top

snip tips

cut in half

MEDIUM SIZE

BABY AND SMALL

kitchen scissors to snip off the sharp pointed tips of the remaining leaves. Rinse under cool running water, letting the water get in among the leaves. Shake out any excess water.

Halving large or jumbo artichokes: Cut the artichoke in half from stem end to top. With the tip of a small knife, carefully cut out and discard the fuzzy choke and thin leaves in the center of each half.

Preparing medium-size artichokes: Although you can use the same method as for large artichokes, I prefer this one. Cut off the stem close to the globe. Use a serrated knife to cut off the top of the artichoke so that all the leaves are the same length and none of them have sharp points. Now pull off the lowest layer of leaves and trim around the stem to remove any dark green or fibrous bits. From this point you may halve or quarter them and cut out the fuzzy chokes or you may leave them whole and scrape out the fuzzy chokes to create hollow centers for stuffing. Rinse well, letting the water get in among the leaves. Shake out any excess water.

Preparing baby and small artichokes: Cut off the stems close to the buds. Peel off leaves until you're down to the ones that are yellow at the stem ends and pale green at the tips. Cut off at least ½ inch of the tip of each artichoke. If necessary, trim around the stem end to remove any dark green or fibrous bits. Rinse well under cool water.

NOTE: *I know it seems as if you're wasting a lot of leaves, but since the whole baby or small artichoke will be eaten, it is essential to peel off all the tough outer leaves.*

Halving baby and small artichokes: Cut each artichoke in half from stem to tip. There are no fuzzy chokes to remove because these artichokes are so young that no chokes have developed.

NOTE: *Most cookbooks will tell you to rub the cut edges of artichokes with lemon to prevent discoloring. It is true that the cut edges darken considerably, but this does not affect the flavor. Frankly, I never bother with the lemon; by the time the artichokes are cooked and dressed, no one notices the edges anyway. On the other hand, I don't cook artichokes in aluminum or iron pans because they turn an unappetizing grayish color.*

CRISP ARTICHOKES

MAKES SIX SERVINGS

Shallow-frying yields deliciously crisp little nuggets without using an enormous amount of fat or creating a lot of smoke and mess. These are really great and very little trouble to make.

24 baby or 15 small artichokes, prepared and halved (see Notes to the Cook)

2 egg whites

1 tablespoon water

½ cup dry bread crumbs

Salt and fresh pepper

Olive oil

1. Bring a saucepan of water to a boil, drop the artichoke halves into the water and simmer for three minutes, until crisp-tender. Rinse under cold water to stop the cooking process, drain well and pat dry on paper towels.

2. In a medium bowl, whisk together the egg whites and water. Add the artichoke halves and stir well.

3. Season the bread crumbs with salt and pepper. Dredge each artichoke half in bread crumbs and place on waxed paper.

4. In a large skillet, heat two tablespoons of olive oil. Place in the skillet as many artichoke hearts as fit comfortably, and sauté over low heat until browned. Turn and brown the other sides. Transfer the crisp artichokes to an ovenproof platter and keep warm in a low oven.

Repeat this process until all the artichokes are cooked, adding more olive oil to the skillet as needed. Serve hot.

MENU SUGGESTIONS

Delicious with a stuffed veal roast and one of the tomato salads on page 324. For a simple vegetarian meal, serve Crisp Artichokes with a pasta primavera that includes whatever parboiled vegetables you like—carrots, broccoli, asparagus, etc.

PANTRY

GARLIC

Garlic is a bulb (or head) composed of individual cloves. When you buy garlic, the bulb should have a dry, papery white outer skin. The cloves inside should be hard and tightly encased in their own tough skins; squeeze them firmly to be sure they are. Don't buy sprouted bulbs with green shoots at the top. Do buy large bulbs with large cloves—small ones are a pain in the neck to peel.

To peel a clove, cut off the nubby end (where it was attached to the main bulb) and do *one* of three things: 1) Place the flat side of a knife on the clove and press down firmly; 2) place the flat side of the

MENU SUGGESTIONS

You might like to try these with thin slices of cold roast pork and a selection of grilled vegetables (page 72), with a basket of good bread. For a vegetarian meal, skip the pork entirely and add a round of goat cheese (or another cheese) or even the White Bean and Goat Cheese Pâté on Greens (page 48).

STUFFED ARTICHOKE HALVES WITH CREAMY HERB DRESSING

MAKES SIX SERVINGS

One of my favorite recipes, it's definitely good enough for company but easy enough to do for family. The herb dressing makes a pungent counterpoint to the satisfying, cheese-nipped stuffing and tender artichokes.

3 large artichokes, prepared and halved (see Notes to the Cook)

6 tablespoons cooked couscous or rice

3 tablespoons dry bread crumbs

3 tablespoons grated Parmesan or Romano cheese

2 tablespoons chopped toasted unsalted cashews (optional)

Creamy Herb Dressing (recipe follows)

1. With the point of a small sharp knife, cut out the fuzzy choke and thin inner leaves of each artichoke half. Rinse well.

Place the halves in the top section of a steamer with 1½ inches of boiling water in the bottom section, and steam until tender, about 30 minutes. Drain on a rack, cut side down, until cool.

2. Meanwhile, in a medium bowl, stir together the couscous, bread crumbs, grated cheese and cashews. Moisten with ¼ cup of Creamy Herb Dressing. Divide this stuffing among the cooled artichokes, pressing it into the cavities where the chokes were. Top the stuffing in each artichoke with a tablespoon of Creamy Herb Dressing. Serve one artichoke half per person and offer the extra dressing in a separate bowl.

Creamy Herb Dressing

MAKES ABOUT ONE CUP

⅓ cup regular or low-fat mayonnaise

⅓ cup regular or light sour cream or plain (unflavored) yogurt

2 tablespoons vegetable or chicken broth

1 tablespoon rice vinegar

1 garlic clove, chunked

2 tablespoons chopped fresh flat-leaf (Italian) parsley

2 tablespoons chopped fresh herbs such as basil or chervil, and/or snipped chives

Salt and fresh pepper

Put all the ingredients in your food processor and process until smooth and creamy. Season with salt and pepper to taste.

knife on the clove and give the knife a sharp thump with the side of your fist; 3) twist the two ends of the clove in opposite directions. The tight skin will peel right off.

Store garlic in a cool dark place if you can, but don't worry if it must be stored at room temperature; you'll probably use it up before it has time to dry out, shrivel or sprout. When you cut open a clove of garlic, throw out any green (bitter) parts you find in the center.

Important: Raw garlic is quite different from cooked garlic. Raw garlic is pungent, sometimes biting, and gives off the strong odor that some people dislike. A certain amount of raw garlic is delicious— even essential—in salad dressings and other highly flavored condiments, but too much may be, well . . . too much.

Sliced, chopped or minced *cooked* garlic is a different story altogether. Cooking tames the harshness and gives your recipes that wonderful and distinctive garlic taste. But take care: Burned garlic is bitter and will ruin any dish.

Roasted garlic is a flavor unto itself; read about it on page 28.

PANTRY

OLIVES

The tastiest olives are found not in jars but in gourmet shops and in Greek, Italian and other ethnic food stores. You'll see many colors, sizes and textures of olives bobbing around in bins of various brines, spicy oils and herbs. Be adventurous and try a few of each to determine which are your favorites. Look for tiny Niçoise olives, meaty cracked Sicilian ones, purplish-brown Kalamatas, smooth Gaetas and many more.

MENU SUGGESTIONS

Nice with grilled chicken or pork sausage and either Browned Leeks and Mushrooms (page 199) or Browned Leeks with Hazelnut Butter (page 200). Alternatively, serve the artichokes with Small Potatoes with Garlic Cream (page 262), a good green salad and crusty French or Italian bread.

ARTICHOKES PROVENÇAL

MAKES SIX SERVINGS

The term "provençal" indicates the presence of typical ingredients of Provence—garlic, olive oil, tomatoes, olives and anchovies.

- **5 medium-size artichokes, prepared (see Notes to the Cook)**
- **2 tablespoons olive oil**
- **2 garlic cloves, minced**
- **1 small onion, chopped**
- **¾ cup white wine**
- **Salt and fresh pepper**
- **6 anchovy fillets**
- **1 large ripe tomato, stem end removed**
- **12 black olives, pitted (*Use Kalamata or any other good black olive; do not use the canned variety.*)**

1. Quarter each artichoke. With the point of a small sharp knife, cut out and discard the fuzzy choke and thin inner leaves of each quarter. Rinse well and shake off any excess water.

In a large skillet, heat the olive oil and sauté the garlic and onion for a few minutes, until soft.

2. Add the wine, artichoke quarters and a good sprinkling of salt and pepper and stir well. Cover tightly and simmer over low heat until the artichoke hearts are tender, 30 to 35 minutes.

Arrange the artichokes on a platter with the hearts toward the center and the leaves toward the outer edge. Set aside.

3. Chop the anchovies and dice the tomato and olives. Add them to the skillet and cook, stirring, until the anchovies dissolve. Spoon this chunky sauce over the artichoke *hearts* and serve at room temperature.

LEMON-BRAISED ARTICHOKES

MAKES SIX SERVINGS

When you've had enough boiled or steamed artichokes with melted butter or vinaigrette, try this tangy recipe instead. It takes just a bit longer but it tastes more than a bit better.

2 tablespoons olive oil

4 shallots, minced

**3 large artichokes, prepared and halved
     (see Notes to the Cook)**

**2 lemons, room temperature or warmed in a bowl of
     hot water** *(Warm lemons yield much more juice.)*

½ cup dry vermouth

Salt and fresh pepper

1. In a skillet large enough to hold the artichoke halves in one layer, heat the olive oil and sauté the shallots until soft.

Meanwhile, with the point of a small sharp knife, cut out the fuzzy choke and thin inner leaves of each artichoke half.

2. Peel a few thin strips of zest from the lemons. To the skillet, add the strips of zest, the juice of the lemons (squeezed through a strainer), the vermouth and a good sprinkling of salt and pepper. Arrange the artichokes in the skillet, cut sides up, baste with the sauce, and cover the skillet tightly.

Cook over low heat, turning several times, for 30 to 35 minutes, until the leaves can be broken off easily and the heart is easily pierced by the point of a knife. Serve hot or warm.

Olives from cans are awful, so don't buy them; olives from jars have their uses, mainly when you can't get loose olives or when you want pimiento-stuffed ones for garnish.

Store olives in plastic containers or glass jars in the refrigerator. If you like, add olive oil or equal parts of water, vinegar and olive oil to fill the containers or jars. Crushed coriander seeds, hot red pepper flakes, crushed garlic cloves, a little mixed pickling spice or several slices of lemon will liven up the olives, too. Shake the container or jar occasionally to mix the ingredients.

MENU SUGGESTIONS

Lamb chops are a fine partner to artichokes, along with Herbed Potatoes Provençal (page 263)—a good spring meal. If you don't want to serve meat, make a big *salade niçoise* and heat up a round country loaf to go with it.

ROASTED GARLIC

Garlic roasted in its skin is so sweet and mellow (never harsh and strong) that you can peel it and pop the soft cloves right into your mouth. It's delicious spread on hot crusty bread or toast—a great substitute for butter or margarine—or added to any number of dishes.

Here is the simplest way to roast garlic: Preheat the oven to 400°. Put one or more whole bulbs of garlic in a small baking dish, place the dish on the middle rack of the oven, and leave it there for 30 to 35 minutes, until the garlic inside the papery skin is soft. You'll know it's soft when you squeeze the bulb (with a pot holder, of course) and feel it give easily under the pressure.

Let the bulb(s) cool until you can handle them. To get whole cloves, separate the roasted cloves and peel each one carefully; if you are planning to mash the roasted garlic, peel off as much of the papery outer skin as you can, then slice off the stem end of the bulb with a serrated knife and squeeze out the pulp.

Try these tricks with roasted garlic:

- STIR PEELED CLOVES INTO RISOTTO (MY FAVORITE) OR PASTA.
- SQUEEZE OUT AND MASH THE PULP WITH A LITTLE BUTTER, MARGARINE OR OLIVE OIL TO MAKE A MILD GARLIC SPREAD.
- MASH THE PULP WITH A LITTLE LOW-FAT MAYONNAISE AND CHICKEN BROTH TO MAKE A RICH-TASTING DIP FOR RAW VEGETABLES.
- PURÉE WITH CREAM OR SOUR CREAM AND A LITTLE CHICKEN OR VEGETABLE BROTH TO MAKE A DELICIOUS SAUCE.
- USE PEELED CLOVES TO GARNISH ROASTED CHICKEN OR PORK.

ARTICHOKE TART WITH ROASTED GARLIC

MAKES ONE 9-INCH TART, PLENTY FOR SIX SERVINGS

Not strictly a side dish, I admit (unless you serve it as part of a buffet), but it's too good to leave out.

12 large unpeeled garlic cloves

1 small red bell pepper, cored, seeded and deveined

1 unbaked readymade 9-inch pie crust, *room temperature*

15 baby artichokes, prepared and halved (see Notes to the Cook)

Olive oil

Salt and fresh pepper

1. Preheat the oven to 375°. Put the garlic cloves in a small baking dish and roast for 20 minutes. Let them cool, then peel carefully and cut each one in half lengthwise; set aside. Leave the oven on for prebaking the pie crust.

Cut the pepper into ¼-inch strips.

2. Turn the pie crust out onto an ungreased baking sheet—just flip it over and let it drop out of the aluminum pie plate onto the baking sheet. Gently flatten the center (easy when the crust is at room temperature), leaving the crimped edge to form the rim of the tart. If the crust tears, dab a little water on the torn edges and press them together. Prick the crust all over with a fork and bake for five minutes.

NOTE: *I know this turning-a-pie-crust-into-a-tart-crust trick sounds a little surprising, but it works and it's terrific. In fact, it's so easy that you'll probably find other ways to use it.*

3. Bring a saucepan of water to a boil. Drop the prepared artichokes into the boiling water and simmer three minutes, until just crisp-tender; keep in mind that the artichokes will be cooked further in the oven. Rinse immediately under cold water to stop the cooking process, then drain well and pat dry on paper towels.

4. Brush olive oil on the partially baked crust, including the crimped edge. Arrange the artichokes and garlic on the crust, cut sides down, and place the pepper strips on top. Lightly brush all the vegetables with olive oil and sprinkle with salt and pepper.

Bake the tart for 35 to 40 minutes, until the peppers are crisp-tender or tender and the crust is golden brown. Be careful not to overbake the crust. Serve at room temperature.

- **HALVE PEELED CLOVES AND ADD THEM TO A VEGETABLE DISH—GREEN BEANS, BABY ARTICHOKES, RUTABAGA, ZUCCHINI.**
- **MASH THE PULP AND ADD IT TO SOUP.**
- **MAKE PEELED ROASTED CLOVES A PART OF AN ANTIPASTO PLATE OR SERVE THEM WITH AN APPETIZER OF ROASTED PEPPERS, MOZZARELLA AND FRESH BASIL.**

MENU SUGGESTIONS

Perfect with simple roasted chicken or Cornish hens and a salad—perhaps My Favorite Belgian Endive Salad (page 76). Or you can parlay this recipe into a real Mediterranean party menu that includes Flageolets with Oven-dried Tomatoes and Crisp-fried Onions (page 52), Green Beans in the Style of Spain (page 62), Simplified Caponata with Sun-dried Tomatoes (page 152) and a platter of pâtés and other charcuterie. Serve lots of good bread, of course.

ASPARAGUS

This is my asparagus rule: When asparagus is in season—and therefore more affordable—eat lots of it.

During the rest of the year asparagus will probably be only an occasional treat, so when it's plentiful I eat it every way I can think of, in embarrassing amounts. I even eat it in sandwiches.

In this section you won't find the standard asparagus recipes—hot with lemon butter or hollandaise sauce, cold with vinaigrette dressing—with the exception of Asparagus Cordon Bleu (page 37). The other recipes here will give you something new and wonderful to try with asparagus when the season arrives.

BUYING AND STORING

Over the season you will see thin, medium and thick spears of asparagus. When they are perfectly fresh, all three are delicious, so feel free to buy any size you find. How much you buy is a tricky matter: For a simple side dish, 6 thick spears per person might be enough, but you'll probably need 8 to 10 medium spears per person and 12 to 14 skinny spears.

When you buy asparagus, the important thing is that the stalks must be firm and really green (not grayish) and that the tips must also be firm, compact and not overgrown. Reject any spears with seeding, bruises or dryness at the tip.

Many markets offer asparagus rubber-banded together in bunches, making it likely that imperfect spears will be mixed in with perfect ones. Do not hesitate to take off the rubber bands and discard the bad guys. Disregard the protests of the produce manager; he shouldn't be selling inferior produce anyway.

Asparagus should be eaten as soon as possible, but if you must store it, keep it unwashed in a plastic bag in the refrigerator for just a day or two.

NOTES TO THE COOK

Trimming: Remove the woody end of each spear simply by bending the spear gently until it snaps. Discard the woody ends.

Peeling: If you've bought skinny asparagus, all you have to do now is wash it well. However, medium and thick stalks make better eating when the lower two or three inches of the spears are peeled. Use a swivel-blade peeler (or any other peeler you prefer) and peel down toward or up from the bottom of the stalk, taking off a little thicker peel toward the bottom.

Cleaning: You never know if grit is lodged under those pointy little scales, so it's a good idea to soak the asparagus in several changes of cool water, then rinse it well.

ASPARAGUS WITH SESAME-GINGER SAUCE

MAKES SIX SERVINGS

A light Asian sauce here, with the merest bite from the hot pepper. The mellow sweetness of the sauce really brings out the asparagus taste.

TIP: If you double the sauce, you can pour the whole thing—including the asparagus—over pasta for a very creditable dish.

FOR THE SAUCE

- 1 tablespoon soy sauce
- 1 tablespoon rice vinegar *(Either Chinese or Japanese rice vinegar is appropriate here; cider vinegar is an acceptable substitute.)*
- 2 tablespoons peanut oil
- 1 tablespoon water
- 1 tablespoon tahini
- 1 teaspoon chopped fresh ginger
- ½ teaspoon chopped garlic
- 1 tablespoon sugar
- Pinch of red pepper flakes

---

48 medium-size asparagus spears (or more if desired), trimmed, peeled and cleaned (see Notes to the Cook)

1. In a food processor, whirl the sauce ingredients until thoroughly blended; set aside.

Cut the asparagus into two-inch pieces, on the diagonal.

2. Fill a large skillet half-full of water, cover and bring to a boil. Add the asparagus and simmer just until crisp-tender, four to five minutes. Drain well but do not rinse in cold water. Transfer to a serving bowl.

Pour the dressing over the hot asparagus and toss to coat. Serve warm or at room temperature.

MENU SUGGESTIONS

Serve with Chinese chicken salad (perked up with chopped water chestnuts and scallions) on a bed of greens or, if you prefer a meat-free meal, with batter-dipped, shallow-fried tofu, Japanese Cucumber Salad (page 146) and rice.

Herb vinegar is a wonderful addition to salad dressings (especially vinaigrette), sauces and marinades. You can buy it, of course, but it's very simple to make—particularly in summer, using fresh herbs from your garden.

To make a pint of herb vinegar, have ready a clean, heatproof quart jar and lid, two cups of vinegar (see the following list) and the chosen *fresh* herb or herbs.

Here are some combinations to try, keeping in mind that there are endless variations on herb vinegar—don't hesitate to experiment by adding more or fewer herbs, a different combination of herbs, a different vinegar altogether or even including a crushed clove of garlic.

ASPARAGUS SALAD WITH YOGURT-DILL SAUCE

MAKES SIX SERVINGS

Serve this sprightly dish as a salad or side dish. It's creamy and mild, with a lift of dill and onion.

FOR THE SAUCE

   5 tablespoons plain (unflavored) yogurt

   3 tablespoons regular or low-fat mayonnaise

   2 teaspoons snipped fresh dill

   2 tablespoons minced red onion

   Fresh pepper to taste

---

   3 ripe, firm plum tomatoes, stem ends removed

   36 medium-size asparagus spears (or more if desired), trimmed, peeled and cleaned (see Notes to the Cook)

   1 small bunch watercress, washed and dried, large tough stems discarded

Salt

Snipped dill for garnish

1. Whisk together the sauce ingredients and set aside to let the flavors develop. Halve the tomatoes and remove the pulp; dice the flesh and set aside.

2. Fill a large skillet half-full of water, cover it, and bring to a boil. Add the asparagus and simmer uncovered until the spears are crisp-tender, about five minutes. While the asparagus is cooking, rotate the spears on the bottom to the top.

Test with the point of a sharp knife; the knife should pierce the stalks easily. Drain well and rinse under cold running water until cool. Pat dry on paper towels.

3. On a serving platter, make a bed of watercress sprigs and arrange the asparagus spears in layers on the watercress. Scatter most of the diced tomatoes over the asparagus. Sprinkle the tomatoes and asparagus with a little salt.

4. Spoon the sauce across the asparagus in a wide band. Scatter the remaining tomatoes on the sauce and garnish with a bit of snipped dill.

- **RED WINE VINEGAR AND ½ CUP OF BASIL OR MARJORAM LEAVES OR DILL SPRIGS**

- **CIDER VINEGAR AND ½ CUP MINT LEAVES**

- **WHITE WINE VINEGAR AND ½ CUP SAGE LEAVES**

- **RICE VINEGAR AND ½ CUP TARRAGON LEAVES**

- **CIDER VINEGAR AND ½ CUP MIXED OREGANO, SAGE AND THYME LEAVES**

- **WHITE WINE VINEGAR AND ½ CUP CHERVIL, PARSLEY AND TARRAGON LEAVES**

Wash and dry the herbs and place them in the jar. Bring the vinegar to a boil and pour it into the jar, completely covering the herbs; boil more if necessary. When the vinegar cools to room temperature, screw the lid on the jar loosely and store in a cool, dry spot (not the refrigerator) for two weeks, swirling the liquid around every day or so.

At the end of two weeks, strain the vinegar into a clean pint jar (with a couple of fresh sprigs or leaves of your herb, if you like), cap the jar and label it.

MENU SUGGESTIONS

I like this asparagus with a spring dinner of baked ham and Mashed Potatoes and Leeks (page 197). For a vegetarian meal, have an Artichoke Tart with Roasted Garlic (page 28) and a salad of cold sliced potatoes and fennel dressed with vinaigrette.

SPRING HOLIDAY VEGETABLE SIDE DISHES

For spring holidays, such as Passover, Easter and Mother's Day, celebrate with seasonal vegetables and traditional dishes.

Asparagus with Sherry Sauce,
page 36

Asparagus Cordon Bleu,
page 37

Stuffed Artichoke Halves
with Creamy Herb Dressing,
page 24

White Bean and Goat Cheese
Pâté on Greens,
page 48

Flageolets with Oven-dried
Tomatoes and Crisp-fried
Onions, page 52

Scallions in Piquant Sauce,
page 198

Browned Leeks with Hazelnut
Butter, page 200

Wild Mushroom Fricassee in
Croustades, page 209

Sugar Snap Peas with
Peppered Orange-Butter Sauce,
page 238

Russian Salad,
page 241

Potato-
Mushroom
Pudding,
page 266

Poached
Spinach
Dumplings,
page 292

ASPARAGUS WITH MUSHROOMS

MAKES SIX SERVINGS

Be choosy when combining herbs with asparagus, to avoid overwhelming the delicate flavor of asparagus; in this recipe the rosemary is unmistakable but not intrusive. Wild mushrooms are great with asparagus, too, and only a little butter is needed for richness.

NOTE: *Read more about mushrooms on pages 201 and 202.*

> 36 medium-size asparagus spears (or more if desired), trimmed, peeled and cleaned (see Notes to the Cook)
>
> ⅓ pound wild mushrooms, cleaned (*Use shiitake, portobello, oyster or cremini mushrooms.*
>
> 2 tablespoons olive oil
>
> 2 tablespoons butter
>
> Salt and fresh pepper to taste
>
> 3 garlic cloves, minced
>
> 1 teaspoon crumbled dried rosemary leaves
>
> ½ cup dry white wine

1. Fill a large skillet half-full of water, cover it, and bring to a boil. Add the asparagus and simmer uncovered until the spears are barely crisp-tender, three to five minutes. While the asparagus is cooking, rotate the spears on the bottom to the top.

Test with the point of a sharp knife; the knife should meet slight resistance when inserted into the stalks. Drain well and rinse under cold running water until cool. Set aside on paper towels.

2. Trim the stems of the mushrooms; slice the mushrooms ¼ inch thick. Melt the olive oil and butter in the large skillet, add the mushrooms and a sprinkling of salt and pepper, and sauté until the mushrooms are limp and lightly browned.

3. Add the garlic and rosemary and sauté until the garlic is soft. Add the wine, stir well, and simmer for one minute to reduce the sauce slightly. Reduce the heat, add the asparagus with a little more salt and pepper, and cook until the liquid is gone and the asparagus is very hot. Do not overcook the asparagus. Correct the seasoning and serve hot.

MENU SUGGESTIONS

Pair this asparagus recipe with a roasted red pepper frittata or with pan-cooked steak. Round out the meal with Small Potatoes with Garlic Cream (page 262) or oven-roasted potatoes (Oven-roasted Rosemary Potatoes minus the powdered rosemary, page 270).

PANTRY

BREAD CRUMBS

There are two kinds of bread crumbs: dry and fresh. Dry bread crumbs are the crunchy ones that look (and are) toasted; fresh ones are soft and untoasted. Recipes usually call for fine crumbs, which are smaller than coarse crumbs.

There is absolutely nothing wrong with using packaged dry bread crumbs, as long as they are of good quality and not stale. I prefer the unseasoned type because the seasoned ones always seem to have an odd metallic flavor; when I want seasoned bread crumbs, I simply add salt, fresh pepper, powdered oregano and basil (or whatever is appropriate) to the unseasoned crumbs.

Homemade crumbs—dry or fresh—are easy to make and taste very good. In fact, when you make them yourself, you can prepare any flavor of crumbs: sourdough, egg bread, rye or whole wheat in addition to white. If you have room in your freezer, it's worthwhile to make up a big batch of whatever

MENU SUGGESTIONS

There are many ways you can go to make up a menu with basic asparagus. For example, serve risotto with the sherry-sauced asparagus or the asparagus with Walnut Dressing, and try pasta with the cheese-topped asparagus. Lamb chops or rosemary chicken is good with orange-butter–sauced asparagus, along with a dish of brown rice with chopped toasted cashews.

THE VEGETABLE EXPRESS

FOUR SIMPLE DRESS-UPS FOR BASIC ASPARAGUS

MAKES SIX SERVINGS

Asparagus is an express vegetable, quick to cook and easy to dress. Prepare 36 thick asparagus spears (or 48 medium-size spears), trimming, peeling and cleaning them as described in Notes to the Cook.

Fill a large skillet half-full of water, cover it, and bring to a boil. Add the asparagus and simmer uncovered until the spears are just crisp-tender, four to five minutes. While the asparagus is cooking, rotate the spears on the bottom to the top.

Test with the point of a sharp knife; the knife should pierce the stalks easily. Drain well, rinse under cold water to halt the cooking, and set aside. Finish the asparagus with any of the following and season with salt and fresh pepper.

SHERRY SAUCE: In the skillet, heat $2\frac{1}{2}$ tablespoons of butter until lightly browned. Swirl in $3\frac{1}{2}$ tablespoons of sweet sherry; add the asparagus and toss gently over low heat until hot.

WALNUT DRESSING: In the skillet, sauté $\frac{1}{4}$ cup finely chopped toasted walnuts in 2 tablespoons of walnut oil. Add the asparagus and toss gently until hot.

CHEESE TOPPING: Heat 2 tablespoons of olive oil in the skillet, add the asparagus, and toss until hot. Remove the asparagus to a platter and sprinkle with $\frac{1}{4}$ cup grated Parmesan cheese.

ORANGE-BUTTER SAUCE: In the skillet, heat 2 tablespoons of butter until lightly browned. Swirl in 2 tablespoons of fresh orange juice and 1 tablespoon of fresh lemon juice. Add the asparagus and toss gently over low heat until hot.

ASPARAGUS CORDON BLEU

MAKES SIX SERVINGS

This is a traditional and festive treatment of asparagus. Your guests feel really pampered when they're served these little bundles of spears, wrapped in prosciutto and sprinkled with cheese and freshly made buttery bread crumbs.

30 to 36 medium-size asparagus spears (or more if desired), trimmed, peeled and cleaned (see Notes to the Cook)

4 tablespoons ($\frac{1}{2}$ stick) butter

$\frac{1}{2}$ cup fine fresh bread crumbs

3 paper-thin slices prosciutto

$\frac{1}{3}$ cup grated or shredded Gruyère cheese

Fresh pepper

1. Butter a baking dish large enough to hold six bundles of asparagus in one layer; preheat the oven to 350° (325° for ovenproof glass).

Fill a large skillet half-full of water, cover, and bring to a boil. Add the asparagus and simmer just until crisp-tender, three to five minutes. Test with the point of a knife; the knife should meet slight resistance. Drain well and rinse under cold running water until cool enough to handle. Set aside on paper towels.

2. In a small skillet, melt the butter and sauté the bread crumbs until golden brown; set aside.

Cut the prosciutto in half lengthwise to make six long narrow pieces.

3. Divide the asparagus into six bundles and wrap one piece of prosciutto around the middle of each bundle. Arrange the bundles side by side in the prepared baking dish and sprinkle with the cheese. Spoon the bread crumbs evenly over the bundles and grind some pepper over them.

Bake just until the asparagus is hot and the cheese melts, about ten minutes. Serve immediately.

kind you like and stash them for later use. Here's how to do it:

Trim the crusts from sliced or unsliced white or whole wheat bread. If you're working with a whole loaf, slice it $\frac{1}{4}$ inch thick.

For fresh crumbs, tear the bread in small pieces and put the pieces in your food processor with the metal blade; pulse several times until the crumbs are the size you need.

For dry crumbs, arrange the sliced bread in one layer on a baking sheet and leave it in a low oven until light brown and completely crisp; break into small pieces and process until the crumbs are the right size.

Store in airtight containers or in heavy plastic bags in the refrigerator or freezer.

MENU SUGGESTIONS

This is a rich dish, so keep the rest of the meal simple. Chicken cutlets or roasted chicken are fine choices, followed by a green salad with a citrus-y vinaigrette dressing. For myself, asparagus, bread and salad are a whole meal.

BEANS,
DRIED

Beans are a big category and in this section you'll find recipes using lentils, split peas, black beans, pink beans, pinto beans, cannellini (white kidney beans), small white beans, chick-peas (also called garbanzos), red kidney beans, black-eyed peas and flageolets. (To be strictly correct, dried beans, lentils and split peas are classified as legumes, but we tend to think of them all as dried beans.)

BUYING AND STORING

I'd better warn you that I'm going to do something unconventional here: I'm recommending using canned beans instead of soaking and cooking dried beans from scratch, a somewhat laborious, time-consuming process. This will probably bring the wrath of the Food Police down on my head, but I'll take the risk in exchange for the time and energy we'll all save.

Canned beans are, in fact, nutritious, delicious, convenient and accessible—and that means you'll prepare beans more often, which will be very good for you and your family.

NOTE: *Preparing lentils and split peas from scratch is an entirely different story, since they are quick-cooking (relatively speaking) and don't require soaking beforehand as dried beans do.*

Dried lentils and split peas: For these recipes, use basic brown or green lentils, not red lentils or any of the lentils used for the Indian dish called *dal.* Brown lentils are the ones you'll find in the supermarket; green ones, usually from France, are found more often in gourmet shops and other stores that sell imported foods. Brown lentils take about 20 minutes to cook, while green lentils take a little longer.

Green or yellow split peas are dried field peas, a kind of pea grown specifically for drying. Use either color—they are interchangeable.

When you buy dried lentils, split peas or any dried beans, you want to see what you're getting, so purchase them in clear plastic bags, windowed boxes or from bins of loose beans at a health food store. The dried lentils or split peas should be whole and roughly uniform in size and color, with none of the tiny pinholes that tell you insects have been at work.

Lentils or split peas (or dried beans) can be stored in airtight containers on a cool pantry shelf for up to a year.

TIP: One pound of uncooked dried lentils or split peas comes to about 2⅓ cups, which cooks up to about 6 cups. Half a pound of uncooked lentils or split peas equals about 1 cup plus 2 to 3 tablespoons, which cooks up to about 3 cups.

Canned beans: The canned beans you want to buy for these recipes are basic beans without sauces or special seasonings. Try a few different brands to find your favorites. One caveat: Some brands of canned beans have a lot of sodium and others even contain preservatives. Avoid these brands if you can, and always rinse canned beans before using. You may also want to refrain from putting any additional salt in the dish you're cooking. Canned beans come in a variety of can sizes, from ten ounces on up, not all of which may be available in your particular supermarket. The cans may be stored in your pantry for up to a year.

NOTES TO THE COOK

Picking over and rinsing lentils and split peas: Measure the amount of dried lentils or split peas you need. Spread them out a handful at a time on a light-colored surface; pick out and discard any pebbles and debris as well as any shriveled lentils or split peas. Put the picked-over group in a strainer and rinse well to remove dust and dirt.

Rinsing canned beans: Turn the entire contents of the can into a large strainer and rinse under cold running water, gently flipping the beans over a few times to be sure the water reaches them all. Rinse until the beans are free of all the canning liquid.

About can sizes and yield: The label information will tell you that a one-pound can of beans contains two cups of ingredients. This is true, but after you rinse off the canning liquid you will have only about 1⅔ cups of beans. A nineteen-ounce can of chick-peas, after the necessary rinsing, yields two cups of chick-peas.

SAVORY BAKED LENTILS

MAKES PLENTY FOR SIX SERVINGS

This hot dish has the rich flavors of Parmesan cheese and smoky bacon—perfect for a chilly night in autumn or winter. The mushrooms are optional but recommended.

1 cup plus 2 tablespoons dried brown or green lentils (about 8 ounces), picked over and rinsed (see Notes to the Cook)

2 tablespoons olive oil

1 large yellow onion, chopped

3 garlic cloves, minced

1 tablespoon butter or margarine

2½ tablespoons flour

2 cups chicken or vegetable broth (or one 13¾-ounce can of broth plus enough water to make 2 cups of liquid)

2 to 4 ounces Canadian bacon, minced

6 tablespoons grated Parmesan cheese

Salt and fresh pepper

Worcestershire sauce

1 cup chopped cremini mushrooms (optional)

1. Butter a 1½-quart baking dish; preheat the oven to 400° (375° for ovenproof glass).

Put the lentils in a saucepan with water to cover, plus one inch. Cover the pan, bring to a boil, lower the heat, and simmer for 20 minutes, until barely tender. Drain well.

2. While the lentils are simmering, heat the olive oil in a large skillet and sauté the onions until lightly browned. Add the garlic, butter and flour, and sauté for one minute. Add the broth and simmer, stirring, until the sauce thickens. Turn off the heat.

3. Stir in the Canadian bacon, grated cheese, a little salt if needed, a good grinding of pepper and Worcestershire sauce to taste. If you're using mushrooms, stir them in, too.

Stir in the drained lentils, correct the seasoning, and spoon the mixture into the prepared baking dish. Bake for 15 to 20 minutes, until the lentils are tender (but not mushy) and the sauce is bubbling. Serve hot.

MENU SUGGESTIONS

This hearty dish can stand alone as the focal point of the menu, accompanied by Cornmeal Pan-fried Okra (page 214), sliced tomatoes and brown rice. If you like, serve a little stewed chicken or pork, too.

PINK BEANS IN CREAMY ONION SAUCE

MAKES PLENTY FOR SIX SERVINGS

This is a super-simple recipe that rewards you with a lot of mellow flavor and good thick texture for very little effort.

2 tablespoons vegetable oil

2 cups diced sweet onion *(Choose Spanish, Bermuda, Vidalia, Walla Walla, etc.)*

¾ cup white wine

½ cup regular or light sour cream

3⅓ cups cooked pink beans (two 1-pound cans), rinsed well and drained (see Notes to the Cook)

Salt and fresh pepper

1. In a large skillet, heat the oil and sauté the onions over low heat for 15 minutes, until very soft and lightly browned. Add the wine, cover the skillet, and simmer for five minutes.

2. Add the sour cream and blend well. Stir in the beans and mash about half of them. Season with salt and pepper and simmer uncovered over low heat for five minutes, stirring constantly. Season with more salt and pepper if needed, and serve hot.

MENU SUGGESTIONS

Try these beans with pan-browned fish fillets and your choice of Okra Fritters with Sauce Ti-Malice (page 212), Swiss Chard Pancakes (page 312) or Chile-Cheese-Corn Pudding (page 136). Tomato salsa and blue corn chips are a good accompaniment.

AVOCADO

Avocados fall into the category of vegetable fruits: Technically they are fruits, but we generally treat them as vegetables, using them in savory dishes (such as guacamole or salad) rather than sweet ones. Avocados are rich, so a little avocado goes a long way. And because they're rich they work especially well with tart or acidic flavors—lemon or lime juice, vinaigrette dressing, tomatoes, oranges and grapefruit.

There are two popular kinds of avocados—Haas, which is small, with a thick, pebbly black skin, and Fuerte, much larger, with a thin bright green skin. The Haas has a creamy, buttery texture and distinct avocado flavor, while the Fuerte is watery, with much less taste.

MENU SUGGESTIONS

Another hearty dish that needs very little more to make a meal. Fluffy Baked Rutabagas with Melted Cheese (page 285) will do it, along with a green salad and good bread. Sautéed Canadian bacon is a lean accompaniment.

SWEET-AND-SOUR LENTILS

MAKES SIX SERVINGS

Think bistro here—a warm or room temperature dish, rather sophisticated but earthy, too, with delicate sweetness from orange juice and brown sugar and mellowness from vinegar and mustard. Add the optionals for a bit of crunch and greenness.

$1\frac{1}{4}$ **cups dried brown or green lentils (about nine ounces), picked over and rinsed (see Notes to the Cook)**

2 medium carrots, peeled and diced

2 cups chicken or vegetable broth (or one $13\frac{3}{4}$-ounce can of broth plus enough water to make 2 cups of liquid)

$\frac{1}{2}$ **cup water**

$\frac{1}{2}$ **cup orange juice**

1 tablespoon cider vinegar

1 tablespoon Dijon mustard

1 tablespoon brown sugar

$\frac{1}{4}$ **cup dark raisins**

Salt and fresh pepper

$\frac{1}{3}$ **cup chopped red onion (optional)**

2 tablespoons minced fresh flat-leaf (Italian) parsley (optional)

1. In a large saucepan, stir together the lentils, carrots, broth and water. Cover the pan and bring to a boil. Lower the heat and simmer for 20 to 25 minutes, until the lentils are firm but cooked. Drain well (saving the liquid for making soup, if you like) and return the hot lentil mixture to the saucepan.

2. Stir in the orange juice, vinegar, mustard, brown sugar and raisins, and season with salt and pepper. Simmer uncovered for five to six minutes, stirring often; the lentils should be tender and the mixture should be just a bit soupy, although most of the liquid will be gone. Add more salt and pepper if needed, and stir in the onion and/or parsley if you are using them. Serve warm or at room temperature—not hot.

Split Pea and Bulgur Wheat Pilaf

Makes six servings

Turmeric is one of the spices used in curry powder, so this dish has a sort of curry flavor. The peas and bulgur are tender, the almonds are crunchy, and the currants add a touch of sweetness.

NOTE: *Omit the currants if you prefer a completely savory pilaf.*

> 2 tablespoons olive oil
>
> ¾ cup coarse or medium bulgur wheat
>
> 2 garlic cloves, minced
>
> 2 cups chicken or vegetable broth (one 13¾-ounce can broth plus enough water to make 2 cups of liquid)
>
> 1 cup water
>
> ¾ cup green or yellow split peas, picked over and rinsed (see Notes to the Cook)
>
> 1 tablespoon butter
>
> ¾ teaspoon turmeric
>
> ½ cup currants
>
> ½ cup toasted chopped almonds
>
> Salt and fresh pepper

1. In a large skillet, heat the oil and sauté the bulgur wheat for about three minutes. Add the garlic and sauté one more minute. Add the broth and water, cover the skillet, and bring to a simmer. Simmer for five minutes.

2. Stir the peas into the bulgur, cover the pan, and return to a simmer. Simmer for about 25 minutes, or until the peas are tender. If all the liquid evaporates before the peas are tender, add a little more water to the skillet—but don't let the peas get mushy.

3. Stir in the remaining ingredients, including salt to taste and a good grinding of pepper. Again, you may want to add a little water if the mixture seems too dry.

Avocados are shipped rock-hard to market and ripen at room temperature in the grocery or in your home. (Only fully ripe avocados should be stored in the refrigerator.) Depending on when you need it, either buy a hard avocado and give it three to six days to soften or search around until you find a ripe or almost-ripe avocado—one that yields to gentle pressure at the stem end. Don't buy overripe Haas avocados with skins that feel detached from the flesh or have loose pits, or Fuerte avocados with bruises or dark spots.

The easiest way to peel an avocado is to slit the skin lengthwise (without piercing the flesh), using the tip of a sharp knife. Do this in four or five places; then cut off the stem end and peel the skin down as you would a banana skin.

After peeling, cut the flesh in half, working around the pit; then pry the halves apart and set aside the pit. Chop, slice or cube the flesh as needed. The exposed flesh discolors rather quickly, so peel, cut and add avocado as close to serving time as possible.

MENU SUGGESTIONS

Point this dish in the direction of India by serving it with Roasted Eggplant with Indian Spices (page 159), Green or Yellow Squash Raita (page 297), any mild or hot chutney and hot Indian or other flat bread.

GUACAMOLE

MAKES ABOUT 1 ½ CUPS

Everyone has a favorite guacamole—there are dozens of variations. Here's one you can alter to your liking.

MENU SUGGESTIONS

The obvious thing to do here is make the beans part of a Mexican feast, with rice, tortillas, and taco ingredients such as chopped onion, shredded lettuce, cheese, chopped tomatoes and salsa (pages 50, 62 and 214). But a different approach is to serve the beans with Quick Spinach Pie (page 291) and Creamy Carrot Slaw with Chives (page 108).

BLACK BEANS WITH BACON AND CHILE

MAKES PLENTY FOR SIX SERVINGS

This recipe for a variation on refried beans uses five cups of beans, which yields a generous but not excessive amount since everyone will love them. If there are any left over, they are delicious reheated the next day.

NOTE: *In this recipe the bacon fat makes the flavor right. No substitutes will really do the trick.*

> 6 slices lean bacon, minced (about ¼ pound)
>
> 9 garlic cloves, minced
>
> 1½ to 2 fresh hot peppers, charred, peeled, seeded and minced (see Working with Hot Peppers, page 246)
>
> 5 cups cooked black beans (three 1-pound cans), rinsed well and drained (see Notes to the Cook)
>
> 1 cup water
>
> Salt and fresh pepper

1. In a large skillet, fry the bacon until crisp. Add the garlic and hot peppers and sauté for one minute.

2. Keeping the heat low, add a cup of beans and a tablespoon or two of water (from the cup of water listed in the ingredients) and mash the beans. The idea is to add just enough water to make the mashing easier and to yield a creamy thick purée of beans. Keep adding more beans and water until you have added about four cups of the beans.

3. Now add the remaining beans and water. Keep stirring and mashing gently for a few more minutes, until you have a thick purée with plenty of whole beans mixed in. Season with salt and black pepper. Add extra water if needed to keep the consistency creamy, or if the mixture is too soupy, cook it down for a few minutes. Serve hot.

KIDNEY BEANS WITH RICE AND CHEESE

MAKES PLENTY FOR SIX SERVINGS

A hearty, stick-to-the-ribs dish with a mellow flavor—sort of a delicious cross between kidney bean chili and what we used to call, in the 1950s, Spanish rice. There are a lot of ingredients here, but they all go in one pot so it's quite easy to make.

2 tablespoons vegetable oil

1 large onion, chopped

1 green bell pepper, cored, seeded, deveined and diced

2 garlic cloves, minced

1 can (14½ ounces) whole tomatoes, with liquid from can (about ¾ cup liquid)

1¾ cups cooked kidney beans (one 1-pound can), rinsed well and drained (see Notes to the Cook)

Salt and fresh pepper to taste

½ cup raw long-grain rice

¾ cup chicken or vegetable broth

½ cup shredded sharp cheddar cheese (about 2 ounces)

1. In a large skillet, heat the oil and sauté the onion and bell pepper over medium heat until the onion is lightly browned. Add the garlic and sauté for another minute or two.

2. Add the tomatoes and their liquid, breaking up or cutting the tomatoes into one-inch pieces. Stir in the beans, salt and pepper and simmer, covered, for ten minutes, stirring occasionally.

3. Stir in the rice and broth, cover the skillet, and cook over low heat for about 25 minutes, until the rice is tender, stirring occasionally.

4. Add the cheese a little at a time, stirring each addition until it melts. Season the mixture with more salt and pepper if needed, simmer for three more minutes, and transfer to a serving bowl. Serve right away.

TIP: Read more about choosing and preparing avocados on page 42.

2 RIPE HAAS AVOCADOS, PEELED AND PITTED

2 TABLESPOONS MINCED ONION

1 GARLIC CLOVE, MINCED

1 TABLESPOON FRESH LIME JUICE

⅛ TEASPOON (OR MORE) PURE CHILE POWDER

SALT TO TASTE

OPTIONAL ADDITIONS:

- 1 FRESH JALAPEÑO, ROASTED, PEELED, STEMMED, SEEDED AND MINCED

- 1 PICKLED JALAPEÑO, STEMMED, SEEDED AND MINCED

- 1 MEDIUM-SIZE RIPE TOMATO, STEM END REMOVED, DICED

- 3 FRESH TOMATILLOS, STEM ENDS REMOVED, DICED

- 1 OR 2 SCALLIONS, WHITE AND GREEN PARTS, MINCED

- 1 TO 2 TABLESPOONS MINCED FRESH CORIANDER

- 1 TABLESPOON REGULAR OR LOW-FAT MAYONNAISE

- 1 TABLESPOON REGULAR OR LIGHT SOUR CREAM

Chunk the avocados and mash them roughly. Stir in the remaining ingredients and any optional additions you like and serve.

MENU SUGGESTIONS

This dish makes a perfect lunch if you serve it with whole grain rolls and a spinach salad with melon (page 344) or a green salad with avocado slices.

SUN-DRIED TOMATOES

Sun-dried tomatoes come in two basic forms: dry halves sold loose by the pound and halves packed in oil in jars. Both have their uses, but the dry kind is far more economical and of course there is no fat.

Dry tomatoes are the ones I mean when I specify sun-dried tomatoes in an ingredients list.

Dry tomatoes vary enormously in quality: They are all wrinkled and salty to some degree, but some sun-dried tomatoes are a beautiful red, with flesh that still has a hint of plumpness. Others have been over-dried and will never reconstitute to softness or meatiness, are too salty, or have an excessive number of seeds. If you have gourmet shops or Italian specialty stores in your area, try their different brands of sun-dried tomatoes to find the one you like best.

Preparing the tomatoes for use in a side dish, sauce or garnish is simple: Rinse the tomatoes well to remove surface dirt and salt. Put them

MENU SUGGESTIONS

I like these beans with something crisp and tangy, such as Tomato Tart (page 320), with little bowls of Giardiniera (page 116) and Marinated Mushrooms (page 204). If you like, offer some cold chicken to round out the meal.

CANNELLINI WITH ESCAROLE PURÉE

MAKES PLENTY FOR SIX SERVINGS

A mild, fresh dish to serve with other dishes of more assertive flavor. Serve it slightly warm or at room temperature.

- 1 medium head escarole (about 1 pound), trimmed, yellow or wilted leaves discarded, remaining leaves washed
- ½ cup chicken or vegetable broth
- 3 tablespoons olive oil
- 3 garlic cloves, minced
- Salt and fresh pepper
- 3 stalks celery, trimmed
- 1 medium-size red bell pepper, cored, seeded and deveined
- 3⅓ cups cooked cannellini (two 1-pound cans), rinsed well and drained (see Notes to the Cook) *(Cannellini are white kidney beans.)*
- Powdered dried rosemary
- Powdered dried sage

1. Stack the escarole leaves and cut them into one-inch strips. Bring a large saucepan of water to a boil, add the escarole, and parboil for three to five minutes, until tender. Rinse under cold water, drain well, and squeeze out the liquid.

In your food processor, purée the escarole with the broth, one tablespoon of the oil, half the minced garlic and a sprinkling of salt and pepper. Set aside.

2. Dice the celery and red pepper. In a large skillet, heat the remaining two tablespoons of oil and sauté the diced celery and pepper until softened. Add the rest of the garlic and sauté for another minute or two.

3. Stir in the beans, escarole purée and a few pinches of rosemary and sage. Stir over low heat until the beans are hot, three to five minutes. Adjust the seasoning, adding more salt, pepper and herbs if needed. Serve warm or at room temperature.

TOMATO-BAKED CHICK-PEAS

MAKES PLENTY FOR SIX SERVINGS

The sun-dried tomatoes and wine give this dish of tender chick-peas a deep, dark flavor and a beautiful color, too. Whole olives add texture and interest.

2 ounces sun-dried tomatoes

1 six-ounce can tomato paste

1 cup water

2 tablespoons olive oil

1 large onion, chopped

2 garlic cloves, minced

½ cup red wine

1 tablespoon balsamic vinegar

1 teaspoon sugar

½ teaspoon powdered dried oregano

1 teaspoon powdered dried basil

4 cups cooked chick-peas (two 19-ounce cans),
   rinsed well and drained (see Notes to the Cook)

½ cup pitted or pimiento-stuffed whole green olives

Salt and fresh pepper

1. Have ready a 1½-quart baking dish or casserole; preheat the oven to 375° (350° for ovenproof glass).

Simmer the sun-dried tomatoes in a small saucepan of water for five to eight minutes, until very soft. Drain, rinse, and squeeze out any excess water. Purée the tomatoes with the tomato paste and the cup of water.

2. In a large skillet, heat the olive oil and brown the onion. Add the tomato mixture, garlic, wine, vinegar, sugar and herbs, and simmer uncovered for ten minutes, stirring often.

3. Stir in the chick-peas, olives and a sprinkling of salt and pepper if needed. Transfer the mixture to the baking dish and bake for 30 minutes. Serve hot.

in a small saucepan of water, bring to a simmer, and continue simmering for three to eight minutes, until the tomatoes are soft without being mushy. (The amount of time depends on the dryness of the tomatoes.) Drain, rinse well in cold water, and drain again. Pat dry on paper towels.

The basic softening method above will remove a lot of salt, but if you want to get rid of even more, try this alternative: Let the tomatoes simmer for one minute, then drain, rinse the tomatoes, add fresh water to the pan, and repeat. Do this several times—much of the salt will rinse away. (You can actually lose too much salt this way and wind up with bland tomatoes, so taste between changes of water.)

TIP: For a great appetizer, purée softened sun-dried tomatoes with some good olive oil and a garlic clove or two. Spread on slices of plain or grilled Italian bread.

MENU SUGGESTIONS

With the chick-peas, you might serve couscous with raisins or currants and a green salad, with shepherd's bread to dunk in the tomato sauce. If you like meat, add lamb shish kebabs or lamb steaks, and a small bowl of the fiery Tunisian sauce called harissa. A cucumber salad would turn this into a full-fledged feast.

FOUR QUICK BEAN SALADS

MAKES SIX SERVINGS
OF EACH SALAD

For each salad, use two 1-pound cans of the required beans, rinsed well and drained.

White Bean Salad: Use small white beans for this salad. Stir in ½ cup sour cream and 2 tablespoons of chopped fresh herbs—parsley, chives, basil. If you like, dice and add a roasted red pepper (from a jar). Season well with salt and fresh pepper.

Black Bean Salad: Dress the black beans with garlicky vinaigrette (page 53) and stir in two tablespoons of small capers (or chopped large capers). Season with additional fresh pepper and a pinch or two of paprika.

Black-eyed Pea Salad: Stir together the black-eyed peas, ½ cup cooked corn kernels and one large ripe tomato that has been cored and diced. Add your favorite vinaigrette to taste, along with a splash of hot pepper sauce.

Pink Bean Salad: Chop fine ¼ cup of mild mango pickle (a salty-spicy Indian condiment). Stir the chopped pickle and ½ cup plain yogurt into the beans and sprinkle with sliced scallion (green part only).

WHITE BEAN AND GOAT CHEESE PÂTÉ ON GREENS

MAKES SIX SERVINGS

An unusual and interesting presentation—and it doesn't take a lot of work. I like to serve these little bean-and-cheese cakes on dressed greens as a side salad, but the pâté is just as good as an appetizer, served in a bowl (or patted into a shape) and spread on bread.

> **3¼ cups cooked small white beans (two 1-pound cans), rinsed well and drained (see Notes to the Cook)**
>
> **2 tablespoons half-and-half, or 1 tablespoon milk plus one tablespoon cream**
>
> **¼ pound creamy goat cheese**
>
> **½ cup minced fresh flat-leaf (Italian) parsley**
>
> **Arugula, slivers of Belgian endive, pale green and white chicory leaves or other lettuce leaves**

Vinaigrette Dressing (recipe follows)

1. Put the beans, half-and-half, cheese and two tablespoons of parsley in a large bowl and mash to a rough texture. The ingredients should not be perfectly blended; there should be nubbins of cheese and pieces of bean here and there in the mixture. A potato masher is the best tool for this job; do not use a food processor.

2. Divide the pâté in 12 equal parts and shape each part into a flat, round cake about an inch high. Pat about ½ tablespoon of the remaining parsley on the top and sides of each cake.

3. Toss the greens with vinaigrette to taste and spread the greens on a platter. Arrange the bean-and-cheese cakes on the greens and serve chilled.

Vinaigrette Dressing

MAKES ABOUT ONE CUP

This basic recipe has more vinegar than classic vinaigrette; to lighten it even more, add two or three tablespoons of water.

⅓ cup red or white wine vinegar

⅔ cup mild olive oil, or ⅓ cup olive oil plus ⅓ cup neutral vegetable oil (corn, safflower, canola, sunflower, etc.)

¼ teaspoon salt

½ teaspoon dry mustard

Fresh pepper to taste

1 garlic clove, split in half

In a food processor or by hand with a whisk, blend all the ingredients except the garlic. Pour the dressing into a jar and add the garlic; let the sauce stand at room temperature for about two hours to develop flavor. Store in the refrigerator, but bring it to room temperature and shake well before using.

MENU SUGGESTIONS

The pâté with greens makes a light but filling supper, served with Sweet-and-Sour Pattypan Squash (page 296) and plenty of good whole wheat or sourdough rolls.

INDIAN BEANS AND GREENS

MAKES SIX SERVINGS

Hot and spicy beans and spinach, with a nip of ginger and garlic and a crunch of mustard seeds. A substantial curry-flavored dish, deep and rich without being fatty.

2 tablespoons vegetable oil

1 large onion, sliced thin

2 garlic cloves, minced

1 teaspoon minced fresh ginger

3⅓ cups cooked pinto beans (two 1-pound cans), rinsed well and drained (see Notes to the Cook)

1 cup chicken or vegetable broth

1 tablespoon mild curry powder

1 tablespoon mustard seeds

¼ teaspoon hot red pepper flakes

1 ten-ounce package frozen chopped spinach, thawed, liquid pressed out

Salt and fresh pepper

1. In a large skillet, heat the vegetable oil and sauté the onions until lightly browned. Add the garlic and ginger and sauté for another minute or two.

2. Stir in the beans, ½ cup of the broth, the curry powder, mustard seeds and hot pepper flakes. Simmer over low heat for 20 minutes, stirring occasionally. Stir in the spinach and remaining broth and simmer for another three minutes. Season with salt and pepper and serve hot.

MENU SUGGESTIONS

Almost any kind of chicken will be tasty with Indian Beans and Greens, along with some kasha or brown rice and Cauliflower with Cheese Sauce (page 114). Alternatively, serve the beans with white rice and a platter of plain cheese nachos topped with any good red or green salsa.

BLACK-EYED PEAS WITH BUTTER AND SCALLIONS

MAKES SIX SERVINGS

This is one of my favorite Vegetable Expresses. Canned black-eyed peas with their comforting softness are definitely best for this tasty dish.

2 tablespoons butter

1 tablespoon vegetable oil

6 scallions (white and green parts), minced

5 cups cooked black-eyed peas (three 1-pound cans), rinsed well and drained (see Notes to the Cook)

Salt and fresh pepper

1 tablespoon cider vinegar

¼ cup water

1. In a large skillet, melt the butter and oil and lightly brown the scallions. Stir in the black-eyed peas, a sprinkling of salt and a good grinding of pepper. Cook over low heat, stirring often, until the peas are hot.

2. Add the vinegar and water, and stir well to get all the brown bits off the pan and make a little sauce. Serve right away, or set aside until needed and reheat quickly over medium heat.

MENU SUGGESTIONS

Pork chops or baked ham is the obvious choice to go with black-eyed peas, I think, but corned beef hash is good, too. If you prefer something vegetarian, a rice dish or an omelet will work well. Creamy Greens and Tomatoes (page 182) are great with any of these.

AIOLI

Aioli is simply garlic mayonnaise. To the French, however, it is no ordinary garlic mayonnaise, but the centerpiece of a traditional Provençal celebration that takes place each summer, in which the aioli is eaten with fish, vegetables, chicken and country bread. Americans enjoy aioli as a dip served with a selection of cooked and raw fresh vegetables, accompanied by a couple of warm crusty loaves and a good wine.

You can have your own aioli feast, with one caveat: In France, the traditional aioli is completely homemade, using raw eggs in the mayonnaise, of course; in our own country, the United States Department of Agriculture no longer considers it safe to use raw eggs (which may be carriers of bacteria) in any recipe.

So your aioli should begin with commercial mayonnaise, which is safe to eat since it is made with pasteurized eggs. Starting with store-bought may seem like heresy, but with a little doctoring, high-quality commercial mayonnaise can be turned into very good aioli. Here's how to make about 1½ cups of aioli:

In your food processor, chop five cloves of raw garlic. Add 1¼ cups of commercial mayonnaise and 1 tablespoon of fresh lemon juice and process until smooth. With the motor on, slowly drizzle 2 tablespoons of fruity, extra virgin olive oil through the feed tube into the mixture, processing until thick and thoroughly combined. Season to taste with salt and freshly ground pepper.

Serve the aioli with any or all of these fresh vegetables (and don't forget the bread and wine):

COMPANY'S COMING

FLAGEOLETS WITH OVEN-DRIED TOMATOES AND CRISP-FRIED ONIONS

MAKES SIX SERVINGS

Small white or pale green flageolets (flahge-oh-LAY) are actually immature kidney beans. The dried beans are easier to find than the canned version, so prepare your own freshly cooked beans for this recipe; it's not difficult because flageolets do not require long soaking and boiling. The beans, tomatoes and onions are made separately and then assembled on a platter for an impressive presentation.

1½ cups dry flageolets (one 9½-ounce package), picked over and rinsed well (*This becomes about four cups of cooked beans.*)

Lemon-Garlic Vinaigrette (recipe follows)

1 large garlic clove, forced through a garlic press

2 tablespoons minced fresh flat-leaf (Italian) parsley

Salt and fresh pepper

6 medium-size ripe plum tomatoes

Powdered marjoram

2 medium onions

Vegetable oil for shallow-frying

1. Put the beans in a saucepan with cold water to cover. Bring the water to a boil, then drain the beans. Return the beans to the pan, add cold water to cover, and bring to a boil. Reduce the heat and simmer, covered, for 45 minutes, until tender but not mushy. *Do not add salt.* Drain, rinse under cold water, and drain again.

In a medium bowl, toss the flageolets with ½ cup dressing, the pressed clove of garlic, the parsley and a sprinkling of salt and pepper. Taste and add more dressing and seasoning, if needed. Set aside to marinate, stirring occasionally.

2. While the beans are cooking, prepare the oven-dried tomatoes: Preheat the oven to 300°; have ready a wire rack placed on a jelly roll pan or baking sheet.

Cut off and discard ¼ inch of each end of each tomato. Slice the tomatoes crosswise, about ¼ inch thick, and place the slices on the wire rack. Sprinkle both sides with salt, pepper and marjoram. Bake for 30 minutes, then turn the slices and bake for another 30 minutes. Let them cool on the wire rack.

3. Slice the onions as thinly as possible; separate the rings. In a medium skillet, heat ¼ inch of oil over high heat until very hot. Add the onions in several batches, stirring and turning to let each batch brown and crisp nicely, adjusting the heat as necessary to keep the onions from burning. Drain the onions on paper towels and set aside.

4. Arrange the tomatoes around the edge of a serving platter, spoon the marinated flageolets into the center, and top with a mound of crisp onions. Serve at room temperature.

Lemon-Garlic Vinaigrette

MAKES ABOUT ONE CUP

This is a very tart dressing, perfect for marinating the beans. If you want to use it for dressing a green salad, add a little more oil and two tablespoons of water.

⅓ cup fresh lemon juice

⅔ cup olive oil, or a combination of olive oil and another vegetable oil

¼ teaspoon salt

2 garlic cloves, forced through a garlic press

Fresh pepper to taste

In a food processor or by hand with a whisk, blend all ingredients until thoroughly combined; adjust seasonings if necessary. Shake or whisk again just before serving.

- **ASPARAGUS, TRIMMED AND BLANCHED OR PARBOILED UNTIL CRISP-TENDER**

- **BABY ARTICHOKES, TRIMMED AND BOILED UNTIL TENDER**

- **GREEN BEANS, PARBOILED UNTIL CRISP-TENDER**

- **RED AND YELLOW PEPPERS, CORED, DEVEINED AND CUT INTO STRIPS**

- **SMALL RED OR WHITE POTATOES, BOILED UNTIL TENDER**

- **FENNEL, TRIMMED AND SLICED**

- **MUSHROOMS, TRIMMED**

- **BEETS, TRIMMED, PEELED AND CUT IN THIN SLICES OR NARROW WEDGES**

MENU SUGGESTIONS

Make this handsome dish part of an elegant buffet that includes Stuffed Artichoke Halves with Creamy Herb Dressing (page 24) or Artichoke Tart with Roasted Garlic (page 28), cold poached salmon, green salad and herb-flecked bread.

BEANS, FRESH

In this section you'll find recipes for green beans (a variety of snap beans) and lima beans (a variety of shell beans). There are several other kinds of snap beans—yellow wax beans, purple beans, flat Italian green beans and Chinese long beans—but I've stayed with green beans because they are available year-round in your supermarket or greengrocer. Feel free to substitute any of the other snap beans if you prefer them and you can find them.

Also, fancier stores usually carry haricots verts (AH-ree-co VAIR), small French green beans that look and taste like very young green beans. Haricots verts are expensive compared to regular green beans, but you'll want them for recipes that require small green beans when you can't find the homegrown item.

Shell beans, such as lima, cranberry and fava, are fresh beans nestled inside throw-away pods. Fresh limas and other shell beans are expensive and hard to find, and when you find them you can't be sure the pods contain the small-size beans that make the best eating. For my money, it makes more sense to use frozen baby limas, which are tender, sweet and quite reasonably priced.

BUYING AND STORING

Green beans: The best green beans are small and narrow, with velvety skin. Cookbooks are always telling you to buy beans that snap crisply when you break them, but I have found that not-so-snappy small beans taste just as good as snappy small ones. In fact, all green beans should be somewhat flexible; stiff ones are too old and dry.

Small green beans are hard to find in quantity (especially in winter), but they are worth the search; they tend to slip between the big beans and fall to the bottom of the grocer's bin, so look for them way below the big beans. If you must buy larger beans, avoid the bulging, tough-skinned biggies, which will contain overdeveloped, mealy seeds. Reject any beans with brown spots, large scars or withered ends.

Store green beans unwashed in a plastic bag in the refrigerator; they'll keep for several days.

Lima beans: Although Fordhook limas (a larger, meatier type of lima) are popular in certain regions of the country, I suggest that for these recipes you stick with frozen baby limas, which are tasty, tender and rarely mealy. Buy only Grade A frozen baby limas and keep them in your freezer until needed.

NOTES TO THE COOK

Preparing green beans: Just nip off the stem ends by hand or with a knife and rinse the beans well.

Thawing frozen baby limas: Remove the packaging and place the block of frozen limas in a bowl of cold water, breaking it up as it defrosts. If the limas are not frozen solid, break into lumps in a strainer and hold under cool running water until they separate into individual beans. Use right away or refrigerate until needed.

PANTRY

Nuts

Nuts pop up in quite a few vegetable recipes, so it makes sense to keep a supply of shelled nuts on hand for cooking. You'll want to stock, at a minimum, whole almonds, peanuts, pecans, pine nuts and walnuts. I like to have a can or jar of whole cooked chestnuts on the pantry shelf, too. (Other nuts you may want to have for other purposes are Brazil nuts, cashews, hazelnuts, macadamias and pistachios.)

Nuts must be fresh—rancid, moldy or stale nuts will ruin any dish. Buy nuts in packages (although that is not an absolute guarantee of freshness) or in bulk from a market with a rapid turnover, and store them in the refrigerator, freezer or another cool place. Always taste nuts before you use them; if they don't taste right, throw them out or—if it's a new package—return them to the store.

Often a recipe will require *toasted* nuts, because toasting gives a wonderful crunch to nuts and also brings out the flavor, aroma and richness. Here's how to toast nuts:

Spread whole or chopped nuts on an ungreased jelly roll pan or other shallow baking pan with sides (not a baking sheet). Place the pan in a preheated 350° oven for five to ten minutes. The nuts are done when they smell toasty and a cooled nut is crunchy. Watch them carefully to avoid burning. Let the nuts cool in the pan on a wire rack.

BUTTERY GREEN BEANS WITH PECAN CRUMBS

MAKES SIX SERVINGS

These beans are elegant without being fussy, with a richness resulting from toasted pecans and—happily—just a little butter. They have a pleasant nip of cayenne, too.

1½ pounds small green beans, stem ends removed, beans rinsed

2 tablespoons butter

1 tablespoon vegetable oil (not olive oil)

½ cup finely chopped pecans

¼ teaspoon cayenne pepper

Salt

1. Bring a large pot of water to a boil and parboil the green beans until crisp-tender, about three minutes. Drain, rinse under cold running water, and drain again. Set aside.

2. In a large skillet, melt the butter with the oil. Add the pecans and cayenne and sauté, stirring constantly, for one minute, until the nuts smell toasty. Be careful not to let the nuts burn.

3. Add the green beans and stir-fry for two to three minutes, until the beans are hot and well coated with butter and pecans. Season with salt to taste and serve immediately.

MENU SUGGESTIONS

Buttery green beans go well with roasted chicken and stuffing, Foil-baked Rutabagas with Butter and Herbs (page 284) and a big salad. Vegetarians can simply leave out the chicken (but keep the stuffing).

STIR-FRIED GREEN BEANS

MAKES SIX SERVINGS

Everybody loves this dish—crisp beans in a Chinese ginger and garlic sauce. I think it's as good as or better than you get in many Chinese restaurants. A wok is the best pan to use, but a skillet or sauté pan will do just fine.

FOR THE STIR-FRY SAUCE

$1\frac{1}{2}$ tablespoons minced garlic

$1\frac{1}{2}$ tablespoons minced fresh ginger

2 scallions (white and green parts), minced

2 tablespoons dry sherry (fino or manzanilla)

2 tablespoons sugar

2 tablespoons soy sauce

1 tablespoon water

———

2 tablespoons peanut oil (or vegetable oil; not olive oil)

$1\frac{1}{4}$ pounds green beans, stem ends removed, beans rinsed

2 tablespoons water

1. Combine the sauce ingredients in a small bowl; set aside.

2. In a large skillet or wok, heat the oil and stir-fry the green beans until barely crisp-tender, about two minutes. Add the water and continue stir-frying for another two minutes, until the beans are crisp-tender and the water has evaporated.

3. Add the sauce and continue stir-frying for five to six more minutes, until the beans are tender but not overcooked. Serve immediately.

MENU SUGGESTIONS

You can make this a Chinese menu, if you like, by serving noodles or rice and any of the recipes in the section on Chinese greens (pages 126 to 134). Stir-fried·chicken, pork or beef will be delicious here, too. On the other hand, these green beans don't have to have Asian accompaniments—they'll go with just about any favorite main course from fish to turkey.

PANTRY

FRESH HERBS

Nowadays many supermarkets carry a small selection of fresh herbs—curly parsley, flat-leaf (Italian) parsley, basil, coriander and perhaps dill or chives. Greengrocers and gourmet shops tend to have a larger variety—all of the above plus sage, oregano, tarragon or rosemary. Occasionally you may find chervil, marjoram, mint or thyme.

MENU SUGGESTIONS

Cold suppers are convenient and make a nice change, so put these beans together with potato salad (page 266) and cold cuts or cold chicken. For a meatless meal, serve with Cheddar-baked Tomatoes (page 323) and popovers.

DILLY BEANS

MAKES SIX SERVINGS

These beans are pungent and tart, almost like pickled green beans. Try them as part of a composed salad, mounded in the center of a platter edged with slices of cucumber and boiled potato.

> 3 tablespoons olive oil
>
> ¾ cup white wine vinegar (or ¾ cup white wine plus 1½ tablespoons fresh lemon juice, for a milder taste)
>
> 1 teaspoon sugar (superfine, if you have it)
>
> 3 tablespoons minced fresh dill
>
> 1¼ pounds green beans, stem ends removed, beans rinsed

Salt and fresh pepper

1. In a large bowl, whisk together the oil, vinegar, sugar and dill. Set aside.

2. Bring a large pot of water to a boil and parboil the green beans until crisp-tender, about three minutes, depending on the size of the beans. Drain well. Add the beans to the bowl of dressing, tossing and stirring to coat the beans. Add salt and pepper to taste, then let the beans come to room temperature, stirring occasionally. Serve immediately or refrigerate until needed.

CREAMY LIMAS

MAKES SIX SERVINGS

Creamy, yes, also rich and buttery—don't have too much or have it too often. Even lima loathers discover they love limas prepared this way.

2½ ten-ounce packages frozen baby lima beans, partially thawed

½ cup half-and-half, or ¼ cup heavy cream plus ¼ cup milk

½ cup regular or light sour cream

½ cup chicken or vegetable broth

Salt and fresh pepper to taste

2 tablespoons butter

⅓ cup dry bread crumbs

1. Butter a 1½-quart casserole or baking dish; preheat the oven to 375° (350° for ovenproof glass).

In a medium saucepan, simmer the lima beans in a couple of inches of water until tender, about 15 minutes. Drain and transfer to the bowl of your food processor.

2. To the processor bowl add the half-and-half, sour cream, broth, and salt and pepper; purée until the limas are smooth. Correct the seasonings and transfer to the prepared casserole.

3. In the saucepan, melt the butter and add the bread crumbs. Sauté for a minute or two. Spread the bread crumbs on the lima bean mixture and bake for 15 minutes, until very hot. Serve right away.

Fresh herbs do give a wonderful flavor to your cooking, but there are two maddening things about them: First, they are expensive—except in summer, if you grow them yourself or have access to a farmstand or farmers' market where fresh herbs are sold. Second, you generally have to buy a whole bunch when you need only a couple of tablespoons of the minced fresh herb.

To minimize the pain of throwing out half-used bunches of herbs, share them with your friends or store them like this: To keep them for a few days, wash and dry the herbs, wrap them in a paper towel and tuck them into a zip-lock bag in the refrigerator.

To store them for longer, trim off a bit of the stem ends and put the herbs in a jar of water as if they were flowers; place a plastic bag over the herbs and jar and refrigerate, changing the water every few days.

MENU SUGGESTIONS

Delicious with beef short ribs, a casserole of barley or brown rice, and Browned Rutabagas with Mustard Sauce (page 281). You can omit the beef and add one of the basic baked squash variations on page 307 to make a vegetarian meal.

BARBECUE LIMAS

MAKES SIX SERVINGS

This makes a lot of lima beans, but I don't think there will be much left over. Leftovers may be successfully reheated for another meal.

TIP: If you don't have a lot of stovetop room, preheat the oven to 375° and bake the beans in their sauce in a covered casserole for 25 minutes, or until they are tender.

FOR THE SAUCE

> 1 six-ounce can tomato paste
>
> 1 cup water
>
> ¼ cup cider vinegar
>
> 2 tablespoons Worcestershire sauce
>
> 1 tablespoon dry mustard
>
> 1 tablespoon chili powder *(Chili powder is a store-bought blend of herbs, spices and chiles.)*
>
> 2 tablespoons sugar
>
> ---
>
> 1½ tablespoons vegetable oil
>
> 1 large onion, chopped
>
> 2 ten-ounce packages frozen baby lima beans, partially thawed
>
> Salt and fresh pepper

1. In a medium bowl, whisk together the sauce ingredients. Set aside.

2. In a large skillet over medium heat, heat the oil and sauté the onions until they are lightly browned. Add the limas and cook, stirring, until they thaw completely. Add the sauce, stir well, and season with salt and pepper. Cover the skillet and cook for 25 minutes, stirring occasionally; add a little water if the sauce begins to stick to the pan. Serve hot.

MENU SUGGESTIONS

Try this dish with old-fashioned potpie or leftover turkey and stuffing, with baked beets and Horseradish Sauce for Hot Beets (page 68). Savory Buttercup Squash and Cheese Gratin (page 305) with the limas and beets makes a good meatless menu.

MAPLE-BAKED LIMAS

MAKES SIX SERVINGS

Here's a smoky-sweet pairing of lean Canadian bacon, mustard and maple syrup with tender limas—a hearty and filling dish for a cold night.

2 ten-ounce packages frozen baby lima beans, thawed

1 tablespoon butter

1 tablespoon vegetable oil (not olive oil)

¼ pound Canadian bacon, diced

1 medium onion, chopped

1 tablespoon flour

1 tablespoon dry mustard

½ cup hot water

¼ cup maple syrup

Salt and fresh pepper

1. Put the lima beans in a 1½-quart casserole or baking dish; preheat the oven to 375° (350° for ovenproof glass).

In a medium skillet, melt the butter and oil and sauté the Canadian bacon and onion until lightly browned. Add the flour and cook, stirring, for one minute. Stir in the mustard, then the hot water and finally the maple syrup. Simmer for several minutes, until slightly thickened.

2. Stir this sauce into the lima beans and season to taste with salt and pepper. Cover and bake for 35 minutes, until the limas are very tender. Serve right away or keep warm in a low oven until needed.

MENU SUGGESTIONS

I like these slightly sweet limas with pork patties or pork roast, as well as Spiked Parsnips (page 231) and a spinach salad or any salad made with strong dark greens.

I love salsa with everything from baked potatoes to green salad. There's hardly a green vegetable that doesn't taste better with a dollop of good salsa, and of course it's great as a dip for tortilla chips or as a sauce for pasta or rice. (There are two more salsa recipes in a sidebar on page 214 and a tomato-mango salsa on page 252.)

Salsa Cruda: Core and chop two large, juicy, ripe tomatoes into a small dice. Mince and add two scallions (white and green parts), as many chopped fresh coriander leaves as you like, and one fresh hot chile (cored, seeded and deveined) or pickled jalapeño. Season to taste with fresh lime juice and salt.

GREEN BEANS IN THE STYLE OF SPAIN

MAKES SIX SERVINGS

If you choose to do the entire recipe, including the garnishes, you'll have a truly impressive salad presentation, suitable for any dinner party or buffet. On the other hand, feel free to make just the beans any time. You must use small beans for this recipe.

FOR THE DRESSING

$\frac{1}{2}$ cup fruity olive oil (preferably Spanish)

$\frac{1}{4}$ cup white wine vinegar

2 garlic cloves, forced through a garlic press

1 teaspoon paprika

$\frac{1}{2}$ teaspoon sugar

Salt and fresh pepper

---

1 pound small green beans or French beans (haricots verts), stem ends removed, beans rinsed

2 tablespoons minced fresh flat-leaf (Italian) parsley

2 tablespoons capers, preferably small ones (nonpareils)

FOR THE GARNISHES

2 medium-size ripe tomatoes, stem ends removed, halved

2 red bell peppers, roasted, peeled, cored, seeded and deveined (page 244), or one 7-ounce jar roasted red peppers

1 hard-cooked egg, peeled and halved

18 to 24 small green pitted Spanish olives (without pimientos)

1. Make the dressing in a large bowl: Whisk together the olive oil, vinegar, garlic, paprika, sugar, and salt and pepper to taste.

2. Bring a pot of water to a boil and parboil the green beans until crisp-tender, five to seven minutes. Drain and transfer to the large bowl; toss and stir the beans in the dressing.

Add the parsley and capers and toss again. Set aside to cool, stirring occasionally. When the mixture is cool, taste it and add more salt and pepper if needed.

3. Prepare the garnishes: Scoop out and discard the pulp and seeds from the tomato halves. (A melon baller works well for this job.) Cut the flesh into ¾-inch squares.

If you are using roasted peppers from a jar, rinse them and pat dry on paper towels. Cut the peppers into ¾-inch squares.

Mince or sieve the egg white and yolk separately.

4. Lift the green beans out of the bowl and arrange them neatly in the center of a large platter; there will be dressing and capers left in the bowl. Surround the green beans with a ring of tomatoes and peppers, and spoon the leftover dressing and capers over them.

Tuck olives among the tomatoes and peppers. Sprinkle minced egg white over the green beans and mound the minced yolk on the very top. Serve chilled or at room temperature.

Tomatillo Salsa: **Husk 12 fresh tomatillos and cook in water to cover until tender but not mushy. Purée with two fresh hot chiles (cored, seeded and deveined), two big cloves of garlic and one small onion (chunked). Heat two tablespoons of oil in a skillet, add the puréed ingredients and sauté, stirring occasionally, until slightly thickened (about 5 minutes) or even thicker (15 to 20 minutes). Cool and add salt to taste.**

MENU SUGGESTIONS

Since this is a rather elaborate dish, keep the main course simple—grilled or pan-fried thin steaks or grilled squid are good choices. Accompany with chewy, herb-topped bread.

BEETS

Fresh beets have a strong sweet earthiness that can stand alone or be enhanced by either sweet or savory seasonings. (Canned beets aren't even a close second in flavor or texture.) And, contrary to popular opinion, they are no more difficult to prepare than, for instance, carrots.

In fact, the process is exactly the same: trim, peel and slice (or dice or whatever). The only thing you have to watch out for with beets is that purple juice: Wear an apron because the juice stains everything it touches (including your insides). It does wash off your hands eventually.

BUYING AND STORING

Beets should be round (for easy peeling), firm and smooth; don't buy soft, flabby specimens and be sure there is no decay at the stem end. It's fine if the beets are dusty or even caked with a bit of earth—they are root vegetables after all. If the greens are attached, they should be fresh and crisp.

TIP: Most beets are plain red-purple inside, but sometimes you can find one of the newer varieties, which are yellow-orange (no purple juice to dodge) or red-and-white-striped.

NOTE: *For the purposes of this book, a large beet is about 2½ inches in diameter, a medium beet is about 2 inches and a baby beet is no more than 1 inch across.*

Before storing beets, cut off the greens, leaving about two inches of red stem attached to the beets. Don't cut off the long skinny root end until you are ready to prepare the beets for cooking. Store the beets unwashed in a plastic bag in the refrigerator, where they will last for more than a week. The greens are highly perishable, so use them as soon as possible.

NOTES TO THE COOK

Trimming: Cut off the stem end, including all the little bumps and ridges; cut off the root end close to the main globe of he beet.

Peeling: Use a vegetable peeler to remove the skin, peeling the beet just as you would an apple.

NOTE: *Many cookbooks will tell you not to peel medium or large beets, but to boil them whole with the skins on, let them cool and then slip the skins right off. This is a smart idea and it* works beautifully—but it takes a long time (at least 45 minutes) to boil a $2\frac{1}{2}$-inch beet, and you still have to peel and cut it. I prefer to spend 5 minutes peeling, 5 minutes cutting and 15 minutes boiling my cut-up beets, especially since I find no appreciable loss of flavor or texture by doing it the shorter way.

Beet greens: Rinse, dry, and cook them like any other greens; see pages 182 and 183 for recipes.

BEET-APPLE-GINGER RELISH

MAKES ABOUT THREE CUPS

One of the great combinations—sweet beets, tangy apples, nippy ginger.

1 POUND BEETS (ABOUT TWO MEDIUM-LARGE), TRIMMED, PEELED AND DICED

1 TABLESPOON MINCED FRESH GINGER

GRATED RIND OF ONE LEMON

JUICE OF ONE LEMON (ABOUT TWO TABLESPOONS)

½ CUP APPLE CIDER OR APPLE JUICE

¼ CUP SUGAR

¼ TEASPOON GROUND ALLSPICE

2 PINCHES SALT

1 POUND TART APPLES (ABOUT THREE MEDIUM), PEELED, QUARTERED, CORED CAREFULLY AND DICED

MENU SUGGESTIONS

Sliced boiled beef or corned beef are fine accompaniments to this meatless red flannel hash, along with Sautéed Swiss Chard with Thick Spicy Yogurt (page 314).

RED FLANNEL HASH

MAKES SIX SERVINGS

Red flannel hash is a mixture of cubed beets, potatoes and onions. Leftover corned beef is sometimes added, but the hash is just as authentic without it. The bacon is optional but adds a nice smoky flavor.

1½ pounds beets (without greens), trimmed and peeled (see Notes to the Cook)

1 pound all-purpose potatoes, scrubbed and peeled

4 slices bacon (optional)

¼ cup vegetable oil (not olive oil)

1 large onion, chopped

Salt and fresh pepper

1. Cube the beets and potatoes (½-inch pieces), keeping them separate. Put them in separate saucepans with water to cover and bring to a boil. Boil until tender, about 5 minutes for the potatoes and 15 minutes for the beets. Drain well and place both in one big bowl.

2. If you are using bacon, fry it in a large skillet until crisp, then drain well and crumble or chop it into small bits. Add the bacon bits to the beet mixture and discard the bacon fat.

In the same skillet, heat half the oil and sauté the onion until lightly browned. Stir the browned onion into the beet mixture and season the mixture with salt and pepper.

3. Add the rest of the oil to the skillet. Spread the beet-potato mixture evenly in the skillet and sauté over medium heat without stirring, until the potatoes are crisp and brown on the bottom. Use a spatula to turn the hash; brown again and repeat until most of the potatoes are browned. Season with more salt and pepper if needed, and serve hot.

SWEET BEET CAVIAR

MAKES SIX SERVINGS

This happy marriage of beets and sour cream (remember borscht?) is balanced by the tart sweetness of orange juice and a little vinegar. I call it caviar because it approximates that delicate nubby caviar texture.

2½ pounds medium or large beets (without greens), trimmed and peeled (see Notes to the Cook)

¼ cup orange juice

¾ cup regular or light sour cream

1 tablespoon balsamic or cider vinegar

½ teaspoon grated orange rind

Salt and fresh pepper

Parsley leaves or strips of orange zest for garnish

1. Depending on how much time you have, slice or quarter the beets. (It takes longer to slice the beets but they'll cook faster; quartering takes less time, but the cooking time increases.) Put them in a saucepan with water to cover, bring to a boil, and simmer until tender, 15 to 25 minutes, covering the pan with a lid slightly tilted to allow steam to escape. Drain well.

2. Whisk together the orange juice, sour cream, vinegar and grated rind.

Purée the beets in batches, in your food processor, adding part of the orange juice mixture to each batch. The texture should be grainy, not smooth—something like caviar. Return the purée to the saucepan, season with salt and pepper, and heat gently. Serve right away, garnished with parsley leaves or narrow strips of orange zest, if you like.

1. Put all the ingredients except the apples in a heavy nonreactive saucepan (stainless steel, enameled, etc.) and bring to a boil. Reduce the heat and simmer, partially covered, for 20 minutes, stirring occasionally. Add a little water if the liquid gets low, so the mixture does not burn.

2. Stir in the apples, cover the pan, and continue cooking over low heat for seven minutes. Let the relish cool, then spoon it into containers. The relish may be refrigerated for up to one week.

MENU SUGGESTIONS

For a meatless meal, prepare cheese or potato blintzes (ready-made frozen blintzes can be quite good) or mushroom or cheese tortellini. Your green vegetable can be Swiss Chard with Lemon and Garlic (page 315) or Swiss Chard in Walnut Oil with Toasted Walnuts (page 316). For a meat meal, try ground turkey meatballs or patties and Minted Zucchini Tabbouleh Salad (page 298).

MATCHMAKING: MEAT LOAF OR HAMBURGERS

You're making meat loaf for dinner. What do you serve with it? Here are some possibilities from which to choose, including the Vegetable Express for hurry-up meals.

Dilly Beans, page 58

Red Flannel Hash, page 66

Creole Corn, page 138

*Savory Baked Lentils,
page 40*

*Red and Green Gazpacho Salad,
page 322*

*Sage-roasted Turnips,
page 328*

*Tomato-baked Chick-Peas,
page 47*

*San Francisco Salad,
page 343*

VEGETABLE EXPRESS

*Oven-roasted
Rosemary Potatoes,
page 270*

*Butter-browned Savoy Cabbage
and Mushrooms,
page 182*

THE VEGETABLE EXPRESS

FOUR SAVORY SAUCES FOR BAKED BEETS

MAKES SIX SERVINGS

The best way to prepare beets is also the simplest: Baking preserves the sweet, earthy flavor and yields a wonderfully tender but firm texture. For six generous servings, you'll need 2 to 2½ pounds of medium beets.

There are two ways to bake beets:

Method 1. All you need for this method is beets and time. Cut off the greens and stems right at the top of the beets; cut off the root ends. Wash the *unpeeled* beets well, place them in a baking dish, and cover tightly with a lid or with foil. Bake at 400° until the beets are tender and easily pierced with a knife, 1¼ to 1½ hours. When the beets are cool enough to handle, slide the skins right off.

Method 2. Trim and peel the beets. Leave them whole or cut large beets in half (or even in quarters); try to get all the pieces approximately the same size. Pat the beets dry, rub or brush them with oil (olive oil is tasty), and place them on a big piece of foil (or two pieces of foil, pinched together to make a tight seal). Enclose the beets securely in foil, bringing the foil up and pinching it closed. Place the foil package on a baking sheet and bake at 400° for 45 to 60 minutes, until the beets are tender and easily pierced with a knife.

Leave the cooked beets whole or cut them in slices, half moons or cubes. Serve hot, dressed with salt, pepper and a bit of butter or margarine, or serve cold, dressed with sour cream or your favorite salad dressing. Better yet, stir in one of these simple sauces for a superlative dish. Each recipe makes enough sauce for 2½ pounds of baked beets, except for the vinaigrette recipe, which makes twice the amount you'll need.

HORSERADISH SAUCE FOR HOT BEETS: Melt two tablespoons of butter and stir in three tablespoons of drained prepared horseradish, one teaspoon of Dijon mustard and one teaspoon of wine vinegar; season well with salt and pepper.

HORSERADISH SAUCE FOR COLD BEETS: Whisk together ½ cup of medium-thick yogurt cheese (page 312), 1½ tablespoons of drained prepared horseradish, 1 teaspoon of mustard seeds and salt and pepper to taste.

BASIL-PARSLEY SAUCE: In your food processor, blend ½ cup (packed) fresh basil leaves, ½ cup (packed) fresh flat-leaf (Italian) parsley leaves, ¼ cup white wine vinegar, ¼ cup olive oil, 2 tablespoons water, 1 garlic clove, 1 tablespoon sugar, ¼ teaspoon hot pepper flakes, and salt and pepper to taste.

ANCHO CHILE VINAIGRETTE: Put one ancho chile in a saucepan with water to cover and bring to a boil. Turn off the heat and let the chile soak, covered, until softened, about five minutes. Remove the stem and seeds, purée the chile with ¾ cup of vinaigrette dressing, and pour through a fine strainer. Season with salt and pepper. Use about half of this amount for 2½ pounds of baked beets.

MENU SUGGESTIONS

With either of the horseradish-sauced beets, make a little smorgasbord of herring, Hot and Cold Cucumbers (page 148), Mashed Rutabaga and Potatoes (page 280) or potato salad (page 266), dark bread, butter and radishes. Chicken and a green salad go well with the Basil-Parsley Sauce. Make a simple vegetarian meal of beets with Ancho Chile Vinaigrette, mushroom and barley casserole, and some sautéed beet or turnip greens or collards.

BABY BEETS
AND BEET GREENS

MAKES SIX SERVINGS

Baby beets are ½ to 1 inch in diameter, with completely edible skin, stems and leaves. The baby beets for this dish must be no more than 1 inch in diameter; the greens (leaves) attached to them will be small and tender. You'll want four beets per person.

24 baby beets, ½ to 1 inch in diameter, with greens

Olive oil for rubbing the beets

2 tablespoons olive oil

2 tablespoons butter

½ large Spanish onion (or other sweet onion)

Salt and fresh pepper

1. Preheat the oven to 400°. Cut off the greens, leaving one inch of stems attached to the beets, and trim the root end close to the globe. Discard any wilted or yellowed leaves. Wash and dry the beets and greens very well.

Cut the beet greens into ½-inch pieces and set aside.

2. Put a little olive oil in your palms and rub it on the beets. Spread the beets on a baking sheet and bake for 30 to 35 minutes, until tender when pierced by a knife point.

3. Meanwhile, chop the onion. In a large skillet, melt together the two tablespoons each of olive oil and butter and brown the onions lightly. Add the chopped greens and sauté for one minute. Season with salt and pepper and set the skillet aside until the beets are done.

4. When the beets are done, reheat the greens quickly and transfer them to a serving platter. Put the beets in the same skillet over low heat, add a tablespoon of water, and stir well to glaze the beets with the oil left in the pan. Season with salt and pepper and arrange the baby beets on the bed of greens. Serve immediately.

MENU SUGGESTIONS

This simple but elegant dish deserves simple but elegant partners—soft-shell crabs or broiled swordfish, Crisp Mushrooms (page 208) and Crisp Artichokes (page 23).

BELGIAN ENDIVE

BUYING AND STORING

Heads of Belgian endive are from four to six inches long, with tightly wrapped leaves that are thick and pearly white at the centers, thin and pale yellow or yellow-green at the edges and tips. The smaller the endive, the sweeter it will be, though even a large one is not very bitter. (Besides, the sharp taste is what makes it interesting and a good mixer.) Avoid leaves with brown edges and tips and stem ends that look rusty or slimy.

Store Belgian endive unwashed in a plastic bag in the refrigerator. After several days the outer leaves begin to deteriorate, but many's the time I've simply pulled off the offending leaves and used the ones underneath.

NOTES TO THE COOK

Trimming: First pull off any split leaves or leaves with brown edges. If the head is to be cut lengthwise (with the stem end holding the leaves together), trim the stem end by slicing off a very thin piece to get a fresh clean surface. If the leaves are going to be cut crosswise, go ahead and cut ½ inch off the stem end. Trim the pointed end only if it is discolored.

Cleaning: Never plunge Belgian endive into water. Simply wipe the outside clean with a damp paper towel.

My favorite thing about Belgian endive is its Flemish name: *witloof*. In addition, I love that slightly bitter taste and succulent texture that give unmistakable character to green salads. Belgian endive can be cooked, too—sautéed, braised, baked or grilled to perfection.

GRILLED VEGETABLES

There is nothing, but nothing, like the taste of vegetables grilled out-doors over charcoal. To make them even more enticing, grilled vegetables could hardly be easier to prepare. All you do is cut your choice of vegetables into manageable pieces, brush them with good olive oil, sprinkle with salt, fresh pepper and chopped fresh herbs, and pop them onto the hot grill.

Always start with the vegetables that take longer to cook: ¾-inch-thick slices of eggplant, fennel and onions; whole pattypan squash; chunks of acorn squash. Give these a 10- to 15-minute start and then add the fast-cooking vegetables: whole or halved bell peppers; halved radicchio or Belgian endive; small heads of bok choy; mushrooms; soft-skinned squash (such as zucchini or yellow summer squash) halved lengthwise.

As the pieces char, turn them often to prevent serious burning and to be sure they are uniformly cooked. Remove each piece when it's done and set aside on an oven-proof platter; if you like, reheat all the vegetables in a hot oven for a few minutes just before serving.

SALAD OF ENDIVE AND PEARS WITH CREAMY GINGER DRESSING

MAKES SIX INDIVIDUAL SALADS

I like to serve these attractive individual salads in autumn, when pears are juicy and flavorful. In summer, make the salad with ripe nectarines instead of pears.

6 small heads Belgian endive, wiped clean

6 large leaves of red leaf lettuce

2 medium-size ripe red Bartlett pears *(Any good pear will do, but red Bartletts look prettiest.)*

Creamy Ginger Dressing (recipe follows)

For the garnish (optional): three tablespoons mild mango chutney, coarsely chopped; whole fresh coriander leaves

1. Trim ½ inch off the stem end of each endive; cut each head lengthwise in eighths. Place one leaf of red leaf lettuce on each of six salad plates and top it with one cut-up head of endive, arranged in a fan shape.

2. Cut each pear in quarters; core the quarters. Slice each quarter lengthwise in three pieces. Arrange four pear slices on each salad, narrow ends at the point of the fan.

Put a tablespoon or two of the dressing on the salad at the point of the fan and garnish, if desired, with ½ tablespoon of chopped chutney and a few coriander leaves. Serve the extra dressing on the side.

Creamy Ginger Dressing

MAKES ABOUT ¾ CUP

⅓ cup regular or light sour cream

⅓ cup regular or low-fat mayonnaise

1 teaspoon grated fresh ginger

1 to 2 tablespoons honey *(Thyme honey is especially good here.)*

½ teaspoon dry mustard

Blend the ingredients in your food processor or by hand with a whisk, adding the second tablespoon of honey if you prefer the dressing a bit sweeter.

MENU SUGGESTIONS

Make a simple luncheon by serving this salad with tasty sandwiches of cream cheese on Boston brown bread or raisin bread. For an autumn dinner, have baked pork chops and Maple-baked Limas (page 61), followed by the endive salad.

BELGIAN ENDIVE BAKED IN WHITE WINE SAUCE

MAKES SIX SERVINGS

This mild, lightly sauced dish is beautifully flecked with orange zest.

6 medium heads Belgian endive, trimmed and wiped clean (see Notes to the Cook)

1 tablespoon butter

1 tablespoon olive oil

2 garlic cloves, minced

1 tablespoon grated orange rind

⅓ cup orange juice

⅓ cup dry white wine

Salt and fresh pepper

1. Cut the endive heads in half lengthwise. Arrange the halves, cut sides up, in a buttered baking dish large enough to hold them in one layer; preheat the oven to 375° (350° for ovenproof glass).

In a small skillet, melt the butter with the oil and sauté the garlic until soft. Add the grated rind, orange juice and wine and simmer for ten minutes.

2. Pour the sauce over the endive, sprinkle with salt and pepper, and bake uncovered for seven minutes. Turn the endive cut sides down, and bake 13 more minutes. Arrange the endive, cut sides up, on a platter and serve hot.

MENU SUGGESTIONS

I like crisp crumb-coated chicken cutlets with this endive or, for a meatless menu, Tomatoes Stuffed with Couscous and Pine Nuts (page 325). Add Asparagus with Mushrooms (page 34) and warm crusty bread.

SAUTÉED BELGIAN ENDIVE WITH BACON AND PECANS

MAKES SIX SERVINGS

An unexpected touch of the South here—Belgian endive quickly sautéed, then stirred with bacon and pecans in a glaze made right in the pan with sugar and pungent vinegar.

6 medium heads Belgian endive, trimmed and wiped clean (see Notes to the Cook)

¼ pound sliced bacon, chopped

1 tablespoon olive oil

⅓ cup chopped pecans

Salt and fresh pepper

¼ cup balsamic vinegar

2 teaspoons sugar

1. Cut each endive crosswise in one-inch slices, discarding the hard cores; set aside.

In a large skillet, sauté the bacon until crisp; drain on paper towels.

2. Pour off most of the bacon fat, add the olive oil to the skillet, and heat. Add the pecans and sauté for one minute. Add the Belgian endive and bacon and sauté for several minutes, until the endive is just tender. Season with salt and plenty of pepper. Transfer to a bowl.

3. Add the vinegar and sugar to the skillet and stir over low heat for about two minutes, until the mixture is a thin syrup. Return the endive mixture to the skillet, stir well to coat with sauce, and serve right away.

MENU SUGGESTIONS:

This endive goes well with Tomato Tart (page 320) and a bean salad (page 48) or Split Pea and Bulgur Wheat Pilaf (page 43). If you like fish, sautéed fillets of red snapper or halibut are another good choice. For a slightly jazzier meal—veal chops and Buttered Okra and Wild Rice (page 217).

You're making pork chops for dinner. What do you serve with them? Here are some possibilities from which to choose, including the Vegetable Express for hurry-up meals.

*Acorn Squash with
Apples and Cider Glaze,
page 303*

*Cornmeal Pan-fried Okra,
page 214*

*Braised Red Cabbage
and Apples, page 99*

MENU SUGGESTIONS

Start your meal with hearty bean soup or clam chowder, then serve the salad with an interesting bread. That's a light supper right there. For a totally different kind of dinner, make individual pizzas with simple toppings (page 172) to go right along with the salad.

MY FAVORITE BELGIAN ENDIVE SALAD

MAKES SIX SERVINGS

The ingredients for this hearty but sophisticated salad are not particularly unusual, but they combine particularly well. The one unusual ingredient is the walnut oil used in the dressing, and the dressing is what makes this salad so special.

> **2 ounces sun-dried tomatoes, rinsed**
>
> **6 medium heads Belgian endive, trimmed and wiped clean (see Notes to the Cook)**
>
> **$\frac{1}{4}$ pound arugula, long stems cut off, washed and dried**
>
> **Walnut Oil Vinaigrette (recipe follows)**
>
> **3 ounces Roquefort cheese, crumbled**

1. Simmer the tomatoes in a small saucepan of water for three to eight minutes, until softened. Rinse well in cold water, pat dry on paper towels, and cut in $\frac{1}{4}$-inch strips. Put the strips in a large salad bowl.

2. Cut the endives crosswise, on the diagonal, in one-inch pieces, discarding the hard cores; break large arugula leaves in half. Put all the endive and arugula in the salad bowl. Chill until needed. Just before serving, toss well with Walnut Oil Vinaigrette to taste, then sprinkle with the crumbled Roquefort.

Walnut Oil Vinaigrette

MAKES ABOUT ONE CUP

¼ cup red or white wine vinegar

½ cup walnut oil *(Taste a bit of the oil to be absolutely sure it is not stale or rancid.)*

2 tablespoons vegetable oil (not olive oil)

1 tablespoon water

1 tablespoon Dijon mustard

Salt and fresh pepper to taste

Whisk the ingredients together until thoroughly blended and slightly thickened. Whisk again right before using.

Belgian Endive Baked in White Wine Sauce,
page 74

Pumpkin and Black Beans,
page 274

Sweet Corn Cakes with Raisins,
page 137

Tzimmes of Parsnips, Carrots and Dried Fruits,
page 229

Pungent Salad,
page 344

VEGETABLE EXPRESS

Maple-baked Limas,
page 61

Creamy Greens and Tomatoes,
page 182

BROCCOLI

Frozen broccoli was the only kind I ate until the early 70s, when suddenly everyone was serving a new appetizer called crudités. Back then, crudités consisted of rock-hard flowerets of raw broccoli, carrot sticks and whole raw mushrooms, with a bowl of sour-cream-and-onion-soup dip. It's a wonder that fresh broccoli survived the crudités phase.

Two kinds of broccoli are included here: regular broccoli (Calabrese) and broccoli rabe, which is also called broccoli raab, broccoli di rape, broccoletti di rape and a few other variations. By any name, broccoli rabe is deliciously bitter stuff, something of an acquired taste but well worth trying if you've never had it.

Note about regular broccoli (Calabrese): Many cookbooks give two- or three-minute cooking times for broccoli and declare it crisp-tender. By my lights, that's blanched broccoli in need of more cooking. My recipes require seven or more minutes of cooking time to render the broccoli perfectly done; if you prefer your broccoli underdone, adjust the cooking times accordingly.

BUYING AND STORING

Regular broccoli: A stalk of regular broccoli (Calabrese) is usually a thick main stem topped by a bunch of flowerets. If available, choose firm, narrow stems since thick stems can have hollow, tough or woody cores; leaves still attached to the stems should be fresh and crisp. The buds of the flowerets should be deep green or purplish green, tightly closed and free from wet, blackened spots. Avoid flowerets with large open buds or yellow buds—that's overmature broccoli.

Broccoli rabe: Broccoli rabe looks rather different from Calabrese. A bunch of broccoli rabe has many narrow, dark green stalks, each with broad, ruffly leaves and some with small flowerets. Stalks should be succulent (not woody), leaves green (not yellow or wilted) and flowerets crisp (not decayed).

Keep either kind of broccoli unwashed in a plastic bag in the refrigerator, where it will remain in good shape for several days.

NOTES TO THE COOK

Trimming regular broccoli: If the main stems are woody or hollow, cut off and discard those parts; otherwise, just trim the stems to get fresh, clean ends. Discard any leaves still attached to the stems.

Peeling regular broccoli: The main stems have thick, tough skin that should be removed. After you have separated the flowerets from the main stems, remove the skin by gripping it at the bottom of the stem between your knife and finger and simply pulling up—the skin will usually peel off easily. (You may prefer not to bother, but be warned that unpeeled stems are tough to chew and will take longer to cook. And longer cooking will render the flowerets mushy.)

Trimming broccoli rabe: Stems may be frayed or hollow, so cut off and discard those parts. Remove any wilted or yellowed leaves.

Peeling broccoli rabe: Unfortunately, the skin on the largest stems is very tough. If you can bear to do it, peel them as described for regular broccoli; if not, cut them in smallish pieces so they're easier to chew.

Rinsing: All broccoli should be carefully rinsed under lukewarm water to get dirt out of the nooks and crannies. If the broccoli is especially grimy, it may first need to be soaked briefly, swishing it around in the lukewarm water to loosen the dirt.

IMPROVING LOW-FAT, LOW-CAL MAYONNAISE

The problem with reduced-fat, reduced-calorie mayonnaise is that it doesn't taste like mayonnaise. It's not bad, it's just different and a little disappointing. The trick is to improve it by altering the taste without plumping it up with too much extra fat or calories. Fortunately, this is easily done: There are any number of herbs and seasonings you can mix into the mayo, adding them gradually, tasting tiny little dabs, until you achieve the desired result.

Use the improved mayonnaise as a spread, sauce or dip, thinning it—if necessary—with a small amount of buttermilk or low-fat milk. Here are some possibilities:

- **FRESH LIME JUICE, A LITTLE SUPERFINE SUGAR AND A LITTLE LOW-FAT SOUR CREAM**

- **PREPARED HORSERADISH AND DIJON MUSTARD**

- **FRESH CHOPPED OR SNIPPED HERBS (TRY BASIL, TARRAGON, DILL OR CHIVES), DIJON MUSTARD AND FRESH PEPPER**

- **CHILI SAUCE (THE BOTTLED, SPICY TOMATO-BASED KIND) OR KETCHUP AND CHOPPED SWEET PICKLES**

BROCCOLI SALAD WITH LEMON-CURRY MAYONNAISE AND PEPPER CONFETTI

MAKES SIX SERVINGS

This salad stays bright and crisp because the curried mayonnaise is used to highlight rather than coat the lemony broccoli.

TIP: Omit the pepper confetti if you're in a hurry.

FOR THE LEMON-CURRY MAYONNAISE

 1 cup regular or low-fat mayonnaise

 Juice of one lemon (about three tablespoons)

 Salt and fresh pepper to taste

 $\frac{1}{2}$ to 1 teaspoon mild curry powder

 $2\frac{1}{2}$ pounds broccoli, trimmed (see Notes to the Cook)

 1 tablespoon fresh lemon juice

 2 tablespoons vegetable oil (not olive oil)

 1 tablespoon water

 1 garlic clove, forced through a garlic press

 Salt and fresh pepper

 $\frac{1}{2}$ red bell pepper, cored, seeded, deveined and diced

 $\frac{1}{2}$ yellow bell pepper, cored, seeded, deveined and diced

1. Whisk together the mayonnaise ingredients, using $\frac{1}{2}$ teaspoon curry powder; set aside for 30 minutes to let the flavor develop. Taste and, if you like, add the remaining $\frac{1}{2}$ teaspoon curry powder.

2. Bring a large saucepan of water to a boil. While it heats, cut the flowerets from the main stems of the broccoli; cut any large flowerets into bite-size chunks. Peel the stems and cut them into $\frac{1}{4}$-inch slices. Rinse and drain well.

Parboil the broccoli for seven minutes, until crisp-tender. Drain, rinse well under cold water, and drain again.

3. In a large bowl, whisk together the lemon juice, oil, water and garlic. Add the broccoli, sprinkle with salt and pepper and toss well. Arrange the broccoli on a serving platter, dot with dollops of mayonnaise, and sprinkle the diced peppers over all. Serve the rest of the mayonnaise on the side, for dipping or for adding to taste.

- CHILI SAUCE, CHOPPED GREEN PEPPER, CHOPPED SCALLIONS
- CHOPPED PICKLED JALAPEÑOS, CHOPPED CORIANDER AND A PINCH OF GROUND CUMIN
- LEMON JUICE, CAPERS AND A SMIDGEN OF ANCHOVY PASTE

MENU SUGGESTIONS

You can put together a simple supper by serving the broccoli salad with slices of smoked turkey and a cold rice salad with raisins or chopped dried fruit. Or create a party menu by adding a couple of these: Artichoke Tart with Roasted Garlic (page 28), Minted Zucchini Tabbouleh Salad (page 298), Mediterranean Cauliflower (page 115), Simplified Caponata with Sun-dried Tomatoes (page 152), Marinated Roasted Red and Yellow Peppers with Fresh Basil (page 244).

Peppery, pungent, biting, sweet, hot—when you bite into a radish you never know just what sensation will happen to your mouth. If you've chosen wisely (squeezing each radish to be sure it is firm and not spongy) you know you'll be rewarded with crunch, but how stinging it will be is anybody's guess.

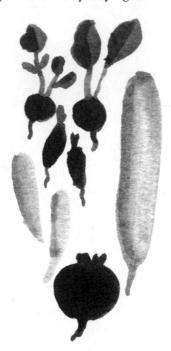

BROCCOLI AND CHINESE MUSHROOMS

MAKES PLENTY FOR SIX SERVINGS

Crisp and richly flavored, with meaty chunks of mushroom. You can prepare this without the mushrooms to make a simpler Chinese-style broccoli dish; if you do, use 2½ pounds of broccoli.

> 12 Chinese dried black mushrooms, stems snapped off and discarded
>
> 2 to 2½ pounds broccoli, trimmed (see Notes to the Cook)

FOR THE SEASONING SAUCE

> ¼ cup oyster sauce (Chinese oyster-flavored sauce)
>
> 2 tablespoons chicken or vegetable broth
>
> 1 tablespoon soy sauce
>
> 2 tablespoons dry sherry (fino or manzanilla)
>
> ¼ cup water
>
> 1 teaspoon sugar

> 3 tablespoons peanut oil
>
> 1 tablespoon minced garlic
>
> 1 tablespoon minced fresh ginger

1. Rinse the mushroom caps well, then soak in a bowl of very hot water for 30 minutes, until soft. Drain and rinse again to remove any sand caught in the gills; squeeze out any excess liquid. Cut each mushroom in quarters, discarding any tough stem ends.

2. While the mushrooms soak, cut the broccoli flowerets from the main stems; cut large flowerets into bite-size pieces. Peel the stems and slice them lengthwise, ¼ inch thick; cut the slices in half crosswise. Rinse the flowerets and stems and drain well.

3. In a small bowl, stir together the ingredients for the seasoning sauce.

4. In a large skillet or wok, heat the peanut oil and sauté the garlic and ginger over low heat for one minute. Add the mushrooms and sauté for one minute. Raise the heat to high, add the broccoli, and stir-fry for two minutes.

5. Lower the heat a bit, carefully pour the seasoning sauce over the broccoli, and continue stirring and cooking for eight to ten more minutes, until the broccoli is crisp-tender. Transfer the broccoli and mushrooms to a platter or bowl and serve immediately.

There are several kinds of radishes available now: the familiar red globe- or oval-shaped radish; the carrot-shaped white icicle radish; the beet-shaped (and beet-size) black radish, which is white inside; and the surprisingly large cream-colored daikon radish so important in Japanese cooking.

When you get your radishes home, trim off any greens and store the radishes in a plastic bag in the refrigerator. When you're ready to eat them, trim off the root ends, wash well and pat dry on paper towels. Icicle and daikon radishes have a thin, somewhat rough skin that may be peeled before eating.

All varieties may be eaten raw, of course, alone or in salads, but the strong black radishes are almost always eaten with some other food (rye or black bread with butter, for instance). All varieties may be steamed, sautéed or boiled.

MENU SUGGESTIONS

Buy some readymade Chinese roast pork to go with the broccoli, add a bowl of rice, and you've got a meal. Steamed Vegetable Dumplings (page 130) are fun, too, when you have the time.

BROCCOLI RABE WITH ANCHOVY AND GARLIC SAUCE

MAKES SIX SERVINGS

Broccoli rabe has such a distinctive flavor that the anchovies and garlic can't overwhelm it—they just complement it and make it more interesting.

2 pounds broccoli rabe, trimmed (and peeled, if you like; see Notes to the Cook)

6 tablespoons olive oil

¼ cup pine nuts (optional)

4 garlic cloves, minced

¼ to ½ teaspoon hot pepper flakes

10 anchovy fillets

½ cup white wine

Salt

1. Cut the broccoli rabe into two-inch pieces (stems, leaves and all); rinse and drain well, shaking off any excess water.

In a large skillet, heat the olive oil over low heat and sauté the pine nuts until lightly browned. Add the garlic and pepper flakes and sauté for another minute. Add the anchovies and cook, mashing them with a wooden spoon until they dissolve. Stir in the wine and simmer 30 seconds.

2. Add the broccoli rabe by the handful, stirring it down as it wilts. Be sure all the pieces are well coated with sauce. Sprinkle with salt (if needed) and continue cooking and stirring over medium-low heat until the broccoli is tender, about five minutes.

With a slotted spoon, remove the broccoli to a platter; simmer the remaining liquid until only a couple of tablespoons are left. Pour this sauce over the broccoli and serve right away.

MENU SUGGESTIONS

I like this with ravioli—meat, cheese or vegetable—and lots of garlic bread. It's also wonderful with Baked Eggplant Slices Rolled with Fontina Cheese (page 160) and that mountain of garlic bread.

BROCCOLI IN CREAMY BROCCOLI PURÉE

MAKES SIX SERVINGS

This is what you cook when you've made a killing in broccoli—two big bunches for 99¢ or whatever—because this simple recipe uses lots of broccoli. The stems become the purée and the flowerets retain their shapes.

3 pounds broccoli, trimmed (see Notes to the Cook)

½ cup regular or light sour cream

½ cup whole milk or part skim ricotta

¼ teaspoon ground nutmeg

Salt and fresh pepper to taste

1. Boil a large pot of water for parboiling the broccoli. While it's heating, cut the broccoli flowerets from the main stems, leaving ½-inch stems on the flowerets; break or cut large flowerets into bite-size ones. Rinse well and set aside.

2. Peel the main stems and slice them ¼ inch thick. Rinse well and parboil the stems until very tender, about seven minutes. Use a slotted spoon to remove stem pieces to a colander, then cool under running water and drain well.

3. Return the pot of water to a boil. Parboil the flowerets until crisp-tender, six to seven minutes. Drain well and set aside.

4. Put the stem pieces in your food processor with the sour cream, ricotta, nutmeg, and salt and pepper and process to a smooth purée, scraping down the bowl once or twice. Transfer the purée to a saucepan.

Add the flowerets to the purée, stir well and heat gently. Correct the seasoning, if necessary, and serve hot.

MENU SUGGESTIONS

Delicious with a simple but elegant dish of angel hair pasta tossed with salmon caviar or bits of smoked salmon. Equally delicious with Caulifritters (page 118), Creole-style Okra (page 215) or Creole Corn (page 138), and a dish of well-seasoned bulgur wheat.

SAUTÉED BROCCOLI RABE WITH PARMESAN

MAKES SIX SERVINGS

This very simple preparation adds interest to the broccoli without detracting from or disguising its unique flavor.

2 pounds broccoli rabe, trimmed (and peeled, if you like; see Notes to the Cook)

2 tablespoons butter

2 tablespoons olive oil

Salt and fresh pepper

6 tablespoons grated Parmesan or Romano cheese or a combination of both

¼ cup seasoned bread crumbs

1. Cut the broccoli rabe into two-inch pieces (stems, leaves and all); rinse and drain well, shaking off any excess water.

In a large skillet, melt the butter and olive oil together. Add the broccoli rabe by the handful, stirring it down as it wilts. Sprinkle with salt and pepper and continue cooking and stirring over medium-low heat until tender, about five minutes. Transfer the broccoli to a serving dish.

2. Sprinkle the broccoli with the grated cheese and bread crumbs, toss well, and serve right away.

MENU SUGGESTIONS

Simple risotto made with onions, garlic and broth is perfect with this broccoli rabe, along with a tomato salad (page 324) and crusty bread. Another good main course is Tuscan Cabbage Soup-Without-the-Soup (page 101) served over fettuccine or wide noodles.

BUCKWHEAT CRÊPES WITH CREAMY BROCCOLI FILLING

MAKES ABOUT 15 CRÊPES, PLENTY FOR 6 SERVINGS

This is a dish for special occasions—partly because the ingredients are so rich and partly because it's a labor-intensive undertaking. Serve these filled crêpes as a side dish in place of potatoes, rice or any other starch. They make a wonderful first course, too.

FOR THE CRÊPES

½ cup buckwheat flour

¼ cup flour

2 eggs plus 1 egg white

1 cup whole or skim milk

¼ cup water

1½ tablespoons butter, melted and cooled

½ teaspoon salt

FOR THE FILLING AND SAUCE

1¼ cups whole or skim milk

2 tablespoons butter

2 tablespoons flour

¼ cup heavy cream or crème fraîche

¾ cup grated cheddar cheese (about 3 ounces)

2¼ cups finely chopped parboiled broccoli (about 1 pound before trimming, peeling and cooking)

2 teaspoons Dijon mustard

Paprika

Salt

MATCHMAKING: LAMB CHOPS OR LAMB ROAST

You're making lamb chops for dinner. What do you serve with them? Here are some possibilities from which to choose, including the Vegetable Express for hurry-up meals.

Peas with Toasted Almonds, page 239

Browned Kohlrabi and Onions, page 189

Sweet-and-Sour Lentils, page 42

Chilled Braised Leeks with Sweet Peppers, page 196

April Salad, page 347

VEGETABLE EXPRESS

Browned Carrots, page 110

Kohlrabi in Poppy Seed Dressing, page 190

PANTRY

GRATED CHEESE

Freshly grated high-quality Parmesan or Romano cheese tastes nothing at all like the poor-quality grated stuff you buy in containers at the supermarket. Do yourself a big favor and grate your own cheese for cooking and for sprinkling on pasta. Here are some of your choices:

- **PARMIGIANO-REGGIANO: COMMONLY CALLED PARMESAN; SWEET, FRAGRANT AND MELT-IN-THE-MOUTH; CONSIDERED THE BEST OF THE GRATING CHEESES**

- **GRANA PADANO: SIMILAR TO PARMIGIANO-REGGIANO AND LESS EXPENSIVE**

- **PECORINO ROMANO: STRONG AND SALTY; GOOD WHEN COMBINED HALF-AND-HALF WITH GRANA PADANO**

- **ASIAGO (AGED): PUNGENT AND FLAVORFUL; SOMETIMES CALLED "THE POOR MAN'S PARMESAN"**

- **DRY JACK: SHARP AND ROBUST; MADE IN CALIFORNIA AND FOUND ONLY IN WELL-STOCKED CHEESE SHOPS**

Buy a block of cheese and keep it wrapped tightly in plastic or foil and stored in an airtight container in the refrigerator. When you need grated cheese, rub the block on the larger grating holes of a box grater or flat grater. Alternatively, cut the cheese

Vegetable oil (not olive oil)

2 tablespoons minced fresh flat-leaf (Italian) parsley for garnish

1. Make the crêpe batter: In a food processor, process all the batter ingredients until completely smooth. Transfer to a bowl and let the batter stand at room temperature for an hour.

2. Make the filling and sauce: Heat the milk in a small saucepan. In a medium saucepan, melt the butter, add the flour, and stir over low heat for one minute. Add the hot milk all at once and whisk over low heat until smooth and thickened. Add the cream and grated cheese and continue stirring over low heat until the cheese melts and the sauce is smooth. Reserve ½ cup of this sauce.

Into the remaining sauce stir the cooked broccoli, mustard, a pinch or two of paprika and salt to taste, to make the filling. Set aside.

3. Make the crêpes: For each crêpe you will use ⅙ cup of batter (half of a ⅓-cup measure). Have ready a baking sheet lined with a couple of paper towels and a crêpe pan or skillet that measures six inches across the bottom.

Heat the crêpe pan or skillet over medium heat and brush oil on the bottom and sides. Lift the pan off the heat, pour in ⅙ cup of batter, and quickly tilt the pan to spread the batter evenly over the bottom. Put the pan back on the heat and brown the crêpe lightly; when the top is dry-looking, turn it carefully and brown the other side for a few seconds.

Slide the crêpe out of the pan onto the baking sheet to cool. Brush a bit more oil in the pan and repeat the process to make the rest of the crêpes, about 16 more. Stack the crêpes as they cool. When cool, choose the 15 prettiest ones.

4. Fill and heat the crêpes: Place two rounded tablespoons of filling just off center on the less attractive side of one crêpe. Fold the crêpe over the filling and press lightly. Repeat this process with the remaining 14 crêpes. Arrange the filled crêpes in a buttered baking dish, slightly overlapping as shown in the illustration.

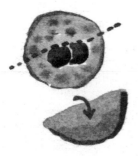

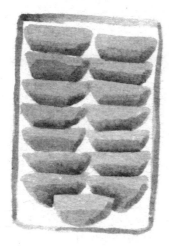

in small pieces and process them with the metal blade in your food processor (taking care not to over-process) or grate the cheese in a hand-operated cheese mill.

NOTE: *I know convenience is important to a busy person and I know it is not always convenient to spend precious minutes grating cheese when you could shake it out of a can. So here are two compromises, one for the table and the other for cooking:*

- **BUY A CHEESE MILL AND GRATE YOUR CHEESE RIGHT AT THE DINING TABLE; THE MILL IS EASY TO USE AND KIDS LOVE DOING IT.**

- **GRATE A CUP OR TWO OF CHEESE AT A TIME AND STORE IT IN THE REFRIGERATOR OR FREEZER IN AN AIRTIGHT CONTAINER. USE IT AS YOU NEED IT, AND WHEN IT'S GONE, GRATE ANOTHER CUP OR TWO.**

(At this point you may refrigerate the filled crêpes. Bring them to room temperature before reheating them.)

Preheat the oven to 325°; cover the baking dish lightly with foil and warm the crêpes for about 20 minutes. Meanwhile, heat the reserved sauce very gently in a small saucepan. When the crêpes are hot, pour sauce down the center of each row and sprinkle with minced parsley. Serve right away.

MENU SUGGESTIONS

This is a complicated production, so you'll want to keep the rest of the meal simple—herb-roasted chicken and Mushrooms Roasted with Butter and Garlic (page 204), followed by a green salad.

BRUSSELS SPROUTS

Brussels sprouts enjoy a rather mixed reputation. (My teen-aged neighbor Jamie calls them shrunken heads.) People who don't like Brussels sprouts usually object to the strong cabbage-y taste, but I guarantee that even skeptics will like these recipes. The trick is either to tame the sprouts with milder flavors or to enhance the strong flavor with equally strong flavors.

BUYING AND STORING

A ten-ounce carton is the most common unit of Brussels sprouts. Unfortunately, ten ounces is an awkward amount, since for six servings you'll need 2½ cartons (about 25 ounces) of sprouts. Be sure to read the ingredients lists carefully to find the right amount of Brussels sprouts for each recipe.

Look for small firm heads (the smaller the better) with tightly wrapped leaves of a beautiful grass green—no yellow or wilted leaves, no insect holes, no splits, nicks or deteriorated stem ends. Store the sprouts unwashed in the refrigerator in the carton or in a closed plastic bag. They should last several days if they were fresh to start with.

NOTES TO THE COOK

To prepare Brussels sprouts for cooking, trim at least ¼ inch from the stem end because the thick core is not particularly pleasant to eat. Good green leaves will fall off when you trim the stem; keep the good ones but discard any yellowed, withered or chewed-up leaves.

POTATO BOATS STUFFED WITH BRUSSELS SPROUTS AND CHEESE

MAKES SIX SERVINGS

These are just great stuffed potatoes with Brussels sprouts added to give them even better flavor.

6 russet potatoes (such as Idahos), each about ½ pound, scrubbed

8 to 10 ounces Brussels sprouts (one 10-ounce carton), trimmed (see Notes to the Cook)

½ cup whole or skim milk

3 ounces Gruyère cheese, grated (about ¾ cup)

Salt and fresh pepper

2 tablespoons grated Parmesan cheese

1. Preheat the oven to 400°; place the potatoes directly on the oven rack and bake until tender, about one hour. Leave the oven on.

Meanwhile, bring a saucepan of water to a boil and chop the sprouts into small pieces (easily done in your food processor if you quarter the sprouts first). Parboil them for two minutes, until crisp-tender, taking care not to overcook them. Drain well.

2. When the potatoes are cool enough to handle, cut a ½-inch slice, lengthwise, from each potato; set aside the slices to munch on at another time. Scoop most of the flesh out of the potatoes, without tearing the potato skins, and put the flesh in a large bowl. Add the milk and Gruyère cheese, and mash to a rough texture. Stir in the Brussels sprouts and season well with salt and pepper.

3. Stuff the mashed potato mixture back into the potato skins, mounding it generously. Sprinkle one teaspoon of the Parmesan cheese on each potato and place the potatoes on a baking sheet. Bake for 20 to 30 minutes, until piping hot and browned on top.

MENU SUGGESTIONS

This is a favorite recipe of my husband's, and we often have it just with other vegetable dishes—baked beets (page 68), broccoli rabe, green salad. If you want a little meat in this meal, try sliced smoked duck or cold meat loaf.

**MATCHMAKING:
BAKED HAM**

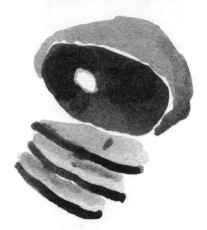

You're making baked ham for dinner. What do you serve with it? Here are some possibilities from which to choose, including the Vegetable Express for hurry-up meals.

*Chinese Broccoli in
Soy-Lemon-Butter Sauce,
page 129*

*Okra Fritters with Sauce
Ti-Malice, page 212*

*Gingered Sweet Potatoes,
page 269*

MENU SUGGESTIONS

Anything involving Russian dressing can also involve turkey, so I serve the sprout salad with turkey, gravy and Maggie's Sweet Potato Casserole (page 268). Instead of the sweet potatoes, you might like to serve Individual Pumpkin-Apricot-Pecan Puddings (page 275) or Oven-fried Potato Cakes (page 271).

BRUSSELS SPROUTS SALAD IN HOMEMADE RUSSIAN DRESSING

MAKES PLENTY FOR SIX SERVINGS

This is a cold salad reminiscent of coleslaw, but the Russian dressing is tangier and the sprouts are tastier.

> 1¼ pounds Brussels sprouts (two 10-ounce cartons), trimmed (see Notes to the Cook)
>
> ½ red bell pepper, diced
>
> **Russian Dressing (recipe follows)**
>
> **Salt and fresh pepper**
>
> **Lettuce leaves**
>
> **1 tablespoon large or small capers for garnish**

1. Slice the sprouts ⅛ inch thick (use your food processor for this job). Bring a pot of water to a boil and parboil the sprouts for five minutes, just until crisp-tender; do not overcook. Immediately run cold water over the sprouts to cool, then drain well and spin dry to remove as much water as possible.

2. In a large bowl, stir together the sprouts, red pepper and ¾ cup of the dressing. Taste and add more dressing, as well as salt and pepper, if needed. Mound the salad on a bed of lettuce and garnish with the capers. Serve chilled or at room temperature.

Russian Dressing

MAKES ABOUT 1¼ CUPS

¾ cup regular or low-fat mayonnaise

3 tablespoons ketchup

3 tablespoons minced sweet pickles (*Don't use India or sweet relish.*)

1 tablespoon drained prepared horseradish

Salt and pepper to taste

Stir the ingredients together until well blended.

SPICY BROWNED BRUSSELS SPROUTS AND CARROTS

MAKES PLENTY FOR SIX SERVINGS

Mustard, beer and the smoky taste of Canadian bacon make this a hearty and lively dish. Vegetarians may omit the Canadian bacon—the sprouts will still be delicious.

1¼ pounds Brussels sprouts (two 10-ounce cartons), trimmed (see Notes to the Cook)

3 medium carrots, trimmed and peeled

3 tablespoons vegetable oil (not olive oil)

1 medium onion, chopped

¼ pound Canadian bacon, diced

2 tablespoons Dijon mustard

¾ cup dark beer

Salt and fresh pepper

1. Cut the sprouts in quarters from top to stem end; rinse well and shake out any excess water. Dice the carrots.

In a large skillet, heat the oil and sauté the onions and carrots until lightly browned. Add the sprouts and Canadian bacon and brown these, too.

2. Stir in the mustard, beer, and salt and pepper to taste. Simmer uncovered, stirring, until the vegetables are crisp-tender and the liquid has almost evaporated. Serve hot.

Stir-fried Cabbage, page 98

Scallions in Piquant Sauce, page 198

Baked Plantains with Chives and Sour Cream, page 253

Squash with Dried Fruits, page 304

Another Spring Salad, page 345

VEGETABLE EXPRESS

Asparagus with Sherry Sauce, page 36

Sautéed Pattypan Squash with Red Pepper Sauce, page 299

MENU SUGGESTIONS

Make a simple meal of these Brussels sprouts with Squash Soufflé (page 308) and corn bread.

THE VEGETABLE EXPRESS

BRUSSELS SPROUTS PAPRIKASH

MAKES PLENTY FOR SIX SERVINGS

The word *paprikash* tells you that the sprouts are in a sauce made with broth, paprika and sour cream. In this recipe the sauce tames the strong flavor of the sprouts.

> 2 tablespoons vegetable oil (not olive oil)
>
> 1 medium onion, chopped
>
> 1½ pounds Brussels sprouts (2½ ten-ounce cartons), trimmed (see Notes to the Cook)
>
> ¾ cup chicken or vegetable broth
>
> ¾ cup regular or light sour cream
>
> 1¼ teaspoons mild paprika, preferably Hungarian
>
> Salt and pepper to taste

1. In a large skillet, heat the oil and brown the onion. While the onion cooks, slice the sprouts ¼ inch thick; rinse and drain well.

2. Add the sprouts to the skillet and sauté for a minute or two. Add the broth, stir well, and cover the skillet. Braise the sprouts over low heat for six to eight minutes, until crisp-tender.

3. Stir in the sour cream, paprika, salt and pepper, and simmer over low heat for several minutes, to warm the sauce. Correct the seasoning and serve right away.

MENU SUGGESTIONS

Veal stew (but not goulash, which is made with paprika and sour cream) with buttered wide noodles and caraway seeds, Basic Baked Squash (page 307) and a hearty bread are very appropriate with the sprouts for this menu. For a vegetarian meal, simply leave out the veal.

BRANDIED BRUSSELS SPROUTS AND CHESTNUTS

MAKES SIX SERVINGS

This is a lovely holiday dish. It's certainly appropriate for special occasions because chestnuts, cream, butter and brandy are not everyday fare.

1¼ pounds Brussels sprouts (two 10-ounce cartons), trimmed (see Notes to the Cook)

18 whole cooked chestnuts (canned, from a jar, or prepared from fresh chestnuts; see the sidebar at right)

4 tablespoons (½ stick) butter

½ cup brandy

¼ cup heavy cream

Salt

1. Cut the sprouts in quarters from top to stem end; rinse and drain well. Chop the chestnuts coarsely.

In a large skillet, melt the butter and sauté the sprouts until lightly browned. Add the chestnuts and continue sautéing for several minutes.

2. Stir in the brandy, cream, and salt to taste and continue cooking over low heat until the sprouts are tender, the liquid is almost gone, and the sauce has become a glaze. Add more salt, if needed, and serve right away.

CHESTNUTS

Fresh chestnuts, boiled or roasted in the shell, are a real treat, but what a tedious job it is to get the meat out of the shell. When I need chestnuts for poultry stuffing or some other recipe, I head straight for the store to buy cans or jars of chestnuts that somebody else has peeled. If you must do it yourself, here's how.

To roast and peel fresh chestnuts: Preheat the oven to 350° and use a sharp knife to cut an **X** in the flat side of each nut. Place the nuts in a roasting or baking pan and roast for 20 to 30 minutes, until the meat feels tender when you poke it with a knife (through the **X** cut). Let the chestnuts cool until you can handle them, and then peel off the hard shell and the inner brown skin. Discard any moldy or buggy nuts.

To boil and peel fresh chestnuts: Make **X** cuts as described above and place the nuts in a saucepan with water to cover. Bring to a boil and simmer, covered, for 15 to 20 minutes, until tender. Remove two or three nuts at a time and peel off the shell and the inner skin. Any nuts that are difficult to peel should be boiled again for a few minutes.

MENU SUGGESTIONS

For a meatless holiday meal, serve with Turnips Rosanna (page 331), Holiday Baked Onions with Double Cheese Sauce (page 224) and a dish of wild rice with chopped toasted almonds. For a holiday meal with meat, simply add your favorite roast—chicken, turkey, ham, pork or beef.

CABBAGE

I think that much of the joking and complaining about cabbage is inspired not, in fact, because it has a strong flavor (so do truffles, after all, and no one complains about them) but because it is considered peasant food. In other words, cabbage is inexpensive, filling, versatile and easy to prepare. That's why it shows up in every cuisine from Indian to Chinese, from Italian to Pennsylvania Dutch, and why Americans eat truckloads of coleslaw and sauerkraut every year.

This section includes green, Savoy and red cabbage, but not Chinese cabbage, which appears in Chinese Greens, pages 126 to 134.

BUYING AND STORING

Newly picked cabbage may come to market with big, loose outer leaves, but most of time—when cabbage is coming from cold storage—you'll find tight heads of green or red cabbage and somewhat looser heads of Savoy. All heads should be firm, heavy for their size, feel solid in the palm of your hand and have no limp, withered or yellowed leaves. Red cabbage leaves should have no blackened edges, but in a pinch you can just peel off the offending leaves.

Store whole cabbage unwashed in a plastic bag in the refrigerator; it will keep at least a week and probably longer. If the outer leaves start looking questionable, simply peel them off and use the remaining cabbage.

Smaller pieces of cabbage can be wrapped tightly in plastic and refrigerated. The flat sides of these leftover halves or quarters will discolor, so just slice off the discolored part and use the rest.

In this book, a small cabbage is 1 to 1½ pounds, a medium head is 1½ to 2 pounds, and a large head is about 2½ pounds. The recipes will tell you exactly how much cabbage to buy.

NOTES TO THE COOK

Preparing: Peel off any loose, darker green outer leaves or any tough, wilted or blemished outer leaves. If you've peeled off enough, you should be down to nice clean leaves.

Coring or quartering and coring: To core a whole cabbage, carefully cut around the tough, hard core with a small, sharp knife, inserting the knife at an angle so you're carving out a conical piece. To quarter and core a head of cabbage, use a large knife to cut the head in four wedge-shaped pieces (cutting down through the core) and then slice the hard core out of each wedge.

Shredding and cutting: To shred the cabbage, cut it in half or in quarters and cut out and discard the core. Lay the cabbage down on the flat side and slice across to make narrow strips. In general, the strips should be about ¼ inch wide, but fine shreds are even narrower. If you're cutting the cabbage in bite-size pieces, halve and core it first; slice in one-inch-wide strips, then cut the strips in approximately one-inch pieces.

Remember: Overcooking is what makes that unpleasant cabbage-y odor. If you follow the timing in the recipes in this chapter, you won't be in any danger of overcooking.

¼-inch strips

1-inch strips

1-inch pieces

core

cut in half

cut in quarters

cut out core

BASIC COLESLAW WITH VARIATIONS

MAKES PLENTY FOR SIX SERVINGS

This is a basic recipe for creamy coleslaw, the kind you think of first when you think of coleslaw. However, in addition to being delicious, it is versatile, so try the variations, too.

> 1 MEDIUM HEAD GREEN CABBAGE (ABOUT TWO POUNDS), PREPARED, QUARTERED AND CORED (SEE NOTES TO THE COOK, PAGE 96)
>
> 1 SMALL ONION, MINCED
>
> 1 MEDIUM CARROT, TRIMMED, PEELED AND SHREDDED OR GRATED
>
> 1 TEASPOON SALT
>
> ½ TEASPOON FRESH PEPPER
>
> ½ CUP WHITE VINEGAR
>
> ⅔ CUP WATER

MENU SUGGESTIONS

I like the cabbage with baked or stir-fried chicken and Hot and Spicy Braised Eggplant (page 156). For a meatless meal, match the cabbage with scallion-flecked Chinese noodles and Braised Chinese Black Mushrooms (page 203).

STIR-FRIED CABBAGE

MAKES SIX SERVINGS

This Chinese-style cabbage is a little hot and spicy. It takes very little time to prepare the ingredients and even less time to cook them in a wok or skillet. In this dish the cabbage loses its crispness and becomes firm and chewy.

FOR THE STIR-FRY SAUCE

> 2 tablespoons soy sauce
>
> 2 tablespoons rice vinegar
>
> 1 tablespoon sugar
>
> 1 tablespoon water
>
> ———————
>
> 1 medium head green cabbage (about 1½ pounds), prepared, quartered and cored (see Notes to the Cook)
>
> 3 tablespoons peanut or other vegetable oil (not olive oil)
>
> 2 garlic cloves, minced
>
> 2 small dried red chiles, snipped in small bits, or ¼ teaspoon hot red pepper flakes

1. In a small bowl, stir together the sauce ingredients; set aside.

2. Cut the cabbage into approximately one-inch pieces.

3. In a wok or large skillet, heat the oil and stir-fry the cabbage over high heat for 3½ minutes, until it loses its crispness and some of the pieces are browned.

Add the garlic and chiles and stir-fry for another minute. Add the sauce and stir-fry for one more minute. Serve immediately.

BRAISED RED CABBAGE AND APPLES

MAKES SIX SERVINGS

The soft, succulent cabbage and apples are deeply flavored with smoky bacon and tart-sweet currant sauce. It's a dish just made to be eaten with pork roast.

4 slices lean bacon

2 tablespoons butter or margarine

1 small head red cabbage (1 to 1¼ pounds), prepared, quartered and cored (see Notes to the Cook)

2 medium-large Granny Smith or other firm, tart apples

⅓ cup red currant or apple jelly

2 tablespoons sugar

3 tablespoons red wine vinegar

Salt and fresh pepper

1. In a large skillet, cook the bacon until crisp; drain on paper towels, crumble, and set aside. Pour off most of the bacon fat and add the butter.

2. Finely shred the cabbage and add it to the skillet. Peel, quarter, and core the apples, taking care to remove all the seeds and hard matter. Dice the apples and add them to the skillet, too. Turn on the heat and sauté until the cabbage is wilted.

3. Add the jelly, sugar, vinegar and crumbled bacon and cook, stirring, over low heat until the jelly and sugar dissolve. Season with salt and pepper, cover the skillet, and continue cooking over low heat for 15 minutes, until the cabbage and apples are quite soft.

Uncover the skillet, raise the heat, and cook until the liquid evaporates and the cabbage and apples are glazed. Serve hot.

2 TABLESPOONS SUGAR

1½ CUPS REGULAR OR LOW-FAT MAYONNAISE

Finely shred the cabbage and put it in a large bowl. Add all the remaining ingredients except the mayonnaise and mix thoroughly. Let the mixture stand for two hours, then drain well. Stir in the mayonnaise and chill until serving time.

For a change of pace, try one of these variations:

- WHEN YOU ADD THE MAYONNAISE, ADD 1½ TEASPOONS CELERY SEEDS AND ONE TABLESPOON DIJON MUSTARD.

- INSTEAD OF USING ALL GREEN CABBAGE, USE HALF A HEAD OF GREEN CABBAGE AND HALF A HEAD OF RED CABBAGE.

- INSTEAD OF 1½ CUPS OF MAYONNAISE, ADD 1 CUP OF MAYONNAISE AND ½ CUP OF REGULAR OR LOW-FAT SOUR CREAM. A TABLESPOON OF CARAWAY SEEDS IS GOOD, TOO.

- INSTEAD OF 1½ CUPS OF MAYONNAISE, ADD ½ CUP OF MAYONNAISE AND 1 CUP OF MEDIUM-THICK YOGURT CHEESE (PAGE 312).

- ADD ABOUT ½ CUP OF DICED RED AND/OR GREEN PEPPER.

MENU SUGGESTIONS

As mentioned in the headnote, pork roast is perfect with this dish. Alternatively, grill or broil some bratwurst to accompany the cabbage and apples, and don't forget the boiled potatoes (see Small Potatoes with Garlic Cream, page 262). Have a green vegetable or a green salad, too.

DELICATE CABBAGE CUSTARD

MAKES PLENTY FOR SIX SERVINGS

This dish—light, feathery and redolent of nutmeg—will surprise you if you expect the taste of cabbage to be strong and the texture to be coarse. Note that it is much lower in fat than an ordinary custard, but just as delicious.

2 tablespoons butter or margarine

2 tablespoons vegetable oil (not olive oil)

6 cups finely chopped green cabbage (about a 1½-pound cabbage) *(Shred the cabbage first, then chop it fine.)*

1 medium onion, minced

2 whole eggs plus 2 egg whites

2 cups buttermilk

¼ teaspoon nutmeg

Salt and fresh pepper

1. Butter a shallow 1½-quart baking dish or casserole; preheat the oven to 350° (325° for ovenproof glass) and bring a kettle of water to a boil.

In a large skillet, melt the butter with the oil and sauté the cabbage and onion until soft but not browned.

2. In a large bowl, whisk together the eggs, egg whites, buttermilk, nutmeg and a sprinkling of salt and pepper. Stir in the cabbage mixture, scraping all the butter and oil from the skillet into the bowl. Pour the mixture into the prepared baking dish.

3. Make a hot water bath for the baking dish: Place the dish in a larger pan (for instance, a roasting pan) on the middle rack of the oven. Carefully pour one inch of boiling water into the larger pan.

Bake for 65 to 70 minutes, until the custard is set and golden on top and a knife inserted in the center comes out almost clean. Serve hot.

MENU SUGGESTIONS

Perfect with a pork roast garnished with prunes, with either Baked Carrots in Honey-Mustard Sauce (page 109) or Turnips Rosanna (page 331). If you omit the meat, add a bean dish, such as Savory Baked Lentils (page 40).

TUSCAN CABBAGE
SOUP-WITHOUT-THE-SOUP

MAKES SIX SERVINGS

Ribollita, the name of the Italian soup from which this dish originates, is served with a slice of bread in the bottom of the soup bowl. This soupless version needs bread, too—warm crusty Italian bread for cleaning your plate.

¼ **pound pancetta, in one whole piece or thickly sliced**

1 **medium head green cabbage (about 2 pounds), prepared, quartered and cored (see Notes to the Cook)**

3 **tablespoons olive oil**

1 **medium onion, chopped**

3 **garlic cloves, minced**

¾ **cup cooked cannellini, rinsed well (*Cannellini are white kidney beans; canned beans are fine for this recipe.*)**

1½ **cups canned whole tomatoes with juice (one 14-ounce can)**

Salt and fresh pepper

¼ **cup minced fresh flat-leaf (Italian) parsley**

3 **tablespoons grated Parmesan or Romano cheese or a combination of both**

1. Dice the pancetta and cut the cabbage into bite-size pieces. In a large skillet, heat the olive oil and brown the pancetta and onion. Add the cabbage and sauté for ten minutes, until the cabbage is soft and glistening.

2. Stir in the garlic, cannellini, tomatoes and their juice and a sprinkling of salt and pepper. Break up the tomatoes into bite-size pieces, cover the skillet, and simmer over low heat for 20 minutes. Taste and add more salt and pepper if needed.

3. Stir in the parsley, transfer the mixture to a serving bowl, and sprinkle with the cheese. Serve right away, with lots of hot crusty Italian bread. You may want to offer more grated cheese with the dish.

MENU SUGGESTIONS

You'll know you've had a meal if you eat this cabbage dish with a bowl of rigatoni or with crusty slices of mushroom-sausage pizza and a big green salad. Here's another tip: Toss with spaghetti or linguine to make a marvelous main dish (with more grated cheese to sprinkle on top), or if you like, add broth to make this dish into a hearty soup.

CONSERVATION IN THE KITCHEN

The kitchen is a prime spot to start (or keep up) your conservation efforts. The following suggestions are easy to carry out—and they make a difference.

Many thanks to my brother, John Javna, and The EarthWorks Group of Berkeley, California, for letting me use this material from *50 Simple Things You Can Do to Save the Earth.*

- **INSTALL A LOW-FLOW FAUCET AERATOR IN YOUR KITCHEN SINK.**

  THIS WILL SAVE HOT WATER. IT WILL ALSO CUT WATER USE BY AS MUCH AS 280 GALLONS PER MONTH FOR A TYPICAL FAMILY OF FOUR. THAT'S OVER 330 GALLONS A YEAR FOR ONE FAMILY. . . . SO IF ONLY 10,000 FOUR-MEMBER FAMILIES INSTALL LOW-FLOW AERATORS, WE'LL STILL SAVE OVER 33 MILLION GALLONS A YEAR.

MENU SUGGESTIONS

For an occasional treat, calf's liver and Crisp Onion and Apple Fritters (page 222) make wonderful accompaniments for this cabbage. Take away the calf's liver and add Mashed Kohlrabi and Potatoes with Tomato Cream Gravy (page 186) to make a meatless meal.

THE VEGETABLE EXPRESS

BUTTER-BROWNED SAVOY CABBAGE AND MUSHROOMS

MAKES SIX SERVINGS

A super-simple dish, intensely flavored with mushrooms and caraway seeds.

1 medium head Savoy cabbage (about 2 pounds), prepared, quartered and cored (see Notes to the Cook)

½ pound white or cremini mushrooms, trimmed and cleaned

2 tablespoons butter

2 tablespoons vegetable oil (not olive oil)

1 tablespoon caraway seeds

Salt and fresh pepper

1. Shred the cabbage and thinly slice the mushrooms.

2. In a large skillet, melt the butter and oil and toast the caraway seeds for two or three minutes.

3. Stir in the cabbage and mushrooms and brown them over medium heat, about ten minutes. (During this time the mushrooms will release their liquid and the liquid will evaporate.)

Season with salt and pepper and serve right away.

COMPANY'S COMING

STUFFED CABBAGE ROLLS ITALIANO

MAKES SIX SERVINGS OF TWO ROLLS EACH

Picture perfect, especially if you arrange the rolls as shown in the illustration. The stuffing is unusual, with a wonderful wild mushroom flavor, and the sauce is fresh and bright.

1 large head green cabbage (about 2½ pounds), cored first, then tough and wilted leaves discarded

½ pound wild mushrooms, trimmed and cleaned (*Shiitake, portobello, oyster or chanterelle are good choices, but feel free to use a combination; there's more about mushrooms on pages 201 to 210.*)

½ cup shredded mozzarella

½ cup cooked lentils

2 garlic cloves, minced

3 tablespoons minced fresh basil or flat-leaf (Italian) parsley, or a combination of both (*If you like, include a little chopped fresh rosemary, sage or oregano.*)

2 tablespoons olive oil

Salt and fresh pepper

1 cup chicken or vegetable broth

6 medium-size ripe plum tomatoes, stem ends removed, diced

- USE REUSABLE CONTAINERS TO STORE FOOD IN YOUR REFRIGERATOR INSTEAD OF HABITUALLY WRAPPING FOOD IN ALUMINUM FOIL OR PLASTIC WRAP.

- USE UNBLEACHED COFFEE FILTERS OR REUSABLE COTTON COFFEE FILTERS.

  YOUR COFFEE FILTERS, PAPER TOWELS, ETC. ARE WHITE BECAUSE THEY'RE BLEACHED. BUT THIS ISN'T A BENIGN AESTHETIC; THE PROCESS OF BLEACHING PAPER IS RESPONSIBLE FOR CREATING DIOXIN, A DEADLY TOXIN THAT HAS BEEN DUMPED INTO AMERICAN WATERWAYS.

- USE BIODEGRADABLE WAX PAPER TO WRAP SANDWICHES INSTEAD OF FOIL OR PLASTIC. OR, FOR SANDWICH AND FREEZER BAG ADDICTS, BIODEGRADABLE NONTOXIC BAGS MADE OF 100 PERCENT CELLULOSE.

- KEEP YOUR EYES OPEN WHEN YOU SHOP. EVERYTHING YOU BUY HAS AN EFFECT ON THE ENVIRONMENT— TRY TO MAKE IT A POSITIVE ONE.

  FOR EXAMPLE, BUY EGGS IN CARDBOARD—NOT STYROFOAM—CARTONS. BUY IN BULK: IT'S CHEAPER AND USES MINIMAL PACKAGING (IN SOME PLACES, YOU CAN EVEN BRING YOUR OWN CONTAINER). BUY CARROTS, ONIONS, POTATOES, ETC. LOOSE AND NOT IN PLASTIC BAGS. AVOID PLASTIC CONTAINERS, ESPECIALLY "SQUEEZABLE" ONES, WHICH ARE MADE UP OF DIFFERENT TYPES OF PLASTIC IN SEVERAL LAYERS AND ARE DRAMATICALLY NON-BIODEGRADABLE.

1. Brush oil in an attractive shallow baking dish large enough to hold 12 cabbage rolls without crowding (a two-quart dish, approximately). You may, of course, use any baking dish, but using a handsome oven-to-table dish makes serving easier. Preheat the oven to 375° (350° for ovenproof glass).

2. Bring a large saucepan of water to a boil. Separate 14 large leaves from the cabbage (the rest of the cabbage may be used for other purposes) and parboil for about 8 minutes, until limp and flexible but not mushy. Drain well and cool the leaves under running water.

Using a small sharp knife, trim off the thick, protruding portion of the center rib on the outside of each leaf. Take care not to cut through the leaf. Set aside.

Important: You need only 12 leaves—the extra 2 were for insurance—so pick out the 12 best and set aside the extras.

3. Make the filling: Mince the mushrooms and combine them in a medium bowl with the mozzarella, lentils, garlic, two tablespoons of the chopped herbs and the olive oil. Stir well and season with salt and pepper. Divide into 12 portions.

4. Stuff each leaf: With the inside of the leaf facing up, place one portion of the filling at the stem end and roll the end over. Fold the sides toward the center and finish rolling. Repeat to make all 12 rolls and place them, seam sides down, in the prepared baking dish.

5. Pour the broth into the baking dish, cover tightly, and bake for 30 minutes. Transfer the cabbage rolls to a plate and pour the broth into a medium saucepan. Return the rolls to the baking dish and keep them warm in a low oven.

6. Stir the tomatoes and remaining tablespoon of herbs into the broth and season well with salt and pepper. Cook over high heat just until the tomatoes soften and begin to look cooked. Use a slotted spoon to remove the tomatoes and arrange them in the center of the dish of cabbage rolls (see the illustration on page 103).

Continue simmering the broth until it is reduced by half. Pour this sauce over the cabbage rolls and serve right away.

MENU SUGGESTIONS

The cabbage rolls are so spectacular that they need only a simple pasta with oil and garlic (or another uncomplicated sauce) to complete the meal. Finish up with a simple green salad dressed with walnut oil vinaigrette.

CARROTS

BUYING AND STORING

Look for the deepest orange carrots you can find, with no sprouting white rootlets, black blemishes, cracks or splits. I think the mature carrots sold in plastic bags are often tastier and sweeter than the unbagged bunches sold with the green tops on, but if you do buy loose bunches, be sure the greens are fresh and not wilted. All carrots, loose or bagged, should be crisp and never rubbery or bendable.

So-called baby or miniature carrots (usually sold in bags at the supermarket or produce store) seem to me bland and uninteresting. On the other hand, sometimes the newest little carrots available at my local farmers' market have a delicate flavor that requires only a bit of butter and salt for seasoning.

If your carrots have green tops, cut them off before storing. Refrigerate carrots in plastic bags; they'll last at least two weeks.

NOTES TO THE COOK

Peeling: Use a swivel-blade peeler (or any other peeler you prefer) to remove the rough skin from mature carrots. Miniature or "baby" carrots may be left unpeeled, if you like.

NOTE: *Yes, you lose some vitamins when you peel, but carrot dishes are better in flavor and texture when made with peeled carrots.*

Trimming: Cut off the top and bottom; this is also called topping and tailing.

Cutting: As you can see in the illustration on the next page, there are many ways to cut a carrot: large or small dice; thick or thin coins sliced straight across or on the diagonal; julienne; sticks; half moons; chunks; or the roll-cut, diamond-shaped pieces favored by Asian cooks.

Carrots, in spite of their reputation as rabbit food and diet munchies, turn out to be one of the tastiest vegetables around. They are also economical and easy to prepare and cook: No leaves to wash, no pods or seeds to remove, no thick skin to cut through, very little waste, and it takes only a few carrots to make a substantial number of servings.

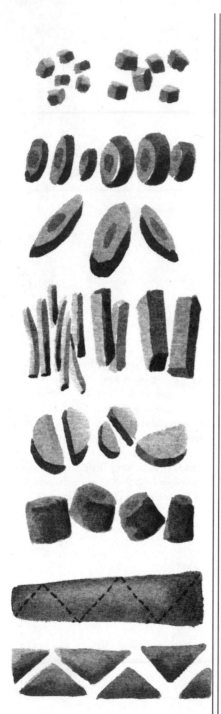

CARROT PANCAKES

MAKES ABOUT 20 PANCAKES, PLENTY FOR 6 SERVINGS

The easiest way to prepare this dish is to use your food processor in the following step-by-step manner. There's no need to wash the food processor bowl between steps. Of course you may do any or all of the steps by hand, if you prefer.

1 medium onion, chunked

Olive oil

1 pound carrots (5 to 6 medium carrots), peeled and trimmed

2 whole eggs plus 1 egg white

¾ cup whole or skim milk

1 cup flour

1 teaspoon baking powder

2 pinches ground nutmeg

½ teaspoon salt

Fresh pepper

1. Mince the onion in your food processor. In a large skillet, heat two tablespoons of olive oil and brown the onion over low heat.

Meanwhile, grate the carrots into the food processor using the grating blade. Transfer the grated carrots to a large mixing bowl.

2. Replace the grating blade with the metal chopping blade. Put the eggs, egg white, milk, flour, baking powder, nutmeg, salt and a good grinding of pepper in the food processor and process to make a smooth batter. Pour the batter over the carrots, add the browned onions—scraping the skillet clean— and stir well.

3. Without cleaning it (unless it has a lot of browned onion stuck to it), heat three tablespoons of olive oil in the skillet. When the oil is very hot, drop rounded tablespoons of carrot batter into it, flattening slightly with the back of the spoon to make raggedy-edged pancakes about two inches in diameter. Don't crowd the pan. (The oil should be sizzling around the edge of each pancake, so adjust the heat if necessary.)

Brown the pancakes on both sides and drain on paper towels. Keep the pancakes warm in a low oven.

Repeat until all the batter is used up, adding oil as needed. Serve hot, as soon as possible.

MENU SUGGESTIONS

These are great with practically anything. Lamb chops or braised lamb shanks are a good choice, with Collards with West Indian Pepper-and-Lime Sauce (page 180) or Not-Too-Hot-and-Spicy Spinach and Chick-Peas (page 288). For a vegetarian dinner, go Indian with the same spinach dish, Red Onion Raita with Coriander (page 221), chutney and basmati rice.

CARROT CHUTNEY

MAKES ABOUT 1½ CUPS

Crisp, tangy Carrot Chutney is a different sort of vegetable side dish, a condiment that is especially good with rich meats such as pork roast, braised beef, baked ham and curried chicken. Chutney can be made ahead and refrigerated until needed.

This recipe makes about 1½ cups; double it if you want more.

½ POUND CARROTS (ABOUT 3 MEDIUM CARROTS), TRIMMED, PEELED AND DICED

¼ CUP DICED RED BELL PEPPER

1 GARLIC CLOVE, MINCED

2 TEASPOONS MINCED FRESH GINGER

1 SMALL ONION, CHOPPED

¼ CUP CIDER VINEGAR

¼ CUP WATER

¼ CUP DARK BROWN SUGAR

¼ CUP GOLDEN RAISINS

¼ TEASPOON DRY MUSTARD

¼ TEASPOON SALT

⅛ TEASPOON HOT RED PEPPER FLAKES

MENU SUGGESTIONS

Wonderful for a picnic or porch supper. Serve with cold oven-fried chicken wings, potato salad (page 266) and buttermilk biscuits.

CREAMY CARROT SLAW WITH CHIVES

MAKES SIX SERVINGS

This is a perfect example of how delicious a dish can be even if you use lower-fat ingredients. It's just creamy enough and the vinegar, sugar and chives give it plenty of flavor.

1½ pounds carrots (8 to 9 medium carrots), peeled and trimmed

½ teaspoon salt

⅓ cup regular or light sour cream

⅓ cup regular or low-fat mayonnaise

1 tablespoon cider vinegar

1 tablespoon sugar

¼ cup snipped fresh chives

Lettuce, watercress, spinach or any other salad greens of your choice

1. Shred or grate the carrots by hand or in your food processor and put them in a large bowl. Stir in the salt and let stand for 15 minutes.

2. Meanwhile, whisk together the sour cream, mayonnaise, vinegar and sugar to make a dressing. Stir the chives into the dressing, pour the dressing over the carrots, and blend well.

Arrange the salad greens on a serving platter, mound the carrot slaw in the center, and serve chilled or at room temperature.

BAKED CARROTS IN HONEY-MUSTARD SAUCE

MAKES SIX SERVINGS

One of my husband's favorites. The combination of sweet carrots and honey punched up with mustard and vinegar is satisfying and rich without being fatty.

2 pounds carrots (10 to 12 medium carrots), peeled and trimmed

1 tablespoon butter or margarine

⅓ cup chicken or vegetable broth

¼ cup honey

3 tablespoons grainy mustard

1 tablespoon cider vinegar

Salt and fresh pepper

1. Cut the carrots into sticks about 3 inches long and ½ inch wide.

Lightly oil or butter a baking dish that will hold the carrots in a shallow layer; preheat the oven to 375° (350° for ovenproof glass). Arrange the carrots neatly in the dish.

2. In a small saucepan over low heat, stir together the butter, broth, honey, mustard and vinegar until well blended. Season to taste with salt and pepper and pour this sauce evenly over the carrots.

Bake for 45 minutes, turning the carrots and basting several times, until the carrots are tender and lightly browned and the liquid has evaporated. Serve hot.

Put all the ingredients in a heavy nonreactive saucepan (stainless steel, enameled, etc.) and bring to a boil. Reduce the heat and simmer, uncovered, for 40 minutes, stirring occasionally. Be sure the mixture does not burn; add a little water if the liquid gets low. Let the chutney cool, then refrigerate until needed. Serve at room temperature.

MENU SUGGESTIONS

Pot roast and Creamy Limas (page 39) make good partners for these carrots. For a meatless dinner, serve Easy Mushroom Timbales (page 206) and Potato Boats Stuffed with Brussels Sprouts and Cheese (page 91). These are hearty meals, so serve a green salad to lighten things up.

BASIC ROOT VEGETABLE BROTH

MAKES 3 QUARTS (12 CUPS)

This broth may be used to make soup or to replace chicken broth in sauces and other recipes.

8 MEDIUM CARROTS, TRIMMED, PEELED AND CHUNKED

2 LARGE PARSNIPS, TRIMMED, PEELED AND CHUNKED

6 TO 8 CELERY STALKS (WITH LEAVES), TRIMMED AND CHUNKED

2 SPANISH OR BERMUDA ONIONS, CHOPPED COARSELY

3 LARGE LEEKS (WHITE AND MOST OF THE GREEN PARTS), TRIMMED, CLEANED CAREFULLY AND CUT IN ONE-INCH SLICES

1 TABLESPOON SALT

FRESH PEPPER TO TASTE

HANDFUL OF FRESH FLAT-LEAF (ITALIAN) PARSLEY LEAVES

3 BAY LEAVES

½ TEASPOON POWDERED THYME

2 GARLIC CLOVES, CRUSHED

MENU SUGGESTIONS

Keep it simple with a frittata and an interesting salad. If you want something more elaborate, make Buckwheat Crêpes with Creamy Broccoli Filling (page 87).

THE VEGETABLE EXPRESS

BROWNED CARROTS

MAKES SIX SERVINGS

Serve the basic carrots—tender, nicely browned and slightly caramelized, thanks to the sugar content of the carrots—or dress them up with a choice of three flavorings.

2 pounds carrots (10 to 12 medium carrots), peeled and trimmed

1 tablespoon butter

2 tablespoons vegetable oil *(Use olive oil for flavoring #1, safflower or another relatively neutral oil for #2 and #3.)*

Salt and fresh pepper

Flavorings (choose one, if desired):

- **2½ tablespoons minced fresh flat-leaf (Italian) parsley plus 2½ tablespoons fresh lime juice**
- **3 tablespoons minced scallions (white and green parts) plus 1 tablespoon Chinese oyster sauce (page 128)**
- **2½ tablespoons bourbon plus 2½ tablespoons brown sugar**

1. Slice the carrots into ¼-inch-thick coins. Heat the butter and oil in a large skillet, add the carrots, and sauté over high heat until lightly browned and tender, 15 to 20 minutes. Season with salt and pepper.

TIP: If you stir the carrots too much, they won't be in contact with the hot skillet long enough to brown.

2. At this point, you may serve the carrots as they are or, if you like, add one of the suggested flavorings (above) to the skillet. If you add one of the flavorings, stir well over low heat until the flavoring is well combined with the carrots and any liquid has evaporated. Serve hot.

SWEET CARROT RING

MAKES ONE 10½-INCH RING, PLENTY FOR SIX SERVINGS

It's hard to describe this luscious dish: It's moist and delicately sweet, rather puddinglike, yet firm and sliceable, with a beautiful crust. Let it take the place of sweet potatoes, rice or any other starch in your company dinner.

1½ **pounds carrots (8 or 9 medium carrots), peeled and trimmed**

2 **eggs, separated**

2 **teaspoons fresh lemon juice**

1 **cup (2 sticks) butter or margarine, or ½ cup (1 stick) of each, room temperature**

1 **cup (packed) light brown sugar**

2½ **cups sifted cake flour**

1 **teaspoon salt**

1 **teaspoon baking powder**

1½ **teaspoons baking soda**

2 **pinches cinnamon**

2 **pinches nutmeg**

1. Preheat the oven to 350°; grease and lightly flour a 10½-inch tube pan.

Chunk the carrots and simmer them in water to cover until very soft, about 20 minutes. Drain well and cool under cold water.

2. In your food processor, purée the carrots with the egg yolks and lemon juice, scraping down the bowl frequently. You should have about 2¾ cups of purée.

3. With an electric mixer or in the food processor, cream the butter and sugar. Add the carrot mixture and blend well.

4. In a separate bowl, whisk together the flour, salt, baking powder, baking soda and spices. Add the dry ingredients to the carrot mixture and blend well.

In a big stockpot, combine the ingredients with 5 quarts (20 cups) of water. Simmer, covered, for 1½ hours. Uncover the pot and continue simmering for 30 minutes more. Strain the resulting broth, discarding the vegetables, and correct the seasoning.

If you prefer a more intense flavor, simmer the broth uncovered for another half an hour to reduce it even further.

Keep refrigerated or freeze for future use.

For an even tastier broth, start with the basics above plus any or all of the following ingredients: one or two white turnips, trimmed, peeled and cubed; one small (or half of one large) rutabaga, trimmed, peeled and cubed; ¼-inch-thick peels from three or four large potatoes; four to five more cloves of garlic, crushed.

If you have been working in the food processor, transfer the mixture to a large mixing bowl.

5. In another bowl, by hand or with clean, dry electric beaters, beat the egg whites until they stand in firm, glossy, moist peaks. Fold into the carrot mixture.

6. Spoon the mixture evenly into the prepared tube pan and smooth the top. Bake for 45 to 50 minutes, or until a toothpick inserted in the ring comes out clean. Allow to cool for ten minutes on a wire rack, then loosen the edges with a sharp knife, cover tightly with an inverted serving platter, and quickly turn over to unmold. Serve hot or warm.

MENU SUGGESTIONS

I think this dish has a holiday feeling, so my menu includes roasted turkey, Brussels Sprouts Paprikash (page 94), and cranberry sauce or Beet-Apple-Ginger Relish (page 66).

CAULIFLOWER

BUYING AND STORING

A good head of cauliflower will be creamy white, firm, compact and heavy for its size. The flowerets should be tightly packed on the main stem and show no signs of yellowing or browning and no black speckles. If leaves are still attached to the stem, they should be bright green, not yellow or withered.

Cauliflower often comes wrapped in cellophane, so you can pop it right into the refrigerator. If it is unwrapped, put it unwashed into a plastic bag and refrigerate for up to several days.

NOTES TO THE COOK

Preparing the flowerets: Turn the whole cauliflower upside down, with the stem end up. You'll see that there is a thick main stem in the center with flowerets or clusters of flowerets branching off. With a small sharp knife, cut away and discard any leaves surrounding the stem. Now cut the flowerets or clusters of flowerets away from the main stem, leaving ½ to 1 inch of thinner stem on each. Break or cut large flowerets into smaller ones so all flowerets are of an approximately uniform size. Trim off any brown or black spots.

Rinsing: Rinse well in a colander and shake out any excess water.

Cauliflower is a vegetable just waiting to be taken in hand: It's incredibly easy to prepare, has an interesting flavor that adapts well to a variety of seasonings, and is quite reasonably priced for the amount you get. Unfortunately, cauliflower is often treated badly and its potential unrealized. You can change all that with the recipes in this section.

My personal preference is for recipes that use individual flowerets, which I think are by far the most attractive shape for cauliflower. A whole head seems to me a rather gross presentation, so you won't find one here.

VEGETABLE MEDLEYS

Vegetable medleys are combinations of three or more vegetables, which may be left over from another recipe or cooked especially for the medley. Uncooked vegetables, such as tomatoes and mushrooms, can be used, too. The suggestions given here are adaptable: Use whatever amounts of vegetables you have, make substitutions according to what you have—and see what you get.

Heat the medley by sautéing the chosen vegetables in a little olive or other oil, adding garlic, salt, pepper, herbs or other seasonings. Here are some possibilities:

- **COOKED CORN AND ZUCCHINI, ROASTED RED PEPPER: SEASON WITH GARLIC, SALT, PEPPER AND A DASH OF HOT PEPPER SAUCE.**
- **COOKED PETITE PEAS AND POTATOES, SAUTÉED ONIONS: SEASON WITH SALT, PEPPER AND A LITTLE CURRY POWDER.**
- **COOKED BROCCOLI AND CAULIFLOWER, SAUTÉED MUSHROOMS: ADD A LIGHT CHEDDAR CHEESE SAUCE AND FRESH PEPPER.**

MENU SUGGESTIONS

With all that cheese sauce, you probably won't want much more animal protein in the meal. Have beans instead—Savory Baked Lentils (page 40) or Tomato-baked Chick-Peas (page 47) are perfect with this cauliflower. A dish of Sautéed Escarole with Bacon and Garlic (page 167) will supply your greens.

CAULIFLOWER WITH CHEESE SAUCE

MAKES SIX SERVINGS

This will remind you of Welsh rarebit, with its mustard-and-beer-laced cheese sauce. Be sure you don't overcook the cauliflower—it should be crisp-tender.

2½ to 3 pounds cauliflower (about 2 small heads), prepared in bite-size flowerets and rinsed (see Notes to the Cook)

2 tablespoons butter or margarine, or 1 tablespoon of each

2 tablespoons flour

½ cup whole or skim milk

½ cup dark beer

1 teaspoon dry mustard

1 tablespoon Worcestershire sauce

⅛ teaspoon paprika

¼ pound sharp cheddar cheese, grated (about 1 cup)

Salt and fresh pepper

1. Grease a shallow 1½-quart casserole or baking dish large enough to hold the cauliflower in a shallow layer; preheat the oven to 400° (375° for ovenproof glass).

Bring a large pot of water to a boil. Parboil the cauliflowerets in the boiling water for about five minutes, until crisp-tender. Drain, cool under cold running water, and drain again. Transfer to the prepared casserole.

2. In a medium skillet or saucepan, melt the butter, add the flour and cook for one minute. Gradually add the milk, whisking constantly over medium heat until thickened and smooth. Stir in the beer, mustard, Worcestershire sauce and paprika and keep stirring until smooth.

3. Lower the heat and stir in the cheese a little at a time, letting it melt after each addition. Season with salt and pepper, pour the sauce evenly over the cauliflower, and bake uncovered for 15 minutes. Serve hot.

MEDITERRANEAN CAULIFLOWER

MAKES SIX SERVINGS

The strong, sweet flavor of cauliflower meets and matches the pungent peppers, anchovies and capers in this dish.

- **2½ pounds cauliflower (about 2 small heads), prepared in bite-size flowerets and rinsed (see Notes to the Cook)**
- **3 tablespoons olive oil**
- **3 garlic cloves, minced**
- **1 small red bell pepper, cored, seeded, deveined and diced**
- **2 tablespoons capers, preferably small ones**
- **1 two-ounce can flat anchovy fillets, drained**
- **Salt and fresh pepper**
- **3 tablespoons fine dry bread crumbs**

1. Grease a shallow ovenproof casserole or baking dish large enough to hold the cauliflowerets; preheat the oven to 400° (375° for ovenproof glass).

Bring a large pot of water to a boil. Parboil the cauliflowerets in the boiling water for about five minutes, until crisp-tender. Drain, cool under cold running water, and drain again.

2. Heat the olive oil in the skillet, add the garlic, bell pepper and capers, and sauté for three minutes. Push the vegetables aside in the pan, add the anchovies and—with the heat still on—mash until they dissolve. Stir the anchovies into the vegetables.

3. With the heat off, stir in the cauliflower and season with salt and pepper. Transfer the mixture to the prepared casserole, sprinkle with the bread crumbs, and bake for 15 minutes, until the cauliflower is tender and piping hot.

- **COOKED PEAS, CARROTS AND ASPARAGUS, FRESH SCALLIONS: ADD A LITTLE CHICKEN BROTH AND SEASON WITH CHOPPED PARSLEY, SALT AND PEPPER.**

- **BRAISED LEEKS, COOKED BABY ARTICHOKES, FRESH FENNEL: SEASON WITH MUSTARD VINAIGRETTE AND FRESH PARSLEY.**

MENU SUGGESTIONS

You might like to begin your dinner with My Favorite Belgian Endive Salad (page 76) and crusty bread. For a simple meal, follow that with a green risotto (with mushrooms, if you like) and the cauliflower. For a meal with meat, serve broiled lamb chops and a rice pilaf instead of risotto.

GIARDINIERA

MAKES ABOUT 5 ½ CUPS

Pucker up and munch your way through these Italian-style pickled vegetables, the perfect little extra to serve with any Italian-style meal. The recipe makes a lot, but it keeps very well in the refrigerator and it makes a great gift when you visit friends for dinner.

½ CUP SALT

2 QUARTS WATER

1 RED BELL PEPPER, ROASTED, CORED, SEEDED AND CUT INTO STRIPS

1 MEDIUM ONION, SLICED ¼ INCH THICK

1 POUND CAULIFLOWER (ABOUT ONE SMALL HEAD), PREPARED IN BITE-SIZE FLOWERETS AND RINSED (SEE NOTES TO THE COOK, PAGE 113)

2 MEDIUM CARROTS, TRIMMED, PEELED AND SLICED THIN

2 STALKS CELERY, TRIMMED AND SLICED THIN

MENU SUGGESTIONS

Pasta and more pasta with this cauliflower—fettuccine with Olive-Herb Pesto (page 198), buttered spinach noodles, spaghetti with white clam sauce. Have a green salad and plenty of garlic bread.

CAULIFLOWER WITH SUN-DRIED TOMATOES

MAKES SIX SERVINGS

Browning the cauliflower gives it a wonderful toasty flavor that is accented by the intense tomatoes, garlic and hot pepper. Tossing it with Parmesan cheese puts a finish on the dish.

2 ounces sun-dried tomatoes

2 to 2½ pounds cauliflower (about 2 small heads), prepared in flowerets and rinsed (see Notes to the Cook)

3 tablespoons olive oil

1 medium onion, chopped

3 garlic cloves, minced

⅓ cup water

½ cup (packed) coarsely chopped fresh flat-leaf (Italian) parsley

Hot red pepper flakes to taste

Salt and fresh pepper to taste

¼ cup grated Parmesan or Romano cheese or a combination of both

1. Put the tomatoes in a small saucepan of boiling water and simmer for three to eight minutes, until softened. Drain, pat dry on paper towels, and cut into ¼-inch strips. Set aside.

2. Slice the cauliflowerets ¼ inch thick. In a large skillet, heat the olive oil and brown the flowerets on both sides over medium heat. Add the onion and garlic and sauté for another minute or two. Add the water and continue cooking, stirring constantly, for a few more minutes, until the cauliflower is crisp-tender, the onion is soft, and all the browning on the skillet is dissolved.

3. Add the tomatoes, parsley, hot pepper flakes and salt and pepper. Stir over low heat until the tomatoes are hot. Transfer to a serving bowl, add the grated cheese, and toss well. Serve right away.

Warm Cauliflower with Creamy Tarragon Dressing

MAKES SIX SERVINGS

Elegant, as tarragon generally is, and quite rich tasting for something so low-fat. We tested it first with light sour cream, light mayonnaise and skim milk and it was great.

FOR THE DRESSING

½ cup regular or light sour cream

2 tablespoons regular or light mayonnaise

¼ cup whole or skim milk

1 tablespoon fresh lemon juice

1 teaspoon powdered dried tarragon

Salt to taste

————————

2½ pounds cauliflower (about 2 small heads), prepared in bite-size flowerets and rinsed (see Notes to the Cook)

Paprika or minced fresh flat-leaf (Italian) parsley for garnish

1. Whisk together all the dressing ingredients; set aside to let the flavor develop.

2. Bring a large pot of water to a boil and parboil the cauliflowerets for seven minutes, until tender. Drain and transfer to a serving bowl.

Pour half the dressing over the hot cauliflower and toss well. Drizzle the rest of the dressing over the cauliflower; do not toss. Garnish with pinches of paprika or parsley, and allow the dish to cool a bit more before serving.

2 CUPS WHITE VINEGAR

2 TABLESPOONS SMALL (NONPAREIL) CAPERS

¼ CUP OLIVE OIL

1 TABLESPOON MUSTARD SEEDS

1 TEASPOON CELERY SEEDS

¼ TEASPOON HOT PEPPER FLAKES

2 TABLESPOONS SUGAR

2 GARLIC CLOVES, CRUSHED

1 CUP GREEN AND/OR BLACK OLIVES (USE GAETA, SICILIAN, KALAMATA OR ANY OTHER GOOD-QUALITY OLIVES.)

1. In a large pot or crock, stir the salt into the water until it dissolves. Add the peppers, onions, cauliflower, carrots and celery and let them stand, covered, for 12 to 18 hours. Drain, rinse, and drain again.

2. In a large nonreactive saucepan (stainless steel, enameled, etc.), stir together the remaining ingredients except the olives and bring to a boil. Cover and simmer for five minutes. Add the vegetables and olives and simmer, covered, for another five minutes. Let the mixture cool, stirring occasionally, then spoon it into containers with liquid to cover and refrigerate until needed.

MENU SUGGESTIONS

This cauliflower lends itself to a sort of sunny-South-of-France bill of fare—Red Pepper Ratatouille (page 246), grilled sausage or cold slices of country pâté, warm baguettes and a little bowl of Niçoise olives.

CAULIFRITTERS

MAKES ABOUT 24 SMALL FRITTERS, PLENTY FOR 6 SERVINGS

Sensational as they come out of the pan—crisp outside and tender inside, with a beautifully irregular perimeter. These fritters are pretty, too, a warm reddish brown flecked with green herbs. For company, serve with an interesting condiment—mild mango pickle, salsa, sour cream or créme fraîche.

1 pound cauliflower (about 1 small head), prepared in flowerets and rinsed (see Notes to the Cook)

¾ cup flour

½ teaspoon salt

Fresh pepper to taste

¼ teaspoon powdered dried oregano

¼ teaspoon cayenne pepper

3 tablespoons tomato paste

1 whole egg plus 1 egg white, separated

1½ tablespoons olive oil

3 tablespoons (packed) minced fresh flat-leaf (Italian) parsley

3 tablespoons (packed) minced fresh basil

Vegetable oil for frying

1. Bring a large pot of water to a boil and parboil the flowerets in the boiling water for seven minutes, until tender. Rinse under cold running water to stop the cooking process; drain well. Chop the cauliflower into small bits.

2. In a large bowl, whisk together the flour, salt, pepper, oregano, cayenne, tomato paste, egg yolk and olive oil until perfectly smooth. Stir in the parsley and basil.

3. In another bowl, by hand or with an electric mixer and clean, dry beaters, beat the egg whites until they hold firm, glossy, moist peaks. Add them to the flour mixture and continue beating briefly until smooth and well blended.

4. Stir the chopped cauliflower into the batter; season with more salt and pepper if necessary.

5. Pour ¼ inch of oil into a large skillet and heat until the oil is very hot and a bit of batter dropped into the pan sizzles right away. To make the fritters, drop heaping tablespoons or soup spoons of cauliflower batter into the skillet; flatten slightly with the back of the spoon. Don't crowd the pan. Brown the fritters on both sides and drain on paper towels; keep warm in a 300° oven.

Repeat the process until you have made as many fritters as needed or until all the batter is used up. Serve hot, as soon as possible.

MENU SUGGESTIONS

Roasted chicken with lemon and herbs will be a very good partner for the fritters, along with a crunchy cucumber salad—either Cucumber Salad with Caper Dressing (page 145) or Hot and Cold Cucumbers (page 148). You can also have the fritters as part of a meatless meal that includes the cucumber salad, Simple Corn and Carrot Sauté (page 140), Red Onion Raita with Coriander (page 221) and lots of rice.

CELERY

Most of us almost always have celery around, but like onions, it's mostly used in the background of other dishes and is rarely served on its own. This is a pity since celery blends so well with both subtle and strong flavors and can be anything from bright and fresh to soft and comforting. In the recipes in this section, the usual positions are reversed, with celery playing the main role.

BUYING AND STORING

Pascal celery, the common green variety, is generally sold either in big loose bunches with the leaves still on or in trimmed bunches in plastic bags. Many stores also sell plastic bags containing only celery hearts.

Bagged or unbagged, the stalks should be crisp and stiff, with no splits, brown spots or yellow tinge. Leaves should be fresh, not limp. Hearts, if sold separately, should have narrow, rather delicate-looking stalks of a pale green or creamy white. Watch out for discoloration or sliminess at the base.

Refrigerate unwashed celery in a plastic bag; it should last for about two weeks.

NOTES TO THE COOK

Trimming: One of the best things about celery is how little preparation it requires. If you need only one or two stalks to mince or slice, simply break them off the bunch and trim both ends, cutting off any little branches of leaves. If you need more than two, first cut off the base of the bunch, removing enough to get rid of the worst dirt, then trim the tops of the stalks and cut off the branches of leaves. (Save the small branches of leaves for seasoning, if you like.)

If you prefer stringless celery, remove the strings by cutting partway through the top of a stalk and pulling the strings down.

When you're using whole celery hearts, just trim a bit off the base and the tops of the stalks to get fresh, clean edges.

Cleaning: Wash the stalks well and dry with paper towels.

TIP: Limp stalks can be somewhat revived by trimming the ends and resting them in a glass or pitcher of icy water.

OLD-FASHIONED CHOPPED CELERY AND APPLE SALAD WITH ORANGE-YOGURT DRESSING

MAKES SIX SERVINGS

If you grew up in the fifties, you'll remember Waldorf salad from your grade school cafeteria. The idea of Waldorf salad is perfectly good, but back in the lunchroom it was usually limp and mayonnaise-y. This bright, fresh dressing makes all the difference.

1 large sweet or tart-sweet apple

1½ cups diced celery (about 3 medium stalks)

3 tablespoons chopped walnuts

3 tablespoons dark raisins

Orange-Yogurt Dressing (recipe follows)

Salad greens of your choice (red leaf, Boston or romaine lettuce; arugula; Belgian endive; etc.)

Quarter and core the apple, making sure to remove all the seeds and hard matter. Dice the apple and combine it in a big bowl with the celery, walnuts, raisins and ⅓ cup of dressing. Taste and add more dressing, if you like.

Serve chilled on a bed of salad greens, with the rest of the dressing in a separate bowl.

Orange-Yogurt Dressing

MAKES ABOUT ONE CUP

⅓ cup regular or low-fat mayonnaise

½ cup plain (unflavored) yogurt

2 tablespoons thawed frozen orange juice concentrate

Pinch (or more) of nutmeg

Salt and pepper to taste

Whisk the ingredients together until smooth.

MENU SUGGESTIONS

For a hot meal, chicken potpie goes well with a celery salad, along with some Sage-roasted Turnips (page 328). For a cold meal, try cold fried chicken and potato salad (page 266).

You're making roasted turkey for dinner. What do you serve with it? Here are some possibilities from which to choose, including the Vegetable Express for hurry-up meals.

Ginger-Orange Parsnips,
page 228

Stir-fried Green Beans,
page 57

Sweet Potato Salad with
Southwest Seasonings,
page 261

Kidney Beans with
Rice and Cheese, page 45

Individual Pumpkin-Apricot-
Pecan Puddings, page 275

MENU SUGGESTIONS

Baked ham sets off this delicate dish of celery very nicely, especially when served with something sweet such as Sweet Beet Caviar (page 67) or any of the baked beets on page 68. If you prefer a vegetable dinner, omit the ham and have Sugar Snap Peas with Peppered Orange-Butter Sauce (page 238).

CELERY-ALMOND TIMBALE

MAKES SIX SERVINGS

Tender, delicate, elegant—did you ever imagine celery could be like this? The onions and almonds make the timbale especially flavorful (like stuffing when it's made with celery, onions, nuts and eggs). This is rich, so go easy.

- 1½ cups whole milk
- 1 cup fresh white bread crumbs
- 3 tablespoons butter, melted and cooled
- 1½ cups minced celery (about 3 medium stalks)
- ½ cup finely chopped onion
- ½ cup finely chopped almonds
- ¾ teaspoon salt
- 2 eggs, lightly beaten

1. Butter a 1½-quart baking dish; preheat the oven to 350° (325° for ovenproof glass) and bring a kettle of water to a boil.

In a medium saucepan, stir together all the ingredients except the eggs. Bring to a boil, stirring constantly. Turn off the heat.

2. Stir ¼ cup of the hot mixture into the eggs to warm them, then return the eggs to the saucepan and mix well. Pour the mixture into the prepared baking dish and place the dish in a larger pan (for instance, a roasting pan) on the middle rack of the oven. Carefully pour one inch of boiling water into the larger pan to make a hot water bath for the baking dish.

Bake for 45 to 50 minutes, until the custard is set and dry on top and a knife inserted in the center comes out almost clean. Carefully lift the baking dish out of the hot water and place it on a wire rack to cool for at least 15 minutes; this is important because it will continue cooking and will firm up as it should.

NOTE: *This is a very delicate custard, so don't try to turn it out of the dish.*

Serve hot, warm or at room temperature.

THE VEGETABLE EXPRESS

CELERY WITH MUSHROOM CREAM SAUCE

MAKES SIX SERVINGS

A true comfort food, soft and rich (but not too rich), which may remind you of homemade cream of celery or cream of mushroom soup.

4½ cups of ¼-inch-thick slices of celery (6 to 8 medium stalks)

1½ cups chicken or vegetable broth

½ pound white or cremini mushrooms, trimmed and cleaned

3 tablespoons butter or margarine

3 tablespoons flour

¼ cup heavy cream

Salt and pepper

1. Put the celery and broth in a saucepan, bring to a boil, and simmer, covered, for ten minutes. Set aside.

2. Chop the mushrooms into pea-size pieces. In a medium skillet, melt the butter and brown the mushrooms. Stir in the flour and cook for one minute.

3. Add the celery and broth and cook, stirring constantly, over medium heat until the sauce is smooth and thickened. Lower the heat, stir in the cream, and cook for another minute or two, until the celery is very tender. Season with salt and pepper and serve hot.

Celery with Mushroom Cream Sauce, page 123

Butternut Squash with Coriander Sauce, page 306

Tex-Mex Salad, page 343

VEGETABLE EXPRESS

Brussels Sprouts Paprikash, page 94

Foil-baked Rutabagas with Butter and Herbs, page 284

MENU SUGGESTIONS

Keep the dinner preparations uncomplicated by baking some turkey drumsticks and sweet potatoes at the same time, to go with the creamy celery. If you have a little more time, turn the baked sweet potatoes into Gingered Sweet Potatoes (page 269).

CROSS-REFERENCE SAUCES

Sesame-Ginger Sauce, page 31

Yogurt-Dill Sauce, page 32

Four Savory Sauces for Baked Beets, page 68

Walnut-Basil Pesto, page 169

Spicy Peanut Sauce, page 134

Ranch Dipping Sauce, page 155

Gorgonzola Cream, page 165

West Indian Pepper-and-Lime Sauce, page 180

Tomato Cream Gravy, page 186

Sauce Ti-Malice, page 213

Fresh Tomato Sauce, page 322

Red Pepper Sauce, page 299

COMPANY'S COMING

BRAISED CELERY HEARTS WITH BLUE CHEESE

MAKES PLENTY FOR SIX SERVINGS

This is unusual and rather impressive, keeping the tender stalks of the heart intact instead of cutting them up in the usual way. The tangy sauce is smooth and silky, glazing the vegetables, and the garnish is elegantly minimal.

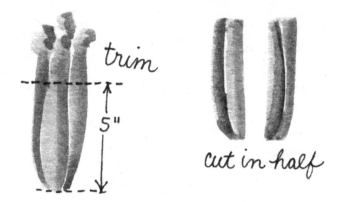

4 celery hearts, tops trimmed to make each heart about 5 inches long, then halved lengthwise

2 tablespoons butter

½ cup chicken or vegetable broth

½ cup medium dry or dry sherry (amontillado or fino)

½ cup crumbled Danish blue cheese

¼ cup chopped toasted walnuts

1. Bring a large saucepan of water to a boil, add the celery hearts, and parboil for four minutes. Drain well.

2. In a large skillet, melt the butter over medium-low heat and add the celery. Sauté for several minutes, turning to coat with butter. Add the broth, cover the skillet, and simmer for five minutes, turning once, until the celery is crisp-tender.

3. Add the sherry to the skillet, swirl it around, and simmer uncovered, turning the celery several times, until the liquid is reduced by half. Transfer the celery hearts to a serving platter and keep warm in a low oven.

4. Add the blue cheese to the skillet and stir over low heat until the cheese dissolves and the sauce is reduced to an almost syrupy consistency. Spoon it over the celery hearts and top with walnuts. Serve hot.

MENU SUGGESTIONS

Your company or family dinner can include a rolled veal or pork roast, Carrot Pancakes (page 106) and either Sweet-and-Sour Lentils (page 42) or rice.

CHINESE GREENS

Chinese broccoli

Chinese cabbage

If you shop, as I do, in the Chinese district of your city or in an Asian market or in a well-stocked super-market, you will find an assortment of Chinese green vegetables that may look strange to you. Look again: The bok choy is not so different from collards and kale, the cabbage is similar to Savoy cabbage, and the broccoli is somewhat like regular broccoli and a lot like broccoli rabe.

There are many different Chinese greens—too many, in fact, to include here. Of these greens, bok choy, Chinese broccoli and Chinese cabbage are the most commonly available and recognizable to the untutored eye. However, the names of these greens can get confusing: Bok choy is sometimes called Chinese white cabbage, which is different from Chinese cabbage—which is also called celery cabbage or Napa cabbage. To make shopping simpler, refer to the drawings and descriptions to identify the greens.

Bok choy (also called bok choi, Chinese white cabbage, Chinese greens, Chinese chard): Though there are quite a few kinds of bok choy in Asia, in the United States we are accustomed to seeing only a few varieties—most often the short and tall versions with pure white stalks and dark green crinkled leaves.

Chinese broccoli (also gai lan, Chinese kale): The flavor of Chinese broccoli is somewhere between ordinary broccoli and broccoli rabe—slightly earthy, a little bitter. It has tapering, dull green, round, smooth stems with dark green leaves, and green flowerets that open to white flowers.

Chinese cabbage (also celery cabbage, Napa cabbage, Tientsin cabbage): Americans are most familiar with two varieties. One is the tall, narrow cabbage whose leaves have wide, white crisp centers and a little frill of green at the edges; the other is the short, fat cabbage whose large, curly, pale green and white leaves have ridged, tapering white centers. The flavors of both are delicate, even bland, so they lend themselves well to combination with other, stronger flavors.

BUYING AND STORING

Look for the same qualities in Chinese greens that you would seek out in any other greens: firm, crisp stems or stalks and fresh-looking leaves with no brown or wilted edges. Avoid limp stems and leaves, dried-out or slimy stem ends or any rotten spots.

Store the greens unwashed in plastic bags in the refrigerator and use them within a few days.

NOTES TO THE COOK

Trimming: Slice off a little of each stem or leaf end to expose a clean, fresh surface. Discard any wilted or yellowed leaves.

Peeling Chinese broccoli: The main stems have thick, tough skin that should be removed; use a swivel-blade peeler (or any other peeler you prefer) to take it off.

Cleaning: Chinese cabbage leaves, once you've peeled off any imperfect ones, are usually quite clean and don't need washing and drying. If they do, rinse well and pat dry on paper towels. The other types of Chinese greens are cleaned under cool running water like any other leafy green vegetables; dry them in a salad spinner or pat dry with paper towels.

bok choy

PANTRY

CHINESE INGREDIENTS

This is my personal list of essential Chinese ingredients, without which I think vegetable cooking would be dull indeed. Look for these items in Asian groceries, gourmet food shops and even some supermarkets.

Soy sauce, light and dark: Dark soy sauce is what you'll find in the supermarket, but light (light in color, not low-sodium "lite") is delicious, too. Try both if you can.

Hoisin sauce: Thick, brown, sweet and spicy—reminiscent of barbecue sauce; buy an authentic Chinese brand for best quality. Comes in cans or jars; if you buy a can, transfer the contents to a jar. Store in the refrigerator.

Oyster sauce: Brown, salty and rich; an authentic Chinese brand will not be fishy tasting.

Ginger: Should be plump and fresh (no shriveling), with dry, light brown skin; cut off the amount you need, peel thinly, and slice or chop. Wrap the remainder tightly in plastic and refrigerate.

Rice vinegar (clear or "white"): Mild, even delicate in flavor; Japanese brands are the most widely available. Black and red Chinese rice vinegars have different and distinctive tastes.

Dark sesame oil: Has a strong, nutty flavor; used for seasoning at the end of cooking rather than for sautéing, since it burns easily.

MENU SUGGESTIONS

Roasted spareribs are a wonderful treat with these greens, along with Thai-style Eggplant (page 151) and brown rice.

MIXED CHINESE GREENS

MAKES SIX SERVINGS

Any combination of Chinese greens will be delicious in this recipe, with Chinese cabbage (either the tall or short variety) as the foundation. As with many Chinese dishes, there's a fair amount of preparation but the cooking is fast.

- ½ tablespoon soy sauce
- 1 tablespoon dry sherry (fino or manzanilla)
- 1½ tablespoons oyster sauce
- 3 tablespoons chicken or vegetable broth
- 1 pound Chinese cabbage, trimmed (and cleaned and dried if necessary; see Notes to the Cook)
- 1 pound other Chinese greens (bok choy, Chinese broccoli, Chinese mustard), trimmed, peeled (Chinese broccoli stems only), cleaned and spin-dried
- 2 tablespoons peanut oil
- 2 garlic cloves, minced

1. In a small bowl, stir together the soy sauce, sherry, oyster sauce and broth; set aside.

Chop the cabbage into bite-size pieces. Chop the thick stems of the greens into one-inch pieces, slit them in half lengthwise, and set aside, keeping them separate. Chop the leaves and flowers of the greens into bite-size pieces.

2. In a wok or large skillet, heat the oil and stir-fry the stems over medium heat for three minutes. Add the garlic and sauce and raise the heat. Add the cabbage and greens by the handful, stirring down as they wilt. When everything is wilted, immediately remove the vegetables with a slotted spoon.

NOTE: *Be careful not to overcook. The leaves should be chewy; the cabbage, stems and flowers crisp-tender.*

3. Simmer the sauce until reduced by half—a couple of minutes. Pour the sauce over the greens and serve right away.

CHINESE BROCCOLI IN SOY-LEMON-BUTTER SAUCE

MAKES SIX SERVINGS

All the parts of the broccoli—leaves, flowers and stems—are used here for a stir-fry in a mellow sauce.

> 2 tablespoons soy sauce
>
> 1 tablespoon fresh lemon juice
>
> 1 tablespoon water
>
> 2 pounds Chinese broccoli, trimmed
>
> 1 tablespoon butter
>
> 1 tablespoon peanut oil

1. Stir together the soy sauce, lemon juice and water; set aside.

Prepare the broccoli: Separate the leaves from the stems; cut off the flowers with about two inches of narrow stem attached; peel the large stems with a vegetable peeler and cut them into one-inch pieces. Cut thick pieces of stem in half lengthwise. Rinse well and shake off any excess water.

2. Put an inch of water in your wok, bring to a boil, and add the stem and flower pieces. Cover and simmer for five minutes, until crisp-tender, stirring once or twice. Pour off the water and shake the pieces in the wok over medium heat until they are fairly dry.

3. Add the butter and oil, and stir the pieces over low heat for one minute. Add the leaves and the sauce mixture alternately, stirring down as the leaves begin to wilt. Stir-fry for a total of about five minutes, until the leaves are completely wilted. Serve immediately.

Water chestnuts: Canned water chestnuts don't have a lot of flavor but they do have an appealingly solid crunch. Buy them whole, packed in water; pour off the water, rinse and pat dry. (Don't buy sliced water chestnuts; they usually have a metallic taste and waterlogged texture.)

Dried black mushrooms: These are actually dark brown to tan, with wrinkled, cracked-looking caps. Buy them loose or in cellophane packages and store in an airtight container. Snap off tough stems, then reconstitute by rinsing well and soaking for 30 minutes in hot water. Rinse again and squeeze out any excess water. Slice or use whole.

MENU SUGGESTIONS

For a main course, choose grilled or pan-browned fish or cold sesame noodles with shredded chicken. Stir-fried Onions (page 223) make a good accompaniment.

Some ingredients used in sophisticated Chinese cooking are unavailable except at sophisticated Asian groceries; however, even supermarkets have most of the following items, and gourmet stores should, too.

Chinese mustard powder: Intensely hot; mix it with water to use for dipping (a dab goes a long way on an untrained palate) or for spicing up a stir-fry dish. Not everyone likes the raw heat, but if you do, here's how to prepare Chinese mustard: Put a tablespoon (or more) of the mustard powder in a small bowl and gradually add water until you have a medium-thin, smooth paste. Set aside for half an hour to let the flavor develop.

Bean curd: Made from soybeans; comes in large and small "cakes," in several textures ranging from the delicate silken to the solid extra-firm; bland in taste but highly compatible with other flavors and textures. You have to see it, taste it and cook with it to understand it.

STEAMED VEGETABLE DUMPLINGS

MAKES 24 OR MORE DUMPLINGS, PLENTY FOR 6 SERVINGS

You'll need a steamer to make these—either a bamboo or a metal rack that fits in your wok, a collapsible metal rack inside a stockpot, or a nested metal pan-plus-rack-plus-lid steamer combination. Dumplings are quite easy to make, though the cooking can be time-consuming if you have to steam the dumplings in several batches.

- **9 leaves of Chinese cabbage, trimmed (and cleaned and dried if needed; see Notes to the Cook)**
- **2 medium scallions (white and green parts), trimmed**
- **12 canned water chestnuts, rinsed and dried (*Use fresh water chestnuts if you can get them.*)**
- **2 teaspoons minced fresh ginger**
- **1½ tablespoons soy sauce**
- **1 tablespoon dry sherry (fino or manzanilla)**
- **1 tablespoon sesame oil**
- **⅛ teaspoon hot red pepper flakes (*Use ¼ teaspoon for really hot and spicy dumplings.*)**
- **24 or more frozen dumpling wrappers (*These are thin rounds of dough about 3½ inches in diameter, sometimes labeled gyoza or shumai wrappers. Buy them in an Asian grocery; keep them frozen until needed.*)**
- **Hoisin sauce, Chinese mustard, and soy sauce for dipping**

1. Make the filling: Cut the cabbage, scallions and water chestnuts into smaller pieces and mince them in your food processor. Combine in a bowl with the ginger, soy sauce, sherry, sesame oil and hot pepper. Let the mixture stand for 15 minutes, then drain off the liquid.

2. Lay out four dumpling wrappers to defrost for a few seconds. (Work quickly in this step since the wrappers tend to dry out at the edges.)

Place a scant tablespoon of filling in the center of each wrapper. Brush water sparingly around the edge of one wrapper. Bring up the dough to encase the filling, fluting and pleating the wrapper and pressing the edges together at the top; the water will make the edges stick together. Set aside on waxed paper.

Repeat this process to make the rest of the dumplings, four at a time.

3. Put one to two inches of water in the bottom of your wok, stockpot or steamer and set the rack above it. Cover and bring the water to a boil.

Steam the dumplings in batches: Arrange dumplings on a lightly oiled heatproof plate, making sure they do not touch each other, and place the plate on the rack. There should be an inch of clearance between the edge of the plate and the steamer, and the plate should be about two inches above the simmering water.

Cover the steamer, lower the heat, and steam the dumplings for about 15 minutes. Keep this batch warm while you repeat the process to steam the remaining dumplings.

NOTE: *Watch the water level in the steamer and replenish as the water evaporates.*

Serve with Hoisin sauce, Chinese mustard, and soy sauce for dipping.

Dried red chiles: **Brittle, terrifically hot dried pepper pods, one to two inches long; use them whole, cut in half, crumbled or snipped crosswise in slivers.**

Chile powder: **A pure powder made from dried red chiles—no other herbs or spices are present; use cautiously since it is usually quite hot.**

Fermented (or salted) black beans: **Soybeans fermented with salt and spices; used for making black bean sauce or combined with garlic and ginger to flavor poultry, seafood and vegetables. Rinse and chop before using (or not, as you choose); store in a jar in the refrigerator indefinitely.**

MENU SUGGESTIONS

The dumplings are a satisfying project to undertake, but keep the rest of the meal simple, with dishes you can make ahead. Hot and sour soup, cold noodles with a simple Chinese sauce, and Japanese Cucumber Salad (page 146) are good choices. If you have a second cook, add Stir-fried Green Beans (page 57) to the menu.

STIR-FRYING

Stir-frying is a Chinese cooking technique that can turn the most commonplace vegetable, such as cabbage, into a sublime side dish or turn a collection of vegetable odds and ends into a coherent accompaniment to rice or noodles.

Stir-frying your vegetables means cooking pieces of vegetable of uniform size over high heat in a wok or heavy skillet that is lubricated with a small amount of oil. The vegetables are then tossed and turned so they are equally exposed to the hot pan. The cooking time is extremely short—just minutes—because of the high heat and the

MENU SUGGESTIONS

Delicious with broiled or pan-browned fish fillets and white rice, or with Braised Chinese Black Mushrooms (page 203) served on Chinese noodles or linguine. Stir-fried Snow Pea Pods (page 240) are good, too, if you have time to make them.

THE VEGETABLE EXPRESS

BOK CHOY WITH GARLIC SAUCE

MAKES SIX SERVINGS

How do you get Chinese vegetables to taste the marvelous way they taste in a Chinese restaurant? This recipe, like the Chinese broccoli on page 129 and the mixed greens on page 128, does it pretty well. Arrange the cooked bok choy with the white parts at the edge of the platter and the green in the center.

- 2 **tablespoons soy sauce**
- 2 **tablespoons rice vinegar**
- 2 **teaspoons sugar**
- 3 **garlic cloves, forced through a garlic press**
- 2 **pounds bok choy (do not trim yet)** *(Use either the tall kind you'll find in the supermarket or the short stubby variety more common in a Chinese market.)*

Peanut oil for sautéing

1. In a small bowl, stir together the soy sauce, vinegar, sugar and garlic to make a sauce; set aside.

Trim a very thin slice from the stem end of each bunch of bok choy; if you're using the tall variety, trim one inch off the leaves. Cut each bunch lengthwise in quarters; wash well and shake off any excess water.

2. In a large skillet, heat one or two tablespoons of peanut oil. Sauté the bok choy in batches over high heat until lightly browned on all sides, adding more oil as needed. Return all the bok choy to the skillet.

3. Brush the sauce on the bok choy, cover the skillet, and braise over low heat for about three minutes, until tender. Transfer the bok choy to a serving platter. Simmer the sauce until reduced by half, pour it over the bok choy, and serve right away.

STUFFED CHINESE CABBAGE ROLLS WITH SPICY PEANUT SAUCE

MAKES 18 ROLLS, PLENTY FOR 6 SERVINGS

Beautiful and unusual—the cabbage-leaf wrappings become translucent when braised, making handsome little packages stuffed with tasty mushrooms, carrots and scallions.

18 medium-size Chinese dried black mushrooms, stems snapped off and discarded

2 medium carrots, trimmed and peeled

5 or 6 scallions (white and green parts), trimmed

18 large leaves of Chinese cabbage, cleaned and dried if needed (*For this dish you must use the short, fat variety of cabbage; see page 126. Make sure the leaves have no tears or splits.*)

2 tablespoons peanut oil

Salt and fresh pepper

¾ cup chicken or vegetable broth

Spicy Peanut Sauce (recipe follows)

18 sprigs of fresh coriander for garnish

1. Rinse the mushroom caps well, then soak in a bowl of very hot water for 30 minutes, until soft. Drain and rinse again to remove any sand caught in the gills. Squeeze out any excess liquid. Cut the mushrooms into ¼-inch strips, discarding any tough stem ends; set aside.

Shred the carrots and mince five scallions. You should have about two loosely packed cups of carrots and scallions; if not, mince and add the sixth scallion.

2. While the mushrooms soak, bring a saucepan of water to a boil. Trim three inches off the stem end of each cabbage leaf, leaving mostly thin leaves and very little thick stem. Blanch the cabbage leaves in the boiling water, two at a time,

way the vegetables are cut. Sometimes garlic and/or ginger is sizzled in the oil before the vegetables are added, and sometimes the vegetables are finished off by the addition of a seasoning sauce that is briskly stirred in during the last minute or two of cooking time.

Here are the points to remember about stir-frying:

- **BEGIN ANY STIR-FRY DISH BY PREPARING ALL THE INGREDIENTS AND SETTING THEM OUT IN BOWLS OR DISHES SO YOU CAN ADD THEM TO THE WOK QUICKLY AND EASILY.**

- **HEAT THE WOK BEFORE YOU EVEN ADD THE OIL. SWIRL THE OIL AROUND TO COAT THE SIDES OF THE WOK AS WELL AS THE BOTTOM.**

- **IF YOU ARE ADDING GINGER, GARLIC OR OTHER SEASONING INGREDIENTS TO THE OIL, HEAT THE OIL BUT DO NOT LET IT REACH THE SMOKING POINT. IF YOU ARE *NOT* ADDING SEASONINGS, GO AHEAD AND HEAT THE OIL ALMOST TO SMOKING.**

- **ADD THE VEGETABLES AND STAND BACK—THERE'S BOUND TO BE A BIG NOISE AND SPLATTER. NOW GET RIGHT IN THERE AND BEGIN MOVING THOSE VEGETABLES AROUND WITH YOUR LONG SPOON, FROM THE CENTER TO THE SIDES.**

- **IF A SEASONING SAUCE IS ADDED AT THE END, DON'T OVERCOOK THE VEGETABLES BY SIMMERING THEM IN THE SAUCE. THE VEGETABLES ARE MEANT TO BE CRISP AND BRIGHT.**

ten seconds per pair. Shake off any excess water and lay them flat to cool.

3. In a large skillet, heat the oil and sauté the mushrooms for five minutes. Add the carrots and scallions and stir-fry for two minutes. Season with salt and pepper and transfer to a bowl to cool slightly. Pour the broth into the skillet.

4. Make the cabbage rolls: Divide the filling mixture into 18 portions (about 1 tablespoon per portion). Lay out a cabbage leaf (on paper towels if it is wet) and place a portion of filling on the stem end. Roll up, tuck the sides under, and place the roll, seam side down, in the skillet. Repeat, using up the remaining cabbage leaves and filling.

5. Cover the skillet and bring the broth to a boil. Lower the heat and simmer the rolls for five minutes, basting once with the broth. Use a slotted spoon to transfer the rolls to a serving platter.

Top each roll with a spoonful of peanut sauce and a sprig of coriander. Serve the rest of the sauce separately.

Spicy Peanut Sauce

MAKES ABOUT ONE CUP

½ cup chunky or smooth peanut butter

2 garlic cloves, quartered

1 tablespoon coarsely chopped fresh ginger

1 small fresh hot pepper, stemmed, seeded, deveined and chunked

¼ cup peanut oil

2 tablespoons soy sauce

2 tablespoons sugar

2 tablespoons rice vinegar

1 tablespoon sesame oil

¼ cup strong tea

In your food processor, purée all the ingredients to make an almost smooth sauce. (If you have used chunky peanut butter, the sauce will be slightly grainier but just as delicious.)

MENU SUGGESTIONS

A company dinner in the Asian style requires several dishes, all presented at the same time, with plenty of white rice. For example, your menu might include cooked and marinated chicken or roast pork, Stir-fried Green Beans (page 57) and pan-browned tofu along with the cabbage rolls.

CORN

BUYING AND STORING

When you're buying locally grown, recently picked corn at a stand or market, look for tightly closed husks of a lovely, dewy grass green, with pliable stems and no wormholes. Peel back the husk at the top of the ear and check to see that the kernels are plump, juicy (the liquid inside each kernel should be milky) and fitting closely on the ear all the way up. The silk should be golden and neither brittle nor decayed at the top of the ear.

If you're not planning to eat the corn immediately, store it husks and all in a plastic bag in the refrigerator and do eat it before 24 hours have passed.

But what if it's the dead of winter and you want to make corn pudding, as I frequently do? Use either fresh ears of corn that have been shipped from someplace far away, frozen ears of corn or frozen corn kernels. The solution is not perfect, but it is perfectly good and you won't be deprived of these delicious treats just because it's December.

NOTES TO THE COOK

Preparing ears of fresh corn: Break off and discard the stem. Peel down the husks, taking most of the silk with them, then carefully pull or rub off any remaining silk.

Stripping kernels off the cob (fresh or frozen): Break the cob in half. Rest the flat end of each half on your cutting board and slice down with a serrated knife, cutting off two or three rows of kernels at a time. Don't cut too close to the cob.

Thawing frozen corn: Remove the packaging and place the block of frozen corn in a bowl of cold water, breaking it up as it defrosts. If the corn is not frozen solid, break into lumps in a strainer and hold under cool running water until it separates into individual kernels. Use right away or refrigerate until needed.

Americans love sweet corn with a passion. Sane people can become absolutely frenzied at the sight of a bin heaped high with fresh juicy ears—I've actually seen it happen at my local farmers' market. Just-picked corn on the cob is a sublime food, but there's plenty of room for tasty side dishes made with fresh corn grown not quite so locally or even corn that grows in the freezer compartment of your supermarket.

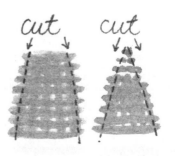

Summer is a perfect time to stage a beach party or backyard social with garden-fresh vegetables as the culinary centerpiece.

Set up some tables under beach umbrellas or shade trees; cover them with brightly checked cloths and baskets holding flatware and napkins. Serve a bountiful array of vegetable dishes, augmented by a variety of cheeses, sausages and crusty breads. Here are some suggestions for the vegetable menu:

Corn on the cob with Lime-Chili Butter Sauce, page 139

Any of the simple tomato salads on page 324

MENU SUGGESTIONS

Delicious garnished with jalapeño jelly and served with a bowl of spicy hot chili. Follow with a cool green salad and plenty of tortilla chips or warm tortillas.

CHILE-CHEESE-CORN PUDDING

MAKES PLENTY FOR SIX SERVINGS

This pudding is comforting and pleasantly solid. It is not hot and spicy—the chiles used are mild.

NOTE: *You'll need three eggs, but you'll use only two of the yolks.*

> 2 whole eggs plus 1 egg white
>
> 1¼ cups buttermilk
>
> ¾ cup yellow cornmeal
>
> ½ teaspoon baking powder
>
> ½ teaspoon baking soda
>
> ½ teaspoon salt
>
> 1 four-ounce can chopped mild green chiles, rinsed and drained
>
> 1 cup grated sharp cheddar cheese (about ¼ pound)
>
> 3 cups raw corn kernels (4 or 5 large ears of corn, stripped of kernels, or 1½ ten-ounce packages frozen corn kernels, thawed)
>
> 2 tablespoons butter or margarine

1. Put a 1½-quart baking dish in the oven and preheat the oven to 400° (375° for ovenproof glass) for 15 minutes.

Meanwhile, in a large bowl, beat together the eggs, egg white, buttermilk, cornmeal, baking powder, baking soda and salt. Stir in the chiles, cheese and corn.

2. Remove the baking dish from the oven, add the butter, and brush it around quickly to coat the sides and bottom of the dish. Stir the corn mixture once more and immediately pour it into the dish. Bake for 35 minutes, or until the pudding is set; it will firm up a bit more as it cools. Serve hot, warm or cold.

Sweet Corn Cakes with Raisins

MAKES ABOUT 30 MEDIUM-SIZE CAKES, PLENTY FOR 6 SERVINGS

The combination of corn and raisins may be a new one to you, but you'll find they go together beautifully. These cakes are as easy to make as pancakes.

6 tablespoons regular or light sour cream

¾ cup whole or skim milk

3 eggs

½ cup plus 1 tablespoon flour

¾ teaspoon baking powder

½ teaspoon salt

Fresh pepper

2 tablespoons sugar

¼ teaspoon cinnamon

⅛ teaspoon nutmeg

2 cups raw corn kernels (about 3 large ears of corn, stripped of kernels, or one 10-ounce package frozen corn kernels, thawed)

¾ cup soft dark raisins

Vegetable oil for frying (not olive oil)

1. Put all ingredients (including a few grinds of pepper) except corn, raisins and vegetable oil in a food processor; process until smooth. Add the corn and process in two or three short bursts until some of the corn is in small bits but some kernels are still whole. Transfer to a bowl and stir in the raisins.

2. In a large skillet, heat two tablespoons of oil. Drop the batter by heaping tablespoons into the hot oil (don't crowd the pan) and cook until the cakes are browned on the bottom. Turn and brown the other sides. Drain on paper towels and keep warm in the oven. Repeat to make the rest of the corn cakes, adding more oil to the skillet as needed. Serve hot.

NOTE: *Using more oil makes the cakes more like fritters; less oil makes them more like pancakes. Delicious either way.*

Dilly Beans, page 58

Cucumbers in Sweet-and-Sour Buttermilk Dressing, page 147

Simplified Caponata with Sun-dried Tomatoes, page 152

Marinated Roasted Red and Yellow Peppers with Fresh Basil, page 244

Herbed Potatoes Provençal, served cold, page 263

MENU SUGGESTIONS

I like an updated down-homey meal with the corn cakes—pork stew, Pumpkin and Black Beans (page 294) with a dab of sour cream, and Scallions in Piquant Sauce (page 198). Buttermilk biscuits are a good idea, too.

CORN ON THE COB

Everyone has his or her own technique for preparing that all-American summer necessity, sweet corn on the cob, and each technique seems to differ slightly from every other one. I use this simple method:

Husk the corn and remove the silk while you bring a big pot of water to a boil. Drop about six ears into the water and cover the pot just until the water boils again. Uncover the pot and let the ears boil for about three minutes, depending on the size of the corn. Lift the ears out with tongs, shaking off the excess water, and—if you're cooking more—add the next batch of six ears to the boiling water. Above all,

MENU SUGGESTIONS

This distinctively flavored dish works well with other southern-style recipes. If you can get catfish, by all means put it on this menu; if not, have any good fish or shrimp dish, plus Browned Okra with Sun-dried Tomatoes (page 216), collard greens and Black-eyed Peas with Butter and Scallions (page 51).

CREOLE CORN

MAKES SIX SERVINGS

Characteristic Louisiana style, with onions, peppers and celery seasoned with bay leaf, garlic and cayenne. This is mildly or very spicy, depending on how much cayenne you add. The tomatoes add brightness and coolness.

- 2 tablespoons vegetable oil (not olive oil)
- 1 cup chopped yellow onion (about 1 medium onion)
- 1 green bell pepper, cored, seeded, deveined and minced
- 2 stalks celery, trimmed and diced (about ¾ cup)
- 3 garlic cloves, minced
- 1 bay leaf
- 3 cups raw corn kernels (4 or 5 large ears of corn, stripped of kernels, or 1½ ten-ounce packages frozen corn kernels, partially thawed)
- ½ cup vegetable or chicken broth
- ¼ to ½ teaspoon cayenne pepper
- Salt and fresh pepper
- 2 medium tomatoes, stem ends removed, seeded and chopped, for garnish

1. In a large skillet, heat the oil over low heat. Add the onions, green pepper, celery, garlic and bay leaf, and sauté until the onion is translucent and the peppers and celery are tender.

2. Stir in the corn and broth, cover, and simmer five minutes. Turn off the heat and remove the bay leaf. Add ¼ teaspoon of the cayenne, plus salt and pepper to taste. If that's not hot enough for you, add the remaining ¼ teaspoon of cayenne pepper.

Mound the corn mixture in the center of a serving platter and surround with chopped tomatoes. Serve right away.

Corn and Lima Succotash in Lemon-Dill Cream

MAKES PLENTY FOR SIX SERVINGS

This new twist on succotash is tart and tangy with the distinctive tastes of fresh dill and lemon. No substitutions—only fresh lemon and dill will do.

1 ten-ounce package frozen baby lima beans, thawed

3 cups raw corn kernels (4 or 5 large ears of corn, stripped of kernels, or 1½ ten-ounce packages frozen corn kernels, thawed)

½ cup regular or light sour cream

2 or 3 tablespoons whole or skim milk

2 tablespoons fresh lemon juice

2 tablespoons minced fresh dill

1 teaspoon sugar

Salt and fresh pepper to taste

1. In a large saucepan or skillet, bring an inch or two of water to a boil. Add the lima beans, cover the pan, and simmer for 5 to 10 minutes, or until barely tender. Add the corn and simmer five more minutes. Drain well and return to the saucepan.

2. Add the remaining ingredients (including two tablespoons of the milk) and stir constantly over low heat until the sauce is hot. If the sauce seems too thick, add the remaining tablespoon of milk. Serve right away.

never add salt to the boiling water; salt toughens the kernels.

Serve the corn right away, with butter, salt and fresh pepper, or prepare one of these two butter sauces and brush it onto the hot ears before serving. These recipes may be doubled if necessary.

Lime-Chili Butter Sauce: In a small saucepan, melt four tablespoons of butter (or two tablespoons butter plus two tablespoons margarine). Stir in the juice of one lime and ½ teaspoon of chili powder (the kind that is a mixture of herbs and powdered chiles, not the pure powder made only of ground chiles). Add salt and fresh pepper to taste.

Brown Butter and Herb Sauce: In a small skillet, melt four tablespoons of butter over medium heat. When the butter foams and then subsides, add ¼ cup minced fresh flat-leaf parsley, basil, chervil or chives and stir well. Season to taste with salt and pepper.

MENU SUGGESTIONS

On a winter night, chicken pot-pie is a hearty and filling partner to succotash. If you prefer vegetables only, try Turnips Rosanna (page 331) and a savory grain casserole.

THE VEGETABLE EXPRESS

SIMPLE CORN AND CARROT SAUTÉ

MAKES SIX SERVINGS

This piquant dish will surprise you; it gets the best out of all the ingredients, including commercial chili sauce.

2 tablespoons olive oil

5 medium carrots, trimmed, peeled and diced

4 cups raw corn kernels (5 to 6 large ears of corn, stripped of kernels, or two 10-ounce packages frozen corn kernels, thawed)

3 garlic cloves, minced

5 tablespoons chili sauce (bottled or homemade) *(Use a tomato-based chili sauce that is seasoned with vinegar, onion and spices.)*

½ cup water

Salt and fresh pepper to taste

1. In a large skillet, heat the olive oil and brown the carrots.

2. Add the remaining ingredients, stir well, and simmer, uncovered, until the carrots are tender and the liquid is almost gone, about five minutes. Correct the seasoning, adding another tablespoon of chili sauce if you like. Serve hot.

MENU SUGGESTIONS

A versatile dish to have with anything from roasted chicken to pork chops to meat loaf, with a green salad and good bread. For a lighter meal, try the corn with Baked Leeks with Bacon and Cheddar Cheese (page 195) and toasted French bread slathered with sun-dried tomato purée.

FRESH CORN SALAD WITH OLIVES AND TOMATOES

MAKES SIX SERVINGS

A bright and crunchy salad that is best in summer but even makes winter tomatoes taste good. It's just as good the second day, after marinating, and the excess dressing in the bottom of the bowl is delicious on a green salad.

4 ears fresh corn (or 2¼ cups thawed frozen corn kernels)

2 medium-size ripe tomatoes, stem ends removed

1 medium-size green tomato, stem ends removed

10 big juicy green olives or Kalamata olives, pitted

2 tablespoons chopped fresh coriander (Use fresh flat-leaf parsley if you don't care for the strong taste of coriander.)

1 fresh jalapeño, roasted, peeled, stemmed, seeded and minced (optional; read Working with Hot Peppers, page 246)

¼ cup balsamic vinegar

¼ cup fruity olive oil

1 garlic clove, minced

½ teaspoon sugar

Salt and fresh pepper

Red leaf lettuce

1. Bring a big pot of water to a boil, add the corn, and cook for three minutes. Drain and set the ears aside to cool.

Cut the tomatoes in half; scoop out and discard the pulp and seeds. Cut the red tomatoes into ¼-inch-wide strips and the green tomato into ½-inch pieces. Chop the olives.

2. Strip the kernels from the ears of corn (see Notes to the Cook) and put them in a big bowl with the tomatoes, olives, coriander and jalapeño.

3. Whisk together the vinegar, oil, garlic and sugar. Pour this dressing over the vegetables and toss gently. Season with salt and pepper to taste. Set aside the salad to marinate for one hour, stirring occasionally.

Line a platter or bowl with whole leaves of red leaf lettuce and use a slotted spoon to mound the salad in the center. Serve chilled or at room temperature.

MENU SUGGESTIONS

Salmon loaf is terrific with this salad, with Marinated Mushrooms (page 204) on the side and a basket of warm focaccia or flour tortillas. An alternative outdoor summer meal featuring corn salad: grilled chicken, a selection of grilled vegetables and grilled Italian bread brushed with olive oil.

CUCUMBERS

BUYING AND STORING

Regular cucumbers: The regular cucumber is usually between six and eight inches long, with smooth, dark green skin and, all too often, a coating of wax that comes off only when you peel the cucumber. Try to find firm cucumbers with no yellow streaks or patches, which indicate maturity and tough, bitter seeds. Avoid shriveled ends, soft or moldy spots and sponginess.

Kirby cucumbers: Kirby (or pickling) cucumbers are small, anywhere from the size of a thumb up to about six inches long. They are naturally bumpy and sometimes irregularly shaped, and the skin (which is never waxed) may range from creamy white to yellow to pale or dark green. Varicolored skin is perfectly acceptable, but watch out for flabbiness and all-over wrinkling, as well as shriveled ends and rotten spots.

Keep Kirbies in a plastic bag in the refrigerator, where they will last from a few days to a week, depending on how fresh they were when you bought them. Regular cukes need not be bagged in the refrigerator; they may last up to two weeks.

Most of the time cucumbers are used as an addition to a green salad, mainly for the crunch. But both common kinds of cucumber, the regular smooth one and the small bumpy Kirby (or pickling) cucumber, are much tastier and more interesting as the main ingredient in a well-dressed cucumber salad.

NOTES TO THE COOK

Cleaning: Even if it is waxed, a regular cucumber should be rinsed well before you go on to trim and peel it. Kirbies should be scrubbed lightly with a soft brush or rough cloth.

Trimming the ends: The ends often seem to collect a certain amount of bitterness, so I always slice an inch off each end of a regular cucumber and ½ inch off each end of a Kirby. You may prefer to trim them less or not at all.

Peeling: Peel a regular cucumber with a swivel-blade vegetable peeler (or any other peeler you prefer) if it is waxed, if the recipe requires it, or if you simply like it better peeled.

QUICK-PICKLED CUKES AND SWEET ONIONS

MAKES ABOUT 3 1/2 CUPS

Tart, sweet and crunchy, these make up in record time. Serve as a relish with any meat or poultry, layer them on sandwiches, or take them along on a picnic.

2/3 CUP CIDER VINEGAR

1/3 CUP WATER

1/4 CUP SUGAR

2 TABLESPOONS OLIVE OIL

1 TEASPOON POWDERED OREGANO

2 BAY LEAVES

1/2 TEASPOON SALT

FRESH PEPPER TO TASTE

2 REGULAR CUCUMBERS, TRIMMED, PEELED, SEEDED AND SLICED THIN

1 MEDIUM-SIZE RED ONION, QUARTERED AND SLICED THIN

Combine all the ingredients except the cucumbers and onions in a large nonreactive saucepan (stainless steel, enameled, etc.) and simmer uncovered for five minutes. Turn off the heat, stir in the cucumbers and onions and let them marinate for 30 to 45 minutes. Remove the bay leaves, spoon the mixture into containers (with liquid) and refrigerate until needed. Serve chilled.

Kirbies, never waxed, need not be peeled unless you like them better that way.

Seeding: Kirbies' seeds are almost always tender and tasty, so you don't have to worry about removing them. Regular cucumbers are more appetizing without their seeds: Remove the seeds by first halving the cukes lengthwise, then scraping out the seeds with a spoon or cutting them out with a knife.

CUCUMBER SALAD
WITH CAPER DRESSING

MAKES PLENTY FOR SIX SERVINGS

This salad has a tangy dressing that is smoothed out by the lovely mellowness of tarragon. It should disappear fast, which is providential because the salad is at peak flavor only on the day it is made.

> **4 regular cucumbers (each about 8 inches long) or 2 pounds Kirby cucumbers (about 6 medium, each 4 to 6 inches long), rinsed and trimmed**
>
> **6 red radishes, trimmed**

FOR THE DRESSING

> **½ cup regular or light sour cream**
>
> **¼ cup plain (unflavored) yogurt**
>
> **1 tablespoon caper liquid (from jar of capers)**
>
> **1 tablespoon Dijon mustard**
>
> **¼ teaspoon powdered tarragon**
>
> **¼ cup loosely packed fresh flat-leaf (Italian) parsley leaves**
>
> **Fresh pepper to taste**
>
> **2 tablespoons drained capers (*Use small [nonpareil] whole capers or chopped large ones.*)**

1. If you're using regular cucumbers, peel them, then halve them lengthwise, and remove the seeds; cut into ¼-inch slices. Well-scrubbed Kirbies may be peeled or not, as you like, then cut into ¼-inch slices.

Cut the radishes into thin slices. Combine the cucumbers and radishes in a large bowl.

2. Put all the dressing ingredients except the capers in a food processor or blender and process until smooth. Correct the seasoning, stir the dressing and the capers into the vegetables, and serve soon.

MENU SUGGESTIONS

A savory tart with layers of cooked vegetables, cheese, fresh tomatoes and a not-too-rich custard makes a fine simple meal, with the cucumber salad on the side. And be sure to include this salad on picnic and other outdoor menus.

PANTRY

A CHOICE OF VINEGARS

Different vinegars are suited to different uses, so you'll want to stock a variety. All vinegars are, of course, acidic and tart, but once you get past the bite, they taste quite different from each other. Some are mild, some are harsh, some have fruity overtones, others are herb-infused.

Distilled white vinegar, for instance, is so harsh that it is used mainly for pickling. At the opposite end of the acid scale, *clear or "white" rice vinegar* is much milder and can be used for delicate salad dressings and sauces as well as the Asian dishes for which it is intended. Between these extremes you'll find a wide range of astringency and flavor.

Cider vinegar is strong and fruity; it cooks well (it's great in chutneys and relishes) and makes a good dressing for robust salads. *Balsamic vinegar* is produced in Italy and is sweet, sour and fruity all at once, with a lovely brown color; use it in dressings, sprinkle it on fruit or vegetables, add a little to tomato sauce.

MENU SUGGESTIONS

This salad is the perfect partner to cold sesame noodles and Stir-fried Peppers and Mushrooms (page 248). For a fancier meal, add Stuffed Chinese Cabbage Rolls with Spicy Peanut Sauce (page 133) and rice; if you'd like a meat dish, try stir-fried beef or chicken.

JAPANESE CUCUMBER SALAD

MAKES PLENTY FOR SIX SERVINGS

You may have tasted cold vegetables similar to this in a Japanese restaurant. The salad is lightly marinated, and the dark rich sesame oil gives it a nutty flavor. If there's any left over, it's great the next day.

TIP: The triangular cut is important, so follow the illustration carefully.

3 tablespoons peanut oil
2 tablespoons sesame seeds
¼ cup rice vinegar
3 tablespoons dry sherry (fino or manzanilla)
1 tablespoon sugar, preferably superfine
1 tablespoon soy sauce
1 tablespoon water
1 teaspoon sesame oil
2 pounds Kirby cucumbers (about 6 medium, each 4 to 6 inches long), scrubbed and trimmed

1. In a small skillet, heat the peanut oil; add the sesame seeds and sauté over medium heat for about one minute, until *light brown;* do not let the seeds get any darker. Set aside to cool.

2. In a large bowl, whisk together all the remaining ingredients except the cucumbers. Add the sesame seeds and any peanut oil you can scrape from the skillet. Whisk again.

3. Peel the cucumbers decoratively, making alternate stripes of green skin and white flesh. Cut into triangular chunks as shown.

Add the cucumbers to the bowl of dressing, stir well, and allow to marinate for several hours, stirring often. Serve chilled or at room temperature.

THE VEGETABLE EXPRESS

CUCUMBERS IN SWEET-AND-SOUR BUTTERMILK DRESSING

MAKES SIX SERVINGS

Buttermilk makes an excellent low-fat foundation for the creamy dressing on this homey, old-fashioned salad, with celery and celery seeds added to give it that extra bit of interest.

4 regular cucumbers (each about 8 inches long) or 2 pounds Kirby cucumbers (about 6 medium, each 4 to 6 inches long), rinsed and trimmed

1 stalk celery, trimmed

FOR THE DRESSING

½ cup buttermilk

2 tablespoons sugar, preferably superfine

¼ teaspoon celery seeds

¼ cup vegetable oil (not olive oil)

Salt and fresh pepper to taste

1. If you're using regular cucumbers, peel them, then halve them lengthwise and remove the seeds; slice thin (a mandoline is great for this). Well-scrubbed Kirbies may be peeled or not, as you like, then sliced thin.

Cut the celery into a small dice. Combine the cucumbers and celery in a bowl.

2. Make the dressing: Whisk together or process (in your food processor) the remaining ingredients until the sugar is dissolved. Pour the dressing over the cucumbers and mix well. Refrigerate until needed.

Wine vinegars, both red and white, can range from pungent to quite tart; use them in vinaigrette dressings, sauces and marinades. *Sherry vinegar*, a kind of wine vinegar that is aged in oak casks, is less acid, richer and mellower, and also makes wonderful vinaigrette.

Fruit vinegars are infusions of fruit, sugar (or honey) and vinegar—wine, cider, sherry or rice vinegar. Sometimes fruits are used in combination with herbs or spices. *Herb vinegar* is an infusion of wine, cider or rice vinegar and one or more fresh herbs such as dill, tarragon, mint, rosemary, thyme, basil, oregano or chives. Some herb vinegars include garlic, too. Use them to enhance vegetable dishes and salads or salad dressings.

TIP: Vinegars vary so widely in strength and flavor that you should, when using an unfamiliar vinegar, add them gradually so you can assess the results as you add.

MENU SUGGESTIONS

You can build whole meals around this cucumber salad. For a cold meal, have slices of cold roast pork, the cucumbers, Fresh Corn Salad with Olives and Tomatoes (page 141) and a basket of dinner rolls. For a hot meal, serve chicken and dumplings or smothered chicken instead of pork.

MENU SUGGESTIONS

Smorgasbord is my first choice for this company menu. Arrange a big table with gravlax or smoked salmon, herring, Pepper and Cabbage Slaw for a Picnic (page 249), potato salad (page 266), cold baked beets with horseradish sauce (#2 on page 69) and Kohlrabi in Poppy Seed Dressing (page 190). You'll also want a selection of cheeses and a big basket of different breads.

COMPANY'S COMING

HOT AND COLD CUCUMBERS

MAKES PLENTY FOR SIX SERVINGS

A very sophisticated pickled salad, unusual and complex in flavor, lime-lemony, gingery, with that unique coriander flavor. On the first day you make it, it's sweet-and-sour with a touch of heat; on the second day, the pepper will have raised the temperature to something a little livelier.

> **2 strips lemon zest, each 3 inches long**
>
> **1 cup rice vinegar**
>
> **⅓ cup water**
>
> **⅓ cup sugar**
>
> **1 teaspoon grated fresh ginger**
>
> **2 teaspoons minced fresh hot pepper (jalapeño, serrano, wax, Fresno, etc.)**
>
> **4 regular cucumbers (each about 8 inches long), rinsed and trimmed**
>
> **3 tablespoons minced fresh coriander**
>
> **⅓ cup fresh lime juice**
>
> **Salt**
>
> **For the garnish: ½ red bell pepper, cut in small dice, and several coriander leaves**

1. In a nonreactive saucepan (stainless steel, enameled, etc.), combine the lemon zest, vinegar, water, sugar, ginger and hot pepper. Bring to a boil and simmer until reduced to ⅔ cup, about 20 minutes.

2. Meanwhile, peel the cucumbers, halve them lengthwise, and remove the seeds. Slice as thin as you can and combine them in a large bowl with the coriander and lime juice.

3. Add the hot vinegar mixture and stir well. Season with salt. Refrigerate the cucumbers for an hour, or until you are ready to serve them, then garnish with diced red pepper and coriander leaves.

EGGPLANT

BUYING AND STORING

The basic plump, purple-skinned eggplant can be small, medium or large, egg-shaped, pear-shaped, straight-sided, rounded or pointy at the bottom. You've probably see them all.

Some supermarkets and produce stores also stock the small purple Italian eggplants that look like miniatures of the large ones, as well as the long, narrow, sweeter Japanese and Chinese eggplants, which may be purple or lavender or striped with both colors. White eggplants may show up, too (usually in the summer), and although some people swear that white is better than purple, I've never been able to detect the difference once it's cooked.

Whichever type you buy, look for firm eggplants that are heavy for their size. Squeeze the eggplant gently—it should be neither spongy nor hard, but nice and springy. The skin should be smooth and unblemished, with no brown patches, soft spots, shriveling or scars. The stem and cap should be fairly green and fresh. When buying ordinary purple eggplants, avoid large ones; small or medium ones are less likely to be bitter.

Refrigerate eggplants in a plastic bag and expect them to last not more than three or four days.

NOTES TO THE COOK

Cleaning: Rinse or wipe the skin well to remove dust and dirt; pat dry.

Trimming: Slice off the stem and spiky cap; pare out or slice off the brown stub at the opposite end.

Peeling: If the recipe requires it, peel the eggplant with a swivel-blade vegetable peeler (or any other peeler you prefer).

A note on salting: The reasons for preparing eggplant by salting and draining it are threefold. The most important is to draw out any bitter liquid; the second reason is to reduce the

Glossy purple eggplant is surely one of the great cross-cultural vegetables. (Actually, it's a fruit by birth, but we always treat it as a vegetable.) You find it in Italian, French, Middle Eastern, Chinese, Indian and Japanese cooking, to name a few cultures, and it has become a staple in regional American cooking, too.

Eggplant is so adaptable that you can go in almost any flavor direction you like: Combine it with tomatoes or goat cheese or curry or hot sauce. It's so satisfying that you can build a vegetarian meal around an eggplant recipe merely by serving it with rice, Asian noodles or pasta.

ASIAN INGREDIENTS

In addition to Chinese ingredients, many of which are used in this book, there are plenty of interesting ingredients from other parts of Asia—ingredients that are now available in America and that work beautifully with vegetables. Many of these ingredients have become familiar and others are beginning to be.

For instance, from Japan we have rice vinegar and soy sauce, of course, but we also have teriyaki sauce, tonkatsu sauce and the potent horseradish powder called wasabi. Sake (rice wine), mirin (sweet cooking wine) and miso (soybean paste) are less known to most people but are well worth investigating.

Aromatic lemongrass, fiery red curry paste, peanutty satay sauce and pungent nam pla, a fish sauce from Thailand—all these and more fascinating Asian flavors are out there waiting for you. Treat yourself to a shopping trip at a couple of Asian groceries to find these specialties.

water content so the texture of the eggplant pieces is somewhat more dense and solid; the third is to prevent the eggplant from absorbing too much oil when you sauté or fry it. Recipes will vary on the matter of salting according to the desired final result, so follow the instructions.

THAI-STYLE EGGPLANT

MAKES SIX SERVINGS

You may be accustomed to Thai food that is rather sweet, but this dish is not. It's a rich, savory and spicy sauce on perfectly roasted, succulent eggplant. Great on noodles, too.

2 pounds eggplant (about 2 medium eggplants), cleaned and trimmed

Vegetable oil (not olive oil)

¼ cup creamy peanut butter

2 tablespoons sesame oil

2 tablespoons rice vinegar

2 tablespoons water

1 teaspoon hot pepper sauce

2 scallions (white and green parts), minced

2 garlic cloves, minced

1 teaspoon minced fresh ginger

1 tablespoon minced fresh coriander

Salt

1. Preheat the oven to 400°. Cut the eggplants in half lengthwise and brush the cut sides with a little oil. Place the halves, cut side down, on a baking sheet and bake for 25 to 30 minutes, until tender but not mushy.

2. Meanwhile, in a medium bowl, mash together the peanut butter and sesame oil. Gradually blend in the vinegar, water and pepper sauce to make a smooth sauce. Stir in the remaining ingredients, including salt to taste, reserving two tablespoons of the scallions for garnish. Set the sauce aside.

3. When the eggplant is cool enough to handle, cut it in bite-size pieces (but don't peel it). Arrange the pieces on a serving platter and pour the sauce over them. Sprinkle with the reserved scallions and serve at room temperature.

MENU SUGGESTIONS

Start the meal with soba or ramen noodles in broth garnished with Chinese greens or escarole. Serve the eggplant with Bok Choy with Garlic Sauce (page 132) and plenty of rice. If you're feeling adventurous, homemade or take-out mee krob—Thai crisp noodles with eggs, chicken and shrimp—is the perfect companion to this eggplant dish.

SIMPLIFIED CAPONATA WITH SUN-DRIED TOMATOES

MAKES SIX SERVINGS

Soft and savory, with the interesting texture contrast of the sun-dried tomatoes. The gradual addition and reduction of water (step 3) is extremely important in marrying the flavors properly, so don't be impatient about it.

1½ pounds eggplant (about 1 medium-large or 2 small eggplants), cleaned and trimmed

Salt

1 medium onion

2 stalks celery, trimmed

2 ounces sun-dried tomatoes, rinsed in hot water

6 to 8 meaty olives, such as Sicilian or Kalamata

6 tablespoons olive oil

1½ tablespoons large or small capers

1 tablespoon red wine vinegar

1 teaspoon sugar

Fresh pepper

¾ cup water

1. Cut the unpeeled eggplant into ½-inch cubes and put the cubes in a colander. Sprinkle with salt, toss to coat, and let drain 30 minutes.

Meanwhile, dice the onion and celery; cut the sun-dried tomatoes into ¼-inch strips. Pit the olives and chop the flesh.

2. In a large skillet, heat half the olive oil and sauté the onions and celery over medium-low heat until translucent and beginning to brown.

Rinse the eggplant and firmly squeeze out the excess liquid. Add the eggplant and the remaining olive oil to the skillet, and sauté with the onions and celery until the eggplant is tender, stirring often.

3. Stir in the sun-dried tomatoes, olives, capers, vinegar, sugar and a generous grinding of pepper. Cook over low heat, stirring, for ten minutes; while you are cooking and stirring, add the water in three parts, letting it evaporate almost completely after each addition. At the end of the ten minutes, the eggplant will be soft (but not mushy) and succulent, and the various flavors will have married and smoothed out.

Let the mixture cool; serve at room temperature.

MENU SUGGESTIONS

Caponata, with its many vegetables, goes nicely with pasta dressed simply with good olive oil and sautéed garlic or with a white clam sauce. If you like, add a dish of Escarole with Gorgonzola Cream (page 164) or some marinated peppers with fresh basil (page 244).

fingers

OVEN-FRIED EGGPLANT FINGERS WITH RANCH DIPPING SAUCE

MAKES SIX SERVINGS

Cracker crumbs, a traditional coating for deep-fried foods, are used here—but there's no deep-frying to add fat. This recipe makes a lot of crisp fingers, but they're so good I don't think you'll have any left over. Serve the dipping sauce on the side.

- **1½ pounds eggplant (about 2 medium-small regular eggplants or 7 small Italian eggplants), cleaned, trimmed and peeled**
- **Salt**
- **2 egg whites**
- **1 tablespoon water**
- **1¼ cups fine Ritz cracker crumbs (about 38 crackers) *(Crush the crackers in a plastic bag with a rolling pin or in your food processor.)***
- **Ranch Dipping Sauce (recipe follows)**

1. Cut the peeled eggplant lengthwise into ¾-inch-thick slices, then cut the slices lengthwise into ¾-inch-wide strips. Cut the long strips in half crosswise to make "fingers." (If you are using Italian eggplants, do not cut the strips in half.)

Put the fingers in a colander, sprinkle with salt, and toss well to coat. Let them drain for 30 minutes.

2. Preheat the oven to 375°; grease a baking sheet. In a medium bowl, beat the egg whites with the tablespoon of water until slightly frothy. Put the cracker crumbs in another bowl.

3. Rinse the eggplant fingers, gently squeeze out any excess liquid, and pat the fingers dry on paper towels. Add them to the bowl of beaten egg whites and stir well to coat. One finger at a time, shake off any excess egg white, dredge in cracker crumbs, and place on the prepared baking sheet.

Bake for 40 minutes, turning once after 20 minutes. Serve immediately, with Ranch Dipping Sauce on the side.

Ranch Dipping Sauce

Ordinarily, I never use garlic or onion powder—only fresh onions or garlic will do. However, it seems that the familiar "ranch" flavor can't be duplicated with anything other than the powdered product.

½ **to 1 teaspoon garlic powder**

½ **to 1 teaspoon onion powder**

1 cup regular or light sour cream

¼ **cup buttermilk**

1 tablespoon minced fresh flat-leaf (Italian) parsley

Salt to taste

Using the smaller amounts of garlic and onion powder, stir the ingredients together until smooth. Let the sauce chill for half an hour to develop the flavor. Taste, and if you like, stir in the rest of the garlic and onion powder. Chill the sauce for another 30 minutes.

MENU SUGGESTIONS

Barbecued beef, beef-and-bean chili or even sloppy joes are good with this dish. Get some greens into the meal by serving Escarole in Tomato Sauce (page 166) or a big salad. If you don't eat meat, substitute Kidney Beans with Rice and Cheese (page 45).

PANTRY

COOKING OIL AND

SALAD OIL

With very little storage space to spare, I keep a fairly simple, pared-down stock of basic supplies. Even so, there are seven kinds of oil I always have on hand: in the pantry closet, extra-virgin Italian olive oil with a light flavor, Spanish olive oil with a fruity flavor, corn oil, safflower oil and peanut oil; in the refrigerator, walnut oil and dark sesame oil.

You may not choose exactly the same array, but your own minimum stock should include a good grade of cold-pressed olive oil (extra-virgin, superfine virgin, fine virgin or virgin) for salads and sautéing, and at least one neutral oil for salads and general cooking purposes. Neutral (almost flavorless) oils include safflower, canola, sunflower, soybean, corn and a lower grade of olive oil labeled "pure."

Depending on your taste preference and the kind of cooking you do, add other oils as you need them: peanut oil and dark sesame oil for Asian and other dishes; light

HOT AND SPICY BRAISED EGGPLANT

MAKES SIX SERVINGS

This is very similar to a dish you'll find on the menu in a Chinese restaurant, in which the eggplant is quite soft and totally infused with the spicy sauce. Make it as hot as you like— $\frac{1}{4}$ teaspoon of hot pepper flakes for a mild kick or $\frac{1}{2}$ teaspoon for Szechuan-style heat.

> 2 pounds eggplant (about 2 medium eggplants), cleaned and trimmed (*If you can get Chinese or Japanese eggplants, this is a good recipe in which to use them.*)

Salt

FOR THE SAUCE

> 2 tablespoons soy sauce
>
> 3 tablespoons hoisin sauce (*See page 128 for more about Chinese ingredients.*)
>
> $\frac{1}{4}$ to $\frac{1}{2}$ teaspoon hot red pepper flakes (*Use $\frac{1}{2}$ teaspoon for a really hot and spicy flavor.*)
>
> $\frac{1}{2}$ cup dry sherry (fino or manzanilla)
>
> $1\frac{1}{2}$ cups water

> 2 tablespoons peanut oil
>
> 2 tablespoons minced garlic
>
> 2 tablespoons minced fresh ginger

Sesame seeds for garnish

1. Cut the unpeeled eggplant lengthwise into $\frac{3}{4}$-inch-thick slices, then lengthwise again into $\frac{3}{4}$-inch-wide strips. Cut the long strips in half crosswise to make shorter strips. Place the strips in a colander, sprinkle with salt, and toss to coat. Let them drain for 30 minutes. Rinse well and squeeze firmly to remove moisture.

(If you are using Japanese or Chinese eggplants, skip the salting and draining process.)

2. In a medium bowl, combine the sauce ingredients; set aside.

In a large skillet or wok, heat the oil; add the eggplant, garlic and ginger and stir-fry over high heat for three minutes.

3. Add the sauce and stir well. Reduce the heat to medium-low and simmer uncovered for 15 minutes, stirring occasionally. Turn up the heat and continue cooking and stirring until the eggplant is quite soft and the sauce is reduced to a thick glaze. Serve immediately, garnished with a sprinkling of sesame seeds.

sesame oil for general use; walnut, almond and/or hazelnut oils (which are often mixed with another oil to tone down the flavor a bit). Keep in mind that the distinctive flavors, high cost and/or low smoking points of walnut, almond, hazelnut and dark Asian sesame oils make them best suited to salads or—if used in cooking—to last-minute addition.

Keep containers in a cool, dark place. Unopened, most oils will keep for a year; opened, use most within six months. Sesame oil and walnut oil are the main exceptions—store them in the refrigerator to avoid their becoming rancid.

MENU SUGGESTIONS

You might like to try sautéed scallops or soft-shell crabs on Chinese noodles and a dish of Mixed Chinese Greens (page 128) with the eggplant. For a more elaborate meal: noodles with scallions and shredded pork or chicken, Chinese Broccoli in Soy-Lemon-Butter Sauce (page 129), stir-fried tofu, and rice.

Christmas, Hannukah and New Year's Eve are the times to go all out and serve the most beautiful and scrumptious party foods. The vegetable dishes listed below will certainly contribute to a luxurious menu.

Buckwheat Crêpes with Creamy Broccoli Filling, page 87

Belgian Endive Baked in White Wine Sauce, page 74

Brandied Brussels Sprouts and Chestnuts, page 95

Sweet Carrot Ring, page 111

Caulifritters, page 118

Braised Celery Hearts with Blue Cheese, page 124

Roasted Fennel with Wild Mushrooms and Crisp Shallots, page 176

THE VEGETABLE EXPRESS

THREE VARIATIONS ON ROASTED EGGPLANT

MAKES SIX SERVINGS

Roasting an eggplant can be a tricky business, but here are two reliable ways to do it. Method #1 yields firm, peeled cubes, while Method #2 gives you softer pieces with the tasty, chewy peel left on.

Roasting Method #1 (firmer): Brush one or two large baking dishes with oil; preheat the oven to 425° (400° for ovenproof glass). Clean, trim and peel the eggplant(s) and cut them into 1- to 1½-inch pieces; brush lightly all over with oil. Arrange the pieces in one layer on the baking dish(es) and cover tightly with foil. Bake for 15 minutes; then remove the foil, turn the pieces, and roast uncovered for 15 more minutes.

Roasting Method #2 (softer): Preheat the oven to 400°. Clean and trim the eggplant(s), cut them in half lengthwise, and brush the cut sides with a little oil. Place the halves, cut side down, on a baking sheet and bake for 25 to 30 minutes, until tender but not mushy. Cut the hot eggplant into 1- to 1½-inch cubes.

Roasted, cubed eggplant can be the foundation for any number of simple side dishes—for example, roasted eggplant tossed with juicy summer tomatoes, chopped fresh basil and a little vinaigrette.

Here are three more simple dishes with very different flavors. For each dish you'll need either one or two pounds of eggplant (one or two medium eggplants; be sure to check the amount required in the recipe). Use whichever roasting method you prefer, cubing the eggplant before or after roasting as described.

ROASTED EGGPLANT WITH MUSHROOMS AND GOAT CHEESE: Brush olive oil on 12 trimmed white or cremini mushrooms and roast them along with one medium eggplant, removing the mushrooms after 20 minutes. Put the hot mushrooms and cubed eggplant in a large bowl, crumble three ounces of goat cheese over them, and toss with 1½ tablespoons of balsamic vinegar, a little salt and a good grinding of fresh pepper.

ROASTED EGGPLANT WITH ROASTED GARLIC AND LEMON: Roast two bulbs of garlic along with two medium eggplants, leaving the garlic in the oven for an extra ten minutes if the cloves are not quite soft. (See page 28 for more on roasted garlic.) Cut the root ends off the garlic bulbs, squeeze the soft garlic out into a large bowl, and mash it with ¼ cup chicken or vegetable broth, one tablespoon regular or light sour cream and the juice of half a lemon. Add the cubed eggplant, mix well, and season to taste with salt and fresh pepper.

ROASTED EGGPLANT WITH INDIAN SPICES: Roast two medium eggplants. In a large bowl, toss the hot cubed eggplant with two tablespoons of butter and set aside. In a small bowl, combine ½ cup plain (unflavored) yogurt, ½ teaspoon each turmeric and paprika, ¼ teaspoon each ground ginger, cayenne, cumin and coriander, and two pinches each cinnamon and ground cloves. Pour the sauce over the eggplant, toss well, and season with salt.

Holiday Baked Onions with Double Cheese Sauce, page 224

Parsnip Purée with Honey and Spice, page 232

Oven-fried Potato Cakes, page 271

Fluffy Baked Rutabagas with Melted Cheese, page 285

Acorn Squash with Apples and Cider Glaze, page 303

Swiss Chard in Walnut Oil with Toasted Walnuts, page 316

Turnips Rosanna, page 331

MENU SUGGESTIONS

The roasted eggplant with mushrooms goes well with fettuccine and broccoli or broccoli rabe; the roasted garlic version is great with pizza or pasta with sausage; serve the Indian-spiced eggplant with basmati rice, lentils and a good raita. Alternatively, roasted chicken and a green salad are fine with any of the recipes.

PANTRY

CHEESE

Cheese (in moderation) is a delicious flavoring for many vegetable dishes. The following descriptions will give you an idea of the taste and texture of many of the cheeses mentioned in the ingredients lists of the recipes in this book.

Boursin: Usually sold in a small round, this triple-cream cheese is white, smooth and buttery, tangy but rather mild.

Cheddar: This familiar cheese, firm and dense, may be mild to sharp in flavor and creamy white to orange in color.

Cottage or pot cheese: White, mild and creamy fresh cheese with large or small curds; if cottage cheese is drained of some liquid, pot cheese results.

Danish blue: Creamy white cheese with blue veins; like most blue cheeses, it is sharp and strong in flavor and smell.

Feta: This Greek cheese is crumbly, salty and quite tangy.

Fontina: A dark yellow, semifirm but smooth cheese with a medium strong, slightly nutty flavor—it melts beautifully.

Goat cheeses (chèvres): There are many varieties—crumbly, creamy, mild and strong; some of the more commonly available kinds

BAKED EGGPLANT SLICES ROLLED WITH FONTINA CHEESE

MAKES 15 ROLLS, PLENTY FOR 6 SERVINGS

This is one of the prettier vegetable dishes—little roll-ups, lightly browned, topped with fresh tomato sauce and parsley leaves. Arrange them on a round platter as shown.

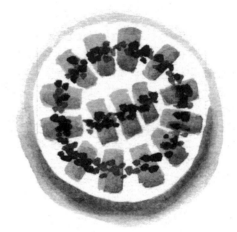

2 medium eggplants, cleaned, trimmed and peeled *(Use long, straight eggplants rather than fat, round ones; this will yield better slices.)*

Salt

Olive oil for sauteing

¼ pound fontina cheese, grated (about 1 cup)

6 tablespoons (packed) minced fresh flat-leaf (Italian) parsley

2 tablespoons finely minced garlic

7 medium-size white or cremini mushrooms, trimmed and thinly sliced

2 roasted red peppers (from a jar, if you like), cored, seeded, deveined and diced

3 ounces prosciutto, chopped

Powdered dried oregano

Fresh pepper

6 ripe plum tomatoes (about 1 pound), stem ends removed

Parsley leaves for garnish

1. Trim the opposite sides of each eggplant as shown, then cut lengthwise in ¼-inch-thick slices—at least 16 to 18 slices in total. Pick the best-looking 15 slices and set aside the rest for another use.

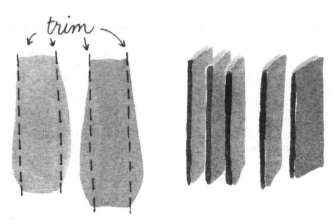

Sprinkle both sides of each slice with salt and place in a colander to drain for 30 minutes. Rinse well, stack the slices, and gently press out the excess liquid, taking care not to break or tear them. Lay out the slices between layers of paper towels and press again to remove more liquid.

2. In a large skillet, heat two tablespoons of olive oil and sauté several of the eggplant slices until lightly browned, about two minutes on each side. Repeat for the remaining slices, adding more oil as needed.

3. Set up an assembly line for filling and rolling the slices. First put each filling ingredient in a bowl: grated fontina cheese, minced parsley, minced garlic, sliced mushrooms, diced peppers and chopped prosciutto. Next lay out all the eggplant slices with narrow ends closest to you.

Stop for a moment at this point and turn the oven on to 400°. Brush olive oil on the bottom and sides of a baking dish large enough to hold the rolled-up slices in one layer.

are Montrachet, boucheron, crottin and Valençay.

Gorgonzola: Famous (or infamous) for its strong taste and smell; young and dolce (sweet) Gorgonzolas are soft and creamy, while the aged cheese is firm and crumbly.

Gruyère: This firm, tan cheese has a strong, nutty flavor; be sure to buy a high-quality product.

Mascarpone: Here's a treat— fresh double- or triple-cream cheese that is so delicate and buttery, it's almost sweet.

Monterey Jack: Jack cheese is usually semisoft, with a mild or mellow flavor slightly reminiscent of cheddar.

Mozzarella and smoked mozzarella: Unfortunately, packaged American mozzarella is rubbery and tasteless. Try to find fresh mozzarella in a gourmet shop or Italian grocery—it's soft and succulent with a subtle flavor. Freshly smoked mozzarella has deliciously smoky brown skin.

Parmesan, Romano and other grating cheeses: See page 88.

Ricotta: Ricotta is a soft, creamy fresh cheese, slightly sweet and very mild in flavor.

Roquefort: A strong and tangy blue cheese, creamy in the center and more crumbly toward the rind—it's great on salads.

4. Now fill all the rolls at once: Sprinkle one tablespoon of cheese evenly down the center of each slice; don't let it get too near the edges or the ends. Sprinkle each slice with 1 teaspoon parsley, then with ½ teaspoon garlic, 4 or 5 slices of mushroom, a little of the roasted peppers, some of the prosciutto, a pinch of oregano, a little salt and a good grinding of fresh pepper. Carefully roll up each slice from the narrow end, ending seam side down.

5. Arrange the rolls, seam side down, in the prepared dish with a little space between them. Brush the rolls with olive oil and cover the dish tightly with a lid or aluminum foil. Bake covered for ten minutes, then uncover and bake ten more minutes.

6. While the eggplant bakes, dice the tomatoes and sauté them in a little olive oil just until softened. Season with salt and pepper. When the eggplant comes out of the oven, place the rolls on a serving platter and top each one with some of the tomato mixture and a parsley leaf. Serve hot.

MENU SUGGESTIONS

It's best not to get too complicated with this menu—the rolls are complicated enough. Serve with sautéed baby artichokes and a simple risotto (or stir the baby artichokes into the risotto), and follow with an arugula salad.

ESCAROLE

BUYING AND STORING

Look for lush, full heads of escarole with deep or bright green outer leaves and pale green or white inner leaves. There should be no blackening or wilting at the edges of the leaves and no browning or yellowing on the leaves. The stem end should be fresh looking and not rusty.

Escarole is stored just like lettuce, refrigerated unwashed in a plastic bag and kept for several days.

NOTES TO THE COOK

Trimming: Pull off and discard the toughest outer leaves. Cut off and discard about an inch of the stem end, which will remove some of the worst dirt and release all the remaining leaves. Tear off any withered or bad spots on any of the leaves.

Washing: Escarole is usually quite sooty, especially at the stem ends of the leaves. Soaking in several changes of cool water will get most of the dirt off, but some will stick and you'll have to rub it off by hand. It's usually easier to forgo soaking and just wash the leaves quickly by hand. After washing, shake the leaves to remove excess water.

Spin-drying: Use your salad spinner and give the escarole a good whirl, until it is dry but not bone dry.

Escarole appears at first glance to be a head of lettuce, but if you look carefully you'll see that the deep green, ruffled leaves are firmer and thicker than lettuce, with no pronounced ribs in the centers. The leaves toward the center of the head are pale green or white and much more tender than the outer leaves— they're wonderful in salad. All the leaves are chewy and slightly bitter, robust enough to combine with other strong flavors.

You may be familiar with escarole as it is frequently prepared in Italian restaurants—braised and served in a little broth, with olive oil, garlic and plenty of salt and pepper. A lovely way to eat escarole, but not the only way.

VEGETABLE SOUP EXPRESS

Like roasting a big plump chicken, one of the best reasons for making vegetable side dishes is having leftovers. They're great for a light lunch or snack the next day, but they're even better added to a hearty quick-cooking vegetable soup.

Start your pot of soup with four to six cups of vegetable, chicken or beef broth or with tomato soup, depending on the kind of leftover vegetables you have. Bring to a simmer and start adding some of the good things listed below:

- **STARCHES TO COOK IN THE BROTH OR ADD, COOKED, TO THE HOT SOUP: WHITE OR BROWN RICE; SMALL PASTA (ORZO OR DITALINI, FOR EXAMPLE); EGG NOODLES; BARLEY; BULGUR WHEAT; DICED POTATOES; SPLIT PEAS; LENTILS**

- **HERBS FOR FLAVORING: CHIVES; PARSLEY; DILL; TARRAGON; THYME; BASIL; OREGANO**

- **COOKED OR FAST-COOKING VEGETABLES TO FILL OUT THE SOUP: SAUTÉED MUSHROOMS; CHOPPED SPINACH OR ESCAROLE; GRATED CARROT; FINELY SHREDDED CABBAGE; ANY KIND OF COOKED BEANS; FROZEN CORN, PEAS OR LIMA BEANS; CANNED TOMATOES**

Now either add all your leftover vegetables and heat them with the rest of the soup, or purée half (or more) of the leftovers and stir both the purée and the remaining leftovers into the soup. If the soup is too thick, add more broth.

If you like, serve the soup garnished with homemade croutons (page 166).

ESCAROLE WITH GORGONZOLA CREAM

MAKES SIX SERVINGS

Escarole is best when cooked simply, in this case dressed up with a rich, silky sauce.

2 medium heads escarole, trimmed and washed (be sure to shake off any excess water; see Notes to the Cook)

2 tablespoons olive oil

2 garlic cloves, minced

½ cup vegetable or chicken broth

Salt and fresh pepper

Gorgonzola Cream (recipe follows)

1. Stack and cut the damp escarole leaves into one-inch strips; set aside. In a large skillet, heat the olive oil; add the escarole by handfuls, stirring it down and sautéing until all the leaves wilt. Add the garlic and sauté for another minute or two.

2. Add the broth, cover the skillet and cook until tender, about two minutes. Season lightly with salt and pepper. Arrange the escarole in a ring on a serving platter and pour the Gorgonzola sauce over it in a zigzag pattern. Serve immediately.

Gorgonzola Cream

MAKES ABOUT ONE CUP

½ cup olive oil

2 tablespoons rice vinegar

3 tablespoons regular sour cream

2 tablespoons water

2 ounces aged Gorgonzola cheese *(Do not use the younger, softer Gorgonzola.)*

½ teaspoon dry mustard

Salt and fresh pepper to taste

Combine all the ingredients in a food processor and process until smooth. Refrigerate until half an hour before needed. Stir well just before using.

MENU SUGGESTIONS

I like this with pasta tossed with Mushroom-Basil Pesto (page 198), with a side of Crisp Artichokes (page 23) or a tomato salad. Focaccia or another Italian bread are essential.

CROUTONS

Croutons are cubes, strips or slices of toasted bread used, among other purposes, to garnish a salad, soup or vegetable side dish. Homemade croutons are significantly better than store-bought ones and very easy to make, too.

Start with a good loaf of sourdough, light whole wheat, French or Italian bread and slice it ½ or ¾ inch thick. Lightly brush both sides of each slice with either olive oil, melted butter or melted margarine, depending on the dish you're plan-

MENU SUGGESTIONS

Delicious alongside pasta tossed with the simplest of dressings—oil, sautéed garlic and lots of chopped fresh flat-leaf parsley. Fried Peppers with Anchovy Butter (page 247) complete the menu.

ESCAROLE IN TOMATO SAUCE

MAKES SIX SERVINGS

Interestingly, the tomato sauce tastes rather harsh until you add the escarole—then the two parts marry and smooth out like magic. This is good served over pasta, too.

- **3 tablespoons olive oil**
- **1 medium onion, coarsely chopped**
- **2 medium heads escarole, trimmed, washed and spin-dried (see Notes to the Cook)**
- **3 garlic cloves, minced**
- **½ cup tomato paste**
- **½ cup red wine**
- **¾ cup water**
- **¼ teaspoon powdered oregano**
- **¼ teaspoon powdered basil**
- **¼ teaspoon hot pepper flakes**
- **Salt and fresh pepper to taste**
- **3 tablespoons grated Parmesan cheese or a combination of Parmesan and Romano cheeses**

1. In a large skillet, heat the olive oil and sauté the onion until lightly browned. While the onion cooks, cut or tear the escarole into bite-size pieces; set aside.

Add the garlic to the skillet and sauté for one minute. Stir in all the remaining ingredients except the escarole and the grated cheese and cook, stirring, for three minutes.

2. Add the escarole by handfuls, stirring it down and sautéing until all the leaves are wilted and tender. Correct the seasoning and transfer to a serving bowl. Sprinkle with Parmesan cheese and serve right away.

SAUTÉED ESCAROLE WITH BACON AND GARLIC

MAKES SIX SERVINGS

Escarole lends itself to a simple sauté because you can wilt the leaves without overcooking them. All it needs is a bit of garlic and bacon and it's a perfect family dish. I like to serve hot pepper sauce on the side.

2 medium heads escarole, trimmed and washed (be sure to shake off excess water; see Notes to the Cook)

4 slices lean bacon

3 tablespoons olive oil

3 garlic cloves, minced

Salt and fresh pepper

1. Stack and cut the damp escarole leaves into ½-inch strips; set aside.

In a large skillet, sauté the bacon until crisp. Drain on paper towels, crumble, and set aside. Discard the bacon fat and wipe out the skillet.

2. Heat the oil in the skillet and sauté the garlic for one minute. Add the escarole by handfuls, stirring down and sautéing until all the leaves are wilted. When the leaves are wilted, sauté for two more minutes.

3. Season with salt and a good grinding of pepper, turn out into a serving bowl, and sprinkle the bacon on top. Serve right away.

ning to garnish. Sprinkle each side with salt, pepper and one or more powdered herbs of your choice (oregano, basil, marjoram, thyme, etc.). If you like, cut the slices into large or small cubes or wide or narrow strips.

In the bad old days, you would now proceed to deep-fry your croutons; in the good new days, you will do one of two things:

- **IN A BIG SKILLET, SAUTÉ THE BREAD UNTIL BROWNED AND CRISP ON BOTH SIDES AND STILL A BIT SOFT IN THE CENTER. YOU MAY HAVE TO ADD A LITTLE MORE OIL TO THE SKILLET TO BROWN (NOT BURN) THE CROUTONS.**

- **IN A PREHEATED 325° OVEN, DRY OUT THE BREAD UNTIL LIGHTLY BROWNED AND QUITE CRISP, ABOUT 10 TO 15 MINUTES ON EACH SIDE.**

Add the croutons to your salad, soup or side dish at the last moment, to preserve the crispness.

MENU SUGGESTIONS

Make an unusual meal by serving some fine veal and Wild Mushroom Fricassee in Croustades (page 209) with this homey escarole. Alternatively, have the escarole with brown rice, beans, and Sautéed Pattypan Squash with Red Pepper Sauce (page 299).

ESCAROLE, RADICCHIO AND WHITE BEANS WITH WALNUT-BASIL PESTO

MAKES SIX SERVINGS

This is an unusual combination, arranged on leaves of radicchio, perfect for adventurous eaters because the textures and flavors are definitely sophisticated.

Be sure to take this salad out of the refrigerator at least half an hour before serving so it will be room temperature or only slightly chilled when you serve it; it should not be cold. And remember—it's a fresh dish, not as good on the second day.

- 1 medium head escarole, trimmed, washed and spin-dried (see Notes to the Cook) *(Be sure to discard all the tough leaves and use only the tender ones; also, leaves should be free of excess water but not bone dry.)*
- 1 large head radicchio (4 to 5 inches in diameter) *(The outer leaves will be used for lining the serving bowl.)*
- 2 tablespoons olive oil
- 2 garlic cloves, minced
- 1¾ cups cooked small white beans (one 1-pound can), rinsed and drained well
- Salt and fresh pepper
- Walnut-Basil Pesto (recipe follows)
- ¼ cup chopped toasted walnuts for garnish

1. Stack and cut the escarole leaves into ½-inch strips; set aside. Core the radicchio and set aside four or five unblemished outer leaves to use for lining the serving bowl; cut the rest of the head in half and then into ¼-inch strips.

2. Heat the olive oil in a large skillet and sauté the garlic for a minute or two. Add the escarole by handfuls, stirring down and sautéing just until all the leaves have wilted slightly. Do not overcook—the leaves should not be fully wilted. Transfer to a large bowl to cool, stirring occasionally to release more heat.

When the escarole is warm (not hot), add the radicchio strips and stir well to wilt them slightly. The radicchio should retain its purple color.

3. Add the beans, a sprinkling of salt and pepper and all the pesto, and mix gently but well. Taste and add more salt and pepper if needed.

Line a shallow serving bowl with the reserved radicchio leaves. Fill the bowl with the escarole mixture and top with the chopped walnuts. Serve slightly chilled or at room temperature.

Walnut-Basil Pesto

MAKES ABOUT ⅓ CUP

This amount of pesto is just enough for the escarole salad. (If you double the ingredients, you'll have enough for saucing a dish of pasta.)

½ cup (packed) fresh basil leaves

1½ tablespoons chopped walnuts

½ garlic clove, chopped

Salt and fresh pepper

3 tablespoons olive oil

3 tablespoons grated Parmesan cheese or a combination of Parmesan and Romano cheeses

1. In a food processor or blender, combine the basil, walnuts, garlic, a shake or two of salt, a good grinding of pepper and half of the olive oil, and process until they make a thick paste.

NOTE: *Use a compact food processor if you have one. If your processor is large, scrape down the sides often as you work.*

2. With the motor running, slowly pour the remaining olive oil through the feed tube. Now add the cheese and mix with several bursts of power. Turn the pesto out into a bowl and correct the seasoning.

MENU SUGGESTIONS

This extravaganza of flavors can be one of the dishes for a fancy party buffet. The others might be Artichokes Provençal (page 26), Tomatoes Stuffed with Couscous and Pine Nuts (page 325), a platter of country pâtés and plenty of crusty rolls and bread. Don't forget the trimmings— grainy mustard, a selection of olives (see page 26), cornichons.

FENNEL

Fennel is not a wildly versatile vegetable, but that's its charm: It has an unusual mild anise flavor that should be reserved for certain kinds of dishes and used in combination with certain other flavors. On the other hand, it is delicious raw (tossed into salads or used for dipping) as well as cooked, so it certainly has some scope.

BUYING AND STORING

Fennel bulbs, creamy white shading to pale green, should be firm and smooth with no cracks or brown patches, and outer leaves should not be dry or withered. Crisp green stalks and bright green feathery leaves are a good sign of freshness. Watch out for a rusty brown color on the bottom of the bulb.

Refrigerate unwashed fennel bulbs in a plastic bag and expect them to last for at least five days and perhaps longer.

NOTES TO THE COOK

Trimming: Cut off the stalks right at the top of the bulb, and cut a thin slice off the bottom of the bulb to expose a fresh, clean surface. The outermost layer of the bulb can be fibrous and tough, so peel off the outer leaf or two to get to the bright white, juicy layer below.

Cleaning: Rinse the trimmed bulbs and pat dry with paper towels.

BAKED FENNEL WITH SOUR CREAM SAUCE

MAKES SIX SERVINGS

You'll need five bulbs here, since the spotlight is on the fennel—no other vegetable or grain to stretch it. It's baked to tenderness and blanketed with a mellow, creamy sauce.

5 medium fennel bulbs, trimmed and cleaned (see Notes to the Cook)

Salt and fresh pepper

¼ cup grated Parmesan cheese or a combination of Parmesan and Romano cheeses

1 cup regular or light sour cream

6 tablespoons chicken or vegetable broth

Paprika to taste

1. Preheat the oven to 400°; bring a large saucepan of water to a boil. Cut each fennel bulb in four wedges, cutting down through the stem end. Butter a baking dish large enough to hold the fennel wedges in one layer.

2. Drop the wedges into the boiling water and simmer just until tender, five to ten minutes; drain well. Arrange the fennel neatly in the prepared dish, and sprinkle with salt, pepper and the grated cheese. Bake for 20 minutes; the cheese will be golden brown.

3. In a small saucepan, whisk together the sour cream, broth and paprika until smooth. Heat gently, stirring, so the sour cream doesn't curdle. Spoon the hot sauce evenly over the baked fennel and serve immediately.

MENU SUGGESTIONS

Serve with braised pork or, if you prefer a meat-free meal, with plain baked potatoes. Either way, have Browned Carrots (page 110) and a green salad.

PIZZA WITH VEGETABLES

Make a ball of pizza dough according to your favorite recipe; preheat the oven to 500° (or slightly lower if your dough recipe suggests it). Punch down and roll out the dough; transfer it to a baking sheet sprinkled with cornmeal.

Brush the dough with olive oil, and if you like, spread with tomato sauce, plain yogurt or sour cream. Arrange any of the following cooked and/or raw vegetables on the dough:

- SAUTÉED SLICES OF EGG-PLANT
- ZUCCHINI OR ANY OTHER SUMMER SQUASH, SLICED OR DICED
- SLICED FRESH TOMATO
- RED OR YELLOW ONION SLICES OR RINGS
- SLICED OR WHOLE COOKED ARTICHOKE HEARTS
- SLICED MUSHROOMS
- SWEET OR HOT PEPPERS, CUT INTO RINGS, STRIPS OR LARGE DICE
- SLICED FENNEL
- PITTED OLIVES, CAPERS, FRESH HERBS (BASIL, PARSLEY, ROSEMARY OR OREGANO)

Sprinkle the vegetables with cheese—grated Parmesan or Romano, crumbled goat or blue cheese, feta, or shredded mozzarella. Bake for 15 to 20 minutes, until the crust is golden.

FENNEL AND CHICK-PEAS IN CUMIN VINAIGRETTE

MAKES SIX SERVINGS

This unusual salad stretches three bulbs of fennel into six servings.

3 medium fennel bulbs, trimmed and cleaned (see Notes to the Cook)

1 medium-size red onion

1 cup canned chick-peas (about half of a 1-pound can), rinsed and drained

Cumin Vinaigrette (recipe follows)

Salt and fresh pepper

Leaves of red leaf or other lettuce

1. Slice the fennel and the red onion as thin as you can, slicing down from top to stem end. (A mandoline works well for the slicing.) Place the slices in a large bowl.

With your fingers, break the chick-peas in halves and add the pieces to the bowl.

2. Stir ½ cup of the dressing into the fennel mixture. Add salt and pepper to taste, plus more dressing if needed. Serve chilled, mounded on a bed of lettuce leaves.

Cumin Vinaigrette

MAKES ABOUT ONE CUP

3 tablespoons red or white wine vinegar

2 tablespoons fresh lime juice

½ teaspoon salt

1 teaspoon ground cumin

½ teaspoon dry mustard

Pinch of cayenne pepper

¾ cup olive oil

1 garlic clove, crushed

In a food processor or by hand with a whisk, blend all the ingredients except the garlic until thoroughly combined. Add more salt if needed, and pour the dressing into a jar with the garlic.

If possible, let the dressing stand for an hour to develop the flavor; if you can't wait, use immediately. Refrigerate any remaining dressing for future use. Shake before using.

MENU SUGGESTIONS

Curried chicken is my first choice to go with this fennel dish, but you could skip the chicken altogether and serve the fennel with Plantains with Curry Sauce and Roasted Peanuts (page 257), any raita in this book, Indian or pita bread and white rice.

LEMON-SAUTÉED FENNEL

MAKES SIX SERVINGS

A simple dish, bright and astringent, good with rich meats or seafood. Keep the texture slightly crisp, not soft as in some other fennel dishes.

> **5 medium fennel bulbs, trimmed and cleaned (see Notes to the Cook)**
>
> **1 tablespoon butter**
>
> **1 tablespoon olive oil**
>
> **Juice of 1 lemon (about 2 tablespoons)**
>
> **¼ cup white wine**
>
> **¼ teaspoon powdered dried thyme**
>
> **Salt and fresh pepper to taste**

1. Cut each fennel bulb in half down through the stem. Slice the halves crosswise, ¼ inch thick, discarding the large pieces of tough core.

In a large skillet, melt together the butter and oil; add the fennel and sauté over medium heat until browned, about ten minutes.

2. Add the remaining ingredients and stir well. Sauté until the fennel is crisp-tender and the liquid is gone, about five minutes. In this dish the fennel should be slightly crisp, so be careful not to overcook it.

Correct the seasoning, if necessary, and serve right away.

MENU SUGGESTIONS

If you like crumb-coated, shallow-fried calamari, this fennel is a good match for it, along with a dish of Sautéed Pattypan Squash with Red Pepper Sauce (page 299). If you don't like squid, flank steak or London broil is a good choice for the same menu.

FENNEL WITH ORANGES AND NIÇOISE OLIVES

MAKES PLENTY FOR SIX SERVINGS

Another delicious salad, to eat right away or even after it marinates for a few days. I discovered this marinating trick when I found—and ate—a small bowl of the leftover salad that had been tucked in the back of the refrigerator.

3 medium fennel bulbs, trimmed and cleaned (see Notes to the Cook)

3 medium-size navel oranges

Salt and fresh pepper

2 garlic cloves

⅓ cup fruity olive oil (Spanish olive oil is perfect)

2 tablespoons balsamic vinegar

18 or more Niçoise olives

1. Slice each fennel bulb crosswise, as thin as you can: a mandoline works perfectly for this job. Peel the oranges (with a sharp knife, if you have time) and cut into ⅛-inch slices.

2. Depending on the shape of your serving platter, overlap the orange slices in rings or rows, with little stacks of fennel between them. Sprinkle with salt and lots of fresh pepper.

3. Force the garlic through a garlic press into the olive oil; stir well. Spoon the oil over the oranges and fennel, and then sprinkle with vinegar. Garnish with olives and serve chilled or at room temperature.

NOTE: *As mentioned in the headnote, you may make this salad ahead if you like and let it marinate for a day or two. Be sure it is well covered so it does not absorb refrigerator odors.*

MENU SUGGESTIONS

Make a super-easy meal of this fennel salad with pan-browned or grilled fish and a cold pasta tossed with creamy dressing (page 342).

BARNABY'S VEGETABLE BROTH

MAKES 3 QUARTS (12 CUPS)

There's no question that the ingredients for this broth are unusual, but the result is utterly delicious, fragrant, complex and comforting all at once. It was invented by painter Barnaby Levy, who lives in New York City but hails from northern California, where they take their fresh vegetables seriously but treat them with great ingenuity.

Sip this broth as is or use it as a basis for other soups. It has a distinctive flavor, so don't use it as an all-purpose broth for cooking.

3 LARGE LEEKS, TRIMMED, WASHED CAREFULLY, AND CUT INTO 1½-INCH SLICES (WHITE AND GREEN PARTS)

1 MEDIUM FENNEL BULB (ABOUT ONE POUND), TRIMMED AND SLICED

5 MEDIUM CARROTS, TRIMMED, PEELED AND GRATED

1 LARGE SPANISH ONION, CUT IN EIGHTHS

1 LARGE DAIKON RADISH (ABOUT 1¼ POUNDS), PEELED AND CUT INTO ½-INCH SLICES

1 POUND CREMINI MUSHROOMS, CLEANED

1 SMALL APPLE, CORED AND CUT IN EIGHTHS

ROASTED FENNEL WITH WILD MUSHROOMS AND CRISP SHALLOTS

MAKES PLENTY FOR SIX SERVINGS

Elegant and interesting, with deep flavors and an unusual combination of textures—tender fennel, soft mushrooms and crisp shallots.

5 medium fennel bulbs, trimmed and cleaned (see Notes to the Cook)

4 tablespoons (½ stick) butter

2 tablespoons olive oil

Salt and fresh pepper

7 or 8 large shallots, trimmed and peeled (to make 1½ cups of rings; see step 2)

½ pound wild mushrooms (such as cèpe, shiitake, portobello, chanterelle, oyster, etc.), cleaned and stemmed

½ cup white wine

Parsley leaves for garnish

1. Preheat the oven to 450°; butter a baking sheet. Cut each fennel bulb in quarters (wedges) down through the stem.

In a medium skillet, melt the butter and oil together. Brush a little of the butter-oil mixture all over the fennel wedges. Arrange the fennel in one layer on the baking sheet, sprinkle with salt and pepper, and roast for 40 minutes, turning twice so all the sides brown.

Lower the oven temperature to 350°.

2. Meanwhile, cut the shallots into ⅛-inch slices and separate the slices into rings. Heat the butter-oil mixture again. When the butter is sizzling, add half the shallots and fry over medium heat, stirring constantly, just until brown and crisp. (This happens suddenly, so you must watch carefully to prevent burning.) Remove the shallots with a slotted spoon and spread them on a plate to cool; do *not* drain on paper towels.

Repeat the process with the remaining shallots. Sprinkle with salt and set aside for now.

The butter-oil mixture in the skillet should not be burned, but if it is, discard it and clean the skillet; heat one tablespoon each of butter and olive oil in the clean skillet.

3. Cut large or thick mushrooms into ¼-inch slices; leave small or thin ones whole. Add the mushrooms to the skillet, with a good sprinkling of salt and pepper, and sauté until browned. Add the wine, stir well, and simmer for 1½ minutes.

4. Pile the roasted fennel in the center of an ovenproof serving platter. Remove the mushrooms from the skillet with a slotted spoon and arrange them in a ring around the fennel. Pour the sauce from the skillet over the fennel. Dot the mushrooms and fennel with little clumps of crisp shallots. Warm the dish in the oven for ten minutes, garnish with a scattering of parsley leaves, and serve immediately.

1 SMALL PEAR, STEMMED, CUT IN EIGHTHS

2 TABLESPOONS FRESH ROSE-MARY LEAVES

2 TABLESPOONS FRESH THYME LEAVES

SALT AND FRESH PEPPER (ADDED GRADUALLY DURING COOKING)

In a big stockpot, combine all of the ingredients with 5 quarts (20 cups) of water. Bring to a boil and simmer, covered, for 1½ hours. Uncover the pot and continue simmering for 30 minutes more. Strain the resulting broth, discarding the vegetables, and correct the seasoning.

Keep refrigerated or freeze for future use.

MENU SUGGESTIONS

For a big holiday meal, start with some cold asparagus to dip in aioli (page 52), then follow with baked ham, the roasted fennel, Gingered Sweet Potatoes (page 269) and a bowl of Beet-Apple-Ginger Relish (page 66). Instead of rolls, offer a basket of miniature corn muffins. Or take a completely different line and start with Tomato Tart (page 320), followed by pasta with Onion-Garlic Pesto (page 198), the roasted fennel and a watercress salad.

GREENS

Some people include spinach, Swiss chard, even watercress and arugula, in this category, but when I say greens I mean the traditional greens: kale, collards, mustard, turnip and beet greens. These are the ones with an earthy quality that you just know is good for you. And it is. All of these vegetables are absolutely packed with vitamins, iron, calcium and other nutritional pluses.

BUYING AND STORING

The colors of these leaves vary from blue-green kale to bright green, purple-veined beet greens, but in all cases the color should be strong and rich. As with most kinds of leafy greens, kale and collards should have fresh, crisp, strong leaves with no limpness or withering; avoid yellowed, brown-edged or bruised leaves, too, and stems that are dry or woody.

The best mustard, turnip or beet greens are young and small; they have a tender rather than strong look about them. Don't buy mustard, turnip or beet greens with brown or yellow patches.

Store greens unwashed in plastic bags in the refrigerator; they should last for several days.

NOTES TO THE COOK

Trimming: Discard any yellowed or deteriorated leaves. Trim ¼ inch off the stem ends.

If you're working with kale, use a sharp knife to cut the foliage away from the stem and the thick center rib of each leaf; this is quite easy to do by holding the end of the stem and skimming the sharp blade right down the center rib. Discard the stems and center ribs.

Rinsing: Greens can be sandy and dirty, so give them a careful rinsing after they are trimmed. Shake off any excess water, spin dry in a salad spinner, or pat dry on paper towels, according to the requirements of the recipe.

SAUTÉED KALE WITH BACON-MOLASSES DRESSING

MAKES SIX SERVINGS

Greens are traditionally prepared with bacon drippings; here I've used bacon but not much of the bacon fat, and combined it with vinegar and molasses to make a sweet-and-sour dressing for the kale.

2 pounds kale, trimmed, center ribs discarded (see Notes to the Cook)

¼ pound sliced bacon

3 tablespoons olive oil

4 shallots, minced

Salt and fresh pepper

1 teaspoon minced fresh ginger

6 tablespoons red wine vinegar

3 tablespoons unsulfured molasses

Hot pepper sauce

1. Rinse the kale leaves very well and shake off any excess water (no need to dry the leaves). Cut or tear the leaves into bite-size pieces and set aside.

2. In a large skillet, cook the bacon until crisp, drain on paper towels, and set aside. Discard most of the bacon fat, leaving only a thin film on the skillet. Add two tablespoons of the olive oil and sauté the shallots until softened.

3. Over medium heat, add the kale by handfuls, stirring it down as the leaves wilt; add ½ cup water if the skillet is dry. Cover the skillet and braise the kale for 10 to 15 minutes, until tender. Pour off any liquid left in the skillet, season the kale with salt and pepper, and transfer it to a bowl.

4. To the skillet, add the last tablespoon of oil, the ginger, vinegar, molasses and a few drops of hot sauce, and stir over low heat. Crumble the bacon into the skillet and stir again. Pour this dressing over the kale and mix well, adding more salt, pepper and hot sauce if needed. Serve right away.

MENU SUGGESTIONS

Kale usually makes you think of southern food, but southwest flavors are also good with these greens—for instance, a layered enchilada casserole and Sweet Potato Salad with Southwest Seasonings (page 261).

PICKLED CHILES

MAKES ABOUT TWO CUPS

1 POUND FRESH HOT CHILES AND SWEET PEPPERS, CLEANED, ROASTED, PEELED, STEMMED AND SEEDED (CHOOSE ANAHEIMS [CALIFORNIA GREEN CHILES], NEW MEXICO GREEN CHILES, POBLANOS, JALAPEÑOS, RED OR YELLOW BELL PEPPERS OR A COMBINATION OF ANY OR ALL OF THESE.)

1 MEDIUM ONION, SLICED ⅛ INCH THICK

½ CUP CIDER VINEGAR

¼ CUP WATER

2 TABLESPOONS OLIVE OIL

½ TEASPOON SALT

2 BAY LEAVES

FRESH PEPPER TO TASTE

Cut the roasted hot chiles and sweet peppers in wide strips or bite-size pieces and combine them with the other ingredients in a nonreactive saucepan (stainless steel, enameled, etc.). Bring to a boil, lower the heat, and simmer, covered, for ten minutes. Let the mixture cool, then spoon it into containers with liquid to cover and refrigerate until needed. The chiles will last for weeks.

COLLARDS WITH WEST INDIAN PEPPER-AND-LIME SAUCE

MAKES SIX SERVINGS

I love this combination of cooked vegetables with a fresh, uncooked sauce. The red pepper in the sauce retains a crunchy, grainy texture that contrasts perfectly with the tender collards and onions.

1½ pounds collard greens, trimmed

2 tablespoons vegetable oil

1 large onion, chopped

Salt and fresh pepper

FOR THE SAUCE

2 small fresh hot peppers (such as jalapeños), cored, seeded and chunked (*If you're not sure how hot you'd like the sauce to be, start with one pepper; you can always add more later.*)

2 medium-size red bell peppers, cored, seeded, deveined and chunked

3 garlic cloves, halved

½ cup olive oil

¼ cup fresh lime juice

Salt and fresh pepper

1. Rinse the greens well and shake off any excess water. Cut the stems into ½-inch lengths, then stack and roll up the leaves and cut them into ½-inch strips. Set aside.

2. In a large skillet, heat the oil and brown the onion. Add the collard stems and leaves by handfuls, stirring them down as they wilt. Add ½ cup water if the skillet is dry, then season the greens with salt and pepper and stir well. Cover the skillet and cook over medium heat for 10 to 15 minutes, until tender. Pour off any liquid left in the skillet, transfer the greens to an ovenproof dish, and keep warm in a low oven.

3. Make the sauce: Purée all the sauce ingredients, including a sprinkling of salt and pepper, in your food processor. (The red pepper will have a grainy texture.) Taste the sauce and add more salt, pepper and/or hot pepper if needed.

Spoon one cup of the sauce over the greens (do not stir) and serve the rest on the side.

MENU SUGGESTIONS

For a hearty meatless meal, serve the collards with Kidney Beans with Rice and Cheese (page 45) and toasted slices of whole grain bread. I like these greens island-style, too, with a chicken fricassee or stew and plenty of rice and beans on the side.

**MATCHMAKING:
ROASTED
CHICKEN**

You're making roasted chicken for dinner. What do you serve with it? Here are some possibilities from which to choose, including the Vegetable Express for hurry-up meals.

*Small Potatoes with
Garlic Cream,
page 262*

*Sautéed Kale with Bacon-
Molasses Dressing,
page 179*

*Sweet Beet Caviar,
page 67*

*Squash with Dried Fruits,
page 304*

MENU SUGGESTIONS

Fish cakes and rice go well with these greens, to make an old-fashioned sort of meal. You can add a little sophistication by serving Browned Kohlrabi and Onions (page 189). Another good—and simpler—main course to serve is manicotti. Hot Italian or French bread supplements either menu.

THE VEGETABLE EXPRESS

CREAMY GREENS AND TOMATOES

MAKES PLENTY FOR SIX SERVINGS

Tomatoes combine particularly well with greens, especially when smoothed out with a small amount of sour cream. My friend Ernie Foster hates greens (for which he blames the school cafeteria in his southern past), but even he makes an exception for this dish.

1½ pounds greens, trimmed (*Choose kale, collards, mustard, turnip or beet greens or any combination of these.*)

1 large can (28 ounces) whole tomatoes in juice

½ cup regular or light sour cream

Salt and fresh pepper

1. If you are using kale, cut out and discard the stems and thick center ribs. Rinse all the greens well and dry them on paper towels or in a salad spinner. Tear the greens into bite-size pieces and set aside.

2. Turn the tomatoes into a strainer over a large saucepan, catching the juice in the pan; set the tomatoes aside for the moment. Bring the juice to a boil and add the greens by handfuls, stirring them down as they wilt. Cover and cook over low heat until almost tender, 10 to 15 minutes.

3. Meanwhile, slit the tomatoes and rinse out the seeds. Chop the tomatoes and add them and the sour cream to the saucepan. Stir well, season with salt and pepper, and cook over low heat for five minutes. Serve hot.

CASSEROLE OF GREENS WITH MOZZARELLA TOPPING

MAKES SIX SERVINGS

Greens may not seem like a very fancy sort of vegetable, but I guarantee that this casserole is rich enough for any company dinner. Serve it with a rather lean main course.

1½ pounds greens, trimmed (*Choose kale, collards, mustard, turnip or beet greens or any combination of these.*)

Salt and fresh pepper

1 cup chicken or vegetable broth

1 cup half-and-half, or ½ cup milk plus ½ cup heavy cream

4 tablespoons (½ stick) butter

¼ cup flour

½ cup grated Parmesan cheese

½ cup whole milk ricotta or part skim ricotta

3 tablespoons dry bread crumbs

2 ounces mozzarella cheese, shredded

1. Butter a 1½-quart baking dish or casserole; preheat the oven to 375° (350° for ovenproof glass).

If you are using kale, cut out and discard the stems and thick center ribs. Rinse all the greens and shake off any excess water. Chop them into ½-inch pieces.

In a large skillet, cook the greens over low heat, adding them by handfuls and stirring them down as they wilt. Add ½ cup of water if the greens seem dry, then cover the skillet and braise the greens for 10 to 15 minutes, until tender. Pour off any liquid left in the skillet, then season the greens with salt and pepper. Transfer to a bowl and set aside.

2. Heat the broth and half-and-half in a saucepan, just until bubbles form around the edge of the pan.

Pan-fried Turnips and Potatoes with Sun-dried Tomato Relish, page 329

Sautéed Swiss Chard with Thick Spicy Yogurt, page 314

Thai-style Eggplant, page 151

Fancy Salad, page 344

VEGETABLE EXPRESS

Black-eyed Peas with Butter and Scallions, page 51

Plátanos Borrachos, page 256

Meanwhile, in the large skillet, melt the butter over low heat. Add the flour and cook, stirring, for one minute. Add the hot broth mixture all at once and stir over medium heat until the sauce is smooth and thickened. Whisk in the grated Parmesan and ricotta.

3. Stir the greens into the cheese sauce and pour the mixture into the prepared baking dish. Sprinkle first the bread crumbs and then the grated mozzarella evenly over the top and bake for 20 minutes, until the sauce is bubbling and the mozzarella is melted and lightly browned. Serve hot.

MENU SUGGESTIONS

Stick to a not-too-rich main course when you serve this casserole—perhaps a simple pasta with a tomato sauce made with red wine and beef broth. Crisp green salad will clear the palate and round out the meal. Spanish tortilla (a sort of frittata with potatoes) is a good choice, too, with a bowl of tomato salsa for brightness.

KOHLRABI

BUYING AND STORING

Kohlrabi is usually pale green but there is also a deep reddish purple variety. Buy only small or medium-size bulbs, two to three inches in diameter or four to eight ounces in weight; larger bulbs are fibrous and tough. Look for round bulbs with no soft spots, splits, cracks or wrinkles. If the leaves are still attached (which I have rarely seen, except in the farmers' market), they should be crisp and green.

Keep kohlrabi in the refrigerator in a plastic bag. Depending on how fresh it was when you bought it, it may last for two weeks.

NOTES TO THE COOK

Trimming: Cut a slice off the top and bottom; snap off the green protrusions (these are the ends of the leaf stalks).

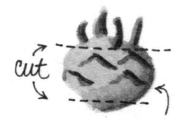

Peeling: Use a sharp knife to peel off a rather thick layer of green skin to get down to the white flesh; the drawing shows the best and fastest way. Keep in mind that the green skin is extremely tough when cooked, so if you don't peel off enough green, you'll end up with little bits of tough, sharp fiber in your finished dish.

My sister-in-law, who has been a vegetarian forever, found in this book only one vegetable she had never tried: kohlrabi, of course. It is kind of an oddball vegetable in American cuisine, but they love it in Europe and you can find it year-round in any Chinese-American greengrocer. Kohlrabi is rather like a milder, sweeter turnip. Give it a try.

When you want an eye-catching decoration, begin with a simple garnish (such as minced parsley) and add one or more of these (or one of the other fancy garnishes on page 190):

Confetti of peppers: Cut fresh red, green and yellow peppers into a tiny dice and scatter them over the surface.

Carrot cutouts: Cut large carrots crosswise into very thin slices; use tiny canapé cutters to cut flower shapes. Alternatively, cut on the diagonal and use a very sharp knife to make parallel cuts.

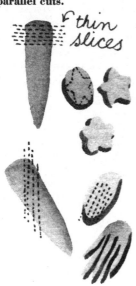

thin slices

MASHED KOHLRABI AND POTATOES WITH TOMATO CREAM GRAVY

MAKES SIX SERVINGS

Serve this the old-fashioned way, by making a well in each scoop of mashed kohlrabi and potatoes and filling it with the hot tomato gravy. Great with meat loaf.

> 1½ pounds kohlrabi, trimmed and peeled (see Notes to the Cook)
>
> 1¼ pounds russet or all-purpose white potatoes (about 4 medium), peeled and quartered

FOR THE GRAVY

> 5 tablespoons butter or margarine
>
> 3 tablespoons flour
>
> 3 tablespoons tomato paste
>
> 1 teaspoon Worcestershire sauce
>
> 1 teaspoon red wine vinegar
>
> 3 tablespoons regular or light sour cream
>
> 1 cup chicken or vegetable broth
>
> Salt and fresh pepper

> ⅓ cup whole or skim milk
>
> Salt and fresh pepper

1. Halve each kohlrabi and cut the halves into ⅛-inch slices. Place the sliced kohlrabi and quartered potatoes in a pan with water to cover, bring to a boil, and simmer partially covered until very tender, 10 to 15 minutes.

2. Meanwhile, make the gravy: In a medium saucepan over low heat, melt three tablespoons of the butter. Add the flour and cook, stirring, for one minute. Turn off the heat and whisk in the tomato paste, Worcestershire, vinegar and sour cream, blending until smooth. Turn the heat back on to medium and gradually whisk in the broth. Continue cooking and stirring until the gravy is thick and smooth. Season with salt and pepper, if needed, and set aside.

3. Drain the kohlrabi and potatoes and transfer them to a large bowl. Add the milk and the remaining two tablespoons of butter and mash by hand until the potatoes are smooth and the kohlrabi is chunky. Season with salt and pepper and keep warm in a low oven.

4. Reheat the gravy gently. On the individual dinner plates or on a serving platter, arrange six mounds of mashed kohlrabi and potatoes. Make an indentation in the top of each mound, fill with hot gravy, and serve right away. Pass around the extra gravy.

Radish fans: Trim the ends of a radish; make parallel cuts $\frac{1}{16}$ inch apart, almost to the bottom of the radish. Soak in salted water for ten minutes, rinse, and squeeze out any excess water. Press gently to fan out the segments.

MENU SUGGESTIONS

Meat loaf, as mentioned in the headnote, is delicious with this kohlrabi and potato dish. Pot roast or beef cubes grilled on skewers with onions and green peppers are also good choices.

KOHLRABI IN GREEN SAUCE

MAKES SIX SERVINGS

The green sauce is pungent and garlicky—a good contrast with the mild, slightly sweet kohlrabi.

3 pounds kohlrabi, trimmed and peeled (see Notes to the Cook)

1 cup (packed) fresh flat-leaf (Italian) parsley leaves

3 garlic cloves, quartered

½ cup dry white wine

½ cup chicken or vegetable broth

¼ cup olive oil

½ cup chopped onion

Salt and fresh pepper

1. Halve each kohlrabi and cut the halves into ⅛- to ¼-inch-thick slices.

NOTE: *Slice the halves from top to bottom (rather than crosswise) to yield short, fat slices. If your food processor has a thick-slicing blade, by all means use it.*

Put the kohlrabi in a saucepan with water to cover and bring to a boil; reduce the heat and simmer uncovered until tender, 10 to 15 minutes. Drain well.

2. Meanwhile, in your food processor, purée the parsley, garlic, wine, broth and two tablespoons of the oil. In a large skillet, heat the remaining oil and sauté the onions until soft. Stir in the purée, season with salt and pepper, and simmer for three minutes.

3. Add the kohlrabi, stirring well to coat with sauce. Simmer uncovered, stirring often, for about eight minutes to reduce the sauce. Correct the seasoning and serve hot.

MENU SUGGESTIONS

Try cheese tortellini here, with good bread on the side. Have an interesting green salad or tomato salad afterward.

BROWNED KOHLRABI AND ONIONS

MAKES PLENTY FOR SIX

The sweetness of this dish will surprise you. Slow browning brings out the sugar in the onions and caramelizes it gently to coat and color both vegetables.

2 pounds kohlrabi, trimmed and peeled
   (see Notes to the Cook)

2 tablespoons butter

2 tablespoons vegetable oil

2 medium Spanish or Bermuda onions
   (about 1½ pounds), chopped coarsely

Salt and fresh pepper

1. Cut the kohlrabi into ½-inch cubes. In a large skillet, melt the butter and oil; add the kohlrabi and onions and sauté over low heat, stirring frequently, for 30 minutes. Season well with salt and pepper.

2. Turn up the heat to medium and continue sautéing until both the onions and the kohlrabi are well browned, about 15 minutes. Serve right away or hold in a low oven for up to half an hour.

MENU SUGGESTIONS

Kohlrabi does have an affinity for beef—thin pan-fried steaks or slices of London broil, for instance—but chicken baked or roasted with other root vegetables will be just right, too.

MORE FANCY GARNISHES

Cornichon or pickle fan: Make parallel cuts $\frac{1}{16}$ inch apart, almost to the end. Press gently to fan out the segments.

Tomato rose: With a very sharp knife, cut a thin slice almost all the way across the stem end of a small tomato and continue to peel it thinly in one long continuous strip. Roll the strip back to sit on the round base, opening out the top edges a bit to make it look more like a rose (see opposite page).

MENU SUGGESTIONS

Since the kohlrabi is sweet and tart, it will go well with smoked lean ham, Canadian bacon or spicy, peppery Italian sausage. With any of these assertive flavors you'll need a foil: mashed potatoes or Creamy Limas (page 59).

THE VEGETABLE EXPRESS

KOHLRABI IN POPPY SEED DRESSING

MAKES PLENTY FOR SIX SERVINGS

Another pungent dressing for kohlrabi, but this one is sweet and tart. The hot kohlrabi absorbs the dressing as you stir it.

3 pounds kohlrabi, trimmed and peeled (see Notes to the Cook)

$\frac{1}{2}$ cup vegetable oil (not olive oil)

3 tablespoons cider vinegar

3 tablespoons honey

1 tablespoon Dijon mustard

1 tablespoon poppy seeds

Salt and fresh pepper to taste

1. Cut the kohlrabi into $\frac{1}{2}$-inch cubes. Put the cubes in a saucepan with water to cover and bring to a boil. Reduce the heat and simmer uncovered until tender, about 15 minutes. Drain well and transfer to a large bowl.

2. Whisk together the remaining ingredients to make the dressing, pour the dressing over the hot kohlrabi, and stir carefully but thoroughly. Set the kohlrabi aside to cool, stirring often; it will absorb most of the dressing as it cools. Add more salt and pepper if needed. Serve at room temperature or slightly chilled.

KOHLRABI
WITH SAGE STUFFING

MAKES PLENTY FOR SIX SERVINGS

This is an unusual dish, so it may indeed be most appropriate for company, when guests are usually willing to try something new. One per person is probably enough, but I've allowed three extra for the big eaters.

9 small-medium kohlrabi, trimmed and peeled (see Notes to the Cook) *(Look for bulbs weighing 6 to 8 ounces each.)*

1 egg white

¼ cup regular or light sour cream

¼ cup chicken or vegetable broth

¼ cup dry whole wheat bread crumbs

¼ teaspoon powdered dried sage

¼ teaspoon powdered dried thyme

2 tablespoons minced shallots

1 tablespoon finely chopped walnuts

½ teaspoon salt

Fresh pepper

1 tablespoon butter or margarine, melted

1. Bring a pot or large saucepan of water to a boil. Add the kohlrabi, return to a boil, and simmer uncovered until the kohlrabi is tender, about 30 minutes. Drain, rinse under cold water, and set aside to cool. Meanwhile, butter a baking dish large enough to hold all the kohlrabi in one layer and preheat the oven to 400° (375° for ovenproof glass).

2. While the kohlrabi cooks, whisk together the egg white, sour cream and broth. Stir in the remaining ingredients (except the melted butter), including a good grinding of pepper. Set aside.

Tic-Tac-Toe: Cut slender strips of carrot and arrange them in a grid; fill in with green peas. Other vegetables work well, too: lemon peel grid filled in with bits of green pepper; zucchini grid with bits of red pepper; roasted red pepper grid with bits of cucumber.

3. Using a melon baller, carefully hollow out each kohlrabi, leaving a shell ¼ to ½ inch thick; reserve the scooped-out flesh. Brush the outsides of the shells with the melted butter or margarine and arrange them in the prepared baking dish.

4. Mince the reserved kohlrabi and stir it into the bread crumb mixture. Mound this stuffing mixture quite high in each kohlrabi shell, using up all the stuffing, and bake for 20 to 30 minutes, until lightly browned on top and very hot. Serve immediately or hold for up to 20 minutes in a warm oven.

MENU SUGGESTIONS

For a festive autumn or winter meal, serve these with roasted turkey, Holiday Baked Onions with Double Cheese Sauce (page 224), and Baby Beets and Beet Greens (page 70) if you can find baby beets or Sweet Beet Caviar (page 67) if you can't. Carrot Chutney (page 108) will put a nice finishing touch on the meal. Vegetarians, after omitting the turkey, might like to omit the chutney, too, and substitute Sweet Carrot Ring (page 111).

LEEKS AND SCALLIONS

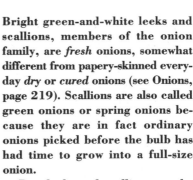

BUYING AND STORING

Leeks: Leeks look rather like giant scallions, though their silhouettes are straight with just a bit of a bulge at the shaggy root end. The white part (which is the part you want to eat) may be anywhere from four to eight inches long and will shade to pale green and then bright green. Leeks may be thick or thin: Slender leeks are about ½ inch in diameter, medium leeks are about 1 inch, and large ones will measure about 1½ inches across.

Avoid wilted or yellowed leaves, although the outermost leaf or two may be tough and dry looking.

Leeks will last from several days to two weeks unwashed in a plastic bag in the refrigerator.

Scallions: Scallions should be bright white at the bottom with a fringe of crisp root ends, and bright green at the top with no withered, dull or darkened stalks.

Store unwashed scallions in plastic bags in the refrigerator. Depending on how fresh they were when you bought them, they'll last from several days to a week or so. Watch out for spoilage because scallions are fragile and the stalks tend to go slimy.

NOTES TO THE COOK

Trimming leeks: Cut off the shaggy root end and remove the outermost leaf. Cut off and discard the green tops about one inch above the white part; for vegetable side dishes you want to use only the white and palest green parts. (You may want to use the entire leek when you make vegetable broth.)

Bright green-and-white leeks and scallions, members of the onion family, are *fresh* onions, somewhat different from papery-skinned everyday *dry* or *cured* onions (see Onions, page 219). Scallions are also called green onions or spring onions because they are in fact ordinary onions picked before the bulb has had time to grow into a full-size onion.

Raw leeks and scallions can be too powerful to eat in any quantity, but cooking tames the pungency of both vegetables. Cooked leeks are usually served as side dishes or in soup, while scallions are—unfortunately—only occasionally eaten on their own; they are mostly added to other dishes or used as garnishes.

Cutting and cleaning leeks: Lots of dirt and sand lodges between the leaves and at the base, so you must clean the leeks well. According to the instructions in the recipe, either cut the leek completely in half lengthwise or slit the leek from the trimmed green end toward the root, ending your cut an inch or two above the root end. Either way will make it possible for you to spread the leaves and wash them thoroughly under cold running water. Shake off any excess water and pat dry on paper towels.

Trimming and cleaning scallions: This is much easier. Cut off the shaggy root end of the scallion and trim the tops of the green stalks to get clean crisp edges. Peel off the outermost leaf if it's tough or blemished. Wash under cold running water, making sure that water runs into and between the hollow stalks. Shake off any excess water and pat dry on paper towels.

BAKED LEEKS WITH BACON AND CHEDDAR CHEESE

MAKES SIX SERVINGS

This is a colorful, simple dish that gets its smoky character from Canadian bacon. It's good made with other cheeses, too—Gruyère, fontina or goat cheese.

½ cup chicken or vegetable broth

¼ cup heavy cream or half-and-half

Salt and fresh pepper

9 medium-to-large leeks, trimmed, cut in half lengthwise and cleaned (see Notes to the Cook)

¼ pound Canadian bacon

2 ounces cheddar cheese

1. Have ready a shallow two-quart baking dish; preheat the oven to 400° (375° for ovenproof glass).

In a large skillet, stir together the broth and cream. Season to taste with salt and pepper. Arrange the halved leeks in one or two layers in the skillet, spooning the broth mixture over them. Bring to a simmer, cover the skillet, and braise for ten minutes, turning once.

Meanwhile, dice the bacon and shred the cheese.

2. Carefully transfer the leeks and sauce to the baking dish, again arranging them in one or two layers; sprinkle evenly with bacon and cheese. (If you've got two layers, sprinkle each layer with half the bacon and half the cheese.) Bake for 20 minutes and serve hot.

MENU SUGGESTIONS

This robust dish doesn't need a lot of accompaniment. Pair it with pasta—either ziti, macaroni or spinach ravioli with tomato sauce.

Chilled Braised Leeks with Sweet Peppers

Makes six servings

Tangy and bright, with strips of mellow sweet pepper for contrast. You'll notice that the lemon juice tastes quite strong when the leeks are hot, but the flavor calms down when the leeks are chilled.

9 medium or 18 slender leeks, trimmed, cut and cleaned (see Notes to the Cook) *(Medium-size leeks should be halved lengthwise; slender ones should be slit to about 2 inches above the trimmed root end.)*

1 cup chicken or vegetable broth

6 anchovy fillets

1 tablespoon olive oil

3 tablespoons fresh lemon juice

Salt and fresh pepper

1 roasted red pepper, homemade or from a jar, stemmed, seeded and deveined

1. Arrange the leeks in a large skillet, pour the broth over them, and bring to a simmer. Lower the heat even more, cover the skillet, and braise for 9 to 12 minutes, until the leeks are tender. Remove the leeks immediately and simmer the remaining liquid until it is reduced by about half.

2. Add the anchovies and olive oil to the skillet and cook over low heat, mashing and stirring until the anchovies dissolve. Turn off the heat, stir in the lemon juice, and add salt and pepper to taste.

3. Return the leeks to the skillet and gently combine them with the sauce. Transfer to a serving platter to cool.

Cut the pepper into ¼-inch strips and scatter the strips over the leeks. Serve chilled or at room temperature.

MENU SUGGESTIONS

Think bistro here and consider serving the leeks with a savory tart and a green salad. Warm or cold Quick Spinach Pie (page 291) is another good choice. In summer, the leeks are good with Simplified Caponata with Sundried Tomatoes (page 152), a fresh tomato salad (page 324) and a selection of cheeses.

MASHED POTATOES AND LEEKS

MAKES SIX SERVINGS

This earthy mixture is no beauty contest winner, but it tastes marvelous. Be sure to season well with salt and pepper.

3 large leeks, trimmed, cut in half lengthwise and cleaned (see Notes to the Cook)

3 scallions, trimmed and cleaned

1 small onion

3 medium or 2 large russet potatoes (such as Idaho; about 1 pound), peeled

1 cup chicken or vegetable broth

2 tablespoons butter

2 tablespoons heavy cream, half-and-half, sour cream or light sour cream, or more to taste

½ teaspoon caraway seeds (optional)

Salt and fresh pepper to taste

1. Coarsely chop the leeks, scallions and onion; dice the potatoes.

2. Put the potatoes and broth in a large skillet or saucepan, bring to a boil, and simmer, covered, five minutes.

3. Add the leeks, scallions, onion and butter and stir to melt the butter. Cover the pan and simmer over low heat for five minutes, or until the leeks and potatoes are tender.

4. Using a potato masher or large fork, mash the potatoes right in the pan until the texture of the mixture is as rough or smooth as you prefer. Add the remaining ingredients, stir well, and reheat gently. Serve hot.

This dish may be made ahead and reheated on top of the stove or in the oven.

MENU SUGGESTIONS

I like this hearty dish for a spring or autumn dinner, with pan-browned salmon steaks and Marinated Roasted Red and Yellow Peppers with Fresh Basil (page 244). Have a green salad with homemade croutons (page 166) at the end of the meal.

THREE SIMPLE PESTOS

Everybody knows about pesto made with fresh summer basil and tossed with hot pasta, but are you aware that pesto—a well-flavored purée or paste—can be made of other fresh herbs, as well as nuts, beans or vegetables? And it doesn't have to be eaten on pasta. Try it spread on toasted Italian bread or warm pita, stirred into risotto or soup, spooned onto hot vegetables (especially baked or mashed potatoes), as a dip for crudités or corn chips—the possibilities are endless.

MENU SUGGESTIONS

Serve with a potato and herb frittata or omelet and the Plantain Salad on page 254. Warm bread or rolls complete the menu.

SCALLIONS IN PIQUANT SAUCE

MAKES SIX SERVINGS

Simple and very effective—a lot of punch for the little work and time involved. Use this dish to perk up a not-too-interesting meal.

1 tablespoon butter

½ cup chicken or vegetable broth

30 medium-to-large scallions, trimmed and cleaned, leaving all of the white part plus 4 inches of green

Salt and fresh pepper

1 tablespoon white wine vinegar

1 teaspoon Dijon mustard

1. In a large skillet, melt the butter with the broth. Arrange the scallions in a layer in the skillet and sprinkle with salt and pepper. Cover the pan and simmer until the scallions are tender, about five minutes. Remove the scallions and keep them warm.

2. Stir the vinegar, mustard and a dash of salt and pepper into the skillet. Simmer uncovered until three to four tablespoons of liquid are left. Pour this sauce over the scallions and serve hot or warm.

THE VEGETABLE EXPRESS

BROWNED LEEKS AND MUSHROOMS

MAKES SIX SERVINGS

Browned leeks can be homely or elegant, as you will see from this recipe and the following one. Either way, they're delicious.

6 medium or 12 slender leeks, trimmed, cut in half lengthwise and cleaned (see Notes to the Cook)

18 medium-size white or cremini mushrooms (about ½ pound), stem ends trimmed, cleaned

2 tablespoons olive oil

Salt and fresh pepper

½ cup white wine

1. Cut the leeks crosswise into ½-inch slices. Slice the mushrooms thinly. (It's neater to slice the mushrooms by hand, but the slicing blade of your food processor is faster.)

In a large skillet, heat the olive oil and sauté the leeks over high heat until lightly browned.

2. Lower the heat, add the mushrooms, and cook, stirring, until the mushrooms have given up their liquid and are limp. Season with salt and lots of pepper. Raise the heat and add the wine a little at a time, letting most of it evaporate before adding more; stir well to get the brown bits off the skillet. Season with more salt and pepper if needed, and serve hot.

The following three pestos are quite different from basil pesto and very easy to make. All you do is put the ingredients in your food processor and process until they form as smooth a paste as possible, scraping down the sides of the bowl frequently. Also, add a spoonful or two of oil or liquid if the mixture is not pasty or loose enough. Each recipe makes about one cup of pesto.

Olive-Herb Pesto: ½ pound cracked green or black olives, *pitted*; 1 garlic clove, chopped; 3 tablespoons olive oil; 1 tablespoon red wine vinegar; ½ teaspoon powdered oregano; ¼ teaspoon powdered thyme

Mushroom-Basil Pesto: ½ pound wild mushrooms (such as cremini, shiitake, portobello or oyster), trimmed, cleaned and sautéed until tender in ¼ cup olive oil; ½ cup (packed) fresh basil leaves; 1 tablespoon pine nuts; salt and fresh pepper to taste

Onion-Garlic Pesto: one large sweet onion, chopped and then sautéed slowly in two tablespoons olive oil until very brown; one whole bulb of garlic, roasted (page 28) and the cloves peeled; salt and fresh pepper to taste

MENU SUGGESTIONS

Veal cutlets or roast lamb will be delicious with these leeks, especially if you add some crisp Oven-roasted Rosemary Potatoes (page 270). For a meatless meal, have the potatoes and a dish of Baked Carrots in Honey-Mustard Sauce (page 109).

HOW TO MAKE GARLIC BROTH

Vegetable or chicken broth enhanced with the mild, mellow flavor of simmered garlic is the perfect base for soups, stews, risottos, sauces and many vegetable dishes. (It's great for poaching chicken, too.) Try it as a substitute for regular vegetable or chicken broth in any appropriate recipe. The formula given here may be doubled or tripled as needed:

Crush six small or five medium garlic cloves and combine them with about two cups of chicken or vegetable broth (one 13¾-ounce can) in a heavy saucepan. Bring to a boil, reduce the heat, and simmer, covered, for 30 minutes. Remove the garlic and use the broth as described.

TIP: To make the broth even better, simmer it for a few minutes with some fresh or dried seasoning: chopped fresh parsley, sage, chervil or dill; dried tarragon, celery seed, fennel or bay leaf.

MENU SUGGESTIONS

One possibility is to match this elegant but simple dish with something equally elegant and simple, such as roasted duck or a fine cut of beef. For a more unusual dinner, serve an eggplant or zucchini roulade with the leeks, with Crisp Mushrooms (page 208) and a salad of crisp greens.

COMPANY'S COMING

BROWNED LEEKS WITH HAZELNUT BUTTER

MAKES SIX SERVINGS

The hazelnuts make this a special dish, so be absolutely sure your nuts are fresh. Taste before buying—a rancid nut announces itself immediately.

9 medium or 18 slender leeks, trimmed, slit to 1 inch above the root end and cleaned (see Notes to the Cook)

6 ounces hazelnuts

4 tablespoons (½ stick) butter

Salt to taste

½ cup dry vermouth

1. Preheat the oven to 350°. While it heats, cut the leeks crosswise into ½-inch slices; set aside.

2. Toast the hazelnuts: Spread the nuts on a jelly roll pan and place them in the preheated oven for five to ten minutes; watch carefully to be sure they don't burn. When the nuts smell toasty and a *cooled* nut is crisp and crunchy, the nuts are properly toasted. Remove the papery skins by rubbing a few nuts at a time between your palms or in a rough dish towel. Chop the nuts into fine bits.

3. In a large skillet, melt two tablespoons of the butter; add the nuts and sauté for about five minutes, until the butter browns. Do not overcook. With a slotted spoon, transfer the nuts to a small bowl and set aside.

4. Melt the remaining two tablespoons of butter in the skillet, add the leeks and salt, and sauté for ten minutes, until the leeks are limp and beginning to brown. (You may stop at this point and do the final step just before serving.)

5. Stir in the chopped nuts and vermouth and cook over medium heat until most of the liquid has evaporated, three to four minutes. Add more salt if needed and serve right away.

MUSHROOMS

BUYING AND STORING

White and cremini mushrooms: A white mushroom (which may actually be tan) should have an even color and a smooth, matte cap with no dark bruising, nicks, pitting or shriveling. Avoid spongy mushrooms or those with a slimy or sweaty look.

At its youngest, the white mushroom has a cap so tightly closed that the gills on the underside are concealed; as the mushroom ages the cap opens and the gills are revealed. Most of us were taught that mushrooms with exposed gills were over the hill, but in fact, exposed light-colored gills simply indicate that the mushroom has a stronger, richer flavor. (If the gills are black, however, the mushroom is too old.)

Creminis have slightly shiny medium or dark brown caps; the same general buying rules apply.

Other mushrooms: The wild mushrooms mentioned in the sidebar vary widely in size, shape, surface texture and color, but all of them should be firm, dry and fresh looking when you buy them.

There are many varieties of dried mushroom, but the one used in this book is the Chinese dried black mushroom, which is actually dark brown to tan, with a wrinkled and cracked-looking cap. In an ordinary mom-and-pop Asian grocery you can buy small packets of these mushrooms, but in a larger Chinese specialty store you'll find bags and bins of different grades of dried mushrooms at different prices; the most expensive grade is excellent, but the less expensive ones are very good, too.

All fresh mushrooms, ordinary or exotic, should be stored in the refrigerator in a paper bag (not a plastic bag), preferably a large one so the mushrooms can spread out in one

Until fairly recently, the only kind of mushrooms most people could or would buy were safe white button mushrooms—eating any other kind seemed like asking for trouble. White mushrooms are still the most common (and the most reasonably priced), but creminis, which have a more intense flavor, are now a close second. Chinese dried black mushrooms are available in every Asian grocery, and the more unusual wild and cultivated mushrooms—shiitake, oyster, portobello, enoki, chanterelle and others—are found in gourmet stores and even some supermarkets from coast to coast.

NOTE: *There's a tricky problem of nomenclature here. Of the more unusual mushrooms mentioned above, some are gathered wild and others are carefully cultivated—but we tend to lump them all together and call them wild. At this point, they are probably called wild mushrooms in your produce or gourmet market, so that's what I call them here.*

or two layers. Never wash the mushrooms before storing. Use them as soon as possible, certainly within a couple of days.

Dried mushrooms will last six months when stored in a dark place in airtight containers.

NOTES TO THE COOK

Trimming fresh mushrooms: The stems of most fresh mushrooms have a ragged, dirty end that should be sliced off. There's no need to remove the whole stem unless it is either soft or woody (like the stems of shiitakes) or the recipe requires it.

Cleaning fresh mushrooms: This is tricky because mushrooms can be quite dirty, but a sustained rinsing will render them soggy and awful. Most books will tell you to wipe mushrooms with a damp paper towel, but all this does is leave bits of lint on the caps without getting them clean and it does nothing to deal with dirt in the gills.

A fast rinse under a thin stream of cool water is the best solution, doing one or two mushrooms at a time, rubbing the dirt off with your fingers as quickly as you can. Gently pat dry with paper towels and, if there's time, let them air-dry, too.

Preparing and reconstituting Chinese dried black mushrooms: Break off and discard the stem of each mushroom—it's too woody to eat. Rinse the mushrooms thoroughly (water won't damage them), rubbing off any dirt you can see. Put the mushrooms in a bowl of very hot water and leave them for 30 minutes, until soft and pliable. Drain well, rinse carefully to remove any remaining grit, and drain again. Squeeze gently to expel more water.

BRAISED CHINESE BLACK MUSHROOMS

MAKES SIX SERVINGS

Chinese dried black mushrooms are my favorites. They are quite different in texture from most fresh mushrooms, of course, being chewy and meaty—even more so than the big meaty portobellos or small meaty shiitakes. Dried mushrooms, once they are reconstituted, will absorb sauce and flavors like a dream when you braise them. Don't miss this recipe.

30 medium and large Chinese dried black mushrooms

1 tablespoon sugar

2 tablespoons soy sauce

1 tablespoon oyster sauce

3 garlic cloves, minced

1 cup low-salt chicken or vegetable broth (*This dish will be too salty if you use regular chicken broth.*)

¼ cup dry sherry (fino or manzanilla)

1 tablespoon peanut oil

1. Snap off the mushroom stems and rinse the mushroom caps well under cold running water. Soak the caps in very hot water for 30 minutes, until soft. Drain and rinse again to remove any remaining sand and dirt. Gently squeeze out any excess liquid; set the mushrooms aside.

2. Put the remaining ingredients in a large skillet and bring to a boil. Stir in the mushrooms, lower the heat, and simmer, covered, for 15 minutes. Remove the cover and continue simmering, stirring often, for 25 more minutes, until the liquid is almost evaporated and the mushrooms are glazed with sauce. Serve hot or warm.

MENU SUGGESTIONS

For a Chinese-style meal, all you need with the mushrooms is Mixed Chinese Greens (page 128) and readymade dumplings or shumai (or Steamed Vegetable Dumplings, page 130). An alternative menu might include baked chicken legs and basic asparagus (page 36) with a bit of butter.

MARINATED MUSHROOMS

MAKES ABOUT THREE CUPS

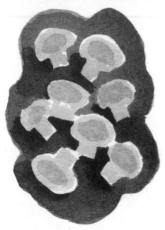

Not your ordinary vinaigrette-soaked mushrooms—these have a decidedly milder but more complex Asian flavor.

1 TEASPOON GRATED FRESH GINGER

1 TEASPOON SUGAR

2 TEASPOONS SOY SAUCE

½ CUP VEGETABLE OIL (PEANUT OIL IS NICE; DO NOT USE OLIVE OIL)

MENU SUGGESTIONS

As mentioned in the headnote, the mushrooms make a wonderful garnish for any roast. They're also great with broiled lamb chops and Peas and Pasta (page 235).

MUSHROOMS ROASTED WITH BUTTER AND GARLIC

MAKES SIX SERVINGS

This is a very simple dish, but rather interesting, especially served with a roast—in fact, these mushrooms make an attractive garnish surrounding roasted beef, pork, turkey or chicken.

Roasted garlic—that's what you have here—is sweet and tasty, not harsh and off-putting as raw garlic can sometimes be. So don't worry about eating these whole cloves; they're mellow and delicious.

24 medium garlic cloves, unpeeled

24 large white or cremini mushrooms, trimmed and cleaned

Salt and fresh pepper

2 tablespoons butter or margarine

1. Preheat the oven to 375°; butter a jelly roll pan or a large, shallow baking dish.

Put the unpeeled garlic cloves in a small baking dish and roast for 20 minutes; set aside until they are cool enough to handle.

Meanwhile, remove the mushroom stems and set them aside for some other purpose. Arrange the mushroom caps, gill sides up, on the baking sheet.

2. Peel the garlic cloves and place one in the center of each mushroom cap; sprinkle with salt and pepper and top with ¼ teaspoon of butter. Bake for 20 to 25 minutes, until the garlic is very soft and the mushrooms are tender. Serve immediately.

SHERRIED MUSHROOMS

MAKES SIX SERVINGS

Basic, tasty and could hardly be simpler. Great as a side dish, of course, or made ahead and added to some sautéed chicken breasts for a quick-and-easy main dish.

2 pounds white or cremini mushrooms, trimmed and cleaned

2 tablespoons butter

Salt and fresh pepper

1 cup dry or medium-dry sherry (fino or amontillado)

¼ cup heavy cream

1. Slice the mushrooms ¼ inch thick. In a large skillet, melt the butter and sauté the mushrooms until lightly browned; there should be no liquid left in the pan.

2. Season with salt and pepper, stir in the sherry, and simmer, stirring often, until the sherry is reduced by half. Stir in the cream and simmer until most of the liquid is gone. Add more salt and pepper, if needed, and serve hot.

¼ CUP BALSAMIC VINEGAR

2 GARLIC CLOVES, CRUSHED

1 POUND SMALL MUSHROOMS (OR LARGE ONES, QUARTERED), TRIMMED AND CLEANED

In a large bowl, whisk together all the ingredients except the garlic and mushrooms. Stir in the garlic and mushrooms. Cover and refrigerate overnight, stirring occasionally, until the mushrooms have given up some of their liquid and are smaller, softer and darker. Serve within two or three days.

MENU SUGGESTIONS

Serve these mushrooms with a veal roast, Kohlrabi in Green Sauce (page 188) and a dish of buttered orzo. If you combine the mushrooms with chicken as suggested in the headnote, garnish with a bit of chopped parsley and serve with broccoli and rice or with rice followed by a mixed green salad.

EASY MUSHROOM TIMBALES

MAKES SIX SERVINGS

These delicate little custards are beautiful enough to serve to guests and easy enough to make for family.

16 to 20 ounces white or cremini mushrooms, cleaned and trimmed

2 tablespoons butter or margarine

Salt and fresh pepper

1 cup whole milk

½ cup chicken or vegetable broth

3 eggs

2 ounces boursin cheese

2 scallions, white and green parts, finely chopped

Chopped scallions and whole parsley leaves for garnish (optional)

1. Preheat the oven to 325°; butter six ½-cup glass custard cups. Bring a kettle of water to a boil.

Chop the mushrooms coarsely. In a medium skillet, melt the butter and brown the mushrooms over medium heat; there should be no liquid left in the pan. Season with salt and pepper and set aside to cool slightly.

2. In a large bowl, whisk together the milk, broth and eggs. Crumble the cheese into the bowl, then stir in the scallions and mushrooms. Divide the mixture among the prepared custard cups, and place the cups in a larger pan (for instance, a roasting pan) on the middle rack of the oven. Carefully pour ¾ inch of boiling water into the larger pan to make a hot water bath for the custard cups.

Bake for 40 minutes, until the custard is set and golden and a knife inserted in the center of one cup comes out clean. Carefully lift the cups out of the hot water and set them on a wire rack to cool for 15 minutes.

Run a sharp knife around the edge of each timbale to loosen it from the glass. Have a serving platter ready. Invert each timbale onto a large pancake turner as shown in the illustration and slide it onto the serving platter—it sounds a little complicated but it's quite easy to do. If you like, garnish the tops with a sprinkling of chopped scallion and a couple of whole parsley leaves.

MENU SUGGESTIONS

These timbales are rich, so serve them with a lean partner—grilled or broiled fish and a good green salad. Or make it an all-vegetable meal, with one of the composed salads on pages 347 to 349 plus toasted whole wheat bread or rolls.

SIMPLE GARNISHES

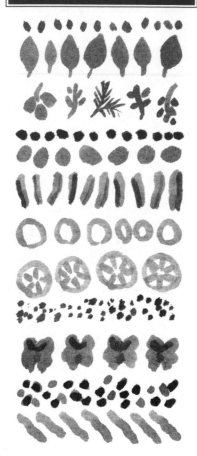

When you've spent time and effort on a dish, it deserves the handsome finishing touch that only a garnish

MENU SUGGESTIONS

If your family likes crunch (without the fat of deep- or shallow-frying), give them a double dose by serving crisp oven-fried chicken along with the crisp mushrooms. I like Barbecue Limas (page 60) with the meal, followed by a simple green salad with blue cheese dressing.

THE VEGETABLE EXPRESS

CRISP MUSHROOMS

MAKES SIX SERVINGS

Okay, so Ritz crackers are not the toniest food in the world, but they make a perfectly delicious cracker coating for these mushrooms.

⅔ cup fine Ritz cracker crumbs (about 20 crackers)
(Crush the crackers in a plastic bag with a rolling pin or in your food processor.)

¼ teaspoon salt

¼ teaspoon paprika

Fresh pepper

1 egg white

1 tablespoon water

30 medium-size white or cremini mushrooms, trimmed and cleaned

1. Preheat the oven to 350°; butter a baking sheet.

In a small bowl, stir the cracker crumbs with the salt, paprika and a good grinding of pepper. In another bowl, whisk together the egg white and water until frothy.

2. Dip each mushroom in the egg white mixture, dredge in the seasoned cracker crumbs, and place on the prepared baking sheet. Bake for 20 minutes, until the mushrooms are tender. Serve hot.

WILD MUSHROOM FRICASSEE IN CROUSTADES

MAKES SIX SERVINGS OF TWO CROUSTADES EACH

Anything (but especially wild mushrooms) served in croustades is bound to feel festive and fun since it's not a treat you get every day. Don't omit the garnish—it's important to the finished look of a sophisticated side dish like this.

TIP: This makes a great first course, too.

12 slices thin-sliced premium whole wheat bread (from a 1-pound loaf)

Olive oil for making the croustades

¾ pound wild mushrooms, trimmed and cleaned (*Try shiitake, cremini, chanterelle, portobello, oyster, etc., or a combination of several kinds.*)

2 tablespoons olive oil

1 tablespoon butter

1 small onion, minced

1 garlic clove, minced

Salt and fresh pepper to taste

¼ teaspoon powdered thyme

¼ teaspoon powdered rosemary

½ cup dry white wine

2 tablespoons grated Parmesan cheese

Whole parsley leaves and several chives for the garnish

1. Preheat the oven to 350°; have ready a medium muffin tin with 12 cups.

Make the croustades: Cut the crusts from the slices of bread to make 3½-inch squares. Flatten each slice with a rolling pin and brush both sides lightly with olive oil. Firmly press one slice into each muffin cup.

can give it. For vegetable side dishes, the simplest garnish, centered on the top, is often the best. Here are some suggestions.

- **A SPRINKLING OF MINCED PARSLEY OR SNIPPED CHIVES**
- **A FEW SCATTERED WHOLE LEAVES OF BASIL OR CORIANDER**
- **SPRIGS OF FRESH DILL, WATERCRESS, OREGANO OR PURSLANE**
- **A SPOONFUL OF CAPERS OR A FEW SMALL OLIVES**
- **SEVERAL NARROW STRIPS OF ROASTED PEPPER, ARRANGED IN A ROW**
- **SOME THINLY SLICED SCALLION OR RED RADISH**
- **SEVERAL THIN SLICES OF LEMON OR LIME**
- **A SPRINKLING OF GRATED LEMON OR ORANGE ZEST**
- **A FEW WALNUT HALVES**
- **A SPOONFUL OF FINELY CHOPPED NUTS, WHOLE PINE NUTS OR TOASTED SESAME SEEDS**
- **SEVERAL NARROW STRIPS OF SUN-DRIED TOMATO**

Bake for 10 to 12 minutes, until lightly crisped. Leave the croustades in the muffin cups.

2. Meanwhile, dice the mushrooms. In a medium skillet, melt the two tablespoons of olive oil with the butter and sauté the onion and garlic until soft. Stir in the diced mushrooms, salt, pepper and herbs. Sauté until the mushrooms give up their liquid and the liquid evaporates.

3. Add the white wine and continue cooking and stirring over low heat until there is almost no liquid left.

4. Divide the mushroom mixture among the croustades and top each with ½ teaspoon of Parmesan cheese. Bake for five minutes, until hot. Remove the croustades from the muffin cups and garnish each with short lengths of chive and whole parsley leaves tucked into the filling. Serve right away.

MENU SUGGESTIONS

Go all out for this meal—starting off with My Favorite Belgian Endive Salad (page 76) or Artichokes Provençal (page 26). Then proceed to roasted duck or Cornish hens with the croustades, fruited wild rice and another green vegetable, perhaps Spinach with Warm Sesame Dressing (page 290).

OKRA

BUYING AND STORING

If you can pick them one at a time, go for small or medium-size pods, not longer than three inches; larger pods will be tough and woody. Okra should be bright green and crisp, with flexible tips. Avoid any pods with bruising, discoloration or withering.

Okra is perishable and moisture will turn the skin slimy, so refrigerate it wrapped in paper towels and use it within a couple of days.

NOTES TO THE COOK

Rinsing: Never wash okra until right before you prepare it; in fact, keep the pods as dry as possible up to the moment you need them. At that time, rinse them in cold water and pat dry on paper towels.

Trimming: Cut the stem off close to the top of the pod; there's no need to cut off the tip unless it is withered or blackened.

I've never met anyone who was neutral about okra, once they'd tasted it. It has an odd—or interesting—texture that excites love or loathing, but never a take-it-or-leave-it shrug. The issue is the sticky goo that begins to ooze from the flesh as soon as the okra is cut, and continues to ooze as you work with it. The drier the preparation (as in Cornmeal Pan-fried Okra, page 214), the less slimy the okra—and in a wetter concoction or one that uses whole pods (Creole-style Okra, page 215), the sliminess is less of a concern. Long cooking of cut pods, as in soups and stews, really develops the slippery stuff.

All this is moot, however: If you don't like okra, you'll be on your way to another vegetable by now, and if you do like okra, no amount of stickiness will put you off and you'll love these recipes, gooey or not.

OKRA FRITTERS WITH SAUCE TI-MALICE

MAKES ABOUT 22 FRITTERS, PLENTY FOR 6 SERVINGS

A good solid fritter, not slippery at all. The peppy Sauce Ti-Malice really makes the dish, but if you can't manage it, serve the fritters with hot sauce and sour cream or even a good hot salsa.

1 pound okra, trimmed (see Notes to the Cook)

1 cup flour

2 teaspoons baking powder

1 teaspoon salt

1 cup whole or skim milk

1 egg

Vegetable oil for frying (not olive oil)

Sauce Ti-Malice (recipe follows)

1. Bring a pot of water to a boil. Cut the okra crosswise into $\frac{1}{4}$-inch-thick slices and parboil for three minutes. Drain, cool the okra under cold water, and then pat dry on paper towels as best you can.

2. In a large bowl, whisk together the flour, baking powder and salt. Add the milk and egg and whisk again until smooth. Stir in the okra.

3. In a large skillet, heat two or three tablespoons of oil. When the oil is very hot, drop spoonfuls of batter and okra in the skillet, not too close together, to make fritters about three inches in diameter. Brown on one side, then turn, flatten with a spatula, and brown the other side. Drain on paper towels and keep warm in one layer in a 300° oven.

Repeat until all the batter is used up. Serve hot, with Sauce Ti-Malice.

Sauce Ti-Malice

MAKES ABOUT ONE CUP

Make this sauce several hours ahead so it has time to macerate.

¾ **cup finely chopped onion (about 1 medium)**

2 shallots, minced

2 garlic cloves, minced

¼ **cup cider vinegar**

¼ **cup fresh lime juice**

¼ **to 1 teaspoon hot pepper sauce**

¼ **cup olive oil**

Salt to taste

1. Combine the onion, shallots, garlic, vinegar and lime juice in a nonreactive saucepan and let stand for one hour. Add the remaining ingredients, starting with ¼ teaspoon hot pepper sauce and adding more until the mixture reaches the degree of fieriness you like.

2. Bring the mixture to a boil and simmer one minute. Let it cool, then add more salt if needed; serve cold.

- CHUTNEY: MILD OR HOT
- ASIAN SAUCES: SOY; HOISIN; OYSTER; TERIYAKI, ETC. (READ MORE ABOUT ASIAN INGREDIENTS ON PAGES 128, 130 AND 150)
- TAHINI (SESAME PASTE)
- PEANUT BUTTER: SMOOTH AND CHUNKY STYLES (USED FOR SAUCES AND SEASONING)

MENU SUGGESTIONS

Broiled or pan-fried bluefish makes a lovely supper with the fritters and Creamy Greens and Tomatoes (page 182). Warm corn bread is an appropriate accompaniment.

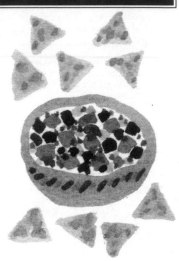

Here are two more salsas to try. It's crucial in the first recipe to snip, not chop, the chives; in the second recipe, it's important to dice the vegetables quite small.

Chive Salsa: Peel, core, seed and devein two fresh hot green chiles. Cut them into pieces and purée them with ½ cup (packed) of fresh coriander leaves, one garlic clove (chunked), two tablespoons of olive oil, two tablespoons of fresh lime juice and ⅓ cup of water. Transfer the mixture to a bowl and stir in one cup of snipped fresh chives and salt to taste. Allow to stand for an hour.

MENU SUGGESTIONS

You might like to try this okra with shrimp jambalaya and plenty of white rice, with a simple tomato salad on the side.

CORNMEAL PAN-FRIED OKRA

MAKES SIX SERVINGS

A simple, tasty and fast way to cook okra, which gives a bit of a crisp coating without a lot of grease or deep-frying. The herbs add interest to the mild okra.

¼ cup yellow cornmeal

¼ teaspoon each powdered dried cumin, coriander, oregano and pure chile

½ teaspoon salt

1¼ pounds okra, rinsed and trimmed (see Notes to the Cook)

Vegetable oil for frying

1. In a large bowl, mix the cornmeal, herbs and salt; set aside. Cut the okra crosswise into ½-inch slices; add them to the bowl of seasoned cornmeal and stir lightly to coat.

2. In a large skillet, heat about three tablespoons of oil. Lift the okra slices out of the bowl with a slotted spoon, shaking off any excess cornmeal, and arrange them in a layer in the skillet. Sauté until brown, then turn and brown again. Continue turning and sautéing until all the pieces are crisp and brown, adding more oil to the skillet if needed.

Correct the seasoning, drain on paper towels, and keep warm in a 300° oven until serving time. Serve hot.

CREOLE-STYLE OKRA

MAKES PLENTY FOR SIX SERVINGS

Down-home flavor the easy way. Since the okra remains whole in this recipe, it's best to use small, tender pods. You can get away with medium-size ones, but nothing over three inches.

3 stalks celery, trimmed

1 green bell pepper, cored, seeded and deveined

1 medium onion

3 tablespoons butter or margarine

1 pound small okra, rinsed and trimmed
   (see Notes to the Cook)

2 medium-size ripe tomatoes, stem ends removed

2 garlic cloves, minced

$\frac{1}{4}$ to $\frac{1}{2}$ teaspoon powdered dried thyme

$\frac{1}{2}$ cup white wine

Salt and fresh pepper to taste

Hot pepper sauce to taste

1. Dice the celery, pepper and onion. In a large skillet, heat the butter and sauté the diced vegetables and whole okra until lightly browned. Meanwhile, dice the tomatoes.

2. Add the tomatoes, garlic and thyme and stir over medium heat until well combined.

3. Stir in the wine, salt, pepper and hot sauce. Cover the skillet and simmer about five minutes, until the okra is tender. Season with more salt and pepper if needed, and serve hot.

Fresh Vegetable Salsa: Peel, core, seed and devein two fresh hot green chiles. Mince the chiles, half of a small red onion and $\frac{1}{4}$ cup (packed) of fresh coriander leaves; put them in a medium bowl. Finely dice one medium-size ripe tomato, four radishes and one Kirby cucumber (trim the ends but don't peel it) and add them to the bowl. Stir in two tablespoons of olive oil, the juice of half a lime and salt and fresh pepper to taste.

MENU SUGGESTIONS

Soft luscious spoon bread is a wonderful partner for this strongly flavored okra. If you need a little more on the menu, add pan-fried fish.

THE VEGETABLE EXPRESS

BROWNED OKRA WITH SUN-DRIED TOMATOES

MAKES SIX SERVINGS

Sun-dried tomatoes add tang and contrasting texture to the nicely browned okra. Be sure to use small, tender pods for this recipe.

1¼ pounds small okra, rinsed and trimmed (see Notes to the Cook)

3 tablespoons olive oil

2 ounces sun-dried tomatoes, rinsed well

¾ cup water

½ teaspoon dried oregano, powdered

2 tablespoons minced fresh flat-leaf (Italian) parsley

Salt and fresh pepper

1. Cut each okra pod in half lengthwise. In a large skillet, heat the oil, add the okra, and sauté over medium-high heat until lightly browned. (It takes a while to get it good and brown.) Meanwhile, cut each tomato into ⅛- to ¼-inch strips.

2. When the okra is browned, add the tomatoes, water and oregano. Continue cooking and stirring over low heat until the tomatoes are soft and the liquid is almost gone. Stir in the parsley, season to taste with salt and pepper, and serve hot.

MENU SUGGESTIONS

For a change from the more obvious chicken or fish, put this quick okra dish on a menu with fettuccine with cream sauce and an interesting green salad dressed with mustard vinaigrette.

BUTTERED OKRA AND WILD RICE

MAKES PLENTY FOR SIX SERVINGS

The beautiful combination of the dark brown wild rice and the yellow-green curried okra make this one of the prettiest dishes I know. Wild rice certainly turns okra into party fare; for family dinners, try it with white or brown rice.

¾ cup uncooked wild rice

1½ cups chicken or vegetable broth

½ cup water

1 pound okra, rinsed and trimmed

3 tablespoons butter

1 tablespoon vegetable oil (not olive oil)

1 cup chopped onion (about one medium-large onion)

1 tablespoon minced fresh ginger

1 teaspoon mild curry powder

2 tablespoons fresh lemon juice

Salt and fresh pepper

1. Rinse the rice in a strainer, stirring it around under cold water for a minute or two. Put it in a saucepan with the broth and water, cover, the pan, and bring to a boil over medium heat.

When the broth boils, uncover the pan, lower the heat, and simmer 35 to 40 minutes, stirring often, until the rice is tender but chewy; watch it closely to be sure it doesn't get mushy. When the rice is done, the pan should be almost dry; if there is liquid left, drain it off. Set the rice aside, stirring occasionally to release more heat.

2. While the rice cooks, cut the okra into ¼-inch slices. In a large skillet, melt the butter and oil and sauté the okra, onions and ginger until the okra is barely tender, about ten minutes.

P A N T R Y

RICE AND OTHER GRAINS

As all vegetarians know, vegetables and grains go together like sunshine and flowers, and I encourage you to invent meals that combine the two. Here is a list of grains and grain products to keep in mind when stocking your pantry for future dinners:

- **RICE**
  WHITE RICE (SHORT OR LONG GRAIN; NOT INSTANT)
  BROWN RICE
  ARBORIO RICE
  BASMATI, WEHANI AND OTHER SPECIAL RICES
- **WILD RICE**
- **PEARL BARLEY**
- **KASHA (BUCKWHEAT GROATS)**
- **CORNMEAL (COARSELY GROUND FOR POLENTA)**
- **HOMINY (FOR POSOLE)**
- **HOMINY GRITS**
- **MILLET**
- **QUINOA**
- **BULGUR WHEAT**
- **CRACKED WHEAT**
- **WHEAT BERRIES**
- **RYE BERRIES**
- **COUSCOUS**

3. Stir in the curry powder, lemon juice and a sprinkling of salt and pepper, and continue sautéing and stirring for three more minutes. Add the wild rice and mix well over low heat to warm the rice. Correct the seasoning and serve right away.

MENU SUGGESTIONS

Begin your company dinner with Tomato Tart (page 320), followed by grilled breasts of duck or chicken and this very beautiful okra dish. If you prefer, omit the duck and serve instead an eggplant soufflé or the Squash Soufflé on page 308. A simple leafy salad is a good idea, too.

ONIONS

BUYING AND STORING

When you see chopped onion on an ingredients list, it means the all-purpose yellow onion, the most common of several kinds of dry onions. Dry onions have been cured after harvesting, which causes them to develop that brittle papery skin. (Scallions and leeks, also members of the onion family, are called fresh onions since they are picked and marketed right away, without being cured; see Leeks and Scallions, pages 193 to 194.)

Dry onions should have no green sprouts poking out at the stem end, no soft spots and no feeling of sponginess when you squeeze them. If an onion has a sort of sweetish, earthy, moldy smell, toss it back.

Onions need not be refrigerated, but if you can keep them in a cool, airy place, so much the better. If not, store in a wire basket and don't buy too many at a time—they'll begin to sprout and rot if they hang around at room temperature for too long.

Here are some other dry onions you should know about:

Red onions can range from mild to very strong; which flavor you'll get is the luck of the draw. They're usually at their best in salads and other raw or cold dishes and they're great when roasted.

Bermuda and Spanish onions are larger and milder than yellow onions, good in salads as well as cooked; if you run out of yellow onions, you can always substitute a Bermuda or Spanish onion.

White onions have silvery-white skins and are 1 to 1½ inches in diameter. They are also called boiling onions, which makes a lot of sense since they are often served boiled. White onions are sometimes called pearl onions, which does not make a lot of sense because you can also buy tiny white onions that really do look like pearls.

Onions are so fixed in our minds as seasonings that it may take a leap of faith to regard them as vegetables in their own right. They are, in fact, both delicious and versatile. When cooked they lose most of their sting and pungent smell; they become much milder—in some cases downright sweet—with an appealing fragrance.

SHALLOTS

The shallot, a member of the onion family, grows either as a small single bulb or as a cluster of several cloves gathered into one bulb; each single bulb or *clove* is considered to be one shallot. They have a hint of garlic flavor, but on the whole shallots taste rather like onions—and when you chop them they may sting your eyes even more than onions.

Buy only firm, plump bulbs or cloves with dry, tight papery skins (which are usually copper-colored or rosy red). Shallots deteriorate faster than garlic or onions, so it's essential to start out with specimens in the best of health. Avoid any that seem shrunken inside their skins, or that have begun to sprout, or that smell too pungent-sweet and feel soft and moist.

Shallots will last longer if you keep them in a cool, dark place, but it still makes sense to buy them in small quantities so that you don't fret about throwing out the ones that inevitably dry up or go bad.

To confuse matters further, these itsy-bitsy *pearl onions* can have white, red or brown skins. They are about ½ inch in diameter and a lot of trouble to work with.

Vidalia, Maui and *Walla Walla* are varieties of naturally sweet onion well worth trying when you can get them. You have to catch them in season (spring and summer) and even then they may be difficult to find; crops seem limited and aren't shipped to every part of the country. Unlike other dry onions, these sweet onions are highly perishable.

NOTES TO THE COOK

You probably have your own way of preparing an ordinary yellow or red onion, but here's my method: Discard any of the papery skin that comes off easily. With a sharp knife, cut off (trim) the stem and root ends. Slit the remaining papery skin and the first layer of onion flesh from top to bottom; peel off the papery skin and the layer underneath to reveal what you hope will be an unblemished onion. (If you see black mold, wash it off; if you see a rotten layer of flesh within the onion, you can halve the onion, pick out the decayed part and salvage the rest. I've done that many times.)

RED ONION RAITA WITH CORIANDER

MAKES SIX SMALL SERVINGS

Raitas are yogurt-based Indian side dishes that accompany a snack or curry or other main course. You don't usually eat a full serving—just a small amount.

⅔ pound red onions, trimmed, peeled and diced

⅔ cup cider vinegar

⅔ cup water

2 teaspoons sugar

¼ teaspoon salt

1 teaspoon mustard seeds

Fresh pepper

1 cup plain (unflavored) yogurt

⅓ cup chopped fresh coriander

Whole coriander leaves for garnish (optional)

1. Put the onions in a saucepan with the vinegar, water, sugar, salt, mustard seeds and a good grinding of pepper. Bring to a boil and simmer for eight minutes, until crisp-tender. Drain well in a fine strainer, to catch the onions and mustard seeds, and transfer them to a bowl.

2. Add the yogurt and coriander and stir well. Season with more salt and pepper, if needed, and serve chilled, garnished with a few coriander leaves.

Shallots are tricky to peel and, as with onions, you'll probably lose a layer of flesh in the peeling: Cut a bit off each end, slit the papery skin (and one layer of flesh, if necessary), and peel it away. Rinse off any dirt and pat dry.

Cook shallots gently, until translucent, soft or lightly browned; don't let them burn or they'll taste bitter.

MENU SUGGESTIONS

You can, of course, use this raita in an Indian-style meal of curry (meat or vegetable), rice and condiments. Another possibility, however, for a light supper, is to serve Indian Beans and Greens (page 50), yellow rice, any good flat bread and the raita.

CRISP ONION AND APPLE FRITTERS

MAKES ABOUT 20 FRITTERS, PLENTY FOR 6 SERVINGS

Delicate and crisp—an absolutely scrumptious fritter, with that characteristically frilled edge and the onions and apples cooked just enough to retain a bit of crunch.

TIP: Be sure to let the first sides brown well or you won't be able to turn the fritters without breaking them.

¼ **cup fine yellow cornmeal**

½ **cup flour**

1 **tablespoon sugar**

2 **teaspoons baking powder**

½ **teaspoon salt**

¾ **cup whole or skim milk**

2 **tablespoons butter or margarine, melted and cooked**

1½ **cups diced yellow onion**

1 **cup peeled, diced apple (any kind)** *(Be sure every bit of the core and seeds are removed before dicing.)*

2 **tablespoons snipped fresh chives**

Vegetable oil for shallow-frying

1. In a large bowl, whisk together the cornmeal, flour, sugar, baking powder and salt. Add the milk and butter and whisk again until smooth. Stir in the onion, apple and chives.

2. In a large skillet, heat ¼ inch of oil until very hot. To make the fritters, drop heaping tablespoons of batter into the skillet, flattening each one slightly with the back of the spoon; don't crowd the pan. Brown well on both sides, then drain on paper towels and keep warm in one layer (don't stack them) in a low oven.

Repeat the process until all the batter is used up. Serve hot.

MENU SUGGESTIONS

A pork roast will be delicious on this menu, and it leaves you free to work on the fritters. Serve Spicy Browned Brussels Sprouts and Carrots (page 93) or—for a jazzier accompaniment—Braised Celery Hearts with Blue Cheese (page 124). For an all-vegetable meal, Zucchini Ribbons in Gorgonzola Sauce (page 295) and a grain casserole or baked sweet potatoes.

STIR-FRIED ONIONS

MAKES SIX SERVINGS

Fresh ginger and Chinese oyster sauce complement the onions, smoothing out any harshness without removing the tang or crunch.

1 tablespoon minced fresh ginger

¼ cup oyster sauce *(Oyster sauce is a bottled Chinese sauce, available in Chinese groceries, gourmet shops and some supermarkets.)*

¼ cup chicken or vegetable broth

3 large or 6 medium-size yellow onions (about 1½ pounds), trimmed and peeled

2 tablespoons peanut oil

1 tablespoon sesame oil

1. Combine the ginger, oyster sauce and broth to make the stir-fry sauce; set aside. Cut the onions in half from stem to root; cut each half into ¾-inch wedges.

2. In a wok or large skillet, heat the peanut oil; add the onion wedges and stir-fry over high heat until the onions are lightly browned on the edges but still crisp. Do not overcook—the onions should not be soft.

3. Add the sauce and stir-fry for three more minutes. Turn off the heat, add the sesame oil, and stir well. Serve immediately.

MENU SUGGESTIONS

Stir-fried vegetables certainly don't have to be eaten with Asian dishes. These onions, for example, may be served with grilled or broiled marinated beef and Mushrooms Roasted with Butter and Garlic (page 204). Have a salad, too, with robust greens and Anchovy Vinaigrette (page 340).

MATCHMAKING: VEAL

You're making veal for dinner. What do you serve with it? Here are some possibilities from which to choose, including the Vegetable Express for hurry-up meals.

Lemon-sautéed Fennel,
page 174

Asparagus with Mushrooms,
page 34

Broccoli in Creamy Broccoli
Purée, page 85

Sugar Snap Peas with Peppered
Orange-Butter Sauce,
page 238

Easy Mushroom Timbales,
page 206

Crisp Onion and Apple Fritters,
page 222

Sweet-and-Sour Pattypan
Squash, page 296

Flavorful Salad,
page 344

VEGETABLE EXPRESS

Basic Baked Squash,
page 307

Roasted Eggplant with
Roasted Garlic and Lemon,
page 159

COMPANY'S COMING

HOLIDAY BAKED ONIONS WITH DOUBLE CHEESE SAUCE

MAKES SIX SERVINGS

Here we have a traditional holiday dish—creamed onions—raised to elegant heights: sweet little onions in a creamy, delicate cheese sauce topped with beautifully browned bread crumbs and cheese.

24 to 28 white (boiling) onions, each about 1¼ inches in diameter

1 cup whole milk

1 cup chicken or vegetable broth

3 tablespoons butter

3 tablespoons flour

2 ounces mascarpone (*This is a rich, creamy Italian cheese.*)

½ cup grated Gruyère cheese (about two ounces)

Salt

3 tablespoons dry bread crumbs

1. Butter a 1½-quart baking dish; preheat the oven to 350° (325° for ovenproof glass).

Peel the onions: Bring a saucepan of water to a boil; turn off the heat and add the onions. Let stand for one minute, then drain and run cold water over them. The skins will slip off easily. Arrange the onions in the prepared baking dish.

2. In a small saucepan, heat the milk and broth. In another saucepan, melt the butter; add the flour and cook, stirring, for one minute. Add the hot milk mixture all at once and stir briskly over moderate heat until thickened and smooth. Reduce the heat to very low, add the mascarpone, and stir until melted and smooth again.

3. Reserve three tablespoons of the Gruyère cheese. Stir the remaining Gruyère into the sauce a little at a time, letting each amount melt before adding more. (You may have to heat the sauce a bit to get it hot enough to melt the Gruyère.)

If necessary, season the sauce with a little salt.

4. Pour the sauce evenly over the onions in the baking dish. Sprinkle with the reserved Gruyère and then with the bread crumbs. Bake for 45 minutes, until the onions are tender. Serve right away or hold the dish (covered lightly with foil) in a warm oven for up to half an hour.

MENU SUGGESTIONS

For a major holiday meal your family will probably want a favorite roast. With the roast and the onions for tradition, the rest of the menu can be a little different—Acorn Squash with Apples and Cider Glaze (page 225), Savory Baked Lentils (page 40) and Buttery Green Beans with Pecan Crumbs (page 56). Vegetarians can have the same basic meal, without the roast, and with the addition of a vegetable pâté to start and an arugula salad to finish.

Parsnips

Parsnips look like creamy beige carrots, taste sweet and rather nutty, and when cooked, have a texture that is smooth and soft, more like sweet potatoes than carrots. They seem like an old-fashioned vegetable to me, something you might have found simmering away in a nineteenth-century stockpot. The truth is that they adapt wonderfully well to contemporary tastes in food, as you will see from the recipes.

BUYING AND STORING

Look for firm, smooth parsnips with no cracks and no rootlets growing along the length. The tops should have no mold or sliminess and the skinny root ends should not be withered or limp.

You might assume that like so many vegetables, smaller is better where parsnips are concerned. This is not true: Big or fat parsnips are just as sweet, tender and tasty as small ones. That being the case, it makes sense to buy large ones because you're going to have to remove the woody cores of every parsnip no matter what size you buy. So you may as well buy the large ones and have the fewest possible cores to remove, with more flesh per core. (Coring the parsnips is explained in Notes to the Cook.)

Store parsnips unwashed in a plastic bag in the refrigerator, where they should last for at least two weeks.

NOTES TO THE COOK

Trimming and peeling: As shown in the illustration on the following page, trim the parsnip by cutting off and discarding the stem end and the skinniest (and sometimes withered) root end. Peel the parsnip as you would a carrot, using a swivel-blade peeler or any other peeler you prefer.

Coring: Once you've discarded the skinny root end of the parsnip, cut off and save the narrow middle section (up to the point where the diameter is about ¾ inch), which is edible with the core left in. The remaining chubby piece has, unfortunately, a tough, woody core that will not soften when cooked. The only way to eliminate the problem is to cut out the core, discard it, and cook only the delicious flesh of the parsnips. Fortunately, this is easy to do and no more laborious than coring an apple.

Core the parsnip by one of two methods: 1) Split the chubby piece lengthwise in quarters and pare out the core in one straight cut per quarter; 2) cut the flesh away from the core in chunks as shown in the illustration.

trim

save

cut flesh away
from core

JERUSALEM ARTICHOKES

Jerusalem artichokes, which are also called sunchokes, are not artichokes from Jerusalem. They are, in fact, a type of sunflower, and the edible part is the tuber—the pale brown, thin-skinned knob that grows underground.

Sunchokes have a texture a bit like water chestnuts and, like water chestnuts, can be eaten raw or cooked. They are crunchy, nutty and mildly sweet. Look for firm, smooth ones with as few bumps as possible (to make peeling easier); avoid cracked, wrinkled or wilted ones. Sunchokes keep well for a week in a plastic bag in the refrigerator. To use them raw in salads, scrub well and peel them (or not, if you prefer—the skin is thin and nutritious), then slice, dice or cut into a julienne. To cook Jerusalem artichokes, do the same and then boil, steam, sauté or stir-fry. Try not to overcook them because they taste best when crunchy; rescue overcooked Jerusalem artichokes by mashing them with butter, salt and fresh pepper.

MENU SUGGESTIONS

Chicken or turkey in some form is always good with parsnips, plus a savory green vegetable to set off the sweetness—Sautéed Broccoli Rabe with Parmesan (page 86) or Spinach with Warm Sesame Dressing (page 290). If you're not eating meat, add Red Flannel Hash (page 66) to the menu.

GINGER-ORANGE PARSNIPS

MAKES SIX SERVINGS

The sweet taste of parsnips is enhanced here by the spiciness of fresh ginger and the tang of orange.

> **2 pounds parsnips, trimmed and peeled (see Notes to the Cook)**
>
> **3 tablespoons butter or margarine or a combination of both**
>
> **1 tablespoon minced fresh ginger**
>
> **1 teaspoon grated orange rind**
>
> **½ cup orange juice**
>
> **Salt**

1. Cut off the narrow end of each parsnip (up to the point where the diameter is about ¾ inch) and split these pieces lengthwise in quarters, to make narrow sticks. Core the remaining chubby pieces of parsnip as described in Notes to the Cook, discard the tough cores, and cut the flesh into 1½-inch sticks.

In a large skillet, melt the butter; add the parsnips and ginger and sauté until the parsnips are lightly browned, 10 to 15 minutes.

2. Stir in the grated orange rind, orange juice and a sprinkling of salt. Cover the skillet and cook over low heat for about five minutes, stirring once, until the parsnips are tender; be sure the parsnips don't burn.

Add more salt if needed, and serve hot.

TZIMMES OF PARSNIPS, CARROTS AND DRIED FRUITS

MAKES SIX SERVINGS

Tzimmes (pronounced TSIM-iss) is a slow-cooking casserole that often includes meat, sweet potatoes, carrots, apples and dried fruit. Tzimmes is sometimes cooked on top of the stove, but I prefer the richness that comes from oven-baking.

1 pound parsnips, trimmed and peeled (see Notes to the Cook)

1 pound carrots, trimmed and peeled

12 pitted prunes

12 large dried apricots (24 apricots if small)

Salt and fresh pepper

1¼ cups chicken or vegetable broth

1 tablespoon butter

1. Butter a 1½-quart casserole or baking dish; preheat the oven to 375° (350° for ovenproof glass).

Cut off the narrow end of each parsnip (up to the point where the diameter is about ¾ inch) and cut these pieces into 1½-inch lengths. Core the remaining chubby pieces of parsnip as described in Notes to the Cook, discard the tough cores, and cut the flesh into one-inch chunks.

Halve the carrots lengthwise and cut into one-inch chunks; if the carrots are very thick, halve them lengthwise again. Cut each prune and apricot in quarters (or cut small apricots in half).

2. Combine the parsnips, carrots, prunes, apricots and a sprinkling of salt and pepper in the prepared baking dish. Pour the broth over the mixture and cover tightly. Bake for 45 minutes. Stir the butter into the tzimmes, add more salt and pepper if needed, and bake uncovered for 20 to 30 more minutes, stirring often. At the end of the baking, the liquid will be greatly reduced and quite syrupy.

The tzimmes may be served immediately or held covered in a warm oven for quite a while—at least an hour.

TIP: Jerusalem artichokes quickly become discolored when peeled or cut; if this concerns you, drop the pieces into acidulated water as you work.

Cooking suggestions:

- **STIR-FRY WITH GARLIC, GINGER AND SOY SAUCE OR TERIYAKI SAUCE.**
- **BRUSH WITH OLIVE OIL, DUST WITH HERBS, AND ROAST IN THE OVEN.**
- **DRESS (RAW OR COOKED) WITH VINAIGRETTE OR CREAMY DRESSING (PAGES 334 AND 336).**
- **FRY AS YOU WOULD HASH BROWNS, ALONG WITH CHOPPED ONIONS AND GREEN BELL PEPPER.**
- **COMBINE WITH ONE OR TWO OTHER COOKED VEGETABLES—CARROTS, PARSNIPS, POTATOES OR ARTICHOKE HEARTS.**

MENU SUGGESTIONS

Nice with the traditional brisket of beef and a kasha or barley casserole. You'll want something green, too—perhaps broccoli, spinach or Swiss chard.

HASH BROWN PARSNIPS WITH SCALLIONS AND JALAPEÑOS

MAKES PLENTY FOR SIX SERVINGS

In this recipe the sweetness of the parsnips plays off the scallions and hot pepper for a wonderfully savory dish. It's a crowd-pleaser, so the yield here is generous.

2½ to 3 pounds parsnips, trimmed and peeled (see Notes to the Cook)

6 medium scallions (white and green parts), trimmed

½ to 1 tablespoon minced pickled jalapeño
(Use ½ tablespoon for a mildly spicy dish, a whole tablespoon for a fiery one.)

Salt and fresh pepper to taste

¼ cup vegetable oil

1. Cut off the narrow end of each parsnip (up to the point where the diameter is about ¾ inch) and cut these pieces into ¼-inch lengths. Core the remaining chubby pieces of parsnip as described in Notes to the Cook, discard the tough cores, and cut the flesh into a ¼-inch dice. Cut the scallions into ¼-inch slices.

In a medium bowl, stir together the parsnips, scallions, jalapeño and a sprinkling of salt and pepper.

2. In a large skillet, heat the vegetable oil and spread the parsnip mixture evenly. Cover the skillet and cook over medium heat until the bottom is brown and crisp, five to ten minutes. Use a spatula to turn the mixture and brown again; turn carefully to keep the parsnip cubes intact. Repeat to brown as much as possible until all the parsnips are very tender, about ten more minutes. Serve right away.

MENU SUGGESTIONS

Play up the spicy parsnips with a Mexican-style dinner of huevos rancheros, Black Beans with Bacon and Chile (page 44) or refried beans, sliced avocado on crisp greens with Tequila Vinaigrette (page 341) and warm tortillas. Salsa, too—see pages 62 and 214.

THE VEGETABLE EXPRESS

SPIKED PARSNIPS

MAKES SIX SERVINGS

Sherry and parsnips have an affinity for each other, both being slightly sweet and slightly nutty.

2 pounds parsnips, trimmed and peeled (see Notes to the Cook)

10 tablespoons sweet sherry (oloroso or cream)

10 tablespoons water

1 tablespoon butter

Salt

1. Cut off the narrow end of each parsnip (up to the point where the diameter is about $\frac{3}{4}$ inch) and cut the pieces into $\frac{1}{4}$-inch slices. Core the remaining chubby pieces of parsnip as described in Notes to the Cook, discard the tough cores, and cut the flesh into $\frac{1}{4}$-inch slices.

In a medium saucepan, combine the parsnips with the sherry and water and bring to a boil. Simmer covered for five minutes, then uncover and continue simmering, stirring often, until the parsnips are tender and the liquid is reduced by half.

2. Stir in the butter and add salt to taste. Serve hot.

MENU SUGGESTIONS

Make a paella-inspired casserole of baked or braised chicken with sliced chorizo over saffron-flavored rice to go with the parsnips. Serve with Peas with Toasted Almonds (page 239) or follow with a lettuce salad.

PARSNIP PURÉE
WITH HONEY AND SPICE

MAKES SIX SERVINGS

Guests will be impressed with this richly spiced combination, but since the purée is so easy to make, you don't have to save it for company.

2¼ pounds parsnips, trimmed and peeled

3 tablespoons butter

3 tablespoons cream or half-and-half

¼ teaspoon cinnamon

¼ teaspoon ground cloves

¼ teaspoon ground ginger

2 tablespoons honey

Salt and fresh pepper to taste

1. Cut off the narrow end of each parsnip (up to the point where the diameter is about ¾ inch) and cut the pieces into ½-inch lengths. Core the remaining chubby pieces of parsnip as described in Notes to the Cook, discard the tough cores, and cut the flesh into ½-inch slices.

Put the parsnips in a saucepan with water to cover, cover the pan, and bring to a boil. Reduce the heat and simmer covered until the parsnips are tender, five to ten minutes. Drain well.

2. In your food processor, purée the hot parsnips with the remaining ingredients. When the mixture is completely smooth, return it to the saucepan and reheat gently. Season with more salt and pepper if needed, and serve hot.

You may keep it warm in a low oven, lightly covered with foil, for half an hour.

MENU SUGGESTIONS

Start with an interesting green salad (pages 342 to 345), perhaps one with crumbled goat cheese. Then have a roasted chicken or duck to go with these luscious parsnips, served with Butter-browned Savoy Cabbage and Mushrooms (page 102), Browned Leeks and Mushrooms (page 199) or Brandied Brussels Sprouts and Chestnuts (page 95).

PEAS

BUYING AND STORING

Petite peas: I have a cooking reference book which states firmly that fresh green peas are available almost year-round. I don't know where the authors of that book do their food shopping, but in New York City fresh peas are available in late spring for about five minutes in the supermarkets and for a few minutes longer in the farmers' market.

The fresh shell peas that do make their way to market are usually large pods containing overgrown, mealy peas. Short of growing them yourself, you'll rarely find the small pods that yield sweet, tender little peas (petite peas or petits pois) and even when you do, they are extremely pricey. And a pound of pods gives you only a cup of peas, barely enough to tease two people.

There are few vegetables more delicious than tiny fresh peas—but given the reality, it makes more sense to rely on frozen petite peas. Buy a good-quality brand, usually in ten-ounce packages, and keep them frozen until you're ready to follow the recipe.

(If you do locate some good fresh peas, shell and cook them right away or store the unwashed pods in a plastic bag in the refrigerator for only a few days.)

Snow pea pods and sugar snap peas: These should be bright green, crisp and as blemish-free as possible—no yellow or brown spots, although lighter green spots are perfectly okay. Like shell peas, edible pods will keep for several days in a plastic bag in the refrigerator; don't wash the pods until you're ready to prepare them.

NOTES TO THE COOK

Thawing frozen petite peas: Remove the packaging and place the block of frozen peas in a bowl of cold water, breaking it up as it defrosts. If the peas are not frozen solid, break them into

This section includes petite peas (also called shell peas, garden peas, English peas or petits pois) and the edible pea pods we know as snow pea pods and sugar snap peas.

Petite peas are really just very young, tender shell peas. Snow pea pods are the flat, crisp pods you often find in Chinese cooking, and sugar snaps are chubbier pods, a sweet and crunchy cross between shell peas and snow peas, usually with tiny peas inside. Snow peas and sugar snaps are equally good cooked or raw.

lumps in a strainer and hold under cool running water until they separate into individual peas. Use right away or refrigerate until needed.

Preparing snow pea pods and sugar snap peas: Cut or break off and discard the stem ends. Rinse, drain and pat the pods dry on paper towels.

PEAS AND PASTA

MAKES SIX SERVINGS

Comforting and nicely flavored with garlic—a very pretty dish flecked with lots of minced parsley. You won't need another carbohydrate dish to complete your dinner menu.

1 cup uncooked ditalini *(Ditalini are tiny [pea-size] tubes of pasta.)*

3 tablespoons olive oil

4 garlic cloves, minced

2 ten-ounce packages frozen petite peas, thawed and drained

2 tablespoons water

Salt and fresh pepper

2 tablespoons minced fresh flat-leaf (Italian) parsley

1. In a large pot of boiling water, cook the ditalini for 10 to 12 minutes, until tender. Drain, rinse under cold water, and drain again. Set aside.

2. In a large skillet, heat the oil and sauté the garlic for two minutes. Add the peas and water, cover the skillet, and continue cooking over low heat for five to seven minutes, until the peas are plump and tender. Season with salt and pepper.

3. Add the ditalini and sauté, uncovered, stirring constantly, until the pasta is hot and any remaining liquid evaporates. Correct the seasoning, stir in the parsley, and serve right away.

MENU SUGGESTIONS

For a spring dinner, have braised lamb shanks with the peas, and any of the asparagus dishes on pages 31 to 37. For a meatless meal, serve the peas with Escarole with Gorgonzola Cream (page 164) and a radish salad. In both cases, warm crusty bread is essential.

JÍCAMA

Jícama (pronounced HEE-ka-ma) is a wonderful vegetable: It's low-cal, inexpensive, easy to prepare and available year-round. Crunchy and sweet, with flesh rather like fresh water chestnuts or apples, jícama can be cooked or eaten raw. Though not as versatile as a potato or tomato (because the texture of jícama stays basically the same whatever you do to it), it is compatible with all kinds of flavors.

When choosing jícama at the market, pick a size you can handle easily—they range from three to eight inches in diameter and six-pounders are not uncommon. Size doesn't affect taste but do look for thin-skinned, smooth specimens without bruises, withering or too many cracks. Cut jícama into manageable pieces, peel thickly with a sharp knife (to take off the brown skin and the thicker underlayer), and cut it to suit your purpose. Wrap leftover pieces in plastic and store in the refrigerator.

Slices or strips of jícama are perfect for dunking in any sort of dip, but don't stop there: Try a combination of cubed jícama, cucumber, sweet and hot peppers with Lime Vinaigrette (page 341). Stir-fry

SUGAR SNAPS WITH DIPS

MAKES PLENTY FOR SIX SERVINGS

Serve one of these dips (Cream Cheese–Horseradish, Spicy Peanut or Pinto Bean) with crunchy sugar snap peas and watch your kids eat their vegetables. Each makes about one cup of dip.

TIP: Other raw and cooked vegetables are good for dunking, too; try whole green beans, sliced Kirby cucumbers, cherry tomatoes, sliced fennel, halved boiled potatoes, asparagus, slices of baked plantain or wedges of beet.

> 1 pound sugar snap peas, stem ends snapped off, rinsed and dried

FOR CREAM CHEESE–HORSERADISH DIP

> 4 ounces (half of an 8-ounce package) light cream cheese (American Neufchâtel cheese)
>
> ¼ cup buttermilk
>
> 2 tablespoons drained prepared horseradish
>
> Few drops Worcestershire sauce
>
> ⅛ teaspoon celery seeds
>
> Salt and fresh pepper to taste

FOR SPICY PEANUT DIP

> ¼ cup tahini (sesame paste)
>
> ¼ cup chunky peanut butter
>
> ½ tablespoon soy sauce
>
> 1 tablespoon rice vinegar or cider vinegar
>
> 1 tablespoon sugar
>
> ¼ cup chicken or vegetable broth
>
> 1 garlic clove, chunked
>
> 1 slice fresh ginger, about the size of a quarter
>
> Hot pepper flakes (optional)

FOR PINTO BEAN DIP

> 1 cup cooked pinto beans, rinsed and drained *(Canned beans are fine for this dip.)*

¼ cup vegetable or chicken broth, water or beer

½ small onion, chunked

2 tablespoons grated Parmesan or cheddar cheese

Salt and fresh pepper to taste

½ pickled jalapeño (optional)

To make any of these dips, simply put the ingredients in your food processor or blender and process until smooth. If necessary to bring the mixture to dipping consistency, add a bit more liquid and process briefly again. Serve in a bowl, surrounded by sugar snap peas.

jícama sticks with snow pea pods, sliced scallions, ginger and garlic, then dress with an Asian sauce (such as Warm Sesame Dressing, page 290). Make a cooling salad of orange sections, honeydew melon balls, cubed mango and diced jícama with Orange-Yogurt Dressing (page 121).

MENU SUGGESTIONS

Dips are usually served before the meal, but there's no reason why you can't serve them along with it, to get the kids munching away. The peas and dips are good for lunch, too, with soup and either quesadillas or pita with melted cheese.

**MATCHMAKING:
BROILED OR
PAN-FRIED FISH**

You're making fish for dinner. What do you serve with it? Here are some possibilities from which to choose, including the Vegetable Express for hurry-up meals.

*Stir-fried Snow Pea Pods,
page 240*

*Spicy Browned Brussels Sprouts
and Carrots, page 93*

*Split Pea and Bulgur Wheat
Pilaf, page 43*

MENU SUGGESTIONS

Baked or grilled fish will be wonderful here—very fresh and light. I like fettuccine as an alternative, perhaps tossed with bits of prosciutto, with a salad to follow.

SUGAR SNAP PEAS WITH PEPPERED ORANGE-BUTTER SAUCE

MAKES SIX SERVINGS

Thanks to Rosanna Gamson for this wonderful idea—an unexpected combination that will delight you. The orange-flavored (but barely sweet) creamy sauce is flecked with tiny bits of green jalapeño, and the sugar snaps are crisp and crunchy.

- **2 tablespoons butter**
- **2 tablespoons flour**
- **1 cup orange juice (fresh, frozen or from a container)**
- **1 pound sugar snap peas, stem ends removed, rinsed and dried**
- **1 teaspoon minced fresh jalapeño pepper (no seeds)**

1. In a large skillet, melt the butter, stir in the flour, and cook over low heat for one minute. Add the orange juice and bring to a boil, whisking constantly to make a smooth sauce. Simmer until thickened.

2. Add the sugar snaps and jalapeño and simmer, stirring, for eight to ten minutes, until the sugar snaps are cooked but still crisp. They can become mushy very suddenly, so be vigilant. Serve right away.

PEAS WITH TOASTED ALMONDS

MAKES SIX SERVINGS

This would be just peas almondine but for the aromatic bite of lemon (rind and juice) and the nip of Dijon mustard. The combination of these ingredients with sautéed almonds makes the dish rather elegant.

3 tablespoons vegetable oil (not olive oil)

½ cup sliced, slivered or chopped almonds (with or without skins)

2½ ten-ounce packages frozen petite peas, partially thawed *(Use the leftover half-package of peas for soup, salad or another recipe.)*

Grated rind of one lemon

2 tablespoons fresh lemon juice

1 teaspoon Dijon mustard

Salt and fresh pepper

1. In a large skillet, heat the oil and sauté the almonds for a few minutes, until they look and smell toasty. Remove with a slotted spoon and set aside. Do not clean the skillet.

2. Add the peas to the skillet, breaking them up. Cover the skillet and cook over low heat for five to seven minutes, until the peas are plump and tender.

3. Add the remaining ingredients, including salt to taste, a good grinding of fresh pepper and the reserved almonds. Cook uncovered, stirring constantly, for another two minutes, until any liquid has evaporated. Serve right away.

Minted Zucchini Tabbouleh Salad, page 298

Cheddar-baked Tomatoes, page 323

Chile-Cheese-Corn Pudding, page 136

Eastern Salad, page 347

VEGETABLE EXPRESS

Simple Corn and Carrot Sauté, page 140

Stir-fried Peppers and Mushrooms, page 248

MENU SUGGESTIONS

Put together an interesting meat-free meal of these peas, Delicate Cabbage Custard (page 100) and a hearty grain pilaf. Another possibility is to serve the peas with Savory Buttercup Squash and Cheese Gratin (page 305) or with sautéed fillets of flounder, sole or bluefish. Finish with a fresh tomato salad (page 324) and a loaf of whole wheat Italian bread.

THE VEGETABLE EXPRESS

STIR-FRIED SNOW PEA PODS

MAKES SIX SERVINGS

This is so simple you won't believe how good it is. Have your ingredients ready before you heat the wok or skillet, and whatever you do, don't overcook the pea pods. Serve the dish immediately or the pods will lose their crunch.

2 tablespoons butter

1 tablespoon peanut oil

2 tablespoons soy sauce

1¼ pounds snow pea pods, stem ends removed, rinsed and dried well

In a large skillet or wok, melt the butter and oil together over low heat. Add the soy sauce and swirl to blend. Add the snow pea pods, raise the heat and stir-fry for three minutes. Serve immediately.

MENU SUGGESTIONS

For a light, satisfying vegetarian dinner, serve the pea pods with Stuffed Chinese Cabbage Rolls with Spicy Peanut Sauce (page 133) and white rice. For a super-simple meal, serve the pea pods with pan-browned chicken cutlets and couscous.

RUSSIAN SALAD

MAKES SIX SERVINGS

In this colorful traditional salad, petite peas are tossed with carrots, potatoes, yellow squash and beets. The vegetables are marinated in vinaigrette first, then bound lightly with mayonnaise.

Important: Don't overcook the vegetables or they'll become mushy and the salad will lose character.

1 medium carrot, trimmed, peeled and diced

2 small red potatoes, diced (do not peel)

1 small yellow summer squash, trimmed and diced

1 ten-ounce package frozen petite peas, partially thawed

Olive Oil Vinaigrette Dressing (recipe follows)

$\frac{1}{4}$ teaspoon powdered dried tarragon

$\frac{1}{4}$ cup minced cornichons or sour gherkins

1 medium beet, trimmed, peeled and diced

$\frac{1}{3}$ cup regular or low-fat mayonnaise

Salt and fresh pepper

Leaves of radicchio

1 tablespoon large or small capers

1. Fill a large saucepan with two or three inches of water and bring to a boil. Add the diced carrots and simmer for three minutes; add the potatoes and simmer three more minutes. Add the squash and the peas (breaking up the clumps of peas) and return the water to a boil. Simmer five to seven minutes, until the peas are plump and all the vegetables are tender. Drain and rinse briefly under cold running water; drain again and transfer to a large bowl.

To the warm vegetables, add $\frac{1}{2}$ cup of the vinaigrette, the tarragon and cornichons, and toss gently but well.

2. Fill a small saucepan with two or three inches of water and bring to a boil. Add the beets, cover the pan, and simmer until tender, about five minutes. Drain, rinse briefly under cold water, and drain again. Transfer the beets to a small bowl and stir in the remaining ¼ cup of vinaigrette.

3. Drain any excess vinaigrette from both large and small bowls. Stir the mayonnaise into the large bowl of vegetables, coating them well; taste and add salt and pepper if needed. Add the beets and toss *briefly* (to prevent the other vegetables from turning pink).

4. Line a platter with the radicchio leaves, mound the salad in the center, and sprinkle the capers on top. Serve at room temperature or chilled.

Olive Oil Vinaigrette Dressing

MAKES ABOUT ¾ CUP

¼ cup balsamic or red wine vinegar

½ cup olive oil

Scant ¼ teaspoon salt

½ teaspoon dry mustard

Fresh pepper to taste

1 garlic clove, split in half

In a food processor or by hand with a whisk, blend all the ingredients except the garlic. Add the garlic and let the dressing stand at room temperature for about two hours to develop flavor. Shake before using.

MENU SUGGESTIONS

Here are three wonderful company dinners to build around the Russian Salad. For the first, serve borscht with cabbage and dumplings (with or without meat), followed by a relish tray, the salad and lots of black bread. For the second, have cold sliced beef with the salad and either Potato-Mushroom Pudding (page 266) or Mashed Potatoes with Cheese and Crispy Potato Skins (page 264). The third menu, for vegetarians, includes the salad, Hot and Cold Cucumbers (page 148), black radishes, a selection of cheeses and that good black bread.

PEPPERS

BUYING AND STORING

Buy firm, crisp peppers with smooth, unblemished skin. Watch out for little dark spots and mushy spots, and don't buy soft, limp or withered peppers. If you're planning to roast your peppers, try to find ones with as few convolutions as possible so the flame can reach every bit of the skin.

The problem with storing peppers is that they don't do really well either in or out of the refrigerator. On the whole, it's better to refrigerate them, unwashed, in a plastic bag; they'll hang on for several days.

NOTES TO THE COOK

Cleaning: Rinse well or scrub gently to remove dust and dirt.

Coring: Make a circular cut around the stem of the pepper, about ½ inch away from the stem. Pull out and discard the stem and the knob of seeds attached to it.

Seeding: Cut the pepper in half from top to bottom. Brush or rinse out the remaining seeds.

Deveining: Open the pepper and trim away the pale veins or ribs, without cutting into the flesh.

This section includes recipes using sweet bell peppers and Italian frying peppers; recipes for and information about hot peppers (chiles) are in the sidebars (pages 180, 248, and 274).

Sweet bell peppers come in a handful of colors these days— yellow, orange, red, purple, green and even chocolate brown. You can do just about anything with sweet peppers—eat them raw, roast them, make sauce out of them or mince them for a multicolored confetti garnish. They are virtually interchangeable (although the green ones seem to me to have the most aggressive flavor), so feel free to use whichever color you prefer.

Sweet Italian frying peppers are pale green or grass green, elongated, and are used almost exclusively for stuffing or frying.

HOW TO ROAST A FRESH PEPPER

The best way to roast a sweet or hot pepper is over the flame of a gas burner on a gas stove or over a fire. (Roasting a pepper under the oven broiler, as is often recommended, results in uneven charring of the skin and overcooked flesh; do it only if you have no flame.) The procedure is simple, if a little time-consuming:

Impale the pepper on a long kitchen fork, pushing the tines into the stem end. Hold the pepper over a medium flame and let the flame blacken the skin. Turn the pepper as each area chars and, when needed, reposition it on the fork to allow the flame to reach every part of the pepper. When the pepper is completely charred, just leave it in a colander in the sink—no need to put it in a bag, since this will steam and overcook it; it will be just as easy to peel without steaming. Repeat this process for any additional peppers.

Run cold water over each pepper while you rub away all the blackening. The skin will come right off and the colander will catch all the bits and pieces. Pat dry and use according to your needs.

NOTE: *The procedure for sweet and hot peppers is exactly the same, except that the skin of a hot pepper is thinner and takes much less time to char and, more important, you must wear rubber gloves while rubbing off the skin.*

MARINATED ROASTED RED AND YELLOW PEPPERS WITH FRESH BASIL

MAKES SIX SERVINGS

This is quick and easy because you roast and marinate the peppers when you have time, and then serve them when you have no time.

3 red bell peppers, cleaned

3 yellow bell peppers, cleaned

Vinaigrette Dressing (recipe follows)

Fresh basil leaves

1. Roast and peel the peppers as described at left. Core, seed and devein them. Cut them into one-inch strips.

2. Layer the peppers in a glass or plastic container, drizzling with Vinaigrette Dressing between layers. When all the peppers are layered, pour over them any remaining vinaigrette. Cover tightly and refrigerate until needed.

NOTE: *Let them marinate at least overnight before serving.*

To serve as a simple side dish, bring to room temperature and arrange the pepper strips on a serving platter; garnish with a chiffonade (very narrow strips) of fresh basil, using as much basil as you like. A more substantial side dish might consist of the peppers, a few marinated mushrooms and artichokes and a garnish of basil.

To make a full-fledged salad, arrange the peppers, along with some thinly sliced fennel and red onion, on a bed of arugula and radicchio. If you like, add a few anchovies and slices of Parmesan cheese. Garnish with basil.

Vinaigrette Dressing

MAKES ABOUT ONE CUP

⅓ cup red or white wine vinegar

⅔ cup mild olive oil, or ⅓ cup olive oil plus ⅓ cup
    neutral vegetable oil (corn, safflower, canola,
    sunflower, etc.)

¼ teaspoon salt

½ teaspoon dry mustard

Fresh pepper to taste

1 garlic clove, split in half

In a food processor or by hand with a whisk, blend all the
ingredients except the garlic. Put the dressing and the garlic
into a jar and let stand at room temperature for about two
hours to develop flavor. Store in the refrigerator but bring it to
room temperature and shake well before using.

MENU SUGGESTIONS

All you need for a complete meal
is this salad and a really great
pizza (page 172) or some Italian
salami, provolone cheese, and
fresh focaccia or grilled Italian
bread.

WORKING WITH HOT PEPPERS

Hot peppers are hot because the veins and central core contain capsaicin, a powerful chemical that can actually give you second-degree burns. Even the seeds of a hot pepper can irritate your skin because they have absorbed capsaicin from the veins.

This chemical is nothing to fool around with. It will stay on your hands—stinging—for hours if you come in direct contact with it, in spite of scrubbing your hands well; you may even notice that when you cut up a very hot pepper, the air

MENU SUGGESTIONS

Lots of vegetables and lots of flavors here, so keep the rest of the dinner simple. Start the meal with chilled braised leeks (page 196; omit the sweet peppers), then serve the ratatouille with baked monkfish or broiled swordfish and pan-fried polenta.

RED PEPPER RATATOUILLE

MAKES SIX SERVINGS

This pepper-based version of ratatouille is a bright, sunny dish that's especially delicious made with fresh tomatoes—although even winter tomatoes make a pretty good showing here.

- 2 medium-size ripe tomatoes, stem ends removed
- 1 medium-size sweet onion (Spanish, Maui, Bermuda, etc.)
- 1 celery stalk, trimmed
- 2 medium-size red bell peppers, cleaned, cored, seeded and deveined
- 1 small zucchini or yellow summer squash, trimmed
- 3 tablespoons olive oil
- 3 garlic cloves, minced
- ½ cup (packed) fresh flat-leaf (Italian) parsley leaves, minced
- ¼ cup balsamic vinegar
- Salt and fresh pepper
- Niçoise olives and parsley leaves for garnish

1. Dice the tomatoes, onion, celery, red peppers and zucchini, keeping them separate from each other.

In a large skillet, heat the oil and add the tomatoes, onions and garlic. Sauté, stirring, until the tomatoes break down and their juice evaporates and the onions are very soft.

2. Add the celery and peppers and cook until the peppers are thoroughly cooked and not crunchy. Stir in the zucchini and continue cooking just until the zucchini is crisp-tender.

3. Add the parsley, vinegar, and salt and pepper to taste. Let the mixture cool, stirring occasionally, then transfer to a bowl or serving platter. Garnish with olives and parsley leaves and serve chilled or at room temperature.

FRIED PEPPERS WITH ANCHOVY BUTTER

MAKES SIX SERVINGS

A twist on the usual fried peppers. In this recipe, some peppers stay crisp, some get soft, all get the flavor of well-browned onion and the bite of anchovy and lemon.

8 large or 10 medium Italian frying peppers, cleaned, cored, seeded and deveined

1 medium-size sweet onion (Spanish, Maui, Bermuda, etc.)

2 tablespoons olive oil

Salt and fresh pepper

2 tablespoons butter

12 anchovy fillets

½ fresh lemon

1. Cut the peppers into ½-inch strips. Cut the onion in half and cut each half in narrow wedges.

2. In a large skillet, heat the olive oil; add the peppers, onions and a little salt and pepper and sauté over medium-high heat until tender, 20 to 25 minutes. Transfer the vegetables to a bowl. Do not clean the skillet.

3. Add the butter and anchovies to the skillet and heat until the anchovies are soft. Squeeze the lemon juice through a strainer into the skillet, scrape up the brown bits in the pan, and mash everything together to make a fairly smooth sauce.

Return the peppers and onions to the skillet and sauté for a minute or two, stirring well to combine the vegetables and sauce. Correct the seasoning, if necessary, and serve hot.

around you irritates your nose and throat. Be smart: Wear rubber gloves when you work with hot peppers and never touch your eyes, nose or lips. Wash the gloves with soap and water when you're done.

Fresh hot peppers should be firm, glossy and bright, with no wrinkles or rotten spots. Slice off the stem end, slit the pepper in half, and carefully cut out the veins. Rinse away the seeds and pat the peppers dry on paper towels. Slice, dice or mince, according to your needs.

If you want to peel a whole fresh hot pepper or give it a nice roasted flavor, impale it on the end of a long kitchen fork and hold it over the flame of a (gas) stove burner, turning slowly until it is blackened all over. Let it cool, then rub off and discard the charred skin. (Remember to wear your rubber gloves when removing the skin.) If you have no flame, do the roasting under the broiler, turning the pepper as it chars.

MENU SUGGESTIONS

Pair the peppers with either a plain or a cheese-filled pasta (such as ravioli or manicotti) topped with Fresh Tomato Sauce (page 322) or a creamy mushroom sauce. Garlic bread is a perfect accompaniment.

A SELECTION
OF CHILES

Unfortunately, calling a particular chile (or hot pepper) by its correct name is a somewhat confusing exercise, since one name may apply to several different peppers and several peppers may have the same name. And, worse yet, some peppers have different names depending on whether they are fresh or dried. To some degree, you just have to figure this out according to what's available in your area. The best strategy I've found is to experiment with whatever chiles I can find, decide which ones what I like and buy them again.

How hot is a chile? One person's hot is another person's mild—so even though chiles can be measured in Scoville Units of heat, you'll have to decide for yourself how much fire you want.

Anaheim (also green chile): fresh; mild heat; also available canned as "whole green chiles" or "chopped green chiles"; a dried Anaheim is called a *California chile*.

Jalapeño: fresh; hot to very hot; also available pickled, in jars; smoke-dried jalapeños are called *chipotles* and are often found canned in adobo sauce.

MENU SUGGESTIONS

Nice with cold sesame noodles and Hot and Spicy Braised Eggplant (page 156). If you like, top the noodles with some sautéed scallops or shrimps.

STIR-FRIED PEPPERS AND MUSHROOMS

MAKES SIX SERVINGS

A dish for lovers of green peppers, this gingery stir-fry is bathed in a robust Chinese-style sauce that combines soy sauce, vinegar and sesame oil.

2 tablespoons soy sauce

1 tablespoon red wine vinegar

1 tablespoon dark sesame oil

$\frac{1}{2}$ pound white or cremini mushrooms, cleaned and stem ends trimmed

3 medium-size green bell peppers, cleaned, cored, seeded and deveined

2 tablespoons peanut oil

1 tablespoon minced ginger

2 scallions (white and green parts), trimmed and sliced thin

1. Stir together the soy sauce, vinegar and sesame oil; set aside. Cut the mushrooms into $\frac{1}{8}$-inch slices. Cut the peppers first into $1\frac{1}{2}$-inch squares, and then cut the squares diagonally into triangles.

2. In a wok or large skillet, heat the peanut oil and stir-fry the ginger and mushrooms over high heat until the mushrooms are browned. Add the peppers and stir-fry until crisp-tender, about five minutes.

3. If there is any liquid in the wok, drain it off. Add the soy sauce mixture and scallions and stir-fry for one minute. Serve immediately.

PEPPER AND CABBAGE SLAW FOR A PICNIC

MAKES PLENTY FOR SIX SERVINGS

Tart and tangy, crunchy and refreshing, a real change from the usual coleslaw you make or buy. This is really pretty, too, with its bright colors, creamy cabbage and pepper-flecked dressing—guaranteed to wake up lazy summer appetites.

TIP: Be sure to start preparation well ahead, since the vegetables must marinate for two hours before being dressed.

½ **cup white vinegar**

⅔ **cup water**

1 **teaspoon salt**

½ **teaspoon ground fresh pepper**

2 **tablespoons sugar**

3 **medium bell peppers in 3 different colors, cleaned, cored, seeded and deveined**

2 **cups finely sliced green cabbage**

1 **small onion, minced**

1 **medium carrot, trimmed, peeled and grated**

½ **cup regular or low-fat mayonnaise**

¼ **cup heavy cream**

1 **tablespoon drained prepared horseradish**

1 **teaspoon celery seeds**

Salt and fresh pepper to taste

1. In a large bowl, stir together the vinegar, water, salt, pepper and sugar. Set aside.

Cut the peppers into julienne strips (easy to do with a mandoline), then add the pepper strips, cabbage, onion and carrot to the vinegar mixture and stir well. Let the mixture stand for two hours.

New Mexico: fresh; mild to hot; these are also available dried.

Poblano: fresh; mild; the dried version is the *ancho* chile.

Serrano: fresh; extremely hot.

Other fresh chiles include banana, güero, Fresno, Santa Fe Grande, Surefire, rocotillo and habañero.

Other dried chiles include mulato, pasilla, Fresno, guajillo, cáscabel, pequín, tepín, japonés and chile de arbol.

2. Drain the liquid from the bowl. Add the remaining ingredients and blend well. Correct the seasoning, chill the slaw, and serve any time.

Important: If you are taking the slaw on a picnic or eating it outdoors on a hot day, keep it well chilled before, during and after serving.

MENU SUGGESTIONS

Go for a classic picnic lunch or supper, with grilled burgers and franks (or a variety of sausage—veal, chicken, chorizo), any cucumber salad (pages 145 to 148), potato salad (page 266) and bean salad, too (page 48). Corn on the cob with Lime-Chili Butter Sauce (page 138) would be a nice addition to the menu.

PLANTAINS

BUYING AND STORING

Plantains are a lot like bananas with one major difference: They are never eaten raw. There's a minor difference, too: Although plantains have similarly thick protective skins that are mottled with black and change color according to the ripeness of the fruit within, the skin of a plantain is much tougher than a banana skin and can't be stripped off quite so easily.

Green plantains are starchy and not at all sweet—they may be an acquired taste. Plantains that are yellow or yellow flecked with black are medium-ripe, sweet but not too sweet; yellow-black to black plantains are fully ripe and sweet indeed.

It takes about two weeks for a plantain to turn from green to black, with mottled yellow right at the midway point, so you can judge what color to buy according to when you want it. Keep plantains at room temperature until ripe, then refrigerate for up to four or five days.

NOTES TO THE COOK

The only special thing you need to know about plantains is how to peel them: First, slice off the ends. Then, if the plantain is very ripe, you may be able to peel the skin off like a banana. If it's not ripe, slit the skin from top to tip and peel it off *sideways* in one big piece.

Plantains are a particular favorite of mine, which partly explains why they are here at all—since plantains are, of course, a variety of banana. The other part of the explanation is that they are often referred to as cooking bananas and treated in a savory way, as if they were vegetables. If you haven't tried plantains before, the menu suggestions at the end of the section will tell you how to use them in your meals.

Indian cooking features a masterful blending of subtle and complex flavors, with each herb and spice carefully chosen to enhance the particular food it will season. In fact, contrary to what Americans may think, in Indian cuisine there is

MENU SUGGESTIONS

Red snapper goes very well with these plantains and salsa. To complete the menu, add a dish of Dilly Beans (page 58) and Butternut Squash with Coriander Sauce (page 306). You'll want some crusty bread or warm corn tortillas, too.

RIPE PLANTAINS WITH TOMATO-MANGO SALSA

MAKES PLENTY FOR SIX SERVINGS

You'll be happy to know that this makes a lot of plantains and a lot of salsa, because it's so good you can't stop eating it. The salsa is sweet (from the mango), a bit spicy and very bright and fresh tasting. It's best made just before serving and it's good for just a day or two, so eat it up right away.

5 ripe plantains (yellow with a lot of black spots or mostly black), peeled (see Notes to the Cook)

¼ cup olive oil

FOR THE SALSA
1 tablespoon olive oil

1 tablespoon fresh lime juice

1 tablespoon rice vinegar

1 ripe mango

2 medium-size ripe tomatoes, stem ends removed

3 scallions, green part only

2 small fresh jalapeños or other hot green chiles

1 garlic clove

Salt

1. Slice the plantains ½ inch thick, on the diagonal. In a large skillet, heat half the oil and brown half the plantain slices on both sides; set aside to cool. Repeat with the remaining oil and plaintains.

2. Make the salsa: In a large bowl, whisk together the oil, lime juice and vinegar. Peel the mango, cut the flesh away from the pit, and chop into small pieces. Dice the tomatoes, saving as much juice as you can. Mince the scallions, chiles and garlic. Add all these to the bowl and stir well. Season with salt to taste.

3. Arrange the plantain slices in overlapping rings on a serving platter and serve at room temperature, accompanied by a bowl of the salsa.

BAKED PLANTAINS WITH CHIVES AND SOUR CREAM

MAKES SIX SERVINGS

You get a lot of result for very little work in this recipe. The hot plantains warm the cool sour cream to give you a lovely rich combination.

²⁄₃ cup regular or light sour cream

1 tablespoon whole or skim milk

½ cup snipped fresh chives

Salt and fresh pepper

5 medium-ripe plantains (yellow with some black spots)

1. Preheat the oven to 350°. While the oven heats, stir together the sour cream, milk and chives, and season to taste with salt and pepper; set aside to let the flavor develop.

2. Cut a lengthwise slit in each plantain, but do not peel; place the plantains on a baking sheet. Bake for about 40 minutes, turning once, until tender when pierced by the point of a knife.

3. When just cool enough to handle, slice off the ends, peel the plantains and cut diagonally into 1½-inch chunks. Arrange the chunks on a serving platter and top with spoonfuls of the sour cream sauce. Serve warm.

no ingredient called "curry powder." No accomplished Indian cook would even consider using the same blend of herbs, spices and ground dried chiles for every so-called curry dish—but very few American cooks have achieved this level of sophistication.

Instead, we are accustomed to using readymade packaged curry powder, mild or hot, for making our favorite chicken, beef or vegetable curries. Since this is the case, it's a good idea to try a few different brands to discover the one you like best. It's an even better idea to try the following homemade mild curry powder—you may find you like it best of all.

Use powdered dried herbs and ground spices (be sure they are not stale): Stir together four teaspoons turmeric, four teaspoons paprika, two teaspoons ginger, two teaspoons cayenne, two teaspoons cumin, two teaspoons coriander, one teaspoon cinnamon, one teaspoon black pepper and ½ teaspoon ground cloves. The recipe makes about six tablespoons, which you should store in an airtight jar.

MENU SUGGESTIONS

I like these plantains in a slightly southern mode, with crisp pan-fried fish and Black-eyed Peas with Butter and Scallions (page 51).

Plantain Salad

Makes six servings

This cold salad is light but filling, almost a meal in itself—especially when served on crisp greens. It has Caribbean origins and is delicious with barbecued pork or chicken.

4 medium-ripe plantains (yellow with some black spots), peeled (see Notes to the Cook)

2 to 4 ounces baked ham *(The amount of ham is your choice.)*

3 hard-cooked egg whites (discard the yolks)

¼ cup diced red onion

½ cup cooked frozen petite peas

Creamy Vinaigrette Dressing (recipe follows)

Salt and fresh pepper

Salad greens

1. Cut the plantains into 1½-inch chunks (four or five chunks per plantain) and put them in a saucepan with enough water to cover. Bring to a boil and simmer, covered, until tender, 10 to 15 minutes. Drain and dry on paper towels.

2. Cut the plantains into ½-inch cubes; cut the ham and the egg whites in a small dice. Put them in a large bowl with the onions and peas and toss with ½ cup dressing and a good sprinkling of salt and pepper. Taste, add more dressing and seasoning if needed, and serve chilled or at room temperature, on a bed of crisp greens.

MENU SUGGESTIONS

This interesting salad goes perfectly with barbecued chicken or pork, as well as with vegetable or chicken curry or pork stew. With any of these, serve black beans and rice on the side. Another possibility, for a simpler meal, is to serve the plantain salad on plenty of greens, with cold poached salmon or boneless chicken breasts.

Creamy
Vinaigrette Dressing

MAKES ABOUT ONE CUP

¼ cup regular or light mayonnaise

2 tablespoons red wine vinegar

2 teaspoons Dijon mustard

⅔ cup olive oil

Salt and fresh pepper to taste

Whisk the ingredients together, then correct the seasoning. Be sure to whisk the dressing again just before using.

CONDIMENTS FOR CURRY

One of the great pleasures of a vegetable, chicken or beef curry dinner is eating it with rice (lots of rice) and accompanying condiments. The condiments, ranged around the curry in small bowls, may be sweet or savory, of varied textures and flavors, hot with chiles or cool with yogurt. Here is a list of possibilities from which to choose; serve two or three for a simple

MENU SUGGESTIONS

Many savory main courses will be delicious here—ham, deviled short ribs, barbecued or broiled chicken or, for a meatless meal, spicy vegetables, beans and rice. Serve a cold green vegetable to round out the meal—cucumber salad or marinated green beans, broccoli or asparagus.

THE VEGETABLE EXPRESS

PLÁTANOS BORRACHOS

MAKES SIX SERVINGS

Sweet and succulent, almost dessertlike, but still perfect with savory main courses.

5 ripe plantains (yellow with a lot of black spots or mostly black), peeled (see Notes to the Cook)

2 tablespoons butter

2 tablespoons vegetable oil (not olive oil)

½ cup dark rum

2 tablespoons honey

Salt and fresh pepper

1. Halve each plantain lengthwise, then cut each piece in half again, crosswise; you now have 20 pieces of plantain. In a large skillet, melt half the butter and oil and brown half the pieces on both sides; set aside. Repeat with the remaining butter, oil and plantains.

2. To the empty skillet, add the rum, honey and a sprinkling of salt and pepper. Simmer, stirring, until the sauce is well blended and slightly reduced. Return all the plantains to the pan, over low heat, and turn gently several times to coat with sauce. Serve hot.

PLANTAINS WITH CURRY SAUCE AND ROASTED PEANUTS

MAKES PLENTY FOR SIX SERVINGS

This is a knockout dish for curry lovers. The complex flavor and chunky texture of the sauce set off the mild sweetness of the plantains to make a luscious combination.

5 medium-ripe plantains (yellow with some black spots), peeled (see Notes to the Cook)

2 tablespoons butter

2 tablespoons vegetable oil (not olive oil)

1 large onion, chopped

2 garlic cloves, minced

2 tablespoons good-quality mild curry powder (*To make your own, see the sidebar on page 252.*)

¼ cup flour

1½ cups chicken or vegetable broth

½ cup half-and-half

Squeeze of fresh lemon or lime juice

¼ teaspoon cayenne pepper

Salt and fresh pepper

½ cup unsalted roasted peanuts, chopped

1. Halve the plantains lengthwise; cut the halves crosswise into ¾-inch slices. Place the slices in a saucepan with enough water to cover; bring to a boil and simmer until tender, 10 to 15 minutes. Drain well and set aside.

2. In a large skillet, melt the butter and oil and sauté the onion until soft. Add the garlic, curry powder and flour and cook, stirring, for one minute. Gradually add the broth and half-and-half, stirring constantly, until thickened.

meal, five or six for a more elaborate one. Some can be made up easily at home, while others may be bought at an Indian market or gourmet food shop.

- SWEET MANGO OR OTHER FRUIT CHUTNEY (MILD OR HOT)
- MANGO PICKLE (TART, SALTY AND HOT)
- CHOPPED ROASTED UNSALTED PEANUTS
- CHOPPED TOASTED ALMONDS
- UNSWEETENED FLAKED OR SHREDDED COCONUT, TOASTED
- CHOPPED SCALLIONS
- CRUMBLED CRISP BACON
- RAITAS (SEE RED ONION RAITA WITH CORIANDER, PAGE 221, AND YELLOW SQUASH RAITA, PAGE 297)
- CHOPPED BANANAS (ADD PLAIN YOGURT TO MAKE BANANA RAITA)
- CHOPPED CUCUMBERS (ADD PLAIN YOGURT TO MAKE CUCUMBER RAITA)
- *DAL* OR ANOTHER LENTIL DISH
- RAISINS SOAKED IN BRANDY OR CURRANTS SOAKED IN PORT
- CHOPPED AVOCADO

3. Add the plantains, lemon juice and cayenne and stir well. Cover the skillet and cook over low heat for 15 minutes. Season with salt and pepper and transfer to a serving bowl. Sprinkle with chopped peanuts and serve hot.

MENU SUGGESTIONS

When you're having company, start with Sugar Snaps with Dips (page 236). Serve the curried plantains with shrimp or chicken and plenty of rice, with a couple of traditional curry condiments—mango chutney, sliced scallions, lentils (or Savory Baked Lentils, page 40)—to make a really special meal. Any good flat bread will be perfect for mopping up the sauce.

POTATOES

BUYING AND STORING

Let's take the white-fleshed potatoes first:

For baking or mashing (or French fries, if you must), choose russet potatoes, one of which is the heavenly Idaho. Russets have that thick, almost leathery brown skin and dry, mealy flesh that makes a fluffy baked potato.

For boiling, choose small or medium-size round red or white potatoes. When these are small and fresh from the earth, we call them new potatoes; when they are small and not so new (and therefore not so sweet), some greengrocers will tell you they are new potatoes even though they have actually been in storage. Small or large, the skin is thin and the flesh is firm and waxy when cooked—perfect for potato salad.

For roasting, choose either russets or round potatoes, depending on whether you prefer a fluffy or firm interior.

And when you haven't decided what you'll be doing with the potatoes, choose the all-purpose long white or large round white, which are firm-textured, with thin skins. Keep in mind that even though they are called all-purpose, they are not good for baking.

Now the orange-fleshed sweet potatoes:

There are two kinds of sweet potatoes, a *dry* type with light yellow or creamy flesh and tan or brown skin and a *moist* type with bright orange flesh and coppery skin. And then there's the yam. Unfortunately, the yam has crept into the language to confuse the sweet potato lover.

True yams are starchy tropical root vegetables and are rarely found in most American markets, but somehow the name "yam" attached itself to the *moist* type of sweet potato. The sweet potato I've used in these recipes is indeed the *moist* type, so look for the coppery skin and orange flesh and don't worry about the name. If you can't tell the difference between the dry and the moist types, ask the produce manager of your market.

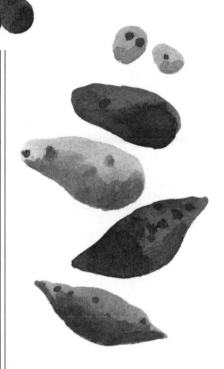

If you think too hard about it, choosing a potato can get very confusing. Thin-skinned, thick-skinned, new, mature, boiling, baking, all-purpose—confusing. And what about the difference between sweet potatoes and yams? Really, it's a lot simpler than it sounds.

In general, any potato you buy should be smooth and free from bruises, nicks, cracks or withering. The skin should have no mold or discoloration and especially no green tinge, which may indicate bitterness and the presence of solanin, a toxic substance. Avoid sprouting eyes if you can, but cut them out if you can't. Sweet potatoes are particularly susceptible to spoilage of all kinds, so choose them carefully.

Actually, you should choose all your potatoes carefully, handpicking them one at a time, but sometimes it's irresistible to buy a ten-pound bag at a terrific price. Just remember that a bag may conceal enough bad specimens to turn that bargain into a mistake.

Store white-fleshed potatoes in a wire basket or any other container that allows air to circulate. It's best to keep the basket in a cool, dark place (not the refrigerator), but even at ordinary room temperature new potatoes will last for up to a week and mature potatoes for a little longer. Sweet potatoes will last for about one week at room temperature; they'll last a little longer if you refrigerate them in a plastic bag.

Notes to the Cook

Washing: Tough-skinned russet potatoes can stand up to a scrubbing—and they often need it. Use a soft brush to get off the dirt, then rinse well. Thin-skinned potatoes and sweet potatoes should be rubbed gently with a sponge or dishcloth or just rinsed well if they are fairly clean. If you're peeling the potatoes, rinse them well after peeling.

Peeling: Peel potatoes just before you need them, using a swivel-blade vegetable peeler (or any other peeler you prefer). You can use the tip of the peeler to remove any eyes or small blemishes, too.

Sweet Potato Salad with Southwest Seasonings

MAKES PLENTY FOR SIX

Instead of the usual white potato salad, try this sweet potato salad perked up with the zingy flavors of lime, cumin, jalapeño and coriander. It's a great marriage of sweet and spicy, without a bit of mayonnaise dressing.

2 pounds sweet potatoes, peeled and rinsed

2 tablespoons fresh lime juice

¼ cup olive oil

1 garlic clove, forced through a garlic press

¼ teaspoon ground cumin

Salt and fresh pepper

½ cup minced red onion

1 medium-size ripe tomato, cored and diced

2 pickled jalapeños, minced

¼ cup (packed) chopped fresh coriander

1. Cut the potatoes into ½-inch cubes; put them in a saucepan with water to cover and bring to a boil. Simmer until tender but not mushy, five to seven minutes. Drain well and then rinse with cold water, just until the cubes are warm. Drain again.

2. Meanwhile, make the dressing by whisking together the lime juice, oil, garlic, cumin, and salt and pepper to taste. Pour the dressing over the warm potatoes and toss lightly but thoroughly.

3. Add the remaining ingredients and toss again. Serve chilled or at room temperature.

MENU SUGGESTIONS

Keep the southwest theme going by making Pink Beans in Creamy Onion Sauce (page 41) and a spicy pork stew. Instead of green salad, offer tomato salsa (page 62) with lots of blue corn tortilla chips and slices of jícama for scooping it up. Or instead of salsa, try the cool and refreshing Red and Green Gazpacho Salad on page 322.

BAKED POTATOES AND TOPPINGS

Years ago, when my husband and I went to Exeter, England, we stumbled upon a hole-in-the-wall shop called Spud-U-Like. Rows of hot baked potatoes were lined up next to containers of toppings and each customer ordered his own favorite combination of spud and stuffing. You, of course, can prepare customized baked potatoes right at home.

Bake one large or medium-size russet potato per person, placing the potatoes directly on the middle rack of the oven set to 375°, for about an hour, or until the potatoes feel soft when squeezed. (About halfway through the baking, use a knife to pierce each potato in a couple of spots to allow steam to escape.) While the potatoes bake,

MENU SUGGESTIONS

Grilled rosemary chicken will be a perfect choice, along with any asparagus dish (pages 31 to 37). For a fancier meal, add Carrot Pancakes (page 106) or Lemon-sautéed Fennel (page 174), a green salad and French bread.

SMALL POTATOES WITH GARLIC CREAM

MAKES SIX SERVINGS

Garlic cream, a slightly rough-textured sauce made with roasted garlic, is neither harsh nor strong, but full of flavor.

2 whole garlic bulbs

18 small round red or white boiling potatoes (1½-inch diameter), washed *(This allows 3 per serving; you may want a few extra, depending on the size of the potatoes and the appetites of your guests.)*

¼ cup chicken or vegetable broth

¼ cup regular or light sour cream

Salt and fresh pepper to taste

1. Preheat the oven to 400°. Put the unpeeled garlic bulbs in a small baking dish and roast in the preheated oven for 30 to 35 minutes, until the cloves are soft. (Squeeze each bulb firmly; if it gives under pressure, the garlic inside is properly cooked.) Set the garlic aside until it is cool enough to handle.

2. Meanwhile, cut the potatoes into quarters, then put them in a saucepan with water to cover and bring to a boil. Simmer until tender, about ten minutes. Drain the potatoes and keep them warm either in the residual heat of the oven (after the garlic is finished roasting and the oven is turned off) or in the oven turned on to a low temperature.

3. Remove as much of the papery skins as will easily come off the bulbs of garlic. Use a serrated knife to slice off about ¼ inch of the root end of each garlic bulb, then squeeze the soft pulp into a bowl. Mash the garlic until fairly smooth, gradually blending in the broth and sour cream. Season with salt and pepper. (Make the garlic cream in your food processor if you prefer a smooth texture.)

Pour the garlic cream over the warm potatoes and toss well. Correct the seasoning and serve hot.

HERBED POTATOES PROVENÇAL

MAKES SIX SERVINGS

This is a very pretty dish, the white potatoes flecked with bits of green zucchini, red pepper, tomato and minced green herbs, glistening with olive oil. Fresh herbs—not dried—are essential here.

5 medium-size round red or white boiling potatoes (2 to 2½ pounds), washed

1 medium zucchini, trimmed

1 red bell pepper, cored, seeded and deveined

1 medium-size ripe tomato, stem end removed

¼ cup olive oil

2 garlic cloves, minced

¼ cup (packed) chopped fresh flat-leaf (Italian) parsley

2 tablespoons minced fresh basil

2 tablespoons minced fresh oregano

Salt and fresh pepper

2 tablespoons balsamic vinegar

1. Slice the potatoes ¼ inch thick, place them in a saucepan with water to cover, and bring to a boil. Simmer the potatoes 10 to 15 minutes, until tender; drain well and set aside in a large bowl.

2. Dice the zucchini, pepper and tomato. In a medium skillet, heat two tablespoons of the olive oil and sauté the zucchini, red pepper and garlic until tender. Add the cooked vegetables to the bowl of potatoes, along with the tomatoes, green herbs and a good sprinkling of salt and pepper. Toss well.

3. Add the rest of the olive oil and the vinegar and toss again, adding more salt and pepper if needed. Serve warm or at room temperature.

prepare the ingredients for your choice of stuffings; when the potatoes are done, slit the tops lengthwise and crosswise and press the ends to open the potatoes. Tuck some of the topping into each potato and serve extra topping on the side, to add as you munch your way through the potato.

Here are some toppings to try for lunch or dinner:

- CHOPPED AVOCADO BLANKETED WITH GRATED CHEDDAR OR MONTEREY JACK CHEESE
- HOT MEAT OR BEAN CHILI WITH A DOLLOP OF SOUR CREAM
- STRIPS OF HOT, THIN-SLICED LEFTOVER MEAT LOAF AND GRAVY
- DICED COOKED ZUCCHINI PLUS GRATED MONTEREY JACK CHEESE AND RED OR GREEN CHILE SAUCE
- CHOPPED COOKED BROCCOLI WITH CHEESE SAUCE
- COTTAGE OR POT CHEESE MIXED WITH CHOPPED SCALLIONS, CHOPPED RED RADISH AND GRATED CARROT
- DICED HAM, CUBED SWISS CHEESE AND CREAMY HERB DRESSING (PAGE 25) OR YOGURT-DILL SAUCE (PAGE 32)
- STRIPS OF SMOKED SALMON, MINCED ONION, MINCED PARSLEY AND SOUR CREAM OR CRÈME FRAÎCHE
- CHOPPED COOKED SPINACH, SAUTÉED MUSHROOMS, CRUMBLED BACON AND BLUE CHEESE DRESSING

MENU SUGGESTIONS

These potatoes are practically a meal in themselves; serve with grilled fresh tuna or cold sliced beef and a crisp green salad with a simple vinaigrette dressing.

PANTRY

DRIED HERBS
AND SPICES

Every cook, no matter how minimal, needs dried herbs and spices. Here are some guidelines and a basic reminder list.

Ground and powdered herbs and spices lose their flavor fairly quickly, so buy small quantities and replace them after six months. Buy them loose or in packages and transfer to small jars or airtight plastic containers.

Since it's difficult to find small enough quantities of some of the less frequently used herbs and spices, you'll probably end up throwing out a lot of items you've barely used. To avoid this, try sharing semiannual purchases of herbs and spices with a friend; otherwise, simply resign yourself to the small cost of replacement—but never resign yourself to using outdated, musty or tasteless herbs and spices.

- ALLSPICE, WHOLE BERRIES AND GROUND
- BASIL, CRUSHED LEAVES (SMALL FLAKES) OR POWDERED
- BAY LEAVES, WHOLE
- CARAWAY SEEDS
- CAYENNE PEPPER, GROUND
- CELERY SEED
- CHERVIL, CRUSHED LEAVES (SMALL FLAKES) OR POWDERED
- CHILE (PURE), GROUND (NOTE: PURE GROUND CHILE IS MADE BY GRINDING DRIED CHILE PEPPERS; IT IS NOT THE COMBINATION OF HERBS AND SPICES WE CALL CHILI POWDER)
- CHILE PEPPER FLAKES (HOT PEPPER FLAKES; RED PEPPER FLAKES)

MASHED POTATOES WITH CHEESE AND CRISPY POTATO SKINS

MAKES PLENTY FOR SIX SERVINGS

This recipe makes a lot of mashed potatoes, but I've never found it to be too much. My nephews Gideon and Sam, the dynamic vegetarian duo, love these potatoes.

5 large russet potatoes (such as Idaho; about $3\frac{1}{2}$ to 4 pounds), washed and dried

2 to 4 tablespoons butter or margarine or a combination of both

$\frac{1}{4}$ cup whole or skim milk heated with $\frac{1}{4}$ cup chicken or vegetable broth

$\frac{1}{2}$ cup regular or low-fat cottage cheese

$\frac{1}{2}$ cup grated sharp cheddar cheese (about 2 ounces)

$\frac{1}{4}$ cup grated Parmesan or Romano cheese

Salt and fresh pepper

Vegetable oil (not olive oil)

1. Peel the potatoes in long strips; cut the potato skins into three-inch lengths. Set aside.

Cut the peeled potatoes into cubes, place them in a saucepan with water to cover, and bring to a boil. Simmer the potatoes until tender, about ten minutes; drain and transfer to a large bowl.

2. Add two tablespoons of the butter, the hot milk and broth, cheeses and a good sprinkling of salt and fresh pepper. Mash by hand for a rough texture or with an electric mixer for a smooth one. (Do *not* try to mash potatoes in your food processor.) Correct the seasonings and add the remaining two tablespoons of butter, if you like. Keep the potatoes warm in a shallow baking dish in a low oven.

3. Heat $\frac{1}{8}$ inch of oil in a small skillet. When the oil is very hot, add half the potato skins and fry, stirring and watch-

ing very carefully to be sure they don't burn. Remove them as they turn crisp and brown; drain on paper towels. Repeat with the second batch, adding a little more oil if necessary. Sprinkle with salt and pepper, and mound the crisp skins on the mashed potatoes. Serve immediately.

- CHILI POWDER (BLEND)
- CINNAMON, POWDERED
- CLOVES, WHOLE AND GROUND
- CORIANDER, POWDERED
- CUMIN, POWDERED
- CURRY POWDER (BLEND)
- DILL, POWDERED
- GINGER, GROUND
- MARJORAM, POWDERED
- MINT, CRUSHED LEAVES (SMALL FLAKES) OR POWDERED
- MUSTARD SEEDS AND POWDER
- NUTMEG, GROUND
- OREGANO, CRUSHED LEAVES (SMALL FLAKES) OR POWDERED
- PAPRIKA, GROUND
- PEPPERCORNS
- POPPY SEEDS
- ROSEMARY, WHOLE NEEDLES OR POWDERED
- SAFFRON, WHOLE THREADS OR POWDERED
- SAGE, CRUSHED LEAVES (SMALL FLAKES) OR POWDERED
- TARRAGON, CRUSHED LEAVES (SMALL FLAKES) OR POWDERED
- THYME, CRUSHED LEAVES (SMALL FLAKES) OR POWDERED
- TURMERIC, POWDERED

MENU SUGGESTIONS

You can make this a meat-free meal since you're already getting some protein from the cheese in the mashed potatoes. Spinach and Mushrooms with Herbs (page 287) and Browned Carrots (page 110) make fine accompaniments.

QUICK POTATO SALADS

For 6 generous servings, halve and boil 24 small red potatoes (about 2 pounds). Drain well, rinse under cold water, and drain again. Set aside until the potatoes are just warm.

Meanwhile, prepare the Basic Creamy Dressing and the ingredients for any variation listed below. Slice the potatoes ¼ inch thick and toss them in a large bowl with the dressing, the prepared ingredients and salt and fresh pepper to taste. Serve chilled.

Basic Creamy Dressing: Whisk together ¾ cup regular or low-fat mayonnaise; ⅓ cup buttermilk, milk or plain yogurt; 1 tablespoon Dijon mustard; salt and fresh pepper to taste.

Variation #1: ¼ cup diced red onion; 2 tablespoons small capers; 2 tablespoons (or more, if you like) sliced pimiento-stuffed green olives; 1 hard-cooked egg, chopped

Variation #2: ¼ pound dry sausage or salami, diced or cut into thin strips; ½ cup diced green pepper; 1 garlic clove, finely minced

Variation #3: 6 slices crisp bacon, crumbled; ½ cup thinly sliced celery; ¼ cup chopped dill pickle; ¼ cup thinly sliced scallions

Variation #4: ½ cup cooked petite peas; ½ cup diced ham; 2 tablespoons snipped fresh chives

Variation #5: ½ bulb of fennel, thinly sliced; 1 medium carrot, grated

POTATO-MUSHROOM PUDDING

MAKES SIX SERVINGS

Based on potato kugel, a traditional Jewish savory pudding with a crisp brown top, soft center and chewy bottom, this version is enhanced with mushrooms and caraway seeds. Serve it in squares, slices or wedges, depending on the shape of the baking dish you use.

NOTE: *If you don't like caraway, just leave it out.*

- 2½ pounds all-purpose potatoes (about 5 medium), peeled and rinsed
- ¾ pound white mushrooms, trimmed and cleaned
- 1 medium onion
- 4 tablespoons (½ stick) butter or margarine or a combination of both
- 3 eggs
- ¼ cup whole milk or half-and-half
- ⅓ cup flour stirred with ½ teaspoon baking powder
- 1 teaspoon salt
- Fresh pepper
- 1 teaspoon caraway seeds

1. Butter a 1½-quart baking dish or casserole; preheat the oven to 375° (350° for ovenproof glass).

Shred the potatoes *by hand* on the large holes of a standard four-sided grater. Transfer to a colander and press or squeeze the potatoes firmly to remove water.

NOTE: *Don't use your food processor for grating the potatoes; the processor cuts long thin pieces that will produce a glutinous pudding with not enough texture.*

2. Thinly slice the mushrooms and chop the onion. In a large skillet, melt the butter and sauté the mushrooms and onion until the mushrooms give up their liquid and the onion is soft. Set aside to cool.

3. In a large bowl, beat the eggs until thick—about like custard sauce—then gradually beat in the milk, flour mixture, salt, a good grinding of pepper and the caraway seeds.

4. Stir in the potatoes, mushrooms and onion, scraping all the butter out of the skillet into the bowl. Blend well and spoon into the prepared baking dish. Bake for one hour, or until the pudding is firm and well browned on top. Serve right away.

MENU SUGGESTIONS

My own inclination is to have some homemade applesauce and a green salad with this hearty dish and call it a meal. To make it part of a grander meal, serve roasted chicken or broiled flank steak, Celery with Mushroom Cream Sauce (page 123), Tzimmes of Parsnips, Carrots and Dried Fruits (page 229) or Braised Red Cabbage and Apples (page 99), and a light cucumber salad.

Maggie's Sweet Potato Casserole

MAKES SIX SERVINGS

A homey, country-ish sort of casserole from my sister-in-law, Maggie Javna. What I like best about it is that each element—sweet potatoes, carrots and apples—retains its own flavor but melds perfectly with the others.

> $1\frac{1}{2}$ **pounds sweet potatoes, peeled and rinsed**
>
> **6 medium or 4 large carrots, trimmed and peeled**
>
> **2 large Granny Smith apples, peeled**
>
> $\frac{1}{4}$ **cup (packed) brown sugar**
>
> $\frac{1}{2}$ **cup apple juice, cider or water**
>
> **2 tablespoons butter or margarine, or one tablespoon of each, room temperature**
>
> **1 teaspoon salt**

1. Cut the potatoes and carrots into one-inch chunks; put them in a saucepan with water to cover and bring to a boil. Simmer until tender, about ten minutes, and then drain well.

Meanwhile, butter a two-quart baking dish; preheat the oven to 375° (350° for ovenproof glass).

2. Quarter and core the apples, being careful to remove all the seeds and hard matter. Cut the apples into $\frac{1}{4}$-inch dice or chop them in your food processor to approximately $\frac{1}{4}$-inch pieces. Transfer the apples to a large bowl.

3. Put the potatoes and carrots in your food processor (in two batches, if necessary) and chop just until the carrots are reduced to approximately $\frac{1}{2}$-inch chunks. Add the mixture to the bowl of apples. Stir in the remaining ingredients and spoon the mixture into the prepared baking dish.

Bake for 20 to 30 minutes, until the apples are crisp-tender and the other ingredients are hot. Serve right away or hold in a warm oven for up to half an hour.

MENU SUGGESTIONS

Great with turkey, of course, and baked beets with any of the sauces described on pages 68 and 69. Swiss Chard in Walnut Oil with Toasted Walnuts (page 316) and hot corn bread will be wonderful for this menu. Vegetarians can omit the turkey and still have a delicious meal.

GINGERED SWEET POTATOES

MAKES PLENTY FOR SIX SERVINGS

Think Thai when you follow this recipe and don't be alarmed by the surprise ingredient—peanut butter. You will be astonished at the wonderful flavor it imparts to the gingery mashed sweets.

2½ **pounds sweet potatoes, washed**

½ **cup chicken broth**

1 **tablespoon rice vinegar**

1 **tablespoon soy sauce**

2 **tablespoons dry sherry (fino or manzanilla)**

1 **tablespoon minced fresh ginger**

2 **garlic cloves, minced**

3 **tablespoons peanut oil**

3 **tablespoons smooth or crunchy peanut butter**

For the garnish (optional): two tablespoons chopped roasted peanuts and two tablespoons sliced scallions (green part)

1. Preheat the oven to 400°. Place the unpeeled sweet potatoes in the oven, directly on the middle rack, and bake until tender, about 60 minutes. Remove from the oven and allow to cool enough to handle.

2. Meanwhile, in a medium saucepan, bring the broth, vinegar, soy sauce, sherry, ginger and garlic to a simmer and cook, uncovered, for five minutes. Turn off the heat and blend in the oil and peanut butter.

3. Peel the warm sweet potatoes and mash them in a large bowl. Bring the broth mixture to a boil again and add it to the potatoes. Stir well and serve immediately or keep warm in a low oven. (This dish can also be successfully reheated the next day in a low oven.) If you like, garnish with chopped peanuts and sliced scallions.

MENU SUGGESTIONS

For an elegant but easy dinner, try a garlic-and-herb–stuffed veal roast with these sweet potatoes, along with a dish of Sautéed Belgian Endive with Bacon and Pecans (page 75). Warm baguettes are good, too.

MATCHMAKING: STEAK

You're making steak for dinner. What do you serve with it? Here are some possibilities from which to choose, including the Vegetable Express for hurry-up meals.

Mashed Kohlrabi and Potatoes with Tomato Cream Gravy, page 186

Collards with West Indian Pepper-and-Lime Sauce, page 180

Baked Carrots in Honey-Mustard Sauce, page 109

Herbed Potatoes Provençal, page 263

MENU SUGGESTIONS

Roasted lamb is great with these potatoes, and since they are so easy to prepare, you may have time to make Russian Salad (page 241)—altogether a perfect spring meal.

THE VEGETABLE EXPRESS

OVEN-ROASTED ROSEMARY POTATOES

MAKES SIX SERVINGS

You may want to make more than six potatoes—these disappear fast. This is not a quick-cooking recipe, but it requires very little preparation time.

6 medium-size russet potatoes (such as Idaho; about 2 pounds), washed and dried

¼ cup olive oil

2 tablespoons minced garlic

1 teaspoon powdered rosemary

Salt and fresh pepper

1. Preheat the oven to 425°; line a large baking sheet with foil and brush with a little of the olive oil. Cut the unpeeled potatoes in half lengthwise; cut each half crosswise into one-inch slices.

2. In a large bowl, mix together the oil, garlic, rosemary and a good sprinkling of salt and pepper. Add the potatoes and toss well to coat with the seasoned oil. Place each piece with one half moon–shaped flat side down on the baking sheet.

Roast for 30 minutes. Using tongs, turn the pieces over and bake for another 30 minutes; the potatoes should be crisp and brown on the outside and soft on the inside. Serve hot.

OVEN-FRIED
POTATO CAKES

MAKES 15 CAKES,
PLENTY FOR 6 SERVINGS

These lacy disks of potato are crisp, golden brown and slightly spicy. They resemble potato pancakes, but they are thinner and crunchier and since they are oven-fried instead of pan-fried, you use less oil and there's no mess and smoke from frying.

For company, top each potato cake with a dab of crème fraîche, a smidgen of caviar and a sprinkling of freshly snipped chives. Alternatively, top each cake with two or three slices of sautéed apple and a dab of sour cream.

2½ pounds russet potatoes (such as Idaho), peeled and rinsed

½ cup minced scallions (white and green parts)

½ teaspoon salt

Fresh pepper

3 tablespoons flour

¼ teaspoon cayenne pepper

Vegetable oil

1. Preheat the oven to 450°; brush oil generously on three baking sheets.

Grate the potatoes *by hand* on a box grater. Place the grated potatoes in a colander, rinse in cold water, and squeeze as dry as you can. Transfer to a large bowl.

NOTE: *Don't use your food processor for grating the potatoes.*

2. Add the scallions, salt, a good grinding of pepper, the flour and cayenne. Mix well with your hands.

Sherried Mushrooms,
page 205

Browned Rutabagas with
Mustard Sauce,
page 281

Winter Salad, page 345

VEGETABLE EXPRESS

Crisp Mushrooms,
page 208

Creamy Turnips,
page 330

3. Divide the mixture into 15 equal portions, placing 5 portions on each prepared baking sheet (one in the center and the other 4 toward the corners). Flatten each portion, patting it out to a ¼-inch-thick round about 5 inches in diameter, and lightly brush oil on the top of each one.

Important: The portions of potato look thick and solid right now, but they will lose a great deal of moisture in the hot oven and will turn out quite thin, crisp and lacy. Also, judging from their appearance, you may think that they won't hold together—but they will.

Bake for 20 minutes on the 2 center shelves of the oven. Turn the cakes over with a spatula, reverse the positions of the baking sheets in the oven (so the cakes cook evenly), and bake for 10 to 15 more minutes, until brown and crisp on both sides. Be careful not to overcook or burn them. Serve hot.

MENU SUGGESTIONS

A rather lean main course is best with these crisp potato cakes—baked chicken with herbs, roasted split Cornish hens or perhaps pot roast with pan juices. With the poultry, serve Artichokes Provençal (page 26), Asparagus with Mushrooms (page 34) or Stir-fried Green Beans (page 57). With pot roast, choose Baked Carrots in Honey-Mustard Sauce (page 109) or Stir-fried Cabbage (page 98). In either case, finish up with green salad.

PUMPKIN

BUYING AND STORING

The pumpkins sold for jack-o'-lanterns are not (usually) the edible variety. For cooking you must be sure to buy edible pumpkins such as pie pumpkins, sugar pumpkins or cheese pumpkins. Miniature pumpkins called Jack Be Littles are also good to eat.

Whatever kind you purchase, look for pumpkins that are heavy for their size, have a dense sound when you rap the shell with your knuckles, and have a smooth skin with no soft or rotten spots.

Store pumpkins in a cool place (not the refrigerator) until needed; they'll last for weeks.

NOTES TO THE COOK

Pumpkin looks virtually unassailable from the outside—how do you cut and peel such a hard, tough character? Actually, it's quite easy to do when you break the pumpkin down (literally) into smaller pieces.

Preparing: With a small sharp knife, cut out and discard the stem end. With a large heavy knife, carefully cut the pumpkin in half crosswise or top to bottom. Scrape out as much stringy matter and seeds as you can with a spoon; leave the rest for now, while you peel.

Peeling: Place the pumpkin, cut side down, on a cutting board and use a sharp serrated knife to slice off the skin, working from top to bottom. When that's done, cut each big piece in half and use your small knife to cut out the remaining strings and any spongy bits of flesh.

Forget jack-o'-lanterns for a moment and think of edible pumpkin as just another kind of winter squash, which of course it is. It's a squash we're more accustomed to carving than cooking, but edible pumpkin makes a handsome side dish in autumn and an interesting change from the other hard-skinned squashes.

Because of its size, pumpkin is a little more awkward to prepare than some of the other winter squashes, but it's still quite manageable. Of the four recipes in this section, two use large fresh pumpkins (easy), one uses mini pumpkins (easier), and a fourth uses canned pumpkin purée (easiest).

NOTE: *Homemade fresh pumpkin purée is reputed to be delicate and wonderful, a revelation compared to canned purée. Sometimes it is, but other times it can be bland and watery. I rarely make it.*

HOT PEPPER IN OTHER FORMS

Fresh hot peppers are wonderful, but you can get that heat and flavor in many other forms, from powder to sauce.

Chile powder: Pure ground chile powder is simply dried chiles ground to a powder. It may be mild, hot or very hot—you'll have to try it to find out which. (Pure chile powder is *not* the same as our American chili powder, which is a readymade blend of ground chiles, cumin, oregano and other herbs and spices.)

Cayenne is ground dried cayenne pepper, very hot indeed. Use it cautiously.

Paprika: Certain sweet red peppers are ground to make paprika, which can be sweet, hot or very hot. Hungarian paprika is the best.

Hot pepper flakes (also called red pepper flakes or crushed red pepper) are flakes of dried red pepper, used for conveniently spicing up any dish—including pizza.

Hot pepper sauce: Where there used to be only a few, now there are many commercially prepared hot sauces, made with different kinds of red or green hot peppers, each sauce seasoned differently, with vinegar, garlic, salt, tomatoes and so on.

MENU SUGGESTIONS

Include this pumpkin dish in a Tex-Mex meal of do-it-yourself tacos, rice and a salsa or two (pages 62 and 214). For the tacos, provide grated Monterey Jack or cheddar cheese, shredded lettuce, chopped tomatoes, sour cream and guacamole (page 44).

PUMPKIN AND BLACK BEANS

MAKES PLENTY FOR SIX SERVINGS

Pumpkin and black beans, used separately, are common in Caribbean cooking and they come together perfectly in this side dish. Perhaps it's because the idea for this dish came from the ingredients used in Cuban-style black bean soup.

- 4 slices bacon
- 2 tablespoons vegetable oil (not olive oil)
- 1 medium onion, chopped
- 2 garlic cloves, minced
- $2\frac{1}{2}$ pounds edible pumpkin, prepared and peeled (see Notes to the Cook)
- $\frac{1}{2}$ teaspoon powdered dried oregano
- $\frac{1}{8}$ teaspoon powdered dried thyme
- Salt and fresh pepper to taste
- Hot pepper sauce to taste
- $\frac{1}{2}$ cup dry sherry (fino or manzanilla)
- $\frac{1}{4}$ cup water
- $1\frac{1}{4}$ cups cooked black beans (one $10\frac{1}{2}$-ounce can), rinsed and drained

1. In a large skillet, cook the bacon until crisp; drain on paper towels and set aside.

2. Pour all but one tablespoon of the bacon fat out of the skillet, and add the vegetable oil. Sauté the onion and garlic over medium-low heat until soft.

Meanwhile, cut the pumpkin in $\frac{1}{2}$-inch cubes.

3. Add the herbs, salt, pepper, hot pepper sauce, sherry and water to the skillet and stir well. Add the pumpkin cubes and black beans and stir again. Cover the skillet and simmer just until the pumpkin is tender, about 20 minutes. Uncover the skillet and simmer, stirring, until most of the liquid has evaporated. Add more salt if needed.

Transfer to a serving dish, crumble the bacon on top, and serve right away.

INDIVIDUAL PUMPKIN-APRICOT-PECAN PUDDINGS

MAKES SIX SERVINGS

It is unusual to have little puddings as side dishes, but these are unusual puddings. Very pumpkin-y, crunchy with pecans—and they have very little sugar, getting their sweetness instead from spices, vanilla and apricots.

$1\frac{1}{2}$ cups canned pumpkin purée (most of a 1-pound can)

3 tablespoons brown sugar

2 tablespoons butter or margarine, melted and cooled

2 eggs

1 tablespoon half-and-half or heavy cream

$\frac{1}{2}$ teaspoon vanilla extract

$\frac{1}{2}$ teaspoon each cinnamon, powdered ginger and nutmeg

$\frac{1}{4}$ teaspoon each ground cloves and allspice

$\frac{1}{8}$ teaspoon salt

$\frac{1}{2}$ cup chopped pecans

$\frac{1}{2}$ cup chopped dried apricots

1. Butter six 6-ounce custard cups; preheat the oven to 375° (350° for ovenproof glass).

In a large bowl, whisk together all the ingredients except the pecans and apricots.

2. Stir in the pecans and apricots, and spoon the mixture into the prepared custard cups. Place the cups on a jelly roll pan (for convenience) and bake for 25 minutes, until a toothpick inserted in the center of a pudding comes out almost clean. Let the puddings cool for ten minutes on a wire rack, then run a knife around each one and turn over onto individual plates.

If you prefer, turn the puddings one at a time onto a large spatula or pancake turner, then slide each one off the spatula onto a serving platter large enough to hold all six. Serve hot or warm.

Chili oil is vegetable oil infused with hot peppers and is an important seasoning in Asian cooking.

Bottled and canned peppers: The proliferation of products, from jars of pickled and unpickled jalapeños to canned whole Anaheims and marinated Tuscan peppers, has made hot peppers available to everyone. Thank heaven.

MENU SUGGESTIONS

Turkey is the obvious choice here and it's a good one, although roasted or baked chicken is great, too. To accompany these, any of the basic asparagus recipes (page 36) will be wonderful, as will greens, green beans or Scallions in Piquant Sauce (page 198). For a meatless dinner, have one of the bean dishes (pages 40 to 53) instead of turkey.

THE VEGETABLE EXPRESS

BAKED MINIATURE PUMPKINS WITH SPICED BUTTER

MAKES SIX SERVINGS

These mini pumpkins are really squashlike, and the preparation could hardly be easier. The spices will remind you of pumpkin pie.

6 miniature edible pumpkins (each about ½ pound)

3 tablespoons butter or margarine or a combination of both

½ teaspoon cinnamon

¼ teaspoon ground ginger

⅛ teaspoon ground cloves

Salt (optional)

1. Preheat the oven to 375°. Cut off the top of each pumpkin about one inch down. Scrape out the seeds and strings.

2. Melt the butter and stir in the spices, adding a little salt if you like. Brush spiced butter inside the tops and bottoms of the pumpkins; spoon any excess butter into the bottoms.

Replace the tops, put the pumpkins on a baking sheet, and bake for 35 to 40 minutes, until the pumpkins can be pierced easily with the point of a knife. Serve hot.

MENU SUGGESTIONS

While the pumpkins bake, prepare Cornmeal Pan-fried Okra (page 214) and sauté some trout. Something green and crunchy is a good idea, too—a lettuce or cucumber salad. If you don't care for fish, Rutabagas and Vegetables in Spicy Tomato Sauce (page 282) works well in the menu.

WEST INDIAN–STYLE CURRIED PUMPKIN

MAKES PLENTY FOR SIX SERVINGS

Give your company menu an ethnic flavor with an unusual vegetable stew that has a fair number of ingredients but is not at all hard to make. Raw tomatoes, added at the very end, give the stew freshness and texture.

1 medium onion

1 red bell pepper, cored, seeded and deveined

2 tablespoons butter

2 tablespoons peanut oil

2 garlic cloves, minced

2½ pounds edible pumpkin, prepared and peeled (see Notes to the Cook)

2 medium-size firm tomatoes, stem ends removed (about 1 pound) *(Even winter plum tomatoes from the supermarket will work here, as long as they are firm and not mushy.)*

2 tablespoons flour

2 teaspoons mild curry powder, or 1 teaspoon mild and 1 teaspoon hot *(To make your own curry powder, see page 252.)*

¼ teaspoon hot red pepper flakes

1 cup white wine

½ cup chicken or vegetable broth

Salt and fresh pepper

1. Chop the onion and dice the pepper. In a large skillet, melt the butter and oil together and sauté the onion, pepper and garlic over low heat until soft.

Meanwhile, cut the pumpkin into one-inch cubes and dice the tomatoes.

TOMATILLOS

Fresh tomatillos (toe-ma-TEE-os), a staple of Mexican cooking, look like little green tomatoes with tissue-thin, papery husks wrapped around them. When raw, they are crisp and tart—delicious in salads, on tostadas or in tacos, or chopped up for un-cooked salsas; cooked tomatillos are soft and more mellow, perfect for puréed sauces or cooked salsa, or for combining with raw vegetables in yet another kind of salsa.

When you buy tomatillos, you'll find a variety of colors from light green to yellow-green to purple-green. The husks are usually still attached, but if they're not, it's no problem as long as the tomatillo itself is firm and glossy with no soft or rotten spots. Store tomatillos in a cool, dry place; they'll last for about two weeks.

Most tomatillo recipes call for you to peel off and discard the papery husks and wash the tomatillos well since the skin has a somewhat sticky, waxy feel; other recipes require dry-roasting the tomatillos in their husks. If you've never eaten tomatillos (or even if you have), try the salsa recipe on page 62 for a terrific introduction.

2. Add the flour and curry powder to the skillet, and cook, stirring, for one minute. Add the hot pepper flakes, wine and broth and stir well. Simmer, stirring, until the sauce is smooth and slightly thickened. Season well with salt and pepper.

3. Stir in the pumpkin, cover the skillet, and simmer until the pumpkin is tender, about 15 minutes. Add the tomatoes and more salt and pepper, if needed, and serve hot.

MENU SUGGESTIONS

This is a strong and interesting dish, so the main course can be simple (roasted pork or chicken, baked ham, fried fish or shrimp), accompanied by rice garnished with chopped peanuts or by a mixture of rice and pigeon peas. Offer a condiment or two, perhaps a chutney or Quick-pickled Cukes and Sweet Onions (page 144).

RUTABAGAS

BUYING AND STORING

Smaller is better where rutabagas are concerned, but small specimens are not so easy to find. Small or medium-size rutabagas—about four inches in diameter—will be sweeter and not quite so aggressively flavored, and the flesh will be more tender, too. Large rutabagas are extremely dense (and therefore harder to cut), may have woody cores, and will probably be bitter tasting.

Buy firm rutabagas that are heavy for their size, with smooth skins and no cracks or splits. The skin may be tan or brown with shadings of purple or green, but unless you buy rutabagas at a farmers' market or health food store, that pretty skin will probably be coated with a film of wax. The wax is disgusting, but happily it comes right off when you peel a rutabaga.

Store rutabagas at room temperature for about a week or in a plastic bag in the refrigerator for at least two weeks and probably longer.

NOTES TO THE COOK

Trimming: Slice off the stem end, including all the bumps and ridges and any little sprouting leaves; cut a slice off the root end, too.

Peeling: Use a swivel-blade vegetable peeler (or any other peeler you prefer) to remove all the wax and the skin below it. Clean off the blade of the peeler a couple of times during the peeling so you aren't depositing wax back on the flesh.

Rutabagas are sometimes (mistakenly) called yellow turnips, and most people feel about rutabagas the way they feel about turnips: They either love them or loathe them. Rutabagas are certainly as strongly flavored as turnips, but they're also sweeter and not as biting. If you're in a crusading mood, a good way to get rutabaga haters to give the vegetable a second chance is to feed them either Mashed Rutabagas and Potatoes (page 280) or Fluffy Baked Rutabaga with Melted Cheese (page 285), both of which tone down the strong flavor into something a lot mellower.

PANTRY

MUSTARDS

Prepared mustards run the gamut from mild to fiery and smooth to grainy. American-style mustards are generally the mildest, but some European mustards can be both mild and sweet (or sweet-sour), for instance Bavarian or Dusseldorf. Dijon mustard (made only in Dijon, France) and Dijon-style mustard (made elsewhere) contain wine and seasonings and tend to have bite, although the amount of bite depends on the brand. English and Chinese mustards are usually the hottest—they can pack quite a punch.

MENU SUGGESTIONS

This robust dish can easily be part of an all-vegetable supper—put it together with Swiss Chard Pancakes (page 312) and one of the composed salads on pages 345 to 349. If you eat meat, a beef-pork-veal meat loaf would be a terrific choice.

MASHED RUTABAGAS AND POTATOES

MAKES SIX SERVINGS

The potatoes tone down the strong flavor of the rutabaga to make a delicious combination, which is then enhanced by sour cream and scallions (and bacon, if you choose to add it).

$1\frac{1}{2}$ pounds rutabagas, trimmed and peeled

1 pound russet potatoes (such as Idahos), peeled

2 cups chicken or vegetable broth (or one $13\frac{3}{4}$-ounce can broth plus enough water to make 2 cups)

4 slices bacon (optional)

$\frac{1}{2}$ cup regular or light sour cream

$\frac{1}{4}$ cup minced scallions (white and green parts)

Salt and fresh pepper

1. Halve the rutabagas and slice them $\frac{1}{4}$ inch thick; slice the potatoes $\frac{1}{4}$ inch thick. Put all the pieces of rutabaga in a large saucepan with the broth, bring to a boil, and simmer, covered, for five minutes. Add the potatoes and simmer ten more minutes, until all the vegetables are very tender. Drain and reserve the broth.

Meanwhile, in a small skillet, cook the bacon until crisp. Drain on paper towels, then crumble or chop in small bits.

2. In the saucepan, mash the rutabagas and potatoes to the texture you prefer—chunky or smooth. Stir in the bacon, sour cream, scallions and $\frac{1}{2}$ cup of the cooking liquid. Season with salt and pepper and reheat gently. Serve hot.

BROWNED RUTABAGAS WITH MUSTARD SAUCE

MAKES SIX SERVINGS

I love these two strong flavors together. Browning the rutabagas brings out the sweetness.

2¼ pounds rutabagas, trimmed and peeled

2 tablespoons butter or margarine

1 tablespoon vegetable oil

2 tablespoons flour

1 cup chicken or vegetable broth

2 to 3 tablespoons good-quality mustard (*Try Dijon, peppercorn or wine mustard or a good grainy mustard that contains whole or crushed mustard seeds; don't use green herb mustard.*)

Salt and fresh pepper

Chopped fresh parsley, chives or dill for garnish (optional)

1. Cut the rutabagas into ½-inch cubes. In a large skillet, melt the butter and oil and brown the cubes; this will take about 20 minutes.

2. Stir in the flour and cook for one minute. Add the broth and simmer, stirring, until slightly thickened. Stir in two or three tablespoons of mustard (according to taste), cover the skillet, and cook over low heat for five minutes, until the cubes of rutabaga are completely tender. Add a little water if needed to prevent burning.

Season with salt and pepper and transfer to a serving bowl. Sprinkle with chopped herbs, if you like, and serve right away.

In addition to these basically straightforward mustards, there are dozens of flavored and herb mustards—champagne or sherry mustard, green peppercorn mustard, tarragon or dill mustard—and a whole category of mustard mixtures: honey mustard; horseradish mustard; jalapeño mustard; miso mustard; chili and garlic mustard; garlic and red pepper mustard, etc.

Prepared mustards can be stored unopened for up to a year; once the jar is open, refrigerate and use within a year.

TIP: Keep a small tin of dry English mustard on hand for vinaigrettes and other recipes that call for powdered mustard. I like to have a container of dry Chinese mustard, too, to mix with water to make a condiment to serve with Asian foods; see the sidebar on page 150.

MENU SUGGESTIONS

There's something robust about rutabagas flavored with mustard, so I like it with roast beef or corned beef and Tomatoes with Orzo and Roquefort (page 319). Follow with a salad and warm bread.

CELERY ROOT

You've probably tasted it or seen it on menus as céleri rémoulade—celery root in a mayonnaise sauce made with mustard, chopped cornichons, capers and fresh herbs. You may know it as celeriac, celeri-rave, knob celery, celery knob, turnip celery or even German celery. Whatever you call it, it's all the same roundish, hairy brown root with a distinctively celerylike flavor and a texture akin to root vegetables like parsnips or turnips.

When you buy it, look for solid, heavy celery roots with no decayed spots. Cut off any stalks or root ends, wash well, and pare off the skin with a sharp knife. Cut in half and cut out the center if you find that it is hollow, soft or fibrous. Slice or cube the flesh or cut it in matchsticks, then boil or steam until tender, 15 to 30 minutes depending on the size of the pieces.

Hot cooked celery root is delicious mashed with sour cream and a little broth, puréed with cream and butter or baked with cheese or cheese sauce. Cold cooked celery root takes well to many salad dressings, from creamy to tart, and it works in combination with other vegetables, too: Try it mixed with diced red pepper, raw or cooked carrot, potatoes, parsnips, turnips or rutabaga. Celery root can be eaten raw, too, as part of a salad or marinated in vinaigrette on its own.

RUTABAGAS AND VEGETABLES IN SPICY TOMATO SAUCE

MAKES PLENTY FOR SIX SERVINGS

This is a filling vegetable stew of rutabagas, carrots, onions and chick-peas, plus your choice of two vegetables from the list below. Served with rice, it makes a substantial vegetarian meal. Great with chicken, fish or pasta, too.

FOR THE SAUCE

1½ cups canned whole tomatoes with juice (one 14-ounce can)

1 six-ounce can tomato paste

½ cup water

1 fresh jalapeño or other hot pepper, stemmed, seeded and minced

3 garlic cloves, minced

1 tablespoon fresh lemon juice

Salt and fresh pepper to taste

¾ pound rutabagas, trimmed and peeled

2 medium carrots, trimmed and peeled

1 medium onion

1 cup cooked chick-peas, rinsed and drained

Any two of the following:

- 1 red bell pepper, stemmed, seeded and cut into 1-inch squares
- 2 medium zucchini, trimmed and cut into 1-inch chunks
- 1 medium all-purpose potato, cut into ½-inch dice
- 3 stalks celery, trimmed and cut into 1-inch pieces
- 1 cup (packed) chopped escarole
- 12 Brussels sprouts, trimmed and halved
- 12 medium-size white mushrooms, trimmed

1. Make the sauce: Combine all the sauce ingredients in a large saucepan or small stockpot, breaking up the tomatoes. Simmer, covered, for ten minutes, stirring occasionally.

2. While the sauce simmers, cut the rutabagas into ½-inch cubes, the carrots into ¼-inch slices and the onion in eighths. Stir these vegetables and the chick-peas into the sauce and simmer, covered, for ten minutes.

3. Stir in the two additional vegetables of your choice and continue simmering until all the vegetables are tender, 15 to 25 minutes. You may have to add a little water if the sauce becomes too thick.

Season with more salt and pepper if needed, and serve hot. This stew can be made ahead and reheated very successfully in the oven or on top of the stove.

MENU SUGGESTIONS

You'll find some menu ideas in the headnote, and here's one more—cheese soufflé, Cucumber Salad with Caper Dressing (page 145) and toasted whole grain bread.

FOIL-BAKED RUTABAGAS WITH BUTTER AND HERBS

MAKES SIX SERVINGS

A reminder: Rutabagas just don't cook very quickly, so the term "express" is a relative one in this case and stretches to include the facts of few ingredients and simple preparation.

1¾ pounds rutabagas, trimmed and peeled

2 tablespoons butter or margarine or a combination of both

2 tablespoons chopped fresh flat-leaf (Italian) parsley

1 tablespoon snipped fresh chives or minced shallots *(If you don't have chives or shallots, give the dish punch with a few pinches of paprika or chili powder—the blend, not the pure chile powder.)*

Salt and fresh pepper to taste

1. Preheat the oven to 400°; bring a large saucepan or pot of water to a boil. Quarter the rutabagas and cut them into ½-inch slices. Parboil the slices in the boiling water for seven minutes. Drain well, then return the slices to the saucepan and toss with the butter, herbs, salt and pepper.

2. Cut six pieces of aluminum foil, each about eight inches long, and divide the rutabaga slices among them. Bring up the ends of the foil and fold them together; pinch the sides together and fold them under to make snug packages. Place the packages on a baking sheet and bake for 20 minutes. Serve one package per person—and watch out for the steam when you open it.

MENU SUGGESTIONS

Start an autumn supper with Salad of Endive and Pears with Creamy Ginger Dressing (page 72), then follow with the rutabagas and pan-braised veal chops or chicken. Browned Carrots (page 110) are a nice touch if you have time.

FLUFFY BAKED RUTABAGAS WITH MELTED CHEESE

MAKES SIX SERVINGS

Here's another recipe in which the strong taste of rutabagas is toned down, in this case by butter, cream and egg. It results in a light, delicate casserole with bits of melted cheese throughout.

2 pounds rutabagas, trimmed and peeled

¼ pound of one of the following cheeses: Gruyère, fontina, Monterey Jack, mild cheddar, Jarlsberg or Cantal

2 tablespoons butter

⅓ cup heavy cream or half-and-half

1 egg, lightly beaten

Salt and fresh pepper to taste

1. Butter a 1½-quart baking dish or casserole; preheat the oven to 375° (350° for ovenproof glass).

Slice the rutabaga thinly and put the slices in a large saucepan with water to cover. Bring to a boil and simmer, covered, for about ten minutes, until tender. Drain well.

Meanwhile, cut the cheese in a ¼-inch dice.

2. Purée the rutabagas and remaining ingredients (except the cheese) in your food processor, in batches if necessary. (Your processor may not be able to get the mixture perfectly smooth; do the best you can.)

3. Add the diced cheese to the processor and pulse several times to combine. Spoon the mixture into the prepared baking dish and bake for 30 minutes. Serve hot.

MENU SUGGESTIONS

This is a little bit rich, so you can opt for a light company menu. Tomato Tart (page 320) is just right, with a big green salad dressed with Herb Vinaigrette (page 340). Be sure to have warm bread, crisp toasts or breadsticks to eat with the salad.

SPINACH

Spinach turned the corner in American cooking when the ubiquitous spinach salad with sliced mushrooms and crumbled bacon arrived. Up to that point, only a few well-trained grown-ups ate spinach; now it's standard fare. Actually, it's an amazingly adaptable vegetable, delicious cooked, barely wilted or raw, seasoned in the style of any number of cuisines. And even though fresh spinach is preferable, frozen spinach is blessedly convenient and quite tasty in cooked dishes.

Important: Don't cook spinach in an aluminum pan—it will discolor and pick up a metallic taste.

BUYING AND STORING

If you have a choice, buy loose fresh spinach rather than packaged fresh spinach; the quality is almost always better and you can see what you're getting. Look for crisp, dark green leaves—no wilting, no yellowing, no bruising and no decay. Once fresh spinach starts to go bad, it goes fast. If you must buy cellophane-bagged spinach, take it out of the bag as soon as you get home and discard any bad leaves.

Store fresh spinach unwashed in plastic bags in the refrigerator; it will last only a short time—a day or two—so eat it soon.

NOTES TO THE COOK

Preparing fresh spinach: Discard any wilted, yellow or decaying leaves. Nip the stems off small and medium leaves; fold big leaves in half and pull the stem away, taking at least some of the large center rib off with the stem.

Washing and drying fresh spinach: Fresh spinach is usually sandy and gritty; if you don't wash it thoroughly, you'll be grinding grains of sand between your teeth. Fill the sink with lukewarm water and slosh the spinach leaves around to loosen the grit. Lift the spinach into a colander, empty the sink, and clean it out; repeat several times with cold water. That should do it, but check the spinach before you dry it, just to be sure.

To dry the spinach, either use a salad spinner or shake off any excess water and pat dry on layers of paper towels. Keep in mind that for a salad, you want the spinach well dried; for wilting or other kinds of cooking, just shaking off the excess water may be adequate.

Thawing frozen spinach: Remove the package, place the block of frozen spinach in a bowl of cold water, and break it up as it defrosts. If the spinach is not frozen solid, break it up in a strainer and hold under cool running water until completely thawed. Use right away or refrigerate until needed.

SPINACH AND MUSHROOMS WITH HERBS

MAKES SIX SERVINGS

A plain, simple, nicely herbed dish—nothing fancy and complicated about it. Don't overcook the spinach; it shouldn't wilt to the point of mushiness—it should be springy and chewy.

1 pound white or cremini mushrooms, trimmed and cleaned

3 tablespoons olive oil

Salt and fresh pepper

1½ to 2 pounds fresh spinach, prepared, washed and well dried (see Notes to the Cook) *(If the spinach you buy is already partially stemmed, with only a few unusable leaves, you'll need only 1½ pounds; if not, you'll need 2 pounds.)*

¼ teaspoon ground rosemary

¼ teaspoon powdered thyme

½ cup white wine

1. Slice the mushrooms thin (by hand or in a food processor with the slicing blade). In a large skillet, heat the oil; add the mushrooms and sprinkle with salt and pepper. Sauté over medium heat until the mushrooms first release their liquid and then turn golden brown.

While the mushrooms cook, tear the spinach into pieces.

2. Add the herbs and wine to the skillet and simmer until the wine is reduced by half, about three minutes. Add the spinach by the handful, stirring it down as it wilts. Do not overcook. Turn off the heat right away, season with more salt and pepper if needed, and serve hot.

MENU SUGGESTIONS

An omelet with Fresh Tomato Sauce (page 322) is the perfect accompaniment for this spinach, along with an onion- or herb-topped flat bread.

VEGETABLE SANDWICHES

- **GRILLED OR SAUTÉED SLICES OF EGGPLANT WITH TOMATOES, SMOKED MOZZARELLA AND CHOPPED FRESH BASIL, ON ITALIAN BREAD OR A HERO ROLL**

- **MIXED GREEN SALAD DRESSED WITH CREAMY VINAIGRETTE, SLICED AVOCADO AND MONTEREY JACK CHEESE, ON WHOLE WHEAT OR SOURDOUGH BREAD**

- **SLICED TOMATOES, CUCUMBERS, SARDINES AND MUSTARD ON RYE**

- **WHOLE WHEAT PITA STUFFED WITH CHOPPED ZUCCHINI, TOMATOES, CUCUMBER AND SCALLIONS, WITH TAHINI DRESSING OR CUMIN VINAIGRETTE (PAGE 172)**

- **REFRIED BEANS, CHEDDAR CHEESE, SALSA, SHREDDED ICEBERG LETTUCE AND CHOPPED ONIONS ON A CRUSTY ROLL**

- **STIR-FRIED VEGETABLES AND SLICED TOFU DRESSED WITH SPICY PEANUT SAUCE (PAGE 134) OR SPRINKLED WITH TERIYAKI SAUCE, STUFFED INTO WHITE PITA BREAD**

- **ROASTED PEPPERS, SUN-DRIED TOMATOES, ARUGULA OR RADICCHIO WITH GARLIC MAYONNAISE ON A BAGUETTE**

NOT-TOO-HOT-AND-SPICY SPINACH AND CHICK-PEAS

MAKES PLENTY FOR SIX SERVINGS

This rich and filling dish has a hint—a slight afterburn—of hot pepper to enhance the rich onion, garlic and tomato sauce. Spinach and chick-peas are a wonderful combination.

> **1½ to 2 pounds fresh spinach, prepared, washed and shaken to remove any excess water (see Notes to the Cook), or two 10-ounce packages frozen chopped spinach, thawed (*If you buy fresh spinach already partially stemmed, with only a few unusable leaves, you'll need only 1½ pounds; if not, you'll need 2 pounds.*)**

> **3 tablespoons olive oil**

> **1 medium onion, chopped**

> **2 garlic cloves, minced**

> **2 tablespoons flour**

> **½ cup water**

> **1 large ripe tomato, stem end removed, chopped**

> **¼ teaspoon hot red pepper flakes**

> **1¾ cups cooked chick-peas, rinsed and drained (one 1-pound can)**

> **Salt and fresh pepper**

1. If you are using fresh spinach, heat a large skillet and add the spinach by the handful, stirring it down as it wilts. (The water clinging to the leaves will be enough to keep it from scorching.) When completely wilted but not mushy, drain the spinach in a strainer, pressing it with a big spoon to remove as much liquid as possible. Let it cool a bit.

If you are using thawed frozen spinach, put it in a strainer and press firmly with a big spoon to remove as much liquid as possible.

Chop the spinach and set aside.

2. In a large skillet, heat the olive oil and sauté the onion and garlic until softened, about five minutes. Add the flour and cook for one minute. Add the water, tomato and hot pepper flakes and cook, stirring, for a minute or two to make a chunky sauce.

3. Add the spinach and chick-peas, mix well, and season with salt and pepper. Stir over low heat until thoroughly heated, about five minutes. Add more salt and pepper if needed and serve immediately.

- **MARINATED MUSHROOMS, GOAT CHEESE AND ARUGULA ON COUNTRY WHITE BREAD OR SOURDOUGH**
- **SLICED BEETS, ROQUEFORT CHEESE AND SOFT LETTUCE ON PUMPERNICKEL, WITH A BIT OF HORSERADISH**
- **CAPONATA WITH CRISP GREENS ON A CRUSTY ROLL**
- **SPINACH, MUSHROOMS, RED ONIONS, FETA CHEESE ON A SOFT ROLL BRUSHED WITH OIL AND VINEGAR DRESSING**
- **SLICED RADISHES, TOMATO AND WATERCRESS ON BUTTERED PUMPERNICKEL**
- **ITALIAN PICKLED VEGETABLES (GIARDINIERA, PAGE 116), SLICED TOMATOES, PROVOLONE CHEESE AND ROMAINE LETTUCE ON ITALIAN BREAD OR A HERO ROLL**

MENU SUGGESTIONS

Pot-roasted chicken is delicious on this menu, with Ginger-Orange Parsnips (page 228) for a contrast in flavor with the spicy spinach. If you prefer a vegetarian meal, skip the chicken and have brown rice and Red Onion Raita with Coriander (page 221) instead.

Spinach with Warm Sesame Dressing

Makes plenty for six servings

Is it a salad or a cooked vegetable? Whichever it is, it could hardly be simpler to make. The sweet-and-tart dressing is a perfect foil for fresh spinach, and wilting gives the spinach a wonderful texture. Perfect for a light lunch or dinner.

1 tablespoon sesame seeds

1 pound fresh spinach, prepared, washed and well dried

2 tablespoons soy sauce

2 tablespoons sugar

2 tablespoons rice vinegar

2 tablespoons sesame oil

2 tablespoons peanut oil

1. In a small skillet, toast the sesame seeds over low heat, stirring constantly, until light brown; be careful not to let them burn. Set aside. Put the spinach in a large bowl.

2. In the same skillet over low heat, combine the remaining ingredients, stirring until the sugar melts. Pour the hot dressing over the spinach and toss lightly to coat and slightly wilt the spinach leaves. Transfer to a serving dish and sprinkle with the toasted sesame seeds. Serve right away.

MENU SUGGESTIONS

This spinach fits neatly into a variety of menus, from stir-fried chicken to baked ham to hamburgers. For a special meal, try it with crisp duck, Oven-roasted Rosemary Potatoes (page 270) and Squash with Dried Fruits (page 304).

THE VEGETABLE EXPRESS

QUICK SPINACH PIE

MAKES SIX SERVINGS

Frozen spinach makes this an express dish. Serve it with other vegetables and salad for a vegetarian meal or in small wedges as a first course.

1 ten-ounce package frozen chopped spinach, thawed

1 nine-inch pie crust, readymade or homemade

Salt and fresh pepper

1 small red onion, chopped

6 ounces feta cheese

1 egg plus 1 egg white

2 tablespoons regular or light sour cream

¼ cup whole or skim milk

1. Preheat the oven to 375°. Squeeze the spinach to remove as much liquid as possible.

Spread half the spinach evenly in the pie crust; sprinkle with a little salt and pepper. Spoon the onion evenly over the spinach, and crumble the feta cheese over the onion. Top with the rest of the spinach and a little more pepper (no salt).

2. Whisk together the egg, egg white, sour cream and milk and pour evenly over the spinach. Bake for about 30 minutes, until the pie is set and the crust is golden. Serve hot, warm or at room temperature.

MENU SUGGESTIONS

If you keep the menu simple, this can be one of your standby meals to make in a hurry. Basic Baked Squash (page 307) takes time to cook but almost none to prepare, so pop that in the oven while you make the spinach pie; the squash finishes cooking while the pie bakes. Meanwhile, put together a simple tomato salad (page 324) and warm some pita bread. That's all.

MATCHMAKING: PASTA WITH CHEESE

You're making pasta with cheese for dinner. What do you serve with it? Here are some possibilities from which to choose, including the Vegetable Express for hurry-up meals.

Fried Peppers with Anchovy Butter, page 247

Escarole in Tomato Sauce, page 166

Spinach and Mushrooms with Herbs, page 287

Broccoli Rabe with Anchovy and Garlic Sauce, page 84

Artichokes Provençal, page 26

Simplified Caponata with Sun-dried Tomatoes, page 152

Hearty Salad, page 342

VEGETABLE EXPRESS

Browned Carrots, page 110

Baked Miniature Pumpkins with Spiced Butter, page 276

COMPANY'S COMING

POACHED SPINACH DUMPLINGS

MAKES ABOUT 18 DUMPLINGS, 6 SERVINGS

Serve as a side dish or use these dumplings to garnish a pork roast, ham, baked fish, Cornish hens, etc. They are a cross between a vegetable and a carbohydrate—light and silky and quite delicate in flavor.

- **1½ pounds fresh spinach, prepared, washed and shaken to remove any excess water (see Notes to the Cook), or two 10-ounce packages frozen chopped spinach, thawed**
- **2 quarts (8 cups) low-salt chicken or vegetable broth**
- **2 whole eggs plus 1 egg white**
- **1¼ cups flour**
- **½ cup whole milk ricotta or part skim ricotta**
- **1 cup grated Parmesan cheese**
- **Salt and fresh pepper**

1. If you are using fresh spinach, heat a large skillet and add the spinach by the handful, stirring it down as it wilts. (The water clinging to the leaves will be enough to keep it from scorching.) When completely wilted but not mushy, drain the spinach in a strainer, pressing it with a big spoon to remove as much liquid as possible. Let it cool a bit.

If you are using thawed frozen spinach, put it in a strainer and press firmly with a big spoon to remove as much liquid as possible.

2. Put the broth in a stockpot, cover, and bring to a boil. Meanwhile, in your food processor, combine the eggs, egg white, flour, ricotta, grated cheese and a sprinkling of salt and pepper and process until smooth.

3. Add the spinach and process with a few bursts of power until the spinach is chopped; do not purée. Transfer the mixture to a bowl and add more salt and pepper if needed.

4. Cook the dumplings in two batches: For the first batch, drop nine rounded tablespoons of batter into the boiling broth, one at a time, making one layer of dumplings. Turn the heat down until the broth just simmers. Cook for ten minutes uncovered, then cover the pot and cook another ten minutes. While the dumplings cook, butter a large baking dish or jelly roll pan; preheat the oven to 325°.

When the first batch is done, remove the dumplings with a slotted spoon and transfer to a plate. Neaten them into nice round shapes by trimming off any tails of spinach or batter. Place them in the prepared baking dish. Repeat the process to make the second batch.

Warm the dumplings in the oven for 10 to 15 minutes, until piping hot. Arrange them around your main dish as a garnish or serve them separately.

MENU SUGGESTIONS

As the headnote says, the dumplings are appealing and tasty edible garnishes around any roast. If you'd rather have an all-vegetable company meal, start with White Bean and Goat Cheese Pâté on Greens (page 48) and hot French bread, followed by the dumplings surrounding Baked Carrots in Honey-Mustard Sauce (page 109), with a dish of Cauliflower with Sun-dried Tomatoes (page 116) on the side.

SQUASH, SUMMER

Summer squashes—zucchini, pattypan and yellow squash—are thin-skinned and have soft flesh that can be eaten raw as well as cooked. They're completely different from winter squashes such as acorn and butternut, which are hard-shelled and must be cooked before they can be eaten. Of course, it's a bit illogical to call them summer or winter squash since we find both kinds in the market year-round, but the names have clung stubbornly.

Along with year-round availability, there's another new wrinkle in the summer squash picture: variety. Zucchini is not just long, narrow and green anymore—it may be miniature or round or yellow. Pattypan can be pale green, white or bright yellow-orange, in sizes ranging from one inch to four or five inches in diameter. And even straightneck yellow squash is now offered in miniature size, too, although crookneck yellow squash seems to be safe for the time being.

BUYING AND STORING

All three kinds of summer squash have the best taste and texture when they are small or—at the most—medium size. Since small ones are hard to find except in summer, look for medium pattypans about three inches in diameter, zucchini that are six to eight inches long and yellow squash about six inches long.

The squash should feel heavy for its size, with no sponginess and no withered ends. The skin should be glossy, with no cuts, bruises or discoloration.

Keep summer squash unwashed in a plastic bag in the refrigerator; it should last four or five days.

NOTES TO THE COOK

Trimming: Cut ¼ to ½ inch off the ends of zucchini and yellow squash; slice off the stem end of pattypan squash.

Cleaning: Summer squash usually needs a gentle scrubbing with a soft brush or rough cloth to remove stuck-on dirt. Take care, though, because the skin is thin and breaks or scrapes off easily. Pat dry on paper towels.

ZUCCHINI RIBBONS IN GORGONZOLA SAUCE

MAKES SIX SERVINGS

There's no getting around it: Gorgonzola is a strange-smelling cheese. But it makes such a luscious sauce that you won't even mind the aroma once you taste this zucchini dish.

2 pounds medium-size zucchini (about 5 or 6, each 6 to 7 inches long), trimmed, cleaned and dried

3 tablespoons olive oil

¼ pound aged Gorgonzola cheese (*Be sure to buy the aged cheese, not the younger "dolce."*)

3 tablespoons regular or light sour cream

1. Using a mandoline or the slicing side of your metal box grater, slice the zucchini into thin lengthwise ribbons.

In a large skillet, heat the olive oil; add the zucchini ribbons and sauté over medium-low heat until tender and flexible. Be careful not to break the ribbons when you stir them during sautéing.

Transfer the zucchini to a colander, draining off any liquid in the skillet; let the ribbons continue to drain while you prepare the sauce.

2. In the same skillet, combine the Gorgonzola and sour cream over the lowest heat, stirring constantly to melt and blend. When the mixture is smooth and completely liquid, return the drained zucchini to the skillet and stir gently until hot and nicely coated with sauce. Serve immediately.

MENU SUGGESTIONS

Simple pasta—perhaps penne or fusilli—is one good choice to go with this strongly flavored dish. Another choice is Pan-fried Turnips and Potatoes with Sun-dried Tomato Relish (page 329), plus salad and good bread.

BABY VEGETABLES

Baby vegetables are having quite a vogue these days. Go to a fancy restaurant and your plate may be decorated with little bitty carrots, beets, zucchini or pattypan squash. Some baby vegetables are actually bred and grown as miniatures, while others are simply the earliest pickings of standard-size vegetables.

MENU SUGGESTIONS

I like this with the mild flavor of grilled or broiled salmon and either Peas with Toasted Almonds (page 239) or Baked Fennel with Sour Cream Sauce (page 171).

SWEET-AND-SOUR PATTYPAN SQUASH

MAKES SIX SERVINGS

A refreshing dish to make with the pretty pattypan squash you find in summer and fall. Slicing them crosswise shows off their scalloped circumference.

1¼ pounds medium-size pattypan squash (about 9 pattypans, each about 3 inches in diameter), trimmed and cleaned

1 small red onion

3 tablespoons superfine sugar

½ teaspoon salt

¼ cup balsamic or red wine vinegar

¼ cup cider vinegar

⅓ cup vegetable oil

Fresh pepper

1. Bring a large pot of water to a boil. Meanwhile, cut the squash crosswise into ⅛- to ¼-inch-thick rounds, to make slices with a pretty scalloped edge. Carefully drop the slices into the pot and parboil until barely tender, about three to five minutes. Drain and set aside.

Slice the onion as thin as possible.

2. In a large bowl, whisk the sugar, salt and vinegars until the sugar dissolves. Whisk in the oil and fresh pepper to taste.

3. Add the squash and onions and toss well. Set aside to marinate for an hour, stirring occasionally. Serve at room temperature or chilled.

YELLOW SQUASH RAITA

MAKES SIX SERVINGS

This is somewhere between a side dish and a relish, so you won't eat as much of it as you would a straight side dish. Raitas are usually served with curry, but have this one whenever you want a tangy condiment to accompany a meal.

1⅓ pounds medium-size yellow squash (about 4), trimmed, cleaned and dried

1½ tablespoons butter or margarine

1 small onion, chopped

1 cup plain (unflavored) yogurt

1 small fresh green chile, cored, seeded, deveined and minced

¼ teaspoon ground cumin

Salt and fresh pepper to taste

1. Shred the squash by hand on the large holes of a box grater; set aside.

In a large skillet, melt the butter and sauté the onion until lightly browned. Add the squash and sauté for about five minutes, until tender. The squash will give up a lot of liquid, so drain it in a colander and press with the back of a spoon to remove even more liquid.

2. In a large bowl, whisk together the yogurt, half of the minced chile, ⅛ teaspoon of the cumin, and salt and pepper. Stir in the onion and squash. Chill the raita until serving time and then, if needed, add more salt and pepper, the remaining ⅛ teaspoon of cumin and the rest of the minced chile.

These babies are cute—but they're also expensive and not always as tasty to eat as they are pretty to look at. Some are tastier than others: Baby green beans, beets (and beet greens), lettuce, potatoes and artichokes are delicious, while baby carrots, broccoli, eggplant and corn are rather bland.

Baby vegetables do make an impressive presentation as crudités, garnishes, side dishes or in salads, so you may want to serve them on special occasions. Look for perfect specimens that are firm, without blemishes or bruises. Sauté them in butter or oil or steam lightly; be very careful not to overcook them. You'll need at least ¼ pound per person for side dish servings.

MENU SUGGESTIONS

Build an Indian-influenced meal around this raita by serving it with lamb or chicken korma, Not-Too-Hot-and-Spicy Spinach and Chick-Peas (page 288), basmati rice and Indian bread. If you want to go all out, offer a variety of condiments (such as chopped scallions, chopped roasted peanuts and chutney) and some baked plantains as well.

RECYCLING IN THE KITCHEN

This information comes to us courtesy of The EarthWorks Group, authors of a wonderful book called *The Recycler's Handbook*. The section quoted here deals with food waste and the simple ways you can recycle leftover food.

1. GIVE IT AWAY

- MOST COMMUNITIES HAVE FOOD BANKS OR HOMELESS SHELTERS. THEY ALWAYS NEED FOOD. IF YOU HAVE A LOT OF EXTRA FRESH FOOD, CONSIDER DONATING IT TO THEM.

2. FIND A PLACE TO PUT IT

- START YOUR OWN COMPOST PILE, OR FIND A NEIGHBOR WHO'S GOT ONE.

- CALL YOUR PUBLIC WORKS DEPARTMENT TO FIND OUT IF THERE'S MUNICIPAL COMPOSTING IN YOUR COMMUNITY.

3. SET UP

- KEEP A LARGE YOGURT-TYPE CONTAINER (HOLDS ABOUT A QUART) BY YOUR SINK OR CUTTING BOARD.

- SOME PEOPLE ALSO KEEP A LARGE CONTAINER—LIKE A FIVE-GALLON PLASTIC BUCKET OR GARBAGE PAIL WITH A TIGHT-FITTING LID (TO KEEP ODORS FROM ESCAPING)—IN THE KITCHEN UNDER THE SINK OR WHEREVER THERE IS ROOM.

MENU SUGGESTIONS

Here's a perfect partner for a delicious Greek Salad (page 344), accompanied by toasted pita bread. If you want to jazz up the meal, add a bowl of taramasalata and a plate of stuffed grape leaves.

MINTED ZUCCHINI TABBOULEH SALAD

MAKES PLENTY FOR SIX SERVINGS

In this version of tabbouleh, zucchini shares the spotlight with bulgur wheat, tomatoes and red onion. Mint, parsley and fresh lemon juice add brightness.

3/4 cup chicken or vegetable broth

6 tablespoons bulgur wheat

2 medium-size zucchini (each 6 to 7 inches long), trimmed and cleaned

1 medium-size ripe tomato, stem end removed

1/4 cup diced red onion

2 tablespoons minced fresh mint

1/4 cup minced fresh flat-leaf (Italian) parsley

2 1/2 tablespoons fresh lemon juice

1/3 cup olive oil

1 garlic clove, minced

Salt and fresh pepper to taste

1. In a small saucepan, bring the broth to a boil. Stir in the bulgur, lower the heat as much as possible, and cover the pan tightly. Cook for 16 to 18 minutes, until the bulgur is tender and chewy (but not mushy) and all the liquid is gone. Uncover the pan and continue cooking and fluffing the bulgur for another minute or two to dry it out.

2. Meanwhile, bring a pot of water to a boil; dice the zucchini and parboil it for three to five minutes, until tender. Dice the tomato.

3. In a large bowl, combine the bulgur, zucchini, tomato and all the remaining ingredients and toss well. Let stand for about half an hour so the flavors have time to mingle, then chill and serve.

THE VEGETABLE EXPRESS

SAUTÉED PATTYPAN SQUASH WITH RED PEPPER SAUCE

MAKES SIX SERVINGS

Bright yellow miniature pattypan squash and bright red roasted peppers from a jar make this a beautiful and speedy dish.

FOR THE SAUCE

1 seven-ounce jar roasted red peppers, drained

1 tablespoon olive oil

1 tablespoon red wine vinegar

½ teaspoon paprika

Salt and fresh pepper to taste

―――――――

30 miniature (baby) pattypan squash, trimmed, cleaned and dried (*If you can't get miniatures, feel free to use small pattypans, trimmed and cut into 1-inch pieces.*)

2 tablespoons olive oil

3 garlic cloves, minced

1. In your food processor or blender, purée the sauce ingredients. Correct the seasoning and set the sauce aside.

2. If any of the squashes are larger than one inch in diameter, cut them in half. In a large skillet, heat the olive oil, add the squash and a sprinkling of salt and pepper, and sauté until crisp-tender and lightly browned. Add the garlic and continue sautéing just until the garlic is lightly browned.

Spoon the sauce onto a serving platter, arrange the squash on top, and serve right away.

4. COMPOST YOUR FOOD

- PUT FOOD SCRAPS IN THE YOGURT CONTAINER WHILE YOU'RE FIXING MEALS.

- WHENEVER THE YOGURT CONTAINER IS FULL, DUMP IT INTO THE LARGER CONTAINER...OR TAKE IT OUT DIRECTLY TO THE COMPOST PILE.

- THE LID ON THE LARGE CONTAINER KEEPS THE SMELL INSIDE; OPEN IT AS LITTLE AS POSSIBLE.

- OTHER WAYS TO KEEP THE SMELL FROM BECOMING A PROBLEM: EMPTY IT FREQUENTLY. AND TRY SPRINKLING SAWDUST ON TOP OF FOOD. IT'S LIKE COMPOST "KITTY LITTER," ABSORBING AND MASKING ODORS. NEED SAWDUST? MOST LUMBER-YARDS GLADLY GIVE IT TO YOU FOR FREE.

- TAKE FOOD SCRAPS FROM YOUR BUCKET TO THE COMPOST PILE REGULARLY AND MIX THEM IN THOROUGHLY.

- REMEMBER: TO AVOID BEES AND FLIES, ALWAYS COVER KITCHEN SCRAPS WITH A LAYER OF LEAVES, GRASS OR DIRT.

MENU SUGGESTIONS

For an express meal, serve the squash with readymade cheese or mushroom ravioli sprinkled with freshly grated Parmesan cheese. Green salad and hot Italian bread complete the menu.

VEGETABLE APPETIZERS

Fancy Canapés: Mash cream cheese with some sour cream and season well with fresh herbs, anchovy paste, jalapeño jelly or any another favorite flavoring. Cut raw carrots and zucchini on the diagonal in $1/8$-inch slices; arrange the slices on a platter and pipe a rosette of seasoned cream cheese on each one. Top with a sliver of pickle, half an olive or a sprig of parsley.

Spring Bites: Cut mini pita pockets across the diameter to make half pockets. Stuff each half pocket with a little mustard-spiked mayonnaise, a narrow strip or two of thinly sliced baked ham and a lightly cooked fresh asparagus tip.

Vegetable Nachos: Arrange blue corn tortilla chips edge to edge on an ovenproof serving platter. Sprinkle generously with grated Monterey Jack cheese or queso blanco. Dot with spoonfuls of highly seasoned ratatouille, caponata, salsa, curried lentils or other favorite vegetable mixture. Heat in a 350° oven until the cheese is bubbling.

COMPANY'S COMING

STUFFED ZUCCHINI BARQUETTES

MAKES SIX SERVINGS OF TWO ZUCCHINI BOATS EACH

Individual presentations make your guests feel special, and these little boats stuffed with a savory rice and pine nut mixture are no exception. You'll detect a light flavor of orange and lime, as well as parsley and capers.

- **2 whole bulbs garlic**
- **3 medium-size zucchini (each 7 to 8 inches long), trimmed and cleaned**
- **2 tablespoons regular or low-fat mayonnaise**
- **2 tablespoons regular or light sour cream**
- **$1/4$ cup orange juice**
- **2 tablespoons fresh lime juice**
- **$1/4$ cup (packed) fresh flat-leaf (Italian) parsley leaves**
- **$3/4$ cup cold cooked rice**
- **$1/2$ cup pine nuts**
- **2 tablespoons small (nonpareil) capers**
- **Salt and fresh pepper**

1. Preheat the oven to 400°. Place the garlic bulbs in a little baking dish and roast for 25 to 30 minutes, until the flesh is soft. (Squeeze each bulb firmly; if it gives under pressure, the garlic inside is properly cooked.) Set aside to cool.

2. Halve each zucchini lengthwise and then crosswise; you'll have 12 pieces. Using a melon baller and a small paring knife, hollow out each piece to make a little boat with $1/4$-inch-thick walls and floor.

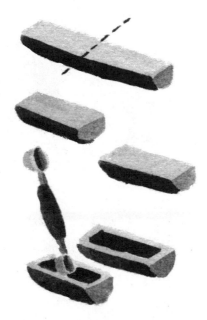

3. Bring one inch of water to a boil in the bottom part of a vegetable steamer; place the boats upside down on the rack above it and steam for about five minutes, just until crisp-tender. Carefully remove the boats, cool them under cold water, and let them drain and finish cooling upside down on a wire rack.

4. Meanwhile, make the dressing: Slice off the stem ends of the roasted garlic bulbs and squeeze out the soft flesh into your food processor (see page 28 for more on roasted garlic). Add the mayonnaise, sour cream, orange and lime juices and parsley and process until smooth.

5. Transfer ½ cup of the dressing to a small bowl and stir in the rice, nuts and capers; season to taste with salt and pepper. Pat the zucchini boats dry and spoon the rice mixture into each one, mounding it neatly. Top each boat with a spoonful of the remaining sauce. Serve chilled or at room temperature.

MENU SUGGESTIONS

Your guests will love these boats served with split, roasted Cornish hens and Fennel and Chick-Peas in Cumin Vinaigrette (page 172). A flat herb-sprinkled bread will be a good accompaniment.

SQUASH, WINTER

Winter squashes are the hard-shelled ones—acorn, butternut, buttercup, delicata, dumpling and so on. They are harvested fully mature in the fall and then kept in cold storage so they are available all winter or, in some cases, all year. Winter squashes range in size from the small dumpling and Golden Nugget to the enormous banana and Hubbard; when you read the recipes in this section, you'll see that my preference is for the smaller squashes.

BUYING AND STORING

Buy nicely shaped squash that is heavy for its size and has good color but a dull (not shiny) finish. Avoid major nicks, cracks and bruises, as well as soft spots or mold. Acorn squash should have some orange patches on the skin; butternut should be an all-over peachy tan with no hint of green.

If you can stash your winter squashes in a cool, dry place (not the refrigerator), they'll last for at least a month.

NOTES TO THE COOK

Scrubbing: Hard-shelled squashes can be quite grimy, even caked with mud, especially if you buy them at a farmstand or farmers' market. Give them a good scrubbing with a vegetable brush.

Cutting: Be careful when cutting winter squash because the skin and flesh are tough to get a knife through. Use a large, heavy knife and work slowly, gently rocking either the knife or the squash as you cut. I find it's easier, when you are cutting a squash in half, to cut off the stem end first (if possible) and then to make two cuts—one down each side—and pull the two halves apart.

ACORN SQUASH WITH APPLES AND CIDER GLAZE

MAKES SIX SERVINGS

This is a perfect autumn dish, sweet and mellow. Apples and squash, especially the mild acorn, complement each other nicely. Great with ham, pork or poultry.

2 pounds small acorn squash, scrubbed

3 cooking apples *(Choose Cortland, Rome Beauty, Northern Spy, Jonathan, Paula Red or Baldwin apples.)*

1 cup apple cider or juice

1 tablespoon butter or margarine

1 tablespoon cider vinegar

1 tablespoon light brown sugar

¼ teaspoon cinnamon

¼ teaspoon ground ginger

Salt and fresh pepper to taste

1. Cut off and discard both ends of each squash. Cut each squash in half lengthwise and scoop out the seeds and strings. Cut each half crosswise into ¾-inch thick-slices; you should have 16 or 18 pieces of squash.

Peel, quarter and core the apples; be sure to remove all the seeds and hard matter. Cut the quarters in half lengthwise.

2. In a large skillet over low heat, combine the remaining ingredients, stirring until the butter and sugar melt. Arrange the squash pieces in the skillet (in one layer if possible) and baste with the sauce. Bring to a boil, cover the skillet, and simmer over low heat for 15 minutes. Turn the squash and simmer, covered, 10 to 15 minutes more, until tender.

3. Turn the squash again, add the apple quarters, and baste with the sauce. Partially cover the skillet and simmer, basting occasionally, until the apples are tender and the sauce has reduced to a glaze, about ten more minutes. (If the sauce is still thin after six to seven minutes of simmering, remove the cover completely for the last few minutes.) Serve hot.

MENU SUGGESTIONS

Ham or pork roast is a clear choice here, but Swedish meatballs or grilled sausages are good matches, too. I like Warm Cauliflower with Creamy Tarragon Dressing (page 117) with any of these. For a meatless meal, take a different tack: Delicate Cabbage Custard (page 100) and Split Pea and Bulgur Wheat Pilaf (page 43).

Thanksgiving dinner requires the fulfillment of family expectations: In my house, it wouldn't be Thanksgiving without mashed potatoes and browned Brussels sprouts. At the same time, festive meals are a good opportunity to show off your cooking skills and try something just a little bit different. Here are some suggestions:

Buttery Green Beans with Pecan Crumbs,
page 56

Baby Beets and Beet Greens,
page 70

MENU SUGGESTIONS:

Lots of rich, sweet flavor here, so make the rest of the meal a counterpoint—sliced pork or turkey, white or wild rice and Corn and Lima Succotash in Lemon-Dill Cream (page 139). Caulifritters (page 118) are good in place of meat.

SQUASH WITH DRIED FRUITS

MAKES SIX SERVINGS

I like this best when it's made with a mix of squashes. Sweet and mellow—absolutely delectable, with a lovely orange and lemon overtone.

- 3 pounds orange-fleshed squash, scrubbed *(These include acorn, buttercup, butternut, dumpling, kabocha, Golden Nugget and delicata.)*

- 3 tablespoons butter or margarine or a combination of both

- 1 cup dried fruit (cut into $\frac{1}{4}$-inch bits) and whole raisins *(Use a selection of your favorites— peaches, apricots, prunes, pears, dark and/or light raisins.)*

- 1 cup orange juice

- Grated rind of one lemon

- Salt

1. Cut each squash in half and scrape out the seeds. Cut each half in four pieces. Put all the pieces in a large saucepan with water to cover. Cover the pan and bring to a boil; uncover the pan and simmer for 10 to 15 minutes, or until just tender when pierced by a knife.

Drain the squash in a colander and run cold water over it until cool enough to handle. Peel or pare the skin from each piece.

2. In a large skillet or saucepan, melt the butter and stir in the dried fruit, orange juice, grated lemon rind and a sprinkling of salt. Simmer for several minutes, until the raisins are plumped and the fruit is soft. Add the squash and stir gently but thoroughly, breaking up the squash somewhat. Simmer, stirring often, until the sauce is reduced to a glaze. Serve hot.

SAVORY BUTTERCUP SQUASH AND CHEESE GRATIN

MAKES SIX SERVINGS

Mild, soft and cheesy—almost baby food. Very comforting.

2 pounds buttercup squash, scrubbed

½ cup chicken or vegetable broth

½ cup regular or light sour cream

Salt and fresh pepper

1 cup (loosely packed) grated sharp cheddar cheese (about 2½ ounces)

¼ cup dry bread crumbs

1 tablespoon cold butter

1. Butter a 1½-quart baking dish; preheat the oven to 375° (350° for ovenproof glass).

Cut the squash in half, scrape out the seeds, and place the halves, cut side down, on a lightly oiled piece of foil on a baking sheet. Bake for 45 minutes, or until just tender when pierced with a knife.

2. When the squash is cool enough to handle, scoop out the flesh and mash it in a large bowl with the broth and sour cream. Season with salt and pepper. Stir in ¾ cup of the grated cheese.

3. Spread the mixture in the prepared baking dish and sprinkle first with the remaining grated cheese and then with the bread crumbs. Dot with bits of cold butter and bake for 20 minutes. Serve hot.

Salad of Endive and Pears with Creamy Ginger Dressing, page 72

Spicy Browned Brussels Sprouts and Carrots, page 93

Carrot Pancakes, page 106

Cauliflower with Cheese Sauce, page 114

Celery-Almond Timbale, page 122

Crisp Onion and Apple Fritters, page 222

Tzimmes of Parsnips, Carrots and Dried Fruits, page 229

Gingered Sweet Potatoes, page 269

Individual Pumpkin-Apricot-Pecan Puddings, page 275

Mashed Rutabagas and Potatoes, page 280

Squash Soufflé, page 308

Stuffed Zucchini Barquettes, page 300

Sage-roasted Turnips, page 328

MENU SUGGESTIONS

This is a light but filling dish to serve with Swiss Chard with Bacon and Black-eyed Peas (page 311) and plenty of corn bread.

VEGETABLE PURÉES

Puréeing is one of the simplest, most satisfying ways to prepare vegetables.

A good purée begins with freshly cooked *hot* vegetables—boiled, steamed, sautéed or baked—or a couple of cups of reheated leftover vegetables. Put the drained hot vegetables in your food processor and pulse until broken down into small bits. Gradually add one or more liquids or semiliquids, salt, fresh pepper and seasonings, processing the mixture until it is thoroughly blended, smooth and almost creamy. (Liquid must be added gradually, in small amounts, so that the purée does not become too soft and loose.)

Vegetables to purée: carrots; parsnips; peas; beans; beets; broccoli; cauliflower; eggplant; escarole, spinach, Swiss chard and other soft greens; rutabaga; turnips; acorn, butternut or other winter squash (without skin). Try some combinations, too: carrots and parsnips, broccoli and cauliflower, acorn squash and carrots.

MENU SUGGESTIONS

Chicken fajitas or burritos go really well with this squash, with rice and beans on the side. If you don't want to serve poultry, substitute Tomato-baked Chick-Peas (page 47).

BUTTERNUT SQUASH WITH CORIANDER SAUCE

MAKES SIX SERVINGS

Squash braised in this manner is firm and moist but not watery (the way steamed squash tends to be). The sauce is spicy but not too hot. Don't forget to sprinkle with lime juice—it makes all the difference.

3 pounds butternut squash, scrubbed

1 cup chicken or vegetable broth

Salt and fresh pepper

½ cup (packed) fresh coriander leaves

1 garlic clove, quartered

2 pickled jalapeños, stemmed and sliced thin

2 tablespoons vegetable oil

1 lime cut in 6 wedges

1. Prepare the squash for cooking: Cut off the stem ends and then cut each squash in two pieces—the bulb and the straight neck. Cut each piece in quarters lengthwise and scrape out the seeds. Peel the pieces with a sharp knife, then cut the flesh into 1½-inch pieces.

2. Place the pieces in a large skillet and pour the broth over them. Sprinkle with salt and pepper. Bring to a simmer, cover the skillet, and cook for 15 minutes, or until the squash is tender. Remove the squash with a slotted spoon and keep it warm on a serving platter in a low oven. Simmer the broth until reduced to about ¼ cup.

3. Make the sauce: In your food processor, mince the coriander leaves with the reduced broth, the garlic, half the slices of jalapeño and the oil. Season with salt and pepper.

Pour the coriander sauce over the hot squash and sprinkle with the juice of two lime wedges. Garnish with the remaining lime wedges and jalapeño slices. Serve hot.

FIVE FILLINGS FOR BASIC BAKED SQUASH

MAKES SIX SERVINGS

Baked squash is one of the world's simplest vegetable side dishes to prepare. For instance, my friend Jenny Snider takes a nice two-pound buttercup squash and puts it—whole—in the oven to bake for 1 to 1½ hours at 375°. She goes about her business and when her kitchen timer rings, she cuts the now-soft squash in half, scrapes out the seeds, and serves the halves with butter. What could be easier?

You can take this a delicious step further by cutting the squash in half before baking and filling each half with a tasty mixture, which will be mashed into the tender cooked flesh. Here you have a choice of five different fillings, savory or sweet.

For six servings you'll need three squashes, each about one pound; the best choices are buttercup, butternut, acorn, dumpling, delicata or kabocha squash. Preheat the oven to 400°. Cut the squashes in half, scrape out the seeds, and place each half, cut side up, on a piece of foil large enough to wrap it completely.

In the hollow of *each* half, put one of the following fillings:

- Sliver of butter, ½ tablespoon honey, 1 teaspoon bourbon
- Sliver of butter, one tablespoon cranberry jelly (whole berry jelly is best) and one teaspoon orange marmalade
- Sliver of butter, one teaspoon brown sugar sprinkled over the flesh, a little grated fresh ginger and a shake of cinnamon
- One tablespoon of your favorite mild or hot mango chutney
- One tablespoon barbecue sauce

Bring two opposite edges of the foil up around the squash and pinch or fold them tightly closed; pinch or fold the open ends closed to make a nice, airtight package. Place the wrapped squash halves on a baking sheet and bake for 45 minutes, or until the squash is soft. Serve immediately or hold in a warm oven for up to half an hour. When you eat the squash, mash the filling right into the flesh.

NOTE: *Potatoes are a special case. They make a delicious purée, but don't blend them alone in the food processor—it turns them into a starchy mess. Instead, mash by hand, then add liquid and beat with an electric mixer. However, potatoes may be puréed successfully in the food processor with a non-starchy vegetable such as carrots or rutabaga.*

Cellular or watery vegetables like fennel or celery are not suitable for puréeing unless combined with a more solid vegetable such as potato.

Liquids or semiliquids to add, depending on the vegetable being puréed: chicken, beef or vegetable broth; milk or cream; sour cream; plain yogurt; buttermilk; wine; fruit juice (not too much); sauce or gravy

Seasonings, depending on the vegetable: butter or margarine; grated Parmesan, cheddar or Gruyère cheese; ricotta cheese; fresh lemon or lime juice; fresh or dried herbs; nutmeg; horseradish; Worcestershire sauce; hot pepper sauce; mustard; creamy salad dressing

MENU SUGGESTIONS

Since most of the fillings are on the sweet side, choose a main course that is either plain or savory—any roast or poultry, grilled fish, pasta or noodles. Add Broccoli Salad with Lemon-Curry Mayonnaise and Pepper Confetti (page 80) and you've got a meal.

CRUNCHY TOPPINGS

A crunchy topping will make many hot vegetable side dishes (and some cold ones) more appealing in texture, taste and appearance. Some are added before cooking and others should be sprinkled on when the vegetables are transferred, still hot, to the serving platter. For cold dishes, think of the crunchy topping as a garnish and choose it accordingly.

- **CRACKER CRUMBS: USE FLAVORFUL CRACKERS, CRUSHED WITH A ROLLING PIN OR WHIRLED IN A FOOD PROCESSOR UNTIL THEY ARE THE RIGHT SIZE. SPRINKLE THEM ON A VEGETABLE DISH BEFORE BAKING.**

- **TOASTED OR FRESH BREAD CRUMBS: READ ABOUT BREAD CRUMBS ON PAGE 36; SPRINKLE THEM ON BEFORE BAKING.**

- **CHOPPED NUTS: SCATTER CHOPPED TOASTED ALMONDS, WALNUTS, PECANS OR PEANUTS OR WHOLE PINE NUTS ON YOUR FINISHED DISH.**

- **CROUTONS: READ ALL ABOUT CROUTONS ON PAGE 166; TOP YOUR FINISHED HOT DISH WITH SMALL CROUTONS; ADD SMALL OR LARGE ONES TO SALADS AND COLD VEGETABLES.**

COMPANY'S COMING

SQUASH SOUFFLÉ

MAKES SIX SERVINGS

A heavenly dish for company—but as with any soufflé, you must rush it to the table the instant it's done. (However, I have to admit that the soufflé is delicious even when it cools and sinks.)

NOTE: *You'll need six eggs, but you'll use only four of the yolks.*

> 2 pounds buttercup, delicata, dumpling, Golden Nugget or kabocha squash, scrubbed *(It's important to use one of these squashes because their flesh is dense and won't become watery when baked.)*

> 1½ cups half-and-half

> 3 tablespoons butter or margarine or a combination of both

> 3 tablespoons flour

> 4 egg yolks, lightly beaten in a small bowl

> ½ cup grated Parmesan cheese

> 6 tablespoons finely minced scallions, green parts only

> Salt and fresh pepper

> 6 egg whites, in a large bowl

1. Preheat the oven to 400°. Cut each squash in half and place the halves, cut side down, on a lightly oiled piece of foil on a baking sheet. Bake for 45 minutes, or until the squash is soft and easily pierced by a knife.

When the squash is cool enough to handle, peel it and mash the flesh; you should have 1½ to 2 cups.

Turn the oven down to 350°; butter a two-quart soufflé dish or straight-sided, three-inch-deep casserole.

2. Heat the half-and-half just until little bubbles form around the edge of the pan; set aside. In a medium saucepan or skillet, melt the butter, stir in the flour, and cook for one minute. Add the hot half-and-half all at once and whisk over medium heat until the sauce is thick and smooth. Transfer to a large bowl.

3. Whisk the mashed squash into the hot sauce; the mixture should now be warm, not hot. (If it is too hot, the yolks may curdle when added, so be sure it is just warm.) Whisk the egg yolks into the mixture, then stir in the grated cheese and scallions. Season well with salt and pepper; the squash mixture must be well seasoned because the flavor will be diluted when the egg whites are folded in.

4. In a large bowl with clean beaters, beat the egg whites until they hold firm, moist, glossy peaks. Fold a third of the whites into the squash mixture to lighten it, then fold the rest of the egg whites into the lightened mixture. Immediately pour the mixture into the prepared soufflé dish.

Bake for 40 to 45 minutes, until the soufflé is puffed, fairly firm and browned. *Serve immediately.*

- **CRISP-FRIED CHINESE NOODLES: IF YOU CAN FIND A NOT-TOO-GREASY PACKAGED BRAND, THESE ARE FUN TO USE FOR TOPPING. BREAK OR CRUSH THEM BEFORE USING ON HOT OR COLD DISHES.**

- **CRISP-FRIED ONIONS OR SHALLOTS: SLICE RAW ONIONS OR SHALLOTS VERY THIN AND SAUTÉ IN $\frac{1}{8}$ INCH OF HOT OIL JUST UNTIL CRISP; TAKE CARE NOT TO LET THEM BURN. DRAIN ON PAPER TOWELS, THEN SCATTER OR MOUND THEM ON HOT OR COLD VEGETABLES.**

- **CHOPPED WATER CHESTNUTS: USE WHOLE CANNED WATER CHESTNUTS, RINSED, DRAINED, PATTED DRY AND CHOPPED IN BITS. ADD BEFORE OR AFTER BAKING, OR SCATTER ON SALADS OR COLD VEGETABLES.**

MENU SUGGESTIONS

To accommodate any soufflé, the menu should be simple and make-ahead, not last-minute. In this case, you might like to have cold roasted chicken, Lemon-braised Artichokes (page 27) served at room temperature, and chilled Sweet Beet Caviar (page 67). Good bread and a green salad round out a company dinner.

SWISS CHARD

If you like mild-tasting greens, Swiss chard—also called chard—is the vegetable for you. Both the stems (which can be white or red) and the dark green leaves are edible and delicious. The stems take a little longer to cook, so it is standard procedure to separate the stem from the leaf and start the stems cooking first.

Like spinach, Swiss chard takes a bit of washing to remove sand, but cleaning Swiss chard is much easier and faster since the dirt washes right off the flat stems and leaves; only the smaller leaves are crinkly and they are generally grit-free.

BUYING AND STORING

A good bunch of Swiss chard will have outer stalks of large, crisp dark green leaves on firm, broad stems surrounding inner stalks of slender stems with more delicate leaves. Avoid stems with brown spots, bruises, splits and insect holes. Yellowed or withered leaves tell you that the chard is old and getting bitter.

Refrigerate unwashed Swiss chard in a plastic bag for up to a few days. Like most leafy greens, this is a perishable vegetable, so use it as soon as you can.

NOTES TO THE COOK

Trimming: Cut a thin slice off the stem ends so you have clean, fresh edges. Now cut off the stems at the base of the leaves, keeping the stems and leaves separate.

Washing: Carefully wash the stems, making sure to remove all the dirt; shake off any excess water and set aside. Do the same with the leaves.

Note on preparation for cooking: The stems are usually cut in shorter lengths for cooking, as shown on the opposite page. The leaves can be stacked, rolled up and cut in ribbons of various widths; the ribbons can be cut down into squares, if required.

Swiss Chard with Bacon and Black-eyed Peas

MAKES PLENTY FOR SIX SERVINGS

Few ingredients, minimal effort, big flavor. This is very hearty fare, almost a meal in itself.

2 tablespoons vegetable oil

3 ounces Canadian bacon, diced

1 pound Swiss chard, trimmed and washed, excess water shaken off

3 garlic cloves, minced

1¾ cups cooked black-eyed peas (one 1-pound can), rinsed and drained

Salt and fresh pepper

1. In a large skillet or saucepan, heat the oil and brown the Canadian bacon. Meanwhile, cut the chard stems into ½-inch pieces and set aside; cut the leaves into one-inch squares.

2. Add the chard stems to the skillet (and two tablespoons of water if there is very little water clinging to the stems), cover, and cook for five minutes. Stir in the chard leaves, garlic, black-eyed peas, and salt and pepper to taste. Cook uncovered, stirring often, for five more minutes, or until the stems and leaves are tender. (You may have to add a little more water to prevent burning.) Serve hot.

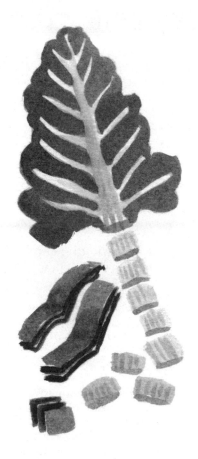

MENU SUGGESTIONS

To complete the meal, serve cheddar cheese spoonbread or Chile-Cheese-Corn Pudding (page 136) and sliced tomatoes. For a meatier meal, have turkey burgers or pork chili, with Hash Brown Parsnips with Scallions and Jalapeños (page 230) on the side.

YOGURT CHEESE

Yogurt cheese is plain (unflavored) yogurt that has been drained of a great deal of liquid. The result is a thick, creamy, smooth, tart "cheese" that can be used in delicious ways:

- ON A BAKED POTATO, ALONG WITH A SPRINKLING OF SNIPPED FRESH CHIVES

- ON CRACKERS, TOPPED WITH ALL-FRUIT PRESERVES

- AS THE BASIS FOR A DIP, WITH CRUDITÉS OR PRETZEL STICKS

- AS A SANDWICH SPREAD

- AS A GARNISH FOR HOT GREEN VEGETABLES

- ON TACOS OR TOSTADAS, INSTEAD OF SOUR CREAM

- STIRRED WITH A LITTLE SUPERFINE SUGAR AND A FEW DROPS OF REAL VANILLA EXTRACT, AS A TOPPING FOR FRESH FRUIT

It takes absolutely no effort to create this versatile food. Here's how it's done:

Put a paper coffee filter in the filter holder of your coffee maker and set the holder over a bowl or other container. (If you don't normally use paper filters or filter holders, buy a small package of filters and set one in a strainer over a bowl.)

Spoon a pint or more (depending on the size of your filter) of plain yogurt into the filter and let it drain

SWISS CHARD PANCAKES

MAKES 20 TO 24 THREE-INCH PANCAKES, PLENTY FOR 6 SERVINGS

A family favorite. Like all pancakes, these are best when they go straight from the pan to the plate, but the first batches will keep nicely in the oven while the last batch cooks.

2 tablespoons olive oil

1 large onion, chopped

1 pound Swiss chard, trimmed and washed, excess water shaken off

¾ cup buttermilk

¼ teaspoon baking powder

½ teaspoon baking soda

1 cup flour

1 egg

Dash of hot pepper sauce (optional)

½ teaspoon salt

Fresh pepper to taste

Vegetable oil for frying

1. In a large skillet, heat the olive oil and brown the onion. Meanwhile, cut the chard stems into one-inch pieces and set aside; cut the leaves into wide ribbons.

2. Add the stems to the browned onions (with two tablespoons of water if there is very little water clinging to the stems). Cover the skillet and cook over low heat for three minutes. Stir the leaves into the onion mixture (adding two more tablespoons of water if needed to prevent burning), cover, and cook for another three minutes.

3. Put the remaining ingredients except the vegetable oil in your food processor and process until smooth. Add the chard mixture (but no liquid from the skillet) and process until coarsely puréed; the batter will be thick. If needed, season with more salt and pepper.

4. In a clean skillet, heat a little vegetable oil, add a big soupspoon of batter, and spread the batter to make a three-inch pancake. Repeat to make several pancakes without crowding the skillet. Brown on both sides, drain on paper towels, and keep the pancakes warm in a low oven.

Repeat the process to use up all the batter, adding oil to the skillet as needed. Serve immediately, plain or garnished with sour cream, yogurt cheese, chutney or salsa.

for about eight hours or overnight in the refrigerator. The longer you let it drain, the thicker the yogurt cheese.

Discard the liquid in the bowl, plop the drained yogurt into a jar or other container, and throw away the paper filter. Store the yogurt cheese in the tightly closed container in the fridge. Two cups of yogurt (one 16-ounce container) yield 1 cup of medium-thick yogurt cheese or ¾ cup of very thick yogurt cheese.

MENU SUGGESTIONS

Chard pancakes go with almost anything from poached fish to curry. Try them with a simple dinner of baked chicken and Baked Miniature Pumpkins with Spiced Butter (page 276).

**MATCHMAKING:
PASTA WITH TOMATO-
BASED SAUCE**

You're making pasta with tomato sauce for dinner. What do you serve with it? Here are some possibilities from which to choose, including the Vegetable Express for hurry-up meals.

Broccoli in Creamy Broccoli Purée, page 85

Mushrooms Roasted with Butter and Garlic, page 204

Cannellini with Escarole Purée, page 46

MENU SUGGESTIONS

There's a lot of flavor going on in this dish, so keep the rest of the menu on the simple side—lamb chops or pan-fried fish will be good, with boiled potatoes or Sweet Corn Cakes with Raisins (page 137).

SAUTÉED SWISS CHARD WITH THICK SPICY YOGURT

MAKES SIX SERVINGS

A simple sauté, rich with onions, garlic and sun-dried tomatoes and topped with tangy, curry-flavored yogurt.

$\frac{1}{2}$ to 1 teaspoon mild or hot curry powder

$\frac{1}{2}$ cup medium-thick yogurt cheese (see page 312) *(You may substitute regular or light sour cream.)*

1 pound Swiss chard, trimmed and washed, excess water shaken off

3 tablespoons vegetable oil (not olive oil)

2 medium onions, sliced $\frac{1}{8}$ inch thick

3 garlic cloves, minced

2 ounces sun-dried tomatoes, diced, then rinsed in hot water

Salt and fresh pepper

1. Stir $\frac{1}{2}$ teaspoon of the curry powder into the yogurt cheese; taste and add the remaining $\frac{1}{2}$ teaspoon if you like. Set aside.

Cut the chard stems into $\frac{1}{2}$-inch pieces and set aside; coarsely chop the chard leaves.

2. In a large skillet, heat the oil and sauté the onions until limp. Add the chard stems and garlic and sauté for five more minutes over medium heat.

3. Stir in the chopped leaves, diced tomatoes, and salt and pepper to taste. Sauté five minutes, or until the leaves are tender, adding a bit of water, if necessary, to prevent burning.

Serve immediately, topped with dollops of the curried yogurt or with the yogurt on the side.

THE VEGETABLE EXPRESS

SWISS CHARD WITH LEMON AND GARLIC

MAKES SIX SERVINGS

This tart, garlicky dish is especially compatible with rich or substantial main courses.

1¾ pounds Swiss chard, trimmed and washed, excess water shaken off

3 tablespoons olive oil

3 garlic cloves, minced

Salt and fresh pepper

Grated rind of one lemon

Juice of half a lemon

1. Cut the chard stems into ½-inch pieces and set aside; chop the leaves coarsely.

In a large skillet, heat the oil and sauté the stems and garlic for five minutes.

2. Add the leaves, season with salt and pepper, and sauté five more minutes, or until the stems and leaves are tender. Stir in the grated rind and lemon juice and serve right away.

Marinated Roasted Red and Yellow Peppers with Fresh Basil, page 244

Zucchini Ribbons in Gorgonzola Sauce, page 295

Italian Salad, page 343

VEGETABLE EXPRESS

Sautéed Broccoli Rabe with Parmesan, page 86

Swiss Chard with Lemon and Garlic, at left

MENU SUGGESTIONS

Perfect with pasta. For an express supper, serve readymade tortellini with tomato sauce; for a robust meal, spaghetti with meat sauce; for a company dinner, fettuccine Alfredo. In all cases, follow with a crisp endive salad and plenty of crusty semolina bread.

SWISS CHARD IN WALNUT OIL WITH TOASTED WALNUTS

MAKES SIX SERVINGS

This is a simple dish with a quick and easy preparation. What makes it worthy of company is the delicious (and expensive) walnut oil and the richness of toasted walnuts. Before you add them, taste the nuts to be absolutely sure they are fresh.

1½ pounds Swiss chard, trimmed and washed, excess water shaken off

3 tablespoons walnut oil

¾ cup chopped walnuts

Salt

1. Cut the chard stems into ½-inch pieces and set aside; cut the leaves into ½-inch-wide ribbons.

In a large skillet, heat half the oil and sauté the walnuts over medium heat until they look and smell toasty, three to four minutes. Use a slotted spoon to remove the walnuts.

2. Without cleaning the skillet, add the remaining oil and the chard stems and sauté five minutes. Stir in the leaves and sauté five to seven more minutes, until the stems and leaves are tender, adding a tablespoon or two of water if needed to prevent burning. Season with salt, add the walnuts, and stir well. Transfer to a serving dish and serve hot.

MENU SUGGESTIONS

Do a simple but impressive menu—the escarole plus wild mushroom ravioli with your own Fresh Tomato Sauce (page 322) and freshly grated Parmesan cheese. Follow with a beautifully composed salad (pages 345 to 349) and great bread.

TOMATOES

BUYING AND STORING

Globe tomatoes (also call slicing or beefsteak tomatoes): These are your basic everyday tomatoes. A small one is four to five ounces, medium-size is six to eight ounces, and a large globe tomato is eight to ten ounces. In general, pick firm (not hard), plump tomatoes with deep red unblemished skin and a good tomato smell; they should feel heavy for their size. Avoid splits in the skin, bruises and rotten spots.

Choose riper tomatoes if you want to eat them right away, of course, and some less ripe ones to mature within a day or two. I always buy a selection, from very ripe to barely ripe, so I'm guaranteed a constantly ripening supply.

Unripe tomatoes must never go in the refrigerator; keep them out of the sunlight, too, in a cool spot, and let them ripen naturally on a big platter or tray. That way you can keep track of which one is ready to be eaten that day. Ripe tomatoes may be refrigerated, but use them as soon as possible. And keep in mind that you can speed the ripening process by paper-bagging an unripe tomato with an apple, which gives off the ethylene gas that does the trick.

Other tomatoes: Green tomatoes are unripe globes and they are delicious when sliced, dusted with flour and salt and pan-fried with a good grinding of fresh pepper. They also make great chutney (page 320).

Bite-size yellow and red cherry tomatoes and teardrop (or pear) tomatoes are sweet and juicy, wonderful during local tomato season and pretty good the rest of the year. Watch out for moldy cherry tomatoes, especially in the boxes you buy out of season.

Plum tomatoes (Italian or Roma tomatoes) are much less juicy—therefore firmer—than globes, but they can be life-savers when you need tomatoes in the winter. Often the centers will be mealy or mushy while the flesh is succulent and

From mid-July through September, fresh tomatoes are my passion. I search the Union Square Farmers' Market like a truffle hound, nosing from stand to stand, hunting down the best flavor, the best texture, the best price. For about ten weeks, my husband and I wallow in toma-toes. Then, suddenly, it's all over for another year. We reconcile our-selves to a winter of plum tomatoes, canned tomatoes and sun-dried tomatoes, and try not to daydream about next summer.

PANTRY

CANNED TOMATOES

No good cook would be caught in the kitchen without a supply of canned tomato products in a variety of sizes. Requirements will differ according to what each family likes to eat and how much cooking is done, but tomatoes in several forms are sure to be on the pantry shelf. Here's a reminder list of canned tomato products:

- **TOMATO PASTE**
- **PREMIUM WHOLE PEELED TOMATOES (GLOBE TOMATOES)**
- **ITALIAN-STYLE PEELED TOMATOES (PLUM TOMATOES)**
- **ITALIAN-STYLE WHOLE TOMATOES IN TOMATO PURÉE**
- **PURÉED TOMATOES**
- **CRUSHED TOMATOES**
- **CUT-UP TOMATOES**
- **STEWED TOMATOES**

The product I haven't listed is tomato sauce. You may have found an acceptable canned tomato sauce, but I haven't. If I need sauce in a hurry, I start with a can of high-quality puréed, crushed or whole tomatoes and add my own sautéed onions, garlic, herbs, spices or other seasonings.

flavorful, so you should remove the mealy part, then dice or sliver the flesh for salads. Plum tomatoes make fine sauce and salsa, too.

Remember: Specialty tomatoes are more available now—hydroponically grown tomatoes, low-acid tomatoes, orange and yellow tomatoes and my favorites, tomatillos (see the sidebar on page 277).

NOTES TO THE COOK

Removing the stem ends: With the tip of a small sharp knife, carve out a little cone with the stem end of the tomato in the center.

Peeling: The recipes in this section do not require peeled tomatoes, but if you prefer them peeled, here's how to do it. Bring a saucepan of water to a boil. Lower two or three medium or large tomatoes at a time into the boiling water and let them sit for 45 to 60 seconds (30 to 45 seconds for small tomatoes). Use a slotted spoon to transfer them to a colander, then run cold water over them immediately. Remove the stem end and peel down the skin. If the skin is stubborn, return the tomato to the hot water for 10 to 15 seconds more.

Seeding: Cut the tomato in half across the equator. Gently squeeze each half, letting the juice and seeds run out; use a small spoon to winkle out any seeds still left in the tomato. (If you want to reserve the juice, do this operation over a strainer set over a bowl.)

TOMATOES WITH ORZO AND ROQUEFORT

MAKES SIX SERVINGS

Light, filling and satisfying—a perfect side dish for a summer meal. Serve on crisp greens for a good contrast in texture.

½ cup uncooked orzo (rice-shaped pasta)

3 medium-size ripe red globe tomatoes (1¼ to 1½ pounds), stem ends removed

¼ pound Roquefort cheese

¼ cup (packed) chopped fresh flat-leaf (Italian) parsley

¼ cup Creamy Vinaigrette Dressing (recipe follows)

Salt and fresh pepper

1. Bring a large saucepan of water to a boil, stir in the orzo, and cook for 9 to 11 minutes, until tender. Drain, rinse well under cold water, and drain again.

Meanwhile, dice the tomatoes and place them in a strainer. Shake the strainer firmly to remove as much tomato juice as possible, then transfer the tomatoes to a large bowl.

2. Add the orzo to the bowl of tomatoes. Crumble the cheese and add it to the bowl, along with the parsley, vinaigrette dressing, and salt and pepper to taste. Toss well, correct the seasoning, and serve chilled or at room temperature.

Creamy Vinaigrette Dressing

MAKES ½ CUP

2 tablespoons regular or light mayonnaise

1 tablespoon red wine vinegar

1 teaspoon Dijon mustard

⅓ cup olive oil

Salt and fresh pepper to taste

Whisk the ingredients together and correct the seasoning. Be sure to whisk the dressing again just before using.

MENU SUGGESTIONS

Bright and tasty, best served with plain grilled chicken quarters or sautéed chicken cutlets. Add a dish of Broccoli Rabe with Anchovy and Garlic Sauce (page 34) or a green salad (if the tomatoes aren't already mounded on a bed of greens).

GREEN TOMATO CHUTNEY

MAKES ABOUT THREE CUPS

1 MEDIUM ONION, CHOPPED

1 CUP DARK RAISINS

1 TABLESPOON MINCED FRESH GINGER

2 GARLIC CLOVES, MINCED

5 TABLESPOONS BROWN SUGAR

½ TEASPOON SALT

¼ TEASPOON EACH CINNAMON, GROUND CLOVES AND NUTMEG

GRATED PEEL OF ONE LEMON

2 TABLESPOONS FRESH LEMON JUICE

¼ CUP WATER

¼ TEASPOON HOT PEPPER FLAKES (OPTIONAL)

1¾ TO 2 POUNDS GREEN TOMATOES (ABOUT 5 MEDIUM), STEM ENDS REMOVED

1. Put all the ingredients except the tomatoes in a heavy saucepan and bring to a simmer, covered, stirring often to prevent burning. Meanwhile, dice the tomatoes.

2. Stir the tomatoes into the simmering mixture and continue cooking, covered, over very low heat for another 15 minutes.

Remove the cover and simmer for 30 more minutes, until thickened. Let the chutney cool, then spoon it into containers and refrigerate until needed, up to several weeks.

TOMATO TART

MAKES ONE 9-INCH TART, PLENTY FOR SIX SERVINGS

This tart is thin and crisp, richly flavored with basil and cheese and, like the artichoke tart on page 28, extremely easy to make because it starts with a readymade pie crust. Serve it along with a big summer or winter salad or even as a first course.

> 2 to 3 medium-size ripe red globe tomatoes (1 to 1½ pounds), stem ends removed *(Depending on the size of the tomatoes, you may need only 2 or 2½ of them.)*
>
> 1 unbaked readymade 9-inch pie crust, room temperature
>
> 1 cup chopped onion (about 1 medium onion)
>
> Olive oil
>
> 2 tablespoons chopped fresh basil
>
> 2½ tablespoons grated Parmesan cheese
>
> Salt and fresh pepper

1. Preheat the oven to 375°.

Slice the tomatoes in half crosswise (across the equator). Gently squeeze the juice and seeds out of each half; then set the halves, cut side down, on a wire rack to drain some more.

2. While the tomatoes drain, turn the pie crust out onto an ungreased baking sheet—just flip it over and let it drop out of the aluminum pie plate onto the baking sheet. Gently flatten the center (easy when the crust is at room temperature), leaving the crimped edge to form the rim of the tart. If the crust tears, dab a little water on the torn edges and press them together. Prick the crust all over with a fork and bake for ten minutes.

NOTE: *This technique for turning a pie crust into a tart crust may surprise you, but it works extremely well—so have faith and give it a try.*

3. Lightly brown the onion in a little olive oil and let it cool. Spread the onion evenly on the partially baked crust, followed by the basil and then the grated cheese.

4. Slice the tomato halves about ⅛ to ¼ inch thick, to get nine good slices; it's a little awkward to cut attractive slices when the tomatoes have been emptied of seeds and juice, but do the best you can. Arrange the slices, slightly overlapping, on the tart as shown. Brush the tomatoes, the crimped rim and any exposed crust with a little olive oil. Sprinkle with salt and pepper and bake for 25 minutes.

Serve warm or cool.

MENU SUGGESTIONS

As suggested in the headnote, Tomato Tart is wonderful with a big composed salad (pages 345 to 349). I like it as part of a cold meal, too, with cold cuts, Dilly Beans (page 58), Cucumbers in Sweet-and-Sour Buttermilk Dressing (page 147) and fresh baguettes.

FRESH TOMATO SAUCE

MAKES ABOUT TWO CUPS

Fresh tomato sauce is one of the world's best uses for fresh tomatoes. It has a simplicity and purity that enlivens whatever it touches, summer or winter. Serve it on vegetables or pasta, perhaps with a sprinkling of chopped basil and freshly grated Parmesan cheese.

1½ POUNDS RIPE RED TOMATOES, STEM ENDS REMOVED (*USE REGULAR GLOBE OR BEEFSTEAK TOMATOES IN SUMMER, PLUM TOMATOES IN WINTER.*)

MENU SUGGESTIONS

If you happen to have a grill, cook some shrimp and a variety of vegetables (page 72) to go with this lively salad. Bean and cheese tostadas are a fine alternative—or make them all when you're entertaining a group of guests.

RED AND GREEN GAZPACHO SALAD

MAKES PLENTY FOR SIX SERVINGS

Here's a gazpacho you can get your teeth into: Instead of the usual cold soup, it's a tart, crunchy, refreshing salad, nippy with garlic and a bit of cayenne.

- **3 medium-size ripe red globe tomatoes (about 1¼ to 1½ pounds), stem ends removed**
- **1 medium-size green globe tomato, stem end removed**
- **1 red bell pepper, cored and seeded**
- **½ cup diced red onion**
- **1 cup diced cucumber (*Trim, peel and seed a regular cucumber before dicing it. Kirby cucumbers are also delicious in this recipe; trim them, peel them if you like, but do not seed them.*)**
- **2 tablespoons balsamic or red wine vinegar**
- **3 tablespoons fruity olive oil (preferably Spanish)**
- **1 garlic clove**
- **2 pinches cayenne pepper**
- **Salt and fresh pepper**

1. Cut the red tomatoes into ½-inch dice, place the pieces in a strainer, and set aside to drain.

2. Cut the green tomato and red pepper into ¼-inch dice and put them in a large bowl with the onion and cucumber.

3. Add the drained tomatoes, vinegar, oil, garlic clove forced through a garlic press, cayenne and a sprinkling of salt and pepper. Stir well, correct the seasoning, and serve chilled or at room temperature.

CHEDDAR-BAKED TOMATOES

MAKES SIX SERVINGS OF ONE TOMATO EACH

Cheese gives this side dish a special taste, and chopped greens and coriander keep the filling light and bright. If you like spicy-hot food, consider adding a little chopped pickled jalapeño pepper—delicious.

TIP: This recipe can be doubled very successfully if you prefer two tomatoes per serving (as for a vegetarian meal).

6 medium-small ripe red globe tomatoes (4 to 6 ounces per tomato)

1 cup grated sharp cheddar cheese (about 4 ounces)

½ cup chopped onion (about 1 small onion)

½ cup (packed) chopped fresh tender greens (spinach, arugula, inner leaves of escarole or chicory)

2 tablespoons chopped fresh coriander

Salt and fresh pepper to taste

1. Butter a baking dish large enough to hold the tomatoes in one layer; preheat the oven to 400° (375° for ovenproof glass).
Cut ½ inch off the top (not the stem end) of each tomato; reserve the cut-off pieces. Scoop out and discard the pulp and seeds of each tomato. (A melon baller works well for this job.) Dice the reserved pieces of tomato and place them in a large bowl.

2. Add ¾ cup of the cheese plus all the remaining ingredients to the bowl and mix well. Divide this stuffing among the tomato shells, packing it in firmly. Press a big pinch of the remaining cheese on top of each stuffed tomato.

3. Place the stuffed tomatoes in the buttered baking dish and bake for 20 minutes. Serve hot.

1 TABLESPOON BUTTER

2 TABLESPOONS OLIVE OIL

1 SMALL ONION, MINCED

1 GARLIC CLOVE, MINCED

SALT AND FRESH PEPPER TO TASTE

2 TABLESPOONS MINCED FRESH FLAT-LEAF (ITALIAN) PARSLEY

1 TEASPOON SUGAR (OPTIONAL)

DASH OF HOT PEPPER SAUCE OR ONE TABLESPOON BALSAMIC VINEGAR (OPTIONAL)

1. Halve the tomatoes crosswise and gently squeeze out the seeds. Dice the tomatoes, saving as much juice as possible, and set aside.

2. In a large skillet, melt the butter with the oil and sauté the onions and garlic for several minutes, until softened. Stir in the tomatoes, salt and pepper. Cook over low heat, stirring, just until the tomatoes begin to soften, about five minutes. Do not overcook.

3. Stir in the parsley and, if the tomatoes are not sweet enough, add the sugar. Add the pepper sauce or vinegar, if you choose. Correct the seasoning and use the sauce hot or cold.

MENU SUGGESTIONS

If you're making a meatless meal, with two tomatoes per person, you might like to serve wedges of herb and mushroom omelet and fresh bread or popovers. Oven-fried Eggplant Fingers with Ranch Dipping Sauce (page 154) is a nice accompaniment.

SIMPLE TOMATO SALADS

Perfect summer globe tomatoes, locally grown, vine-ripened and trucked to market, deserve the best treatment—which is very little treatment indeed. Just core and slice the tomatoes (which are at room temperature, of course) and serve them simply, as suggested below. And don't bother trying these ideas with bland winter tomatoes, plum tomatoes or cherry tomatoes—they can't stand up to such minimalism.

- Drizzle with wonderful olive oil, a few drops of balsamic vinegar and a chiffonade (very narrow strips) of fresh basil.

- Sprinkle with fresh lime juice, chopped fresh coriander and very thin slices of fresh or pickled jalapeño pepper.

- Top the tomato slices with a little crumbled goat cheese, a handful of fresh garlic croutons and a mere drizzle of vinaigrette.

- Whisk together 3 tablespoons cider vinegar, $1\frac{1}{2}$ tablespoons water, $\frac{1}{4}$ cup olive oil, $\frac{1}{4}$ teaspoon dry mustard, $1\frac{1}{2}$ teaspoons sugar and $\frac{1}{4}$ teaspoon salt to make a sweet-and-sour sauce to sprinkle on the tomatoes.

- For a salad extravaganza, arrange slices of tomato, whole anchovies, homemade roasted peppers, sliced mozzarella, olives and thinly sliced red onion on a bed of greens and drizzle with olive oil or vinaigrette.

MENU SUGGESTIONS

When tomatoes are great, they can be the focal point of the menu. Depending on which salad you're making, serve simple pasta, chicken, grilled sausage or cold cuts. Add the appropriate bread and dive right into the tomatoes.

TOMATOES STUFFED WITH COUSCOUS AND PINE NUTS

MAKES SIX SERVINGS

This is an elegant chilled version of stuffed tomatoes, suitable for any dinner party and so good you might need more than six. If you want to make 12 tomatoes, simply double the recipe.

NOTE: Fresh *dill is essential—dried won't do—but you may substitute fresh coriander, basil or chives if you like.*

- **1 tablespoon olive oil**
- **½ cup pine nuts**
- **2 garlic cloves, minced**
- **½ cup vegetable or chicken broth**
- **½ cup uncooked couscous**
- **Salt and fresh pepper**
- **6 medium-small ripe red globe tomatoes (about 1½ to 2 pounds)**
- **3 tablespoons plain (unflavored) yogurt**
- **1 tablespoon Dijon mustard**
- **1 tablespoon chopped fresh dill**
- **6 sprigs of fresh dill and 6 small black or green olives for garnish**

1. In a medium skillet over medium heat, heat the olive oil; add the pine nuts and sauté until lightly browned. Watch the nuts carefully to be sure they don't burn.

2. Add the garlic and broth and bring to a boil. Turn off the heat, stir in the couscous, and cover the skillet; let stand for five minutes, until all the liquid is absorbed and the couscous is soft. (If the couscous is still a bit hard, stir in ¼ cup boiling water, cover the skillet, and let stand another minute or two.)

Uncover the skillet, fluff the couscous with a fork, and season with salt and pepper. Transfer to a large bowl and let the coucous cool.

3. Meanwhile, cut one inch off the top (not the stem end) of each tomato; reserve the cut-off pieces. Scoop out and discard the pulp and seeds of each tomato. (A melon baller works well for this job.)

4. Dice the reserved pieces of tomato and add them to the bowl of couscous, along with the yogurt, mustard and chopped dill. Mix lightly but well, adding more salt and pepper if needed. Divide this stuffing mixture among the tomato shells, packing it in firmly and mounding it slightly.

Garnish each tomato with sprig of dill and a small olive. Serve chilled or at room temperature.

MENU SUGGESTIONS

These gems would look handsome surrounding a cold poached bass or fish mousse, or a platter of sliced steak or spicy chicken. Grilled swordfish or a vegetarian moussaka is a good choice, too. Follow the meal with a green salad.

TURNIPS

BUYING AND STORING

Look for small or medium-size turnips, not more than 2½ inches in diameter; larger turnips tend to be woody and too strongly flavored. Skins should be smooth and creamy white (no brown spots), with a purple, pink or green blush toward the stem end. Good turnips are firm and heavy for their size; if a turnip feels light and gives when you squeeze it, it's spongy inside. If greens are attached, they should be crisp and fresh.

Before storing turnips, cut off any greens. Keep the unwashed greens and turnips in separate plastic bags in the refrigerator. Greens are perishable and will last only a few days; turnips will last for at least a week.

NOTES TO THE COOK

Trimming: Cut off the stem end, including all the little bumps and ridges; cut off the root end close to the main globe of the turnip.

Peeling: Use a swivel-blade peeler (or any other peeler you prefer) to remove the skin, peeling the turnip just as you would an apple.

Turnips, though not as aggressively flavored as some would have you believe, are definitely not wishy-washy vegetables. Their sharp taste makes them ideal for combining with either equally strong flavors (such as ginger, in Turnips Rosanna, page 331) or more mellow ones (such as sour cream and ricotta cheese, in Creamy Turnips, page 330).

Turnips, especially if they are small, will sometimes have stems and leaves attached. These turnip greens are delicious and can be cooked like any other greens; for recipes, see the Greens section on page 178.

MAKES ABOUT 1 1/4 CUPS

1/4 POUND DRY (NOT OIL-PACKED) SUN-DRIED TOMATOES, HALVED (OR QUARTERED, IF LARGE) AND RINSED

1 GARLIC CLOVE, QUARTERED

1/2 CUP (PACKED) FRESH BASIL LEAVES

1/4 CUP OLIVE OIL

2 TABLESPOONS WATER

2 TABLESPOONS BALSAMIC VINEGAR

1 TABLESPOON SMALL (NONPAREIL) CAPERS

SALT AND FRESH PEPPER

MENU SUGGESTIONS

A veal-and-ham loaf or turkey loaf will be delicious with these simple turnips, with Poached Spinach Dumplings (page 292) or Spinach and Mushrooms with Herbs (page 287). If you prefer a vegetarian meal, serve with Zucchini Ribbons in Gorgonzola Sauce (page 295) and Swiss Chard Pancakes (page 312).

SAGE-ROASTED TURNIPS

MAKES SIX SERVINGS

A simple preparation, each slice crisp on the outside and tender within, lightly flavored with sage.

8 medium-size turnips (about 3 pounds), trimmed and peeled

Olive oil

Salt and fresh pepper

Powdered sage

1. Preheat the oven to 400°. Cut each turnip into three thick slices and spread them out on a baking sheet. Brush all over with olive oil, sprinkle both sides with salt and pepper, and dust lightly with sage.

2. Bake the pieces flat side down on the baking sheet for 30 minutes. Turn and continue roasting for another 20 to 30 minutes, until tender and nicely browned. Serve hot.

PAN-FRIED TURNIPS AND POTATOES WITH SUN-DRIED TOMATO RELISH

MAKES SIX SERVINGS

This is really a variation on hash browns—chunks of turnip and potato, crisp on the outside, moist and soft on the inside. Especially good when topped with the tangy relish.

1 pound medium-size turnips, trimmed, peeled and halved

1 large russet potato (such as Idaho; about ¾ pound), peeled and quartered

1 egg plus 1 egg white

2 tablespoons whole or skim milk

3 tablespoons flour

1 medium onion, minced

Salt and fresh pepper

3 tablespoons vegetable oil

Sun-Dried Tomato Relish (see sidebar)

1. Grate the turnips and potato in your food processor, using the grating blade.

In a large bowl, whisk together the egg, egg white, milk and flour. Add the turnips, potato, onion and a good sprinkling of salt and pepper. Mix well (with your hands, if you like).

2. In a large skillet, heat the oil over low heat. Add the turnip mixture, pressing it out to fill the skillet. Cover the skillet and cook for 15 minutes, until the bottom is well browned. Be sure *all* of the bottom is browned.

3. Loosen the edge with a spatula, cut into several pieces, and turn each piece over. Partially cover the skillet and cook for about 15 more minutes, until the bottom is brown and the vegetables are thoroughly cooked. Season with more salt and pepper, if needed, and serve right away, accompanied by the relish.

1. Put the tomatoes in a small saucepan with water to cover, bring to a boil, and simmer until soft, about five minutes. Drain, rinse, and pat dry on paper towels.

2. Whirl the garlic, basil, oil, water and vinegar in your food processor until the basil is minced. Add the tomatoes and pulse several times, until the tomatoes are chopped in small bits. Transfer the mixture to a bowl and stir in the capers and salt and pepper to taste.

MENU SUGGESTIONS

Try skirt steak and an interesting salad with this turnip dish, or omit the meat and serve a hearty Casserole of Greens with Mozzarella Topping (page 183).

MORE VEGETABLE MEDLEYS

Like the suggestions on page 114, these vegetable medleys are combinations of three or more vegetables, either left over from another recipe or cooked especially for the medley. Adapt these ideas freely, using whatever amounts of vegetables you have and making substitutions according to your family's preferences.

MENU SUGGESTIONS

Pair your creamy turnips with roasted chicken or Cornish hens, and add one of the recipes for baked beets (page 68) or Baby Beets and Beet Greens (page 70) to complete the menu.

THE VEGETABLE EXPRESS

CREAMY TURNIPS

MAKES SIX SERVINGS

Sophisticated baby food—comforting and soothing on a cold winter night.

> **1½ pounds medium-size turnips, trimmed and peeled**
>
> **⅓ cup regular or light sour cream**
>
> **⅓ cup whole milk ricotta or part skim ricotta**
>
> **1 tablespoon Dijon mustard**
>
> **Salt and fresh pepper**

1. Cut the turnips into ½-inch pieces. Put them in a saucepan with water to cover and bring to a boil. Simmer, covered, until tender, 10 to 15 minutes. Drain well.

2. Put the turnips, sour cream, ricotta, mustard and a good sprinkling of salt and pepper in your food processor and purée to the desired smoothness. Reheat in the saucepan over low heat. Serve right away.

TURNIPS ROSANNA

MAKES PLENTY FOR SIX SERVINGS

The natural sweetness of turnips is enhanced by molasses and ginger in this sophisticated recipe. Thin-sliced turnips are spiraled in a wide pan, then baked and inverted for presentation and served in wedges.

NOTE: *You'll need metal pie weights for this preparation.*

2 to 2¼ pounds medium-size turnips (each about 2½ inches in diameter), trimmed and peeled

2 tablespoons unsulfured molasses

1 tablespoon grated fresh ginger

2 tablespoons dark rum

2 tablespoons butter

Salt and fresh pepper

1. Line an 11- or 12-inch cake or tart pan with two layers of foil and butter the foil generously; preheat the oven to 400°.

Cut off and discard enough of each end of each turnip so that the first official slice you cut at each end will be about 1½ inches in diameter; slice the turnips ⅛ inch thick. (A mandoline works well for the slicing.) Divide the slices into four equal portions.

2. Simmer the molasses with the ginger and rum, until the mixture is reduced by about half. Add the butter and stir until melted. Pour the resulting sauce into a measuring cup.

3. Arrange one portion of turnip slices in a spiral on the bottom of the pan, overlapping the slices as shown on page 332. The appearance of the spiral is important, because when you invert the vegetables onto a serving platter, that's what you'll see.

Drizzle with a third of the sauce and sprinkle with salt and pepper.

Heat the medley by sautéing the chosen vegetables with a little olive or other oil, and add garlic, salt, pepper, herbs or other seasonings.

- **ROASTED EGGPLANT AND PEPPERS, COOKED ZUCCHINI, FRESH TOMATOES: SEASON WITH OLIVE OIL, BALSAMIC VINEGAR, CHOPPED BASIL, SALT AND PEPPER.**

- **CUBED COOKED SWEET POTATOES, TURNIPS AND PARSNIPS: SEASON WITH MINCED GINGER, NUTMEG, SALT AND PEPPER, PLUS A LITTLE BUTTER AND BROTH.**

- **COOKED SPINACH (OR SWISS CHARD), POTATOES AND CAULIFLOWER: SEASON WITH GARLIC, MINCED HOT GREEN PEPPER AND SALT; STIR IN SOME PLAIN YOGURT JUST BEFORE SERVING.**

- **BRUSSELS SPROUTS, SMALL WHITE BEANS AND FRESH RED PEPPER: SEASON WITH SHALLOTS, WHITE WINE, SALT AND PEPPER.**

- **COOKED LENTILS, CARROTS, CELERY AND GREEN BEANS: SEASON WITH GARLIC, TARRAGON, SALT AND PEPPER.**

4. Using another portion of the turnip slices, make a simple even layer on top of the spiral and drizzle with half the remaining sauce. Sprinkle with salt and pepper.

Repeat with the third portion of turnips and the remaining sauce; end with a layer of the last portion of turnips. Cover the last layer with a piece of foil, then press the mixture down firmly and weight it with pie weights. Place the pan on a baking sheet.

Bake for 45 to 50 minutes, until tender and easily pierced with the point of a knife. Set the cake pan on a rack, remove the weights and foil, and let the turnips cool for ten minutes. Cover the pan tightly with an inverted serving platter and quickly flip over to unmold the turnip cake. Remove the pan and foil and serve right away, or if necessary, hold for up to 20 minutes in a very low oven.

MENU SUGGESTIONS

This gorgeous dish deserves a great company menu—stuffed pork loin or nicely sauced duck, Broccoli in Creamy Broccoli Purée (page 85) and wild rice. For family, roasted chicken legs and plain rice will make a fine meal.

SALADS

Salads have a special section of their own because, even though they are not exactly vegetable side dishes, they are excellent alternatives.

There are two basic kinds of side salads: mixed green salads and composed vegetable salads. Mixed green salads, as you know, are usually composed mostly of lettuce and other greens but may also contain additional ingredients, such as tomatoes, cucumbers and so on. They are almost invariably served chilled, and generally taste best when they are tossed or drizzled with a good dressing.

Composed vegetable salads are combinations of raw and/or cooked vegetables, without lettuce or greens (although a composed vegetable salad may be presented on a bed of lettuce leaves).

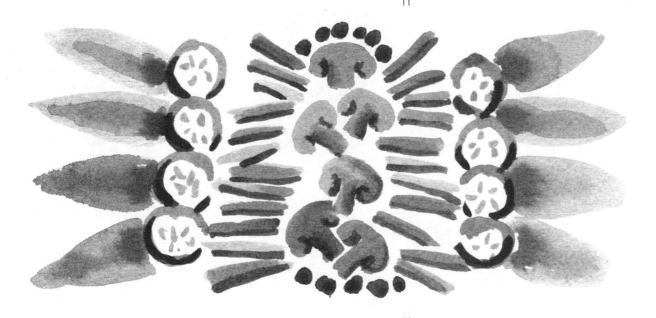

SALAD DRESSING: BASIC VINAIGRETTE

Vinaigrette dressing appears regularly on fresh green salads, but it is just as useful for dressing composed salads (pages 345 to 349) and cooked vegetables. This versatile sauce can be spicy, salty, tangy, gingery, tomato-y, garlicky or a dozen other flavors. How you alter the basic recipe and what other ingredients you introduce depends entirely on the salad or vegetables you're dressing; see page 340 for a slew of variations, and don't be afraid to invent some of your own.

A *traditional* composed salad is a combination of vegetables cut in bite-size pieces and gently tossed together with mayonnaise or some other dressing. Now, however, we have a new style of composed salad comprising vegetables that are left whole (if they are small) or cut in attractive shapes and then arranged beautifully on a platter, with dressing served separately. These salads are usually served at room temperature or chilled.

No elaborate recipes are required for either mixed green salads or composed salads, so this section is organized as an easy-to-use compilation of ideas. You'll also find a sidebar with cross-references to other salads in the book.

As for salad dressings, in this section there are four sidebars of recipes for vinaigrette and creamy dressings, as well as a sidebar with cross-references to the other salad dressings scattered throughout the rest of the book.

MIXED GREEN SALADS

All too often we put together the same old green salad and then wonder why no one wants to eat it. The intriguing combinations suggested on pages 342 to 345 should convince you that it is entirely unnecessary to make boring salads.

In addition to choosing interesting ingredients, presentation is important in salad making, too. If you usually throw the lettuce and tomatoes into your basic salad bowl, add the dressing and toss, consider trying a new approach: Make a bed of bite-size pieces of lettuce and greens on a pretty platter or in a shallow bowl, then arrange the additional ingredients attractively on top. The illustrations will give you an idea of what I mean.

When you're ready to eat the salad, simply spoon or drizzle the dressing evenly over the ingredients (no need to toss them) and serve, making sure each person gets plenty of lettuce and a good selection of the other ingredients.

Keep in mind that the basic recipe may be altered simply by varying the basic ingredients: Instead of wine vinegar, try balsamic or sherry vinegar, herb vinegar, rice vinegar or lemon juice. Fruity olive oil or a touch of walnut or sesame oil can make a big difference, too.

NOTE: *This basic recipe (which makes about one cup of dressing) is a little lighter than classic vinaigrette, with less oil and a bit more vinegar. If you like, lighten it even more by adding a tablespoon or two of water when you blend the ingredients.*

⅓ CUP RED OR WHITE WINE VINEGAR

⅔ CUP MILD OLIVE OIL, OR ⅓ CUP OLIVE OIL PLUS ⅓ CUP NEUTRAL VEGETABLE OIL (CORN, SAFFLOWER, CANOLA, SUNFLOWER, ETC.)

¼ TEASPOON SALT

½ TEASPOON DRY MUSTARD

FRESH PEPPER TO TASTE

1 GARLIC CLOVE, SPLIT IN HALF

In a food processor or by hand with a whisk, blend all the ingredients except the garlic. Pour the dressing into a jar and add the garlic; let it stand at room temperature for about two hours to develop flavor. Store in the refrigerator, but bring it to room temperature and shake well before using.

SALAD DRESSING: BASIC CREAMY DRESSING

Creamy dressings are usually ambushes of delicious but fattening ingredients—mayonnaise, sour cream, heavy cream and so on. The recipe here is easily convertible to lower fat and fewer calories simply by using the low-fat versions of the ingredients and—very important—flavoring the creamy mixture with herbs, mustard, lemon and other good tastes. For example, add a little tomato-based chili sauce, chopped pickles, minced onions and green pepper and you've got a delicious version of Thousand Island Dressing. Check the list on page 342 for more ideas.

Basic Creamy Dressing: To make 1 cup, whisk together ⅓ cup regular or low-fat mayonnaise, ⅓ cup regular or light sour cream and ⅓ cup low-fat buttermilk. Add any of the suggested flavorings and mix to blend. If the dressing is too thick for your purpose, thin with a little more buttermilk.

If you prefer, substitute plain (unflavored) yogurt or yogurt cheese for the sour cream and skim milk for the buttermilk. (Plain yogurt is thinner than sour cream, so add just enough of the milk to achieve the best texture.)

Basic Preparation of Mixed Green Salads

As always, buy the best ingredients you can find. When you're choosing tight-leaved greens such as Bibb, Boston, Belgian endive, cabbage and radicchio, look for firm, compact heads that seem heavy for their size. Loose-leaved greens, such as arugula, mâche, red leaf, chicory and watercress, should be crisp and lively, never limp or droopy. Both types of greens should be free of wilted, bruised or discolored leaves and free of mushy brown spots or sliminess (including on the stem end).

Lettuce and greens must be rinsed thoroughly to remove all dirt and sand, then dried on paper towels or in small batches in a salad spinner—a better choice, ecologically speaking. At this point you may either store the leaves whole (and tear them into bite-size pieces later, before putting the salad together) or you may tear or cut them into bite-size pieces before storing.

To store, put a paper towel or two in the bottom of a ziplock plastic bag, add the dry greens—loosely packed—and close the bag; use several bags if needed, and refrigerate until you are ready to make the salad. (Rinse and reuse those bags when the greens are gone.)

Prepare any other ingredients by cleaning, trimming, peeling (if needed) and cutting into bite-size or smaller pieces. How you make these preparations depends, of course, on which ingredients you are using. Carrots, for instance, must be peeled, topped and tailed and then diced, shredded, sliced thinly or cut into matchsticks; snow pea pods need only be rinsed, dried and cut in half (if they are large).

Allow about two loosely packed cups (or two big handfuls) of prepared greens for each person, plus about ¼ cup of other ingredients.

Lettuce and Greens

Here is a reminder list of lettuce and greens from which to choose when you plan your salad. If you're combining two or more kinds, you may want to mix contrasting textures, flavors and colors. On the other hand, it is sometimes interesting (and sophisticated) to serve a salad that duplicates textures, flavors or colors—arugula, watercress and dandelion greens for a peppery salad, for instance, or Belgian endive, Boston lettuce and frisée for a pale green salad.

About iceberg lettuce: Iceberg is so bland that, if you must use it, you should combine it with more assertive greens. Try shredding it instead of tearing it into bite-size pieces.

ARUGULA (ROCKET, RUGULA): Keep small leaves whole; tear larger ones in half.

BABY DANDELION, TURNIP OR BEET GREENS: Keep small leaves whole, tear larger ones in half.

BELGIAN ENDIVE: Trim and core; cut into wide or narrow slices, shred, or cut into wide or narrow sticks.

BIBB LETTUCE (LIMESTONE): Tear into bite-size pieces or use small leaves whole.

BOSTON LETTUCE (BUTTER, BUTTERHEAD): Tear into bite-size pieces or shred; small leaves can be used whole.

CABBAGE (RED, GREEN, SAVOY): Discard tough outer leaves, then shred or slice thin.

CHICORY (CURLY ENDIVE): Use the inner leaves only; chop or tear into bite-size pieces.

CHINESE CABBAGE (CELERY CABBAGE, NAPA CABBAGE, TIENTSIN CABBAGE): Shred finely or slice into thin or thick strips.

ESCAROLE: Use the inner leaves only; chop, slice or tear into bite-size pieces.

FRISÉE: Tear into bite-size pieces.

ICEBERG LETTUCE: Shred or, occasionally, tear into bite-size pieces.

LEAF LETTUCE (OR LOOSE-LEAF, INCLUDING RED, OAK AND GREEN LEAF): Tear into bite-size pieces.

MÂCHE (FIELD LETTUCE, CORN SALAD, LAMB'S LETTUCE): Keep small leaves whole; tear larger ones in half.

MIZUNA: Tear into bite-size pieces.

RADICCHIO: Tear into bite-size pieces or shred.

ROMAINE LETTUCE (COS): Shred, tear into bite-size pieces, or slit leaves in half and cut into wide or narrow slices.

SPINACH: Chop, slice, or tear into bite-size pieces.

WATERCRESS: Remove thick stems and use remaining leaves and sprigs.

Additions: Raw Vegetables

Add two or three of these to your basic greens, choosing carefully to make an interesting but compatible mix. If you are planning to add some other ingredient, such as croutons or any of the other ones on the next reminder list (page 340), include only one or two kinds of these raw vegetables.

Most raw vegetables can be cut in a variety of shapes. The illustrations will give you some ideas.

AVOCADO (PREFERABLY HASS), PEELED AND SEEDED: Cube or cut in slices.

BABY VEGETABLES (GREEN BEANS, SOFT-SKINNED SQUASH, CARROTS, GREEN PEAS), TRIMMED: Leave whole.

BEAN SPROUTS (ALFALFA, RADISH, MUNG): Cut off roots (if still attached) and use the rest.

BEETS, TRIMMED AND PEELED: Dice or cut into matchsticks.

BELL PEPPERS (RED, GREEN AND YELLOW), CORED, SEEDED AND DEVEINED: Dice, sliver, or cut into sticks or rings.

CARROTS, TRIMMED AND PEELED: Dice, grate, slice thin or cut into matchsticks.

CELERY, TRIMMED AND STRINGS REMOVED: Dice or slice thin.

CUCUMBERS (REGULAR CUKES, KIRBIES, ENGLISH OR HOTHOUSE SEEDLESS CUCUMBERS), TRIMMED, PEELED AND SEEDED: Slice, dice, chop coarsely or cut into sticks.

FENNEL, TRIMMED: Slice thin.

HERBS, FRESH (PARSLEY, BASIL, CHERVIL, CHIVES, DILL, TARRAGON, CORIANDER, OREGANO, MINT, ROSEMARY, MARJORAM), STEMS DISCARDED: Chop, mince or, in some cases, use the leaves shredded or whole.

ITALIAN FRYING PEPPERS, CORED, SEEDED AND DEVEINED: Dice, sliver or cut into sticks or rings.

JERUSALEM ARTICHOKES (SUNCHOKES), TRIMMED AND PEELED: Dice, slice thin or cut into matchsticks.

JÍCAMA, TRIMMED AND PEELED: Dice, slice thin or cut in matchsticks.

MUSHROOMS (WHITE, CREMINI, ENOKI), TRIMMED AND CLEANED: Slice thin or cut in quarters (or halves if small); enokis may be used whole.

SALAD DRESSING: VARIATIONS ON VINAIGRETTE

Whisk or process the ingredients listed for each variation (adding one or two tablespoons of water if you want to lighten the dressing a bit), adding salt and fresh pepper to taste.

Mustard Vinaigrette: 1/3 cup red or white wine vinegar; 1/3 cup olive oil; 1/3 cup neutral oil; 2 teaspoons Dijon mustard; salt and pepper to taste. After whisking, add 1 split clove of garlic.

Garlic Vinaigrette: 1/3 cup red or white wine vinegar; 1/3 cup olive oil; 1/3 cup neutral oil; 4 garlic cloves that have been boiled for about 15 minutes (until tender), then mashed; 1/2 teaspoon dry mustard; salt and pepper

Shallot Vinaigrette: 1/3 cup sherry vinegar; 1/3 cup olive oil; 1/3 cup neutral oil; 2 tablespoons finely minced shallots; salt and pepper

Herb Vinaigrette: 1/3 cup sherry vinegar; 1/3 cup olive oil; 1/3 cup neutral oil; 1/2 teaspoon dry mustard; 1 tablespoon minced fresh basil, chervil, tarragon, chives or dill; 1 tablespoon minced fresh flat-leaf (Italian) parsley; salt and pepper. After whisking, add 1 split clove of garlic.

Curry Vinaigrette: 1/3 cup cider vinegar; 2/3 cup neutral oil; 1/2 to 1 teaspoon mild curry powder; salt and pepper

Tomato Vinaigrette: 1/3 cup balsamic or red wine vinegar; 2/3 cup mild olive oil; 2 tablespoons tomato paste; 1/4 teaspoon powdered oregano; salt and pepper. After whisking, add 1 split clove of garlic.

Anchovy Vinaigrette: 1/3 cup fresh lemon juice; 2/3 cup olive oil;

OLIVES (BLACK, GREEN, STUFFED): Use whole or sliced.

ONIONS (RED, SPANISH, BERMUDA, VIDALIA, MAUI, WALLA WALLA), TRIMMED AND PEELED: Dice, mince or slice thin.

RADISHES (RED, WHITE ICICLE, BLACK, DAIKON), TRIMMED: Quarter, chop or slice thin.

SCALLIONS, TRIMMED: Mince, chop, slice thin or cut into thicker slices on the diagonal.

SNOW PEA PODS, TRIMMED: Cut into matchsticks, slice on the diagonal, or use whole.

SQUASH, SUMMER (ZUCCHINI, YELLOW SQUASH, PATTYPAN), TRIMMED: Dice, slice, cut in half moons or matchsticks.

SUGAR SNAP PEAS, TRIMMED: Slice on the diagonal or use whole.

TOMATOES (SUMMER GLOBE TOMATOES, PLUM TOMATOES, PEAR TOMATOES, RED OR YELLOW CHERRY TOMATOES): Slice, dice or cut in wedges; if you like, first scoop out the pulp and seeds and use only the flesh. Cherry tomatoes should be halved or quartered.

Additions: Cooked Vegetables, Beans, Condiments and More

These are the ingredients that add pep to your salads. They can also become too much of a good thing, so don't go overboard unless you want the salad to dominate your menu.

NOTE: *All the vegetables mentioned in this list (except water chestnuts) are meant be cooked and chilled before use.*

ANCHOVIES: Chop, halve or leave whole.

APPLES (PEELED OR UNPEELED): Cube or slice.

ARTICHOKE HEARTS: Quarter (if the tender leaves are still attached) or slice (if only the hearts are used).

ASPARAGUS: Use the tips only or slice the whole stalk on the diagonal.

BACON, CRISP: Crumble or chop.

BEETS: Dice, cube, slice or cut into matchsticks.

BROCCOLI FLOWERETS: Cut or break into smaller flowerets.

CAPERS

CARROTS: Dice, slice thin or cut into sticks or matchsticks.

CELERY ROOT: Dice, cube, slice or cut into sticks or matchsticks.

CHEESE, FIRM (CHEDDAR, MONTEREY JACK, GRUYÈRE, JARLSBERG, PROVOLONE): Shred or cube.

CHEESE, CRUMBLED (DANISH BLUE, ROQUEFORT, FETA, RICOTTA SALATA, FARMER, LEICESTER, SOME GOAT CHEESES)

CHEESE, GRATED OR SHAVED (PARMESAN, ROMANO, ASIAGO)

CORN KERNELS

CROUTONS (HOMEMADE OR PACKAGED, SEASONED OR UNSEASONED)

DRIED BEANS, COOKED (BLACK, PINK, PINTO, CHICK-PEAS, SMALL WHITE, CANNELLINI, GREAT NORTHERN, RED KIDNEY, BLACK-EYED PEAS)

EGGS, HARD-COOKED: Slice, chop or sieve.

GARLIC, ROASTED CLOVES: Cut in half or leave whole.

GIARDINIERA: Cut large pieces down to bite-size, leave small pieces whole.

GRAPEFRUIT SECTIONS

GRAPES (SEEDLESS RED OR GREEN): Halve or leave whole.

1 teaspoon anchovy paste; 1 tablespoon minced fresh flat-leaf (Italian) parsley; salt (if needed) and pepper. After whisking, add 1 split clove of garlic.

Soy-Ginger Vinaigrette: $\frac{1}{3}$ cup rice vinegar; $\frac{1}{3}$ cup peanut oil; $\frac{1}{3}$ cup neutral oil; 1 tablespoon soy sauce; $\frac{1}{4}$ teaspoon sugar. After whisking, add 2 thin slices of peeled fresh ginger and 1 split clove of garlic.

Tequila Vinaigrette: $\frac{1}{4}$ cup fresh lime juice; 2 tablespoons tequila; $\frac{1}{2}$ cup neutral vegetable oil; salt and pepper

Lime Vinaigrette: $\frac{1}{3}$ cup fresh lime juice; $\frac{2}{3}$ cup olive oil or $\frac{1}{3}$ cup olive oil and $\frac{1}{3}$ cup neutral oil; $\frac{1}{2}$ teaspoon dry mustard; salt and pepper

Jalapeño Vinaigrette: $\frac{1}{2}$ to 1 fresh or pickled jalapeño pepper, minced (start with half a pepper and add more to taste); $\frac{1}{3}$ cup red or white wine vinegar; $\frac{2}{3}$ cup neutral vegetable oil; salt and pepper. After whisking, add 1 split clove of garlic.

SALAD DRESSING: VARIATIONS ON CREAMY DRESSING

Many salads and plain cooked vegetables are vastly improved by the addition of a dollop or two of tasty creamy dressing. Basic Creamy Dressing (page 336) takes just a minute to make and can then be flavored to suit whatever salad or vegetable you're serving. For instance, try a little Creamy Mustard Dressing on chilled asparagus, Creamy Three-Pepper Dressing on Brussels sprouts, or Creamy Dill Dressing on carrots or a mixed green salad.

Simply stir together one recipe of Basic Creamy Dressing with the ingredients listed for one of the variations below. If you have time, it's a good idea to let the mixture stand for 30 minutes to let the flavor develop.

Creamy Curry Dressing: two teaspoons mild curry powder; one tablespoon orange or apple juice concentrate; salt and fresh pepper to taste

Creamy Mustard Dressing: one tablespoon Dijon mustard; one teaspoon cider or sherry vinegar; salt and fresh pepper to taste

Creamy Chutney Dressing: ¼ cup chopped mild mango chutney; 1 tablespoon fresh lime juice; salt and fresh pepper to taste

Creamy Dill Dressing: two tablespoons minced *fresh* dill; one teaspoon Dijon mustard; salt and fresh pepper to taste

Creamy Three-Pepper Dressing: ½ to 1 minced fresh hot pepper (according to taste); 1 tablespoon minced green bell pepper; 1 tablespoon minced red bell pepper; ¼ teaspoon celery seeds; salt and fresh pepper to taste

Creamy Horseradish Dressing: 1 tablespoon drained prepared horseradish; 1 tablespoon minced onion; salt and fresh pepper to taste

GREEN BEANS OR BABY GREEN BEANS: Cut large beans into bite-size pieces, leave small ones whole.

JALAPEÑOS, PICKLED: Mince, chop or slice.

JERUSALEM ARTICHOKES (SUNCHOKES): Dice, cube, slice or cut into sticks or matchsticks.

LENTILS

MANDARIN ORANGE SECTIONS

NAVEL ORANGES (PEELED): Slice or section.

NUTS (TOASTED WALNUTS, PECANS, PINE NUTS OR ALMONDS; ROASTED PEANUTS OR CASHEWS): Chop, sliver or break into small pieces.

PEARS (SLIGHTLY UNDERRIPE, PEELED OR UNPEELED): Cube or slice.

PEPPERS, ROASTED RED OR YELLOW (HOMEMADE OR FROM A JAR): Dice, chop or cut into strips.

PETITE PEAS (BABY GREEN PEAS)

PICKLES, SWEET OR SOUR: Chop or slice.

POTATOES: Dice, cube or slice.

RAISINS

SESAME SEEDS, TOASTED

TOFU: Dice or cube.

WATER CHESTNUTS (CANNED OR FRESH): Quarter, chop or slice.

Mixed Green Salad Suggestions

This is a series of short takes, suggestions for fresh green salad combinations using ingredients from the lists on the previous pages. The possibilities are endless, but here are 25 salads culled from my own list of dozens.

HEARTY SALAD: Toss together bite-size pieces of romaine, radicchio and the tender inner leaves of chicory; top with chopped toasted walnuts and red onion rings, and dress with Mustard Vinaigrette (page 340).

PEPPERY SALAD: Combine arugula and watercress with radish sprouts; dress with Sweet-and-Sour Buttermilk Dressing (page 147). If you like, top with crumbled goat cheese.

TEX-MEX SALAD: Mix red leaf and green leaf lettuce with diced tomatoes, thinly sliced pickled jalapeños and chopped fresh coriander; dress with Cumin Vinaigrette (page 172).

SAN FRANCISCO SALAD: Toss together a variety of tender greens—arugula, baby lettuce, mâche, frisée, etc.—and dress with a good vinaigrette; sprinkle with sourdough croutons and shredded Monterey Jack cheese.

AUTUMN SALAD: Take bite-size pieces of romaine and beet (or turnip) greens, finely shredded red cabbage, thinly sliced apple and matchsticks of jícama, and toss with Creamy Herb Dressing (page 24).

SPICY SALAD: Combine romaine, spinach and grated carrot in a creamy curry dressing or curry vinaigrette; sprinkle with chopped unsalted peanuts and minced fresh coriander.

JAPANESE SALAD: Make a bed of watercress and spinach; top with diced tofu and enoki mushrooms; drizzle with Soy-Ginger Vinaigrette (page 341).

ITALIAN SALAD: Toss tender inner leaves of escarole with arugula, rings of Italian pepper and slivers of giardiniera or cracked Sicilian olives; dress with Garlic Vinaigrette (page 340). If you like, add shavings of Parmesan cheese.

ELEGANT SALAD: Arrange leaves of Bibb lettuce on a platter and top with thin slices of almost-ripe pear; sprinkle with chopped toasted hazelnuts and crumbled Roquefort cheese; drizzle with simple vinaigrette.

CONFETTI SALAD: Combine pale green lettuces, such as Boston, Belgian endive and frisée; dress with vinaigrette and garnish with a sprinkling of several of these—diced ham, corn kernels, diced red pepper, diced carrot, diced beets, tiny cooked limas, petite peas, diced red radish.

CROSS-REFERENCE: SALAD DRESSINGS

Ancho Chile Vinaigrette, page 69

Caper Dressing, page 145

Creamy Ginger Dressing, page 73

Creamy Herb Dressing, page 24

Creamy Tarragon Dressing, page 117

Creamy Vinaigrette Dressing, page 255 and page 319

Cumin Vinaigrette page 172

Lemon-Curry Mayonnaise, page 80

Lemon-Garlic Vinaigrette Dressing, page 53

Olive Oil Vinaigrette Dressing, page 242

Orange-Yogurt Dressing, page 121

Poppy Seed Dressing, page 190

Russian Dressing, page 92

Sweet-and-Sour Buttermilk Dressing, page 147

Vinaigrette Dressing, page 49 and page 245

Walnut Oil Vinaigrette, page 77

CHINESE SALAD: Mix finely shredded Chinese cabbage and whole snow pea pods; dress with Warm Sesame Dressing (page 290), and top with toasted sesame seeds.

SPRING SALAD: Toss together a variety of greens, including some tender lettuce; add whole sugar snap peas and uncooked petite peas, and dress with Lemon-Garlic Vinaigrette (page 53).

FANCY SALAD: Dress a bowl of mâche with Walnut Oil Vinaigrette (page 77); divide it among individual salad plates and top each with matchsticks of raw beets and homemade croutons.

UNUSUAL SALAD: Make a bed of small leaves and bite-size pieces of spinach; arrange thinly sliced mushrooms and thin slices of cantaloupe on it, and drizzle with vinaigrette made with balsamic vinegar.

MIDEAST SALAD: Combine leaf lettuce, finely shredded Savoy cabbage and cooked bulgur wheat or couscous; dress with Orange-Yogurt Dressing (page 121), and garnish with chopped cucumber and minced parsley.

FLAVORFUL SALAD: Mix sliced Belgian endive, torn Boston lettuce, thinly sliced fennel and slivers of red bell pepper in a creamy mustard dressing.

PUNGENT SALAD: Toss watercress, beet greens and romaine with paper-thin slices of red radish, daikon radish and Kirby cucumber; dress with Creamy Herb Dressing (page 25).

GREEK SALAD: Combine shredded iceberg lettuce and bite-size pieces of romaine with diced cucumber, tomato, green bell pepper, sliced sweet onion, black olives and crumbled feta cheese; dress with oil, vinegar, salt and fresh pepper.

WILTED SALAD: Cook, drain, and crumble several slices of bacon; toss the bacon with lots of soft lettuce (Boston, Bibb, red leaf, oak leaf) and Warm Sesame Dressing (page 290); garnish with sliced scallions.

SUMMER SALAD: Tear up leaves of the youngest, freshest lettuce you can find at a farmstand; combine with thinly sliced peaches or nectarines, and dress with Chive Salsa (page 214) or Creamy Ginger Dressing (page 73).

WINTER SALAD: Put together a mix of strong greens—escarole, chicory, spinach, romaine—and top with cooked lentils and halved cherry tomatoes; dress with Shallot Vinaigrette (page 340).

NIPPY SALAD: Toss baby dandelion, beet and/or turnip greens with a milder lettuce (such as red leaf); add strips of roasted red pepper, anchovies and capers, and dress with a basic vinaigrette.

L.A. SALAD: Prepare a bed of bite-size pieces of red and green leaf lettuce; sprinkle with cubed avocado, chopped hard-cooked egg, alfalfa sprouts and crumbled blue cheese; drizzle with Creamy Vinaigrette Dressing (page 255).

CHILE SALAD: Combine romaine with finely shredded green cabbage; top with black beans, cooked corn kernels and chopped mild green chiles; dress with Ancho Chile Vinaigrette (page 69).

ANOTHER SPRING SALAD: On individual salad plates, arrange small whole leaves of Bibb and Boston lettuce; garnish each with asparagus tips, artichoke hearts and a few pine nuts; add dollops of Lemon-Curry Mayonnaise (page 80).

COMPOSED VEGETABLE SALADS

As you know from reading the beginning of this section, composed vegetable salads are cold salads made up of cooked and/or raw vegetables. Traditional composed salads are mixtures of vegetables bound with mayonnaise or salad dressing and served in a bowl. Salade Russe (carrots, potatoes, turnips, beets and peas bound with vinaigrette and mayonnaise) is a good example of this kind of salad. There's a newer style of composed vegetable salads, too—handsome arrangements of

whole and cut vegetables on a platter, with dressing served on the side. In this case, a picture explains it best:

Following the information on basic preparation, here are suggestions for ten composed salads, five of each type.

Basic Preparation of Composed Vegetable Salads

You may, of course, cook or prepare vegetables for the express purpose of using them in composed vegetable salads. However, quite often you can make use of leftover cooked or raw vegetables, combining them with freshly prepared ones to create a beautiful salad with an appropriate dressing.

Whether you're starting from scratch or using up leftovers (or both), the most important part of preparing composed vegetable salads is cutting the vegetables in attractive sizes and shapes. Bite-size or smaller pieces are generally best, unless you are making an arrangement in which you want larger pieces to contrast dramatically with smaller ones. You can see in the illustrations (on pages 12 to 14) that there are many ways to cut vegetables.

Keep in mind that some vegetables do look prettier when they are left whole—for instance, blanched or raw snow pea pods, baby vegetables, cherry tomatoes, asparagus (though you may want to trim long stems), enoki mushrooms or small white mushrooms and so on.

The second part of basic preparation is to make a fresh dressing to toss with or drizzle over the vegetables. Check the sidebars in this section for a variety of vinaigrettes and creamy dressings to use.

Composed Vegetable Salad Suggestions

WINTER BEET SALAD: Toss diced cooked beets and potatoes with Caper Dressing (page 145) and snipped fresh chives. For a more substantial salad, arrange the dressed vegetables on shredded fresh raw spinach.

LATE SUMMER SALAD: Combine small cooked green beans, cooked sweet corn kernels and diced red bell pepper. Dress with Ancho Chile Vinaigrette (page 69) or Yogurt-Dill Sauce (page 32).

APRIL SALAD: Gently toss cooked asparagus tips, tiny new potatoes, petite peas and sliced sautéed wild mushrooms with vinaigrette dressing. If you like, serve the salad on a bed of tender lettuce leaves.

ZUCCHINI SALAD: Mix diced cooked zucchini, carrots and celery with small white beans and diced raw tomatoes. Stir in some garlic mayonnaise (aioli, page 52) and sprinkle with minced fresh basil.

ROOT VEGETABLE SALAD: Combine cooked cubes of parsnip, carrot, sweet potato and rutabaga with sliced fresh scallions. Dress with Creamy Vinaigrette Dressing (page 255).

EASTERN SALAD: On a bed of finely shredded Chinese cabbage, arrange spears of cooked broccoli, whole snow pea

CROSS-REFERENCE: SALADS

Asparagus Salad with Yogurt-Dill Sauce, page 32

Basic Coleslaw with Variations, page 98

Broccoli Salad with Lemon-Curry Mayonnaise and Pepper Confetti, page 80

Brussels Sprouts Salad in Homemade Russian Dressing, page 92

Creamy Carrot Slaw with Chives, page 108

Cucumber Salad with Caper Dressing, page 145

Cucumbers in Sweet-and-Sour Buttermilk Dressing, page 147

Dilly Beans, page 58

Escarole, Radicchio and White Beans with Walnut-Basil Pesto, page 168

Fennel and Chick-Peas in Cumin Vinaigrette, page 172

Fennel with Oranges and Niçoise Olives, page 175

Four Quick Bean Salads, page 48

Fresh Corn Salad with Olives and Tomatoes, page 141

Green Beans in the Style of Spain, page 62

Hot and Cold Cucumbers, page 148

Japanese Cucumber Salad, page 146

Minted Zucchini Tabbouleh Salad, page 298

pods, carrot matchsticks and sliced water chestnuts. Drizzle with Sesame-Ginger Sauce (page 31) or Spicy Peanut Sauce (page 134). Sprinkle with toasted sesame seeds.

EGGPLANT SALAD: Cut roasted eggplant and zucchini in long strips and place them on a platter; brush with olive oil and sprinkle with salt and pepper. Add narrow strips of roasted red peppers, capers, black olives and chopped fresh basil or arugula.

RIVIERA SALAD: Prepare a bed of romaine lettuce leaves. Arrange on it cooked baby green beans, halved cherry tomatoes, quartered new potatoes, slivers of red bell pepper, red onion rings and Niçoise olives. Sprinkle with a variety of chopped fresh herbs such as parsley, chervil, oregano, rosemary, sage or tarragon. Offer Anchovy Vinaigrette (page 340) on the side.

MAY SALAD: Arrange baby dandelion leaves on a platter. Top with braised leeks, fresh scallions (with the greens cut short), pencil-thin asparagus and tiny radishes. Serve with Walnut Oil Vinaigrette (page 77).

ARTICHOKE SALAD: Make a bed of thin slices of radicchio and top this with a ring of individual spears of Belgian endive. In the center of the salad put a mound of cooked artichoke hearts surrounded by small white mushrooms and roasted yellow peppers. Serve with Creamy Herb Dressing (page 25).

My Favorite Belgian Endive Salad, page 76

Old-fashioned Chopped Celery and Apple Salad with Orange-Yogurt Dressing, page 121

Pepper and Cabbage Slaw for a Picnic, page 249

Plantain Salad, page 254

Quick Potato Salads, page 266

Red and Green Gazpacho Salad, page 322

Russian Salad, page 241

Salad of Endive and Pears with Creamy Ginger Dressing,

page 72

Simple Tomato Salads, page 324

Sweet Potato Salad with Southwest Seasonings, page 261

I n d e x

✿ denotes The Vegetable Express entry
♦ denotes Company's Coming entry

Acorn Squash with Apples and Cider
    Glaze, 303
aioli, 52–53
Ancho Chile Vinaigrette for Beets, 69
appetizers, vegetable, 300
Artichoke(s), 21–29. *See also* Jerusalem
    artichokes
    about buying and storing, 21;
        discoloring, 22; preparing,
        21–22; varieties, 21
    Crisp, 23
    Halves with Creamy Herb Dressing,
        Stuffed, 24
    Lemon-Braised, 27✿
    Provençal, 26
    Tart with Roasted Garlic, 28♦
Asian ingredients, 150. *See also* Chinese
    ingredients
Asparagus, 30–37
    about buying and storing, 30;
        preparing, 30
    Basic, Four Simple Dress-Ups for,
        36✿
    Cordon Bleu, 37♦
    with Mushrooms, 34
    Salad with Yogurt-Dill Sauce, 32
    with Sesame-Ginger Sauce, 31
autumn holiday side dishes, 304–5
avocados
    Guacamole, 44
    peeling and using, 42–43

baby vegetables, 296
Barbecue Limas, 60
Barnaby's Vegetable Broth, 176–77
basic information about vegetables, 6–19
    cooking equipment, 7–11
    cooking techniques and terms,
        15–17
    ingredients, 17–19
    non-cooking techniques and terms,
        11–15
    preparation, 6
Basic Root Vegetable Broth, 110
Basil-Parsley Sauce for Beets, 69
Beans, Dried, 38–53
    about buying and storing, 38–39;
        preparing, 39

black bean salad, 48
Black Beans with Bacon and Chile,
    44
Black Beans and Pumpkin, 274
black-eyed pea salad, 48
Black-eyed Peas with Butter and
    Scallions, 51✿
Black-eyed Peas, Swiss Chard with
    Bacon and, 311
Cannellini with Escarole Purée, 46
Chick-Peas and Fennel in Cumin
    Vinaigrette, 172
Chick-Peas and Spinach, Not-Too-
    Hot, Spicy, 288
Chick-Peas, Tomato-baked, 47
Flageolets with Oven-dried Tomatoes
    and Crisp-fried Onions, 52♦
four quick salads, 48
Indian Beans and Greens, 50
Kidney Beans with Rice and Cheese,
    45
Lentils, Savory Baked, 40
Lentils, Sweet-and-Sour, 42
pink bean salad, 48
Pink Beans in Creamy Onion Sauce,
    41
Split Pea and Bulgur Wheat Pilaf, 43
White Bean and Goat Cheese Pâté
    on Greens, 48
white bean salad, 48
White Beans, Escarole and
    Radicchio with Walnut-Basil
    Pesto, 168
Beans, Fresh, 54–63. *See also* Green
    Beans; Lima Bean(s)
    about buying and storing, 54;
        preparing, 54–55; varieties, 54
beef. *See* steak
Beet(s)
    about buying and storing, 64;
        preparing, 64–65
    -Apple-Ginger Relish, 66
    Baby, and Beet Greens, 70♦
    baking, 68
    beet greens, preparing, 65
    Caviar, Sweet, 67
    Four Savory Sauces for, 68✿
    Red Flannel Hash, 66
Belgian Endive, 71–77
    about buying and storing, 71;
        preparing, 71

Baked in White Wine Sauce, 74
Salad of Endive and Pears with
    Creamy Ginger Dressing, 72
Salad, My Favorite, 76♦
Sautéed, with Bacon and Pecans,
    75✿
Black Bean(s)
    with Bacon and Chile, 44
    and Pumpkin, 274
    salad, 48
Black-eyed Pea(s)
    with Butter and Scallions, 51
    salad, 48
    Swiss Chard with Bacon and, 311
Bok Choy with Garlic Sauce, 132
Brandied Brussels Sprouts and
    Chestnuts, 95
bread crumbs, about making and using,
    36–37
Broccoli, 78–89
    about buying and storing, 78;
        preparing, 78–79
    and Chinese Mushrooms, 82
    Chinese, in Soy-Lemon-Butter
        Sauce, 129
    in Creamy Broccoli Purée, 85
    Filling, Creamy, Buckwheat Crêpes
        with, 87♦
    Salad with Lemon-Curry Mayonnaise
        and Pepper Confetti, 80
Broccoli Rabe, 78
    with Anchovy and Garlic Sauce,
        84
    Sautéed, with Parmesan, 86✿
Broth
    garlic, 200
    Root Vegetable, Basic, 110
    Vegetable, Barnaby's, 176–77
Brussels Sprouts, 90–95
    about buying and storing, 90;
        preparing, 90
    Brandied, and Chestnuts, 95♦
    and Cheese, Potato Boats Stuffed
        with, 91
    Paprikash, 94✿
    Salad in Homemade Russian
        Dressing, 92
    Spicy Browned, and Carrots, 93
Buckwheat Crêpes with Creamy Broccoli
    Filling, 87♦
Bulgur Wheat and Split Pea Pilaf, 43

Buttercup Squash, Savory, and Cheese Gratin, 305
Butternut Squash with Coriander Sauce, 306

Cabbage, 96–104
    about buying and storing, 96; preparing, 96–97
    Chinese, Stuffed Rolls, with Spicy Peanut Sauce, 133
    Coleslaw, 98; Variations, 99
    Custard, Delicate, 100
    Pepper and, Slaw for a Picnic, 249❂
    Red, Braised, and Apples, 99
    Rolls Italiano, Stuffed, 103♦
    Savoy, Butter-Browned, and Mushrooms, 102❂
    Soup-Without-the-Soup, Tuscan, 101
    Stir-fried, 98
Cannellini with Escarole Purée, 46
Caponata with Sun-dried Tomatoes, Simplified, 152
Carrot(s), 105–12
    about buying and storing, 105; preparing, 105
    Baked, in Honey-Mustard Sauce, 109
    Browned, 110❂
    Chutney, 108
    and Corn Sauté, Simple, 140❂
    Pancakes, 106
    Parsnips and Dried Fruits, Tzimmes of, 229
    Ring, Sweet, 111♦
    Slaw with Chives, Creamy, 108
    Spicy Browned Brussels Sprouts and, 93
Cauliflower, 113–19
    about buying and storing, 112; preparing, 113
    Caulifritters, 118♦
    with Cheese Sauce, 114
    with Creamy Tarragon Dressing, Warm, 117❂
    Mediterranean, 115
    with Sun-dried Tomatoes, 116
Celery, 120–25
    about buying and storing, 120; preparing, 120
    -Almond Timbale, 122
    and Apple Salad, Old-fashioned Chopped, with Orange-Yogurt Dressing, 121
    Hearts, Braised, with Blue Cheese, 124♦
    with Mushroom Cream Sauce, 123❂
celery root, 282
Cheddar-baked Tomatoes, 323
cheese
    Blue Cheese, Braised Celery Hearts with, 124♦
    Cheddar-baked Tomatoes, 323

Cheddar Cheese, Baked Leeks with Bacon and, 195
Cheese-, Chile-, Corn Pudding, 136
Cheese, Kidney Beans with Rice and, 45
Cheese, Mashed Potatoes with, and Crispy Potato Skins, 264
Cheese, Melted, Fluffy Baked Rutabagas with, 285♦
cheese, pasta with, 292
Cheese, Potato Boats Stuffed with Brussels Sprouts and, 91
Cheese Gratin, Savory Buttercup Squash and, 305
Cheese Sauce, Cauliflower with, 114
Cheese Sauce, Holiday Baked Onions with Double, 224♦
Fontina Cheese, Baked, Eggplant Slices Rolled with, 160
Goat Cheese, Roasted Eggplant with Mushrooms and, 158
Goat Cheese Pâté on Greens, White Beans and, 48
Gorgonzola Cream, 165
Gorgonzola Cream, Escarole with, 174
Gorgonzola Sauce, Zucchini Ribbons in, 295
grated, 88–89
Mozzarella Topping, Casserole of Greens with, 183♦
Parmesan, Sautéed Broccoli Rabe with, 86
Roquefort, Tomatoes with Orzo and, 319
yogurt, 312–13
chestnuts, preparing (peeling, roasting, etc.), 95
chicken, roasted, vegetable side dishes for, 182–83
Chick-Peas
    and Fennel in Cumin Vinaigrette, 172
    and Spinach, Not-Too-Hot-Spicy, 288
    Tomato-baked, 47
Chile-Cheese-Corn Pudding, 136
Chiles
    Pickled, 180
    varieties of, 248–49
    working with, 246–47
Chinese
    Black Mushrooms, Braised, 203
    cooking technique, stir-frying, 131–32
    ingredients (soy sauce, hoisin sauce, etc.), 128–31. *See also* Asian ingredients
Chinese Greens (bok choy, Chinese broccoli, Chinese cabbage), 126–34. *See also* Greens

about buying and storing, 126–27; preparing, 127
Bok Choy with Garlic Sauce, 132❂
Broccoli in Soy-Lemon-Butter Sauce, 129
Cabbage Rolls, Stuffed, with Spicy Peanut Sauce, 133♦
Mixed, 128
Vegetable Dumplings, Steamed, 130
chive salsa, 214
Chutney. *See also* Relish
    Carrot, 108
    green tomato, 320
Coleslaw, Basic, 98
    Variations, 99
Collards with West Indian Pepper-and-Lime Sauce, 180
Composed Vegetable Salads, 345–49; basic preparation of, 346–47; variations, 347–49
condiments, 212–13. *See also* mustard(s); Relish
    for curry, 256–57
conservation in the kitchen, tips for, 102–3
cooking
    equipment for vegetables, basic, 7–11
    techniques and terms, 15–17; non-cooking terms, 11–15
Corn, 135–42
    about buying and storing, 135; preparing, 135
    Cakes with Raisins, Sweet, 137
    and Carrot Sauté, Simple, 140❂
    on the cob, 138; butter sauces, 139
    Creole, 138
    and Lima Succotash in Lemon-Dill Cream, 139
    Pudding, Chile-Cheese-, 136
    Salad with Olives and Tomatoes, Fresh, 141♦
Couscous and Pine Nuts, Tomatoes Stuffed with, 325
creamy dressing, basic, 336; variations, 342
Creole
    Corn, 138
    -style Okra, 215
Crêpes, Buckwheat, with Creamy Broccoli Filling, 87♦
cross-reference
    basic ingredients, 18–19
    salad dressings, 343–44
    salads, 348–49
    sauces for vegetables, 124–25
croutons, 166–67
crunchy toppings for vegetables, 308–9
Cucumber(s), 143–48
    about buying and storing, 143; preparing, 143–44

Cucumber(s) (*cont.*)
  Hot and Cold, 148◆
  Quick-Pickled Cukes and Sweet
    Onions, 144
  Salad with Caper Dressing, 145
  Salad, Japanese, 146
  in Sweet-and-Sour Buttermilk
    Dressing, 147✿
Cumin Vinaigrette, 172
Curried Pumpkin, West Indian–style,
  277
Curry
  condiments for, 256–57
  powder, do-it-yourself, 252–53
  Sauce and Roasted Peanuts,
    Plantains with, 257

Dilly Beans, 58
Dressing. *See also* Sauce(s); Vinaigrette
  aioli, 52–53
  Creamy Ginger, 73
  dress-ups, four simple, for basic
    asparagus; 36✿
  Herb, Creamy, 25
  mayonnaise, low-fat, low-calorie,
    80–81
  Orange-Yogurt, 121
  Russian, 92
  Salad, basic creamy, 336; variations,
    342
  Salad, basic vinaigrette, 334–35;
    variations, 340–41
Dried Beans. *See* Beans, Dried

Eggplant, 149–62
  about buying and storing, 149;
    preparing, 149–50
  Baked Slices, Rolled with Fontina
    Cheese, 160◆
  Caponata with Sun-dried Tomatoes,
    Simplified, 152
  Fingers, Oven-fried, with Ranch
    Dipping Sauce, 154
  Hot and Spicy Braised, 156
  with Indian Spices, Roasted, 159
  with Mushrooms and Goat Cheese,
    Roasted, 158
  Roasted, with Roasted Garlic, 159
  Roasted, Three Variations on, 158✿
  Thai-style, 151
Endive. *See* Belgian Endive
Escarole, 163–69
  about buying and storing, 163;
    preparing, 163
  with Gorgonzola Cream, 164
  Purée, Cannellini with, 46
  Radicchio and White Beans with
    Walnut-Basil Pesto, 168◆
  Sautéed, with Bacon and Garlic,
    167✿
  in Tomato Sauce, 166

Fennel, 170–77
  about buying and storing, 170;
    preparing, 170
  Baked, with Sour Cream Sauce, 171
  and Chick-Peas in Cumin
    Vinaigrette, 172
  Lemon-sautéed, 174
  with Oranges and Niçoise Olives,
    175✿
  Roasted, with Wild Mushrooms and
    Crisp Shallots, 176◆
fish, broiled or pan-fried, vegetable side
  dishes for, 238–39
Flageolets with Oven-dried Tomatoes
  and Crisp-fried Onions, 52◆

garlic, 24–25; roasted, 28–29
  Roasted, Artichoke Tart with, 28
  broth, 200
garnishes
  fancy, 186–87, 190–91
  simple, 208–9
Gazpacho Salad, Red and Green, 322
Giardiniera, 116
Ginger-Orange Parsnips, 228
Gingered Sweet Potatoes, 269
Gorgonzola Cream, 165
Grains, 217
Green Beans, 54–58, 62
  about preparing, 54
  Buttery, with Pecan Crumbs, 56
  Dilly Beans, 58
  Stir-fried, 57
  in the Style of Spain, 62◆
Greens (beet, collard, kale, mustard,
    turnip), 178–84. *See also* Chinese
    Greens
  about buying and storing, 178;
    preparing, 178
  beet, about preparing, 65
  Beet, and Baby Beets, 70
  Casserole of, with Mozzarella
    Topping, 183◆
  Collards with West Indian Pepper-
    and-Lime Sauce, 180
  Kale, Sautéed, with Bacon-Molasses
    Dressing, 179
  for salad, basic preparation of,
    336–38; names of, 337–38
  and Tomatoes, Creamy, 182✿
Green Salads. *See also* Salad(s)
  Mixed, 335–45
  mixed combinations, 342–45
green tomato chutney, 320
Grilled Vegetables, 72
Guacamole, 44. *See also* avocados

ham, baked, vegetable side dishes for,
  92–93
hamburgers or meatloaf, vegetable side
  dishes for, 68

herb(s)
  curry powder, do-it-yourself, 252
  fresh, 58–59
  and spices, dried, 264–65
  vinegar, making, 32–33
Herbed Potatoes Provençal, 263
Horseradish Sauce for Beets, 68–69
hot pepper powder and sauce, 274–75
hot peppers. *See* Pepper(s)

Indian Beans and Greens, 50

Japanese Cucumber Salad, 146
Jerusalem artichokes (sunchokes),
  228–29
jícama, 236–37

Kale, Sautéed, with Bacon-Molasses
  Dressing, 179
Kidney Beans with Rice and Cheese,
  45
kitchen
  conservation tips, 102–3
  equipment for cooking vegetables,
    7–11
  recycling, 298–99
Kohlrabi, 185–92
  about buying and storing, 185;
    preparing, 185
  Browned, and Onions, 189
  in Green Sauce, 188
  in Poppy Seed Dressing, 190✿
  and Potatoes, Mashed, with Tomato
    Cream Gravy, 186
  with Sage Stuffing, 191◆

lamb chops or lamb roast, vegetable side
  dishes for, 87
Leeks, 193–200. *See also* Scallions
  about buying and storing, 193;
    preparing, 193–94
  Baked, with Bacon and Cheddar
    Cheese, 195
  Browned, with Hazelnut Butter,
    200◆
  Browned, and Mushrooms, 199✿
  Chilled Braised, with Sweet Peppers,
    196
  and Potatoes, Mashed, 197
Lemon
  -Braised Artichokes, 27✿
  -Garlic Vinaigrette, 53
Lentils
  Savory Baked, 40
  Sweet-and-Sour, 42
lettuce and greens, names of, 337–38
Lima Bean(s) (Limas)
  Barbecue, 60
  and Corn Succotash in Lemon-Dill
    Cream, 139
  Creamy, 59

Maple-baked, 61✿
thawing, 55

Maple-baked Limas, 61✿
Marinated Roasted Red and Yellow
    Peppers with Fresh Basil, 244
matching vegetable side dishes with
    chicken, roasted, 182–83
    fish, broiled or panfried, 238–39
    ham, baked, 276–77
    lamb chops or lamb roast, 188
    meatloaf or hamburgers, 68
    pasta with cheese, 292
    pasta with tomato-based sauce,
        314–15
    pork chops or pork roast, 76–77
    steak, 270–71
    turkey, roasted, 122–23
    veal, 224
mayonnaise
    aioli, 172–73
    low-fat, low-calorie, 80–81
meatloaf or hamburgers, vegetable side
    dishes for, 68
Mediterranean Cauliflower, 115
medleys, vegetable, 114–15, 330–31
Mushroom(s), 201–10
    about buying and storing, 201;
        preparing, 202; varieties, 201
    Asparagus with, 34
    -basil pesto, 199
    Browned Leeks and, 199✿
    Butter-Browned Savoy Cabbage and,
        102✿
    Chinese, and Broccoli, 82
    Chinese Black, Braised, 203
    Crisp, 208✿
    and Goat Cheese, Roasted Eggplant
        with, 158
    Marinated, 204–5
    Potato-, Pudding, 266
    Roasted with Butter and Garlic, 204
    Sherried, 205
    and Spinach, with Herbs, 287
    Stir-fried Peppers and, 248✿
    Timbales, Easy, 206
    Wild, and Crisp Shallots, Roasted
        Fennel with, 176♦
    Wild, Fricassee in Croustades, 209♦
mustard(s), 280–81. *See also* condiments

non-cooking techniques and terms,
    basic, 11–15
nuts, using, 55; toasting, 55

oil, cooking and salad, 156–57
Okra, 211–18
    about buying and storing, 211;
        preparing, 211
    Browned, with Sun-dried Tomatoes,
        216✿

Buttered, and Wild Rice, 217♦
Cornmeal Pan-fried, 214
Creole-style, 215
Fritters with Sauce Ti-Malice, 212
olive-herb pesto, 198
Olive Oil Vinaigrette Dressing, 242
olives, 26–27; storing, 27
Onion(s), 219–25. *See also* Leeks;
    Scallions; and shallots
    about buying and storing, 219;
        preparing, 219–20
    Browned Kohlrabi and, 189
    Crisp, and Apple Fritters, 222
    Crisp-fried, and Oven-dried
        Tomatoes, Flageolets with, 52♦
    -garlic pesto, 199
    Holiday Baked, with Double Cheese
        Sauce, 224♦
    Raita, Red, with Coriander, 221
    Stir-fried, 223✿
    Sweet, Quick-Pickled Cukes and,
        144
Orzo and Roquefort, Tomatoes with, 319

Parsnip(s), 226–32
    about buying and storing, 226;
        preparing, 226–27
    Carrots and Dried Fruit, Tzimmes of,
        229
    Ginger-Orange, 228
    Hash Brown with Scallions and
        Jalapeños, 230
    Purée with Honey and Spice, 232♦
    Spiked, 231✿
Pasta
    with cheese, vegetable side dishes
        for, 292
    and Peas, 235
    with tomato-based sauce, vegetable
        side dishes for, 314–15
Pattypan Squash,
    Sautéed, with Red Pepper Sauce,
        299
    Sweet-and-Sour, 296
Pea(s), 233–42. *See also* Chick-Peas
    about buying and storing, 233;
        preparing, 233–34
    Black-eyed, with Butter and
        Scallions, 51✿
    black-eyed, salad, 48
    Black-eyed, Swiss Chard with Bacon
        and, 311
    and Pasta, 235
    Pods, Snow, Stir-fried, 240✿
    Russian Salad, 241♦
    Sugar Snap, with Peppered Orange-
        Butter Sauce, 238
    Sugar Snaps with Dips, 236
    with Toasted Almonds, 239
Peanut Sauce, Spicy, 134
pepper, hot (powder and sauce), 274–75

Pepper(s), 243–50
    about buying and storing, 243;
        preparing, 243
    and Cabbage Slaw for a Picnic,
        249✿
    Fried, with Anchovy Butter, 247
    hot, working with, 246–47
    how to roast, 244
    Red, Ratatouille, 246
    Red and Yellow, Marinated Roasted,
        with Fresh Basil, 244
    roasting, 244
    Stir-fried, and Mushrooms, 248✿
    Sweet, Chilled Braised Leeks with,
        196
Pesto, Walnut-Basil, 169
pestos, three simple (olive-herb,
    mushroom-basil, onion-garlic),
    198–99
Pickled
    Chiles, 180
    Quick-, Cukes and Sweet Onions,
        144
Pink Bean(s)
    in Creamy Onion Sauce, 41
    salad, 48
pizza with vegetables, 172
Plantain(s), 251–58
    about buying and storing, 251;
        preparing, 251
    Baked, with Chives and Sour Cream,
        253
    with Curry Sauce and Roasted
        Peanuts, 257♦
    Plátanos Borrachos, 256✿
    Ripe, with Tomato-Mango Salsa, 252
    Salad, 254
pork. *See also* ham
    chops or roast, vegetable side dishes
        for, 76–77
Potato(es), 259–72. *See also* Sweet
    Potatoe(s)
    about buying and storing, 259–60;
        preparing, 260; varieties, 259
    baked, and toppings, 262–63
    Boats Stuffed with Brussels Sprouts
        and Cheese, 91
    Cakes, Oven-fried, 271♦
    Herbed Provençal, 263
    and Kohlrabi, Mashed, with Tomato
        Cream Gravy, 186
    and Leeks, Mashed, 197
    Mashed, with Cheese and Crispy
        Potato Skins, 264
    -Mushroom Pudding, 266
    Oven-roasted Rosemary, 270✿
    and Rutabagas, Mashed, 280
    salads, quick, 266
    Small, with Garlic Cream, 262
    and Turnips with Sun-dried Tomato
        Relish, Pan-fried, 329

presentation (and portions) of
    vegetables, 20
Pumpkin(s), 273–78
    about buying and storing, 273;
        preparing, 273
    -Apricot-Pecan Puddings,
        Individual, 275
    Baked Miniature, with Spiced Butter,
        276❂
    and Black Beans, 274
    Curried, West Indian–style, 277◆
Purée(s)
    Creamy Broccoli, Broccoli in, 85
    Escarole, Cannellini with, 46
    Parsnips with Honey and Spice,
        232
    vegetable, 306–7

Radicchio, Escarole, and White Beans
    with Walnut-Basil Pesto, 168◆
radishes, varieties of, 82–83
Raita
    Red Onion, with Coriander, 221
    Yellow Squash, 297
Ranch Dipping Sauce, 155
Ratatouille, Red Pepper, 246
recycling in the kitchen, tips for,
    298–99
Red Cabbage. See also Cabbage
    Braised, and Apples, 99
Red Flannel Hash, 66
Relish. See also Chutney; condiments;
        mustard(s)
    Beet-Apple-Ginger, 66
    Pickled Chiles, 180
    Quick-Pickled Cukes and Sweet
        Onions, 144
    Red Onion Raita with Coriander,
        221
    Sun-dried Tomato, 328–29
    Yellow Squash Raita, 297
Rice
    and Cheese, Kidney Beans with, 45
    varieties of, 217; other grains, 217
roasted garlic, 28–29
    Artichoke Tart with, 28◆
Root Vegetable Broth, Basic, 110
Russian Salad, 241
Rutabagas, 279–85
    about buying and storing, 279;
        preparing, 279
    Browned, with Mustard Sauce, 281
    Fluffy Baked, with Melted Cheese,
        285◆
    Foil-baked, with Butter and Herbs,
        284❂
    Mashed, and Potatoes, 280
    and Vegetables in Spicy Tomato
        Sauce, 282

Sage-roasted Turnips, 328

Salad(s), 333–49
    about, 333–34
    Asparagus, with Yogurt-Dill Sauce,
        32
    bean, four quick, 48
    Belgian Endive, My Favorite, 76
    Broccoli, with Lemon-Curry
        Mayonnaise and Pepper Confetti,
        80
    Brussels Sprouts, in Homemade
        Russian Dressing, 92
    Carrot Slaw with Chives, Creamy,
        108
    Celery and Apple, Old-fashioned
        Chopped, with Orange-Yogurt
        Dressing, 121
    Coleslaw, 98; Variations, 99
    composed vegetable, 345–49; basic
        preparation of, 346–47;
        variations, 347–49
    cross-reference of, 348–49
    Cucumber, with Caper Dressing,
        145
    Cucumber, Japanese, 146
    of Endive and Pears with Creamy
        Ginger Dressing, 72
    Gazpacho, Red and Green, 322
    Green(s), Mixed, 335–45
        additions to (beans, cooked
            vegetables, fruit, etc.),
            340–42
        basic preparation of, 336–38
        combinations of, 342–45
        names of, 337–38
        raw vegetables addition to,
            338–40
    Minted Zucchini Tabbouleh, 298
    Pepper and Cabbage Slaw for a
        Picnic, 249
    Plantain, 254
    potato, quick, 266
    Russian, 241
    Spinach with Warm Sesame
        Dressing, 290
    Sweet Potato, with Southwest
        Seasonings, 261
    Tomato, Simple, 324
Salad Dressing. See also Dressing;
        Vinaigrette
    basic creamy, 336; variations, 342
    basic vinaigrette, 334–35; variations,
        340–41
    cross-reference of, 343
salsa(s)
    chive, 214
    cruda, 62
    fresh vegetable, 214
    spicy, 62–63, 158
    tomatillo, 63
    Tomato-Mango, Ripe Plantains with,
        252

sandwiches, vegetable, 288–89
Sauce(s). See also Dressing; Pesto;
        Salsa(s)
    Basil-Parsley, 69
    cross-reference of, 124–25
    fresh tomato, 322–23
    Gorgonzola Cream, 165
    Horseradish, for Beets, 68, 69
    Peanut, Spicy, 134
    Ranch Dipping, 155
    Ti-Malice, 213
    for vegetables, 124
Scallions. See also Leeks
    and Butter, Black-eyed Peas with,
        51❂
    and Jalapeños, Hash Brown Parsnips
        with, 230
    in Piquant Sauce, 198
shallots, 220–21
    Crisp, Roasted Fennel with Wild
        Mushrooms and, 176◆
shell beans. See Lima Bean(s)
snap beans. See Green Beans
Snow Pea Pods, Stir-fried, 240
Soup. See also Broth
    express, vegetable (for leftovers), 164
spices and herbs
    curry powder, do-it-yourself, 252
    dried, 264–65
Spinach, 286–93
    about buying and storing, 286;
        preparing, 286
    and Chick-Peas, Not-Too-Hot-and-
        Spicy, 288
    Dumplings, Poached, 292◆
    Indian Beans and Greens, 50
    and Mushrooms with Herbs, 287
    Pie, Quick, 291❂
    with Warm Sesame Dressing, 290
Split Pea and Bulgur Wheat Pilaf, 43
spring holidays, vegetable side
    dishes for, 34
Squash, Summer, 294–301. See also
        Zucchini
    about buying and storing, 294;
        preparing, 294
    Pattypan, Sautéed, with Red Pepper
        Sauce, 299❂
    Pattypan, Sweet-and-Sour, 296
    Yellow, Raita, 297
Squash, Winter, 302–9
    about buying and storing, 302;
        preparing, 302; varieties, 302
    Acorn, with Apples and Cider Glaze,
        303
    Buttercup, Savory, and Cheese
        Gratin, 305
    Butternut, with Coriander Sauce, 306
    with Dried Fruits, 304
    Five Fillings for Basic Baked, 307❂
    Soufflé, 308◆

steak, vegetable side dishes for, 270–71
Stir-fried
    Cabbage, 98
    Green Beans, 57
    Onions, 223
    Peppers and Mushrooms, 248
    Snow Pea Pods, 240
stir-frying, 132–33
Sugar Snap(s)
    with Dips, 236
    Peas with Peppered Orange-Butter
        Sauce, 238
Summer Squash. *See* Squash, Summer
summer vegetable feast, 136–37
Sun-dried Tomato(es)
    about reconstituting and using,
        46–47
    Browned Okra with, 216❂
    Caponata with, Simplified, 152
    Cauliflower with, 116
    Relish, 328–29
Sunchokes. *See* Jerusalem artichokes
Sweet-and-Sour
    Cucumbers in Buttermilk Dressing,
        147
    Lentils, 42
    Pattypan Squash, 296
Sweet Potato(es)
    about, 259
    Casserole, Maggie's, 268
    Gingered, 269
    Salad with Southwest Seasonings,
        261
Swiss Chard, 310–16
    about buying and storing, 310;
        preparing, 310
    with Bacon and Black-eyed Peas,
        311
    with Lemon and Garlic, 315❂
    Pancakes, 312
    Sautéed, with Thick Spicy Yogurt,
        314
    in Walnut Oil with Toasted Walnuts,
        316◆

Tabbouleh Salad, Minted Zucchini, 298
Thai-style Eggplant, 151
Ti-Malice Sauce, 213
tomatillo(s), 277
    salsa, 62
Tomato(es), 317–24. *See also* Sun-dried
    Tomato(es)
    about buying and storing, 317–18;
        preparing, 318; varieties, 317
    -baked Chick-Peas, 47
    canned, 318
    Cheddar-baked, 323
    Corn Salad with Olives and, Fresh,
        141◆

Creamy Greens and, 182❂
    green, chutney, 320
    -Mango Salsa, Ripe Plantains with,
        252
    with Orzo and Roquefort, 319
    Oven-dried, and Crisp-fried Onions,
        Flageolets with, 52◆
    Red and Green Gazpacho Salad, 322
    Salads, Simple, 324❂
    salsa cruda, 50
    sauce, fresh, 322–23
    Stuffed with Couscous and Pine
        Nuts, 325◆
    Tart, 320
turkey, roasted, vegetable side dishes
    for, 122–23
Turnips, 327–32
    about buying and storing, 327;
        preparing, 327
    Creamy, 330❂
    and Potatoes with Sun-dried Tomato
        Relish, Pan-fried, 329
    Rosanna, 331◆
    Sage-roasted, 328
Tuscan Cabbage Soup-Without-the-
    Soup, 101
Tzimmes of Parsnips, Carrots and Dried
    Fruits, 229

veal, vegetable side dishes for, 224
Vegetable(s)
    about, 2; names of, 4
    appetizers, 300
    autumn holiday side dishes, 304–5
    baby, 296
    for baked ham, 276–77
    basic ingredients, 17–19
    basic preparation of, 6
    for broiled or pan-fried fish, 238–39
    Broth, Barnaby's, 176–77
    buying, 5–6
    combinations (medleys), 114–15,
        330–31
    cooked additions to salad, 340–42
    cooking techniques and terms,
        15–17
    crunchy toppings for, 308–9
    cuts of, *illus.* 12–15
    equipment for cooking, 7–11
    grilled, 72
    for lamb chops or lamb roast,
        188–89
    for meatloaf or hamburgers, 68
    medleys, 114–15, 330–31
    non-cooking techniques and terms,
        11–15
    for pasta with cheese, 292
    for pasta with tomato-based sauce,
        314–15

pizza with, 152
    for pork chops or pork roast, 74–75
    presentation (and portions) of, 20
    purées, 306–7
    raw, additions to salad, 338–40
    for roasted chicken, 182–83
    for roasted turkey, 122–23
    Root, Basic Broth, 110
    salads, composed, 345–49
    salads, mixed, 335–45
    salsa, fresh, 214
    sandwiches, 288–89
    sauces for, 124
    soup express (for leftovers), 164
    spring holiday side dishes, 34
    for steak, 270–71
    stir-frying, 132–33
    summer feast, 136–37
    for veal, 224–25
    winter holiday side dishes, 158–59
Vinaigrette
    Ancho Chile, for Beets, 69
    Basic, Salad Dressing, 334–35;
        Variations, 340–41
    Cumin, 172
    Dressing, 49, 245
    Dressing, Creamy, 255
    Dressing, Olive Oil, 242
    Lemon-Garlic, 53
    Walnut Oil, 77
vinegar(s)
    choice of (wine, fruit, etc.), 146–47
    herb, making, 32–33

Walnut-Basil Pesto, 169
Walnut Oil Vinaigrette, 77
White Bean(s)
    Escarole, Radicchio and, with
        Walnut-Basil Pesto, 168◆
    and Goat Cheese Pâté on Greens, 48
    salad, 48
Wild Mushroom(s). *See also*
        Mushroom(s)
    Fricassee in Croustades, 209
    Roasted Fennel with, and Crisp
        Shallots, 176
Wild Rice, Buttered Okra and, 217❂
winter holiday side dishes, 158–59
Winter Squash. See Squash, Winter

yams, about, 259. *See also* Sweet
        Potato(es)
Yellow Squash Raita, 297
yogurt cheese, 312–13

Zucchini. *See also* Squash, Summer
    Barquettes, Stuffed, 300❂
    Ribbons in Gorgonzola Sauce, 295
    Tabbouleh Salad, Minted, 298

Conversion Chart

Equivalent Imperial and Metric Measurements

American cooks use standard containers, the 8-ounce cup and a tablespoon that takes exactly 16 level fillings to fill that cup level. Measuring by cup makes it very difficult to give weight equivalents, as a cup of densely packed butter will weigh considerably more than a cup of flour. The easiest way therefore to deal with cup measurements in recipes is to take the amount by volume rather than by weight. Thus the equation reads:

1 cup = 240 ml = 8 fl. oz.   ½ cup = 120 ml = 4 fl. oz.

It is possible to buy a set of American cup measures in major stores around the world.

In the States, butter is often measured in sticks. One stick is the equivalent of 8 tablespoons. One tablespoon of butter is therefore the equivalent to ½ ounce/15 grams.

Linear Measure

1 inch	2.54 centimeters
1 foot	0.3048 meters
1 yard	0.9144 meters
1 mile	1.609 meters

Area Measure

1 square inch	6.4516 square centimeters
1 square foot	929.03 square centimeters
1 square yard	0.836 square meters
1 square mile	2.5899 square kilometers

Liquid Measures

Fluid Ounces	U.S. Measures	Imperial Measures	Milliliters
	1 teaspoon	1 teaspoon	5
¼	2 teaspoons	1 dessertspoon	7
½	1 tablespoon	1 tablespoon	14
1	2 tablespoons	2 tablespoons	28
2	¼ cup	4 tablespoons	56
4	½ cup or ¼ pint		110
5		¼ pint or 1 gill	140
6	¾ cup		170
8	1 cup or ½ pint		225
9			250, ¼ liter
10	1¼ cups	½ pint	280
12	1½ cups or ¾ pint		340
15		¾ pint	420
16	2 cups or 1 pint		450
18	2¼ cups		500, ½ liter
20	2½ cups	1 pint	560
24	3 cups or 1½ pints		675
25		1¼ pints	700
27	3½ cups		750
30	3¾ cups	1½ pints	840
32	4 cups or 2 pints or 1 quart		900
35		1¾ pints	980
36	4½ cups		1000, 1 liter
40	5 cups or 2½ pints	2 pints or 1 quart	1120
48	6 cups or 3 pints		1350
50		2½ pints	1400
60	7½ cups	3 pints	1680
64	8 cups or 4 pints or 2 quarts		1800
72	9 cups		2000, 2 liters
80	10 cups or 5 pints	4 pints	2250

Solid Measures

U.S. and Imperial Measures		Metric Measures	
OUNCES	POUNDS	GRAMS	KILOS
1		28	
2		56	
3		100	
4	¼	112	
5		140	
6		168	
8	½	225	
9		250	¼
12	¾	340	
16	1	450	
18		500	½
20	1¼	560	
24	1½	675	
27		750	¾
28	1¾	780	
32	2	900	
36	2¼	1000	1
40	2½	1100	
48	3	1350	
54		1500	1½
64	4	1800	
72	4½	2000	2
80	5	2250	2¼
90		2500	2½
100	6	2800	2¾

Suggested Equivalents and Substitutes for Ingredients

all-purpose flour—plain flour
arugula—rocket
beet—beetroot
confectioner's sugar—icing sugar
cornstarch—cornflour
eggplant—aubergine
granulated sugar—caster sugar
kielbasa—Polish sausage
lima beans—broad beans
pearl onions—pickling onions
scallion—spring onion
shortening—white fat
snow pea—mangetout
sour cherry—morello cherry

squash—courgettes or marrow
unbleached flour—strong, white flour
vanilla bean—vanilla pod
zest—rind
zucchini—courgettes
light cream—single cream
heavy cream—double cream
half and half—12% fat milk
buttermilk—ordinary milk
sour milk—add 1 tablespoon vinegar or lemon juice to 1 cup minus 1 tablespoon lukewarm milk. Let stand for 5 minutes.
cheesecloth—muslin

Oven Temperature Equivalents

Fahrenheit	Celsius	Gas Mark	Description
225	110	¼	Cool
250	130	½	
275	140	1	Very Slow
300	150	2	
325	170	3	Slow
350	180	4	Moderate
375	190	5	
400	200	6	Moderately Hot
425	220	7	Fairly Hot
450	230	8	Hot
475	240	9	Very Hot
500	250	10	Extremely Hot

Any broiling recipes can be used with the grill of the oven, but beware of high-temperature grills.